Sequencing Financial Sector Reforms

Sequencing Financial Sector Reforms

Country Experiences and Issues

Editors
R. Barry Johnston
V. Sundararajan

International Monetary Fund
Washington, D.C.

Production: IMF Graphics Section
Cover design: Sanaa Elaroussi
Cover photo: Padraic Hughes
Typesetting: Joseph A. Kumar and Choon Lee

Library of Congress Cataloging-in-Publication Data

Sequencing Financial Sector Reforms: Country Experience and Issues / editors,
R. Barry Johnston and V. Sundarajan.
p. cm.
Includes bibliographical references.
ISBN 1-55775-779-8
1. Fiscal policy—case studies. 2. Finance—Economic aspects—case studies.
I. Johnston, R. B. (Robert Barry) II. Sundararajan, Vasudevan.
HJ192.5.S47 1999
336—dc21 98–32060
CIP

Price: $27.50

Address orders to:
International Monetary Fund, Publication Services
700 19th Street, N.W., Washington D.C. 20431, U.S.A.
Telephone: (202) 623-7430
Telefax: (202) 623-7201
E-mail: publications@imf.org
Internet: http://www.imf.org

Foreword

Financial sector liberalization can spur economic growth and development. But reforms to liberalize the financial sector also entail risks if they are not appropriately designed and implemented. One of the central policy and operational questions for countries reforming their financial systems is how to sequence the reforms so as to maximize the benefits of liberalization and contain its risks.

This book is concerned with the analytical and operational aspects of sequencing financial sector reforms. The IMF has for a number of years provided assistance to its members on their financial sector policies and operations. Issues related to the appropriate sequencing of financial sector reforms have been a central concern in the design of the IMF's technical assistance programs. In seeking to reach a better understanding of the factors that should be taken into account in the design of financial sector reform programs, the IMF has engaged in an ongoing research effort drawing on the practical experiences of its members. This book brings together a number of these studies.

The papers presented in this volume have been prepared over a period of nearly 10 years in the Monetary and Exchange Affairs Department (formerly the Central Banking Department) of the IMF. While the topics covered in the papers reflect some of the critical concerns that confronted technical assistance on financial sectors at the time the papers were written, the recent experiences in the Asian currency crisis countries have served to highlight again the critical role of many of these issues and of the orderly sequencing of financial sector reforms, thus underscoring their continued relevance. The papers focus on monetary control, banking and supervision issues, the macroeconomic and real sector effects of reforms, and the liberalization of the capital account. Some of the lessons drawn from the Asian economies have confirmed what had already been well illustrated during earlier experiences with financial sector reforms, such as the risks of liberalization with a weak and poorly supervised financial system; they have also served to highlight the role of appropriate management of the liberalization of the capital account. Some of the original papers have been updated to reflect more recent critical experiences in Asia.

By bringing together the papers in this volume, the objective is to make more widely available the research that has contributed to the development of approaches to the sequencing of financial sector reform, and therefore to contribute to the ongoing discussion on how best to manage and sequence such reforms. As such, the book offers policymakers and researchers a unique presentation of specific country experiences, and of the lessons that can be drawn from those experiences.

MANUEL GUITIÁN
Director, 1995–1998,
Monetary and Exchange Affairs Department

Acknowledgments

A number of people have contributed directly and indirectly to this book. We wish to thank our coauthors, a number of whom assisted in updating earlier versions of the papers for inclusion in this volume.

We would particularly like to express our gratitude to the directors of the IMF's Monetary and Exchange Affairs Department, formerly the Central Banking Department, initially Justin B. Zulu, and subsequently Manuel Guitián. The papers included in this volume reflect work that the department undertook over a nearly 10-year period, during which time the department directors consistently encouraged and supported this work.

Also to be acknowledged are our colleagues—too many to be mentioned by name—who commented on various drafts of the papers and who contributed ideas during their participation in numerous technical assistance missions and department discussions.

Special thanks go to Francine Koch and Maria Tramuttola for their excellent secretarial assistance in preparing this volume and to Natalie Baumer for her contribution in editing the manuscript. Jeff Hayden of the External Relations Department edited the final version of the volume and coordinated its production.

Contents

1

Managing Financial Sector Liberalization: An Overview

R. BARRY JOHNSTON AND V. SUNDARARAJAN

The papers in this volume illustrate the structural linkages among different components of financial sector reforms and the impact of these reforms on macroeconomic performance, based on country experiences. An underlying theme throughout the volume is that specific financial sector reforms should be properly sequenced and coordinated in order to complement and support macrostabilization objectives, and to reflect the technical linkages among various components of financial sector reform. An appropriate sequencing of financial sector reforms that supports stabilization can help to derive the full benefits of these reforms in terms of efficiency and growth. The book is therefore concerned with the elements that contribute to orderly liberalizations of financial systems, and with avoiding the pitfalls from inappropriately sequenced or insufficiently supported financial reforms.

The objective of developing the monetary and exchange system, and more broadly the financial system, derives from the simple proposition that the more efficient and more stable such systems are, the better a country's economic performance will be. Stable and efficient financial systems will provide the foundation for implementing effective stabilization policies and successfully mobilizing capital and putting it to efficient use, and, therefore, achieving higher rates of economic growth. This proposition will be valid not only in the mobilization and use of national savings but also in harnessing foreign savings. In a world of increasing capital mobility, capital will move not only as a response to competing monetary policies but also to competing financial systems. Inefficient and unstable monetary and exchange systems are likely to be increasingly penalized, placing a premium on developing financial sector institutions and sound macroeconomic policies.

The *efficiency* of financial systems is governed by the range of intermediaries and the role of markets in mobilizing and allocating financial resources; in providing liquidity and payment services, including through the convertibility of currencies; and in gathering information on which to base investment and savings decisions and influence corporate governance. *Stability* is concerned with safeguarding the value of liabilities of financial institutions that serve as stores of value and wealth, and media of domestic and international exchange. It is also concerned with the interrelationship between financial systems and macroeconomic management. This aspect involves questions of monetary control, prudential supervision and financial regulation, and broader questions of good governance.

Figure 1.1 illustrates the types of trade-offs that might be thought to exist between stability and efficiency depending on the nature of market arrangements and type of governance. Market-based systems with strong internal governance (upper right quadrant) are likely to have better economic performance than those in the lower left quadrant. Nonmarket-based systems that rely on direct controls may or may not involve instability, depending upon the quality of governance, but invariably involve inefficiency compared with market-based arrangements. Maintenance of direct controls for prolonged periods is more likely to be associated with instability given the scope for avoidance of direct controls. Seriously repressed financial systems are more likely to be associated with instability and inefficiency and lower economic growth. Success in moving toward higher rates of growth will depend on the sequencing of reforms. An inept approach to sequencing reforms may result in instability and weaker improvements in efficiency than better sequenced reforms. A banking crisis, associated with poorly managed reforms, would damage economic performance. The "quality" of financial reform matters.

Against this background, financial sector liberalization can be viewed as a set of operational reforms and policy measures designed to deregulate and transform the financial system and its structure with

Figure 1.1 Factors Influencing Financial Sector Efficiency and Stability

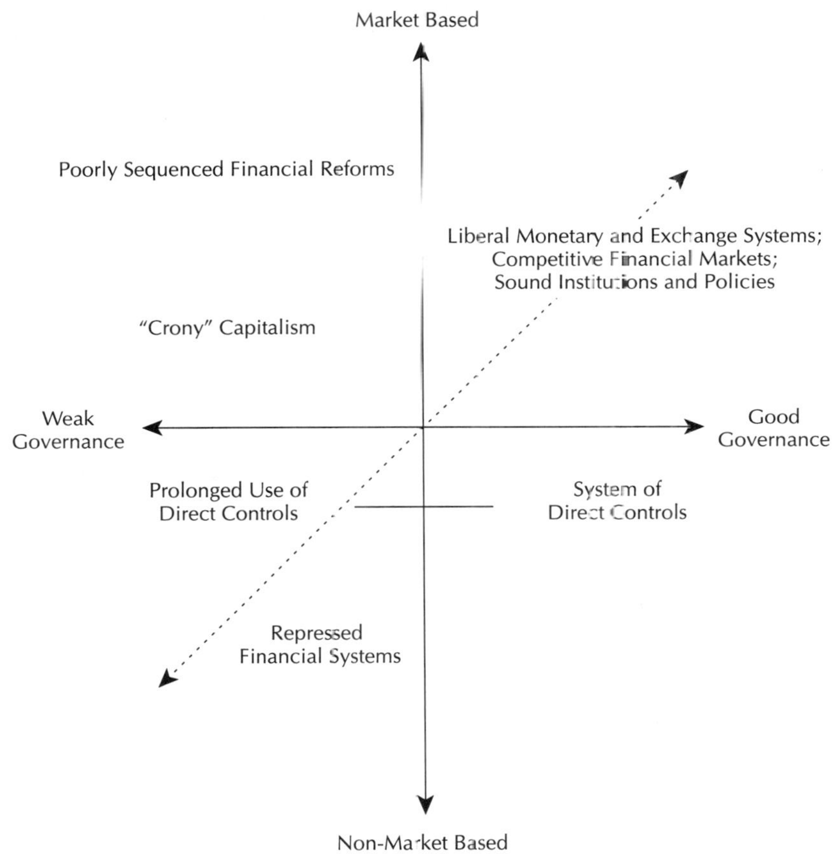

the view to achieving a liberalized market-oriented system within an appropriate regulatory framework. Such worldwide financial sector reforms have led to greater flexibility in interest rates, an enhanced role for markets in credit and foreign exchange allocation, increased autonomy to commercial banks, a greater depth for the money, securities, and foreign exchange markets, and significant increases in cross-border flows of capital. In parallel, the framework for monetary and exchange policy has undergone major changes. Bank-specific credit ceilings and selective credit allocations have been replaced by market-based instruments to implement monetary policy. Prudential supervision systems have been put in place to foster sound credit decisions and effective management of market risks. A regime of strong exchange and trade restrictions and limited foreign exchange markets has given way to a multilateral international exchange and payment system with significant progress toward currency convertibility and active interbank foreign exchange markets.

In support of such a transition, financial sector reforms have, in varying degrees, involved:

- Increasing autonomy to central banks in monetary management.
- Developing market-based monetary control procedures and money and interbank markets to bolster interest rate regimes.
- Reforming prudential regulations and the banking supervision system.
- Recapitalizing and restructuring weak financial institutions, supported by enterprise restructuring policies.
- Reforming selective credit regulations and reducing the scope of directed credit and interest subsidies.
- Fostering autonomy and competition in the financial system, and promoting institutional development of both banks and nonbank financial intermediaries (NBFIs).
- Developing long-term capital markets, including domestic public debt management and government securities markets.
- Reforming clearing and settlement system for payments.
- Developing foreign exchange markets supported by appropriate prudential regulations on foreign exchange exposure.
- Eliminating restrictions on payments and transfers for current international transactions and liberalizing controls on capital movements.

The relative importance of these components and the specific measures within each component have varied from country to country, depending upon, among other things, the prevailing initial conditions, the commitment to reform on the part of the authorities, and the speed of reform process. Examination of country experiences shows that there are close structural linkages among specific components of financial sector reforms, and these linkages have implications for the appropriate sequencing of reforms. Smooth implementation of financial sector reforms would typically also require a wide range of legislative measures and organizational changes. In particular, the organization and functioning of the central bank would need significant strengthening to facilitate implementation of financial sector reforms.

In all cases, however, these reforms have been motivated by the need to pursue stabilization and broader structural reforms in an efficient and effective manner, and thereby step up savings mobilization, improve the efficiency of investment allocation, and achieve sustainable growth. These broader issues are reviewed briefly in the next section, before outlining the structure of the book and the main themes.

The Link Between Stabilization and Financial Sector Reforms

The resurgence in academic interest in the role of financial systems in economic development dates to the early work of Gurley and Shaw (1960) on the interaction between financial structure and economic activity, and especially on the role of intermediaries in the credit supply process. Many authors have argued that credit market conditions and balance sheet developments such as debt-equity ratios, ratio of net worth to liabilities, and other similar ratios can have important effects on output and investment (see, for example, Gertler, 1988; and Sundararajan, 1987). In addition, the information asymmetries and the resulting market failures, such as equilibrium credit rationing, credit market collapse, bank runs, and weak secondary markets, suggest that governments can, through appropriate regulations, improve on the types of contractual arrangements that would arise in an unfettered private economy.[1] Empirical literature has also increasingly emphasized the importance of financial sector variables in economic cycles.[2] Recently, several studies have reported positive correlations between

[1]For example, Cho (1986) shows that the development of equity markets should accompany the liberalization process in order to overcome credit rationing of productive projects due to information frictions. Also, recent literature on banking crisis (Sundararajan and Baliño, 1990) shows that structural measures to strengthen prudential regulations and correct portfolio weaknesses in the financial sector are important for the effectiveness of stabilization policies, in particular monetary policies.

[2]For example, Mishkin (1978) and Bernanke (1983) analyzed data from the Great Depression and concluded that financial sector variables had a significant impact on economic activity. See Gertler (1988) for a recent survey.

levels of financial development and economic growth (e.g., King and Levine, 1993a; and Japelli and Pagano, 1992).

It is widely recognized that certain structural adjustments are necessary to support the effectiveness of stabilization, and at the same time, the successful pursuit of stabilization policies is necessary for the effectiveness of broader structural reforms—price reforms, exchange and trade reforms, industrial restructuring and enterprise reforms (see Barth, Roe, and Wong, 1994). Both stabilization and general structural reform policies, however, need to be supported by complementary financial sector reforms. As discussed later in this volume, wide-ranging structural changes in the financial sector are often needed for the effective and efficient conduct of monetary and exchange policies, without which sustained progress toward macroeconomic and financial stability would be difficult to achieve.

The policy implications of this work are that important gains for economic performance are to be had from financial sector reforms, and therefore these reforms should be accelerated. Countries wishing to attract or retain private savings so as to achieve adequate rates of economic growth have little option but to reform their financial systems and to follow policies that will maintain financial stability. Often, rapid financial liberalization can overcome inertia and be a catalyst for broader economic reforms. Moreover, rapid reforms can add credibility to the government's commitment to carry out reforms and help the mobilization of external resources. This realization comes in the form of both tangible evidence that the authorities are moving ahead with reforms and the evidence of increased willingness of the government to subject itself to discipline from markets.

Nevertheless, financial reforms carry risks if they are sequenced inappropriately or insufficiently supported, and the academic literature has tended to place financial sector reform relatively late in the overall sequence of reform and to favor a gradual approach.[3] The litera-

[3]The literature on interaction between financial reforms (both domestic markets and external capital accounts) and stabilization programs is quite extensive. On the Southern Cone, see Corbo and De Melo (1985); Connolly and Gonzalez-Vega (1987); Calvo (1983); and Corbo, De Melo, and Tybout (1986). For the Pacific Basin countries, see Cheng (1986). See also Diaz-Alejandro (1985) for a more general discussion. The "conventional" approach suggests that fiscal adjustment should occur before financial sector liberalization and the elimination of controls on capital movements should occur after the domestic financial system is liberalized. See, for example, McKinnon (1991).

ture suggests broad propositions on the optimal sequencing of economic reforms, including that: (1) macroeconomic stabilization is a prerequisite to successful structural adjustments; (2) the liberalization of domestic financial markets should precede the removal of controls on international capital flows; and (3) trade liberalization and real sector adjustments should precede capital account liberalization. Nevertheless, the potential role of financial systems in improving economic performance argues for examining ways of accelerating the financial sector reforms while seeking to reduce the possible adverse consequences for macroeconomic control and resource allocation of poorly sequenced or managed reforms. Acceleration of reforms is especially important where restrictive financial systems have failed to deliver adequate economic performance; people appear to be circumventing existing controls; and countries are confronting critical macroeconomic and structural problems that make it difficult to delay reform.

The challenge of financial sector reform is to evolve strategies that can improve financial sector efficiency while achieving or maintaining financial stability—or at least to identify the risks and trade-offs between the efficiency and stability of different strategies. The first task often is to understand the costs of maintaining a high degree of financial repression and the benefits of proceeding with financial sector reform. The second task is to design reforms that can help minimize the costs and risks and, thus, promote more successful transitions to market-oriented financial systems and better economic performance. The development of such strategies requires taking into account the interrelationships among different structural components of financial systems, and between the microeconomic and structural features of financial markets and institutions on the one hand and macroeconomic policy on the other. In particular, conditions in the financial sector could influence the instrument mix and effectiveness of macro policies, while macroeconomic developments could, in turn, affect financial sector soundness and efficiency. These interrelations are complex, however, and the dependence of outcomes on specific institutional structures and policy mixes so far has not been amenable to theoretical analysis. Nevertheless, the experience of different countries with financial reform is rich in information and lessons about the feasibility and risks of different strategies.

Sequencing of Reforms: Country Experiences

This book brings together a number of research papers that address the issue of pace and sequencing of financial sector reforms based on country experiences. Discussions focus on what is feasible in terms of financial sector reform to support stabilization and avoid major risks, and on the practical approaches that can be followed for this purpose. The chapters take a pragmatic and empirical approach aimed at understanding the operational experiences and institutional reforms that shape the financial liberalization process. More specifically, the papers address issues of monetary control and money market development, sequencing of financial sector reforms, sequencing of prudential supervision and bank and enterprise restructuring policies, exchange market and capital account liberalization, and real sector consequences of financial sector reform. Collectively, these papers are the result of work over nearly a 10-year period (1988–97), building on years of advisory work provided by IMF staff.[4]

Chapter 2 examines the development of monetary control procedures and the supporting institutional reforms. It reviews the experiences of nine developing countries that have introduced such instruments, and provides quantitative estimates of their importance in monetary management. It also discusses the implications of increased capital flows for the design of monetary policy frameworks and the effectiveness of monetary policy instruments.

Chapter 3 reviews the historical experiences of five developing countries—Argentina, Chile, Indonesia, Korea, and the Philippines—regarding the sequencing of financial sector reforms. Each country's approach varied considerably, but their results showed a great deal of commonality. Three of these five countries experienced a banking crisis following the reforms, and this chapter examines the background leading up to the crises, and the lessons learned concerning the design of monetary and prudential regulatory policy and the avoidance of financial crisis.

Chapter 4 considers issues in the sequencing of prudential supervision and financial restructuring of banks in the course of financial lib-

[4]These papers were prepared in the IMF's Central Bank Department, and subsequently in the expanded and renamed Monetary and Exchange Affairs Department, drawing on the technical assistance experience of the department.

eralization. The recognition of major two-way linkages between banking soundness and macroeconomic policy calls for appropriate strategies to foster banking soundness in the course of transition to market-based monetary and exchange systems.

To understand the benefits and potential risks of financial sector reforms more fully, Chapter 5 examines the links between financial sector reform and economic growth and efficiency. The research reported is based on an examination of panel data from 40 countries that reformed their financial systems. This chapter also analyzes prefinancial reform, reform, and postreform data for countries that had successful financial liberalizations, as well as countries that faced a financial crisis following the reforms.

Finally, Chapter 6 evaluates the sequencing of capital account liberalization, drawing lessons from four emerging market economies that have experienced large capital inflows—those of Chile, Indonesia, Korea, and Thailand. The impact of capital account liberalization on economic performance varied, and three of the countries experienced a currency crisis. This survey leads to broad conclusions about the conceptual framework for an orderly liberalization of the capital account. This survey also reviews the role of capital account liberalization in the currency crisis in Asia, and draws lessons for the sequencing of liberalizations.

Main Themes and Findings

The major themes and findings are summarized below, as they refer to the sequencing of monetary reforms and managing the shocks associated with liberalizations; the sequencing of banking restructuring and strengthening prudential regulation; the impact of financial sector reform on the real sector; and the sequencing of capital account liberalization.

Monetary Reforms

Many countries with repressed financial systems face problems of monetary control associated with the ineffectiveness of direct credit and interest rate controls. Administered interest rates and credit allocation have tended to be eroded over time, and are inflexible in the face of substantial international capital flows. Moreover, they are associated with inefficiency in resource allocation. The modification of monetary policy instruments in order to achieve more effective monetary control is an important motivation of financial sector reform, and the freeing of direct controls on interest rates and credit is central to most financial sector reforms.

More indirect, market-based approaches have increased the scope for macroeconomic control while allowing for a deregulation of interest rates and the allocation of credit, which can improve resource allocation efficiency. The experience of countries with reforming monetary controls indicates that the introduction of indirect approaches has often been accompanied by an initial active use of reserve requirements and refinance facilities, and for a time, guidance on interest rates and bank credit were continued because of concern over the weak institutional capacity of financial markets (Chapter 2). The introduction of indirect instruments by itself stimulated money and interbank markets, but the successful adoption of indirect instruments required parallel reforms to strengthen money market structures and trading arrangements, and the supporting clearing and settlement system for interbank payments. Where a deregulation of interest rates and credit controls occurred abruptly after a long period of control, countries have experienced significant financial deepening but also some problems of a loss of monetary control. Other countries that liberalized administered controls over bank credit more gradually did not experience the same loss of control (Chapter 3), but the pace of development of financial markets was correspondingly slow.

Two types of monetary and portfolio shocks are evident from the experience of various countries. The first relates to the credit creation process, with rapid credit expansions tending to follow the liberalization of controls on the banking system (Chapter 3). The second relates to external sector liberalizations, with evidence that external liberalization can lead to a reflow of capital flight, improvements in countries' capital accounts, and additional constraints on monetary and exchange rate policies (Chapter 6).

First, in nearly all countries, financial liberalization has been followed by a period in which credit growth exceeded the growth of deposits, and in several countries, the gap between the growth of credit and the growth of deposits widened following the reforms. The initial tendency for credit to grow more rapidly than deposits is perhaps not surprising where credit growth was previously constrained by direct controls with an excess demand for credit. Once the direct controls are removed, the tendency is for financial institutions to respond by running down holdings of excess reserves built up under credit controls, with credit expanding rapidly thereafter. In the prereform period, deposits were not limited by direct controls, and so a similar excess demand did not exist. Deposit growth, however, responds to the adjustments in interest rates.

The adjustment of interest rates to positive real levels and the adoption of interest rate flexibility to contain inflationary pressures appear to be critical policy actions in the reform period to deal with the credit and monetary effects of reform. When the authorities maintain positive real interest rates, the experiences of various countries suggest that the tendency for credit to grow more rapidly than deposits will be temporary. Following the initial stock adjustment, credit growth slows down, while deposit growth continues in response to the ongoing financial deepening. After an adjustment period, the growth of deposits and credit converge, allowing for balanced growth with a higher level of overall resource mobilization (Chapter 3). Thus, over time liberalization of the financial system results in increased financial savings, and the economy can tolerate a somewhat more rapid growth of money and credit without increasing inflationary pressures. In those countries that did not increase their real interest rates, however, financial reforms often impeded economic growth and efficiency. In these cases, the credit expansion resulted in inflation, unproductive investment, and weak bank credit portfolios (Chapters 3 and 5).

Second, eliminating controls on capital inflows has generally, at least initially, resulted in stronger capital inflows as international investors (and local residents with capital abroad) react to the improved investment environment. Such inflows can help support the balance of payments, reduce costs of borrowing, and, therefore, support more rapid economic growth.[5] Increased freedom of capital movements also reduces the capacity to conduct independent monetary and exchange rate policies. High capital mobility also alters the effectiveness of different monetary instruments in achieving the objectives of monetary

[5]Capital inflows in the form of foreign direct investment can also support growth through transfers of technology and management skills, while portfolio capital flows can help to diversify and deepen financial markets.

policy. Instruments that impose a high cost or administrative constraint on the banks—for example, credit or interest rate ceilings or high unremunerated reserve requirements—may be circumvented more easily by disintermediation through the capital account, and therefore become less effective (Chapter 2).

To manage the monetary and credit shocks and the potential foreign capital inflow effectively, the authorities would need to develop indirect instruments of monetary control; the development of such instruments has generally occurred very early in the reform process (Chapters 3 and 6). Because of the close technical and operational linkages between the design of monetary policy instruments and operations, and the structure and depth of money markets, including the supporting payment systems, reforms of monetary control procedures are accompanied by parallel measures to strengthen money and interbank markets, and payment systems (Chapter 2).

Countries with successful financial reforms have tended to liberalize monetary controls in stages, ensuring that necessary concomitant reforms are implemented in a timely manner, and relying on a range of monetary control instruments during the initial stages of reform (Chapters 2 and 3). For example, it may be necessary to phase in the post-liberalization credit expansion because of its potentially destabilizing effects on both the macroeconomic variables and the balance sheets of commercial banks. An attempt to constrain credit demand solely through interest rates could result in high real interest rates, thereby encouraging substantial foreign capital inflows, while weakening a bank's loan portfolio. Countries have generally found it necessary to speed up the introduction of and reliance on indirect monetary controls to help manage the effects of foreign inflows of capital (Chapters 2 and 6).

Monetary and credit aggregates have usually become less stable in the aftermath of financial sector reforms (Chapter 2). Therefore, the authorities have to use a broader range of monetary and macroeconomic indicators to guide monetary and exchange policy and to coordinate monetary, public debt, and exchange market operations.[6] Some of the aggregates at the level of the central banks' balance sheet may be more reliable guides to the stance of monetary policy than broader

[6]This often requires central banks to strengthen their monetary analysis and research functions to develop short-term information systems and liquidity forecasting.

monetary and credit aggregates during the reforms. With increased capital mobility, the external counterpart of money supply may become more volatile, and the demand for domestically defined monetary aggregates may become more sensitive to international interest rate differentials, thus making it more difficult to identify a stable domestic monetary aggregate. Capital account liberalization, therefore, reinforces the trend toward the adoption of a more eclectic monetary framework, and toward giving more weight to exchange rates in monetary assessments (Chapter 6).

Banking Crises and Prudential Supervision

Experiences with financial sector reforms highlight the critical importance of addressing early in the reform process problems in financial system soundness, particularly in the banking industry. Serious banking sector problems are often the legacy of prolonged financial repression. A failure to address these problems weakens the effectiveness of reforms in improving resource allocation, and risks a banking crisis that could seriously disrupt stability and economic growth. The evidence from cross-country experiences indicates that only those countries that avoided financial crisis were able to benefit significantly in the short run from financial sector reform (Chapter 5). Financial sector problems were also a significant component of the currency crises in countries that liberalized their capital accounts (Chapter 6).

Several countries—for example, Argentina, Chile, and the Philippines—experienced financial crises following financial sector reforms (Chapter 3). These crises disrupted the financial sector and were accompanied by a sharp contraction in gross domestic product (GDP) and a reversal of the financial deepening that initially followed the financial reforms. Banking sector problems and weaknesses contributed to an inefficient use of capital inflows and were an important element of the currency crises in Asia (Chapter 6). These episodes indicated the significant two-way correlation between banking soundness and macrostability, and the importance of implementing financial sector reforms with due regard to stability.

The major common elements of these financial crises were the unsound asset structures of banks (reflecting, for example, subsidized credit and insider loans); changes in relative prices, including interest rates and exchange rates, that influenced the viability of borrowers;

and weaknesses in the institutional structure of banking, including weak prudential regulation and banking supervision, that facilitated risk taking. Certain characteristics of the reform may have contributed to the crises. First, the very rapid growth of bank credit following the domestic liberalizations and strong capital inflows may have strained the credit approval process and resulted in an increase in lending to more high-risk projects. This was a particular problem because of extensive lending to interrelated entities and the lack of regulation of loan classification, provisioning, and interest capitalization. Second, in some cases the abruptness of the financial liberalization did not give the private financial institutions time to develop the necessary internal monitoring, credit appraisal, and risk-management procedures, nor did it give the public sector banks time to create a more commercial approach. Third, information systems—accounting, financial disclosure rules, company analysis, credit-rating systems, etc.—that are necessary for an efficient allocation of resources were not developed. At the same time, while prudential supervision was not well formed, market discipline remained weak because of explicit or implicit government guarantees, with depositors and creditors being largely indifferent to bank credit risks. Insolvent banks were able to attract deposits and to disguise their true financial positions by continuing to pay interest and dividends out of deposit receipts.

Early and timely attention to developing vigilant bank supervision and well-designed prudential regulations could have helped detect and contain the buildup of financial fragility. In some countries, financial reform was accompanied by a strengthening in prudential regulations; however, implementation of the regulations was weak and some critical regulations—for example, restrictions on lending to interrelated entities, on loan classification and provisions, and on accounting rules on interest accruals—did not exist and others were rescinded because of an inability to implement them. This underlines the importance of having not only adequate regulations but also the capacity to implement them. Such a capacity is in part technical, but also requires the absence of political interference. The achievement of such a capacity takes time and often involves the strengthening of key public institutions, particularly the central bank, as part of the process of financial reform.

In practice, policies to restructure banks (and enterprises) and strengthen prudential supervision can be phased in to support the interest rate and capital account liberalization process, and thereby avoid either undue delays in liberalization or its abrupt interruptions due to financial crisis. Appropriate sequencing of banking restructuring and supervision policies can help to set up initially a critical mass of reforms in prudential supervision and bank balance sheets, and these can be progressively refined and adjusted in line with the evolution of financial markets and internal governance in commercial banks.

Nevertheless, the speed and nature of interest rate and capital account liberalization also has to take into account the financial structure of nonfinancial firms, and the pace with which problem banks and their assets can be restructured. If nonfinancial firms are highly leveraged, any sharp increase in real interest rates could further weaken the repayment capacity of these firms and the condition of banks. Allowing weak banks to expand their balance sheets through domestic or foreign sources is likely to risk a banking crisis. The preferable option would be to recapitalize the banks and restructure their asset portfolios. This may require corporate restructuring and budgetary transfers and, therefore, a larger fiscal adjustment in support of the financial reforms. Where banking sector reforms are delayed it may then be desirable to liberalize bank interest rates and banks' capacity to borrow abroad only gradually, while pushing ahead with industrial sector restructuring and the recapitalization of banks.

Where banking sector weaknesses are not well perceived by financial markets, or where banks are considered to be explicitly or implicitly guaranteed, so that the markets exercise only weak discipline on the borrower, there would be a case for more direct measures to limit bank balance sheet growth, including controls on the banks' capacity to borrow internationally. In such circumstances, it would be risky to liberalize banks' access to foreign finance until the government addresses banking weaknesses and concerns about moral hazard and implements appropriate supervisory standards.[7] Similar concerns may also arise when providing corporate borrowers access to overseas finance, if the financial sector guarantees are perceived as extending to the corporate sector.

[7]Regulation and supervision must be adequate and effective, yet it should also be designed in ways that will let private markets function efficiently. Over-regulation stifles the efficient functioning of markets and can lead to moral hazard problems since private financial institutions do not take adequate responsibility for their actions.

Nevertheless, policies to restructure banking systems have often proved quite difficult to implement. This can create an important dilemma for the pace and sequencing of financial sector reforms. Should the authorities move forward with reforms in other areas—such as interest rate liberalization—in the expectation that these will be a catalyst to broader financial sector reforms? The country experiences reviewed illustrate the risks of proceeding with partial reforms and the need for supporting measures in a broad range of areas. Partial liberalizations of the financial system without supporting banking sector reforms have frequently led to banking crises. The very large loan losses that have become evident in the episodes of financial crisis in the 1990s, including the recent experience in Asia, have again highlighted the critical importance of phasing in bank supervision and restructuring policies to support domestic and external liberalization. These experiences also highlight that a comprehensive and well-sequenced approach is needed to prevent crisis or to minimize public costs of restructuring during crisis. Such an approach should coordinate the strategies to strengthen prudential supervision with those to restructure banks and banking systems, and to foster efficient institutional arrangements for loan recovery and enterprise restructuring and adopt prudential supervision to meet the emerging circumstances of the market (Chapter 4).

Financial reforms have tended to broaden initially banks' gross lending margins, reflecting, among other things, the removal of interest rate controls, which allowed banks to price credits and risks more appropriately, and increased use of non-interest-bearing reserve requirements. Margins have tended to decline subsequently as more reliance has been placed on indirect monetary controls, and financial sector competition gradually increases. Portfolio weaknesses in banking, however, can result in a widening of lending margins for a prolonged period of time. Not only is this detrimental to economic performance but it can also encourage unsustainable foreign inflows, and thus requires that domestic financial sector restructuring be sequenced appropriately with the opening of the capital account.

Capital market development has tended to lag reforms in the banking systems, although capital markets could play an important role in enhancing competition and intermediating domestic and foreign investment funds, and promoting longer-term capital flows. Although the papers do not provide direct evidence on the importance of capital markets for financial sector reform, they do indicate the importance of following a balanced approach to financial sector development that would involve the simultaneous development of the capital market and the liberalization of the banking system. This is a conclusion that is reinforced by the experiences with capital account liberalizations in Asian economies, where an over-reliance on the intermediation of capital flows through banks rather than capital markets contributed to the short-term composition of capital inflows, and increased the vulnerability to reversals of capital flows (Chapter 6).

Failure to strengthen bank supervision appears to have been a critical weakness in a number of financial sector reforms. In some countries, evident market failures resulted from institutional weaknesses and inappropriate incentives. The critical need to address these difficulties through effective prudential supervision and adequate internal governance was identified only late in the reform process, as was the need to reform deposit insurance as a means of increasing market discipline on financial institutions. In some other countries, such as Argentina, Chile, Indonesia, and Thailand, new prudential regulations were introduced in the initial stage of the reforms, but they were ineffective. The latter underlines the importance of the implementation of the standards as well as the adequacy of the standards themselves.

Real Sector Effects of Financial Reform

A large body of theoretical literature analyzes the extent of financial intermediation in an economy as an important determinant of its real growth rate.[8] Empirical tests using a large sample of countries have also concluded that financial variables have an important impact on economic growth.[9] But, as already noted, the transition from repressed to more market-oriented financial systems involves shocks to interest rates, the exchange rate, and financial flows, and the authorities' reactions to these shocks can affect economic performance and the transitional costs of financial sector reform. Many countries have had successful financial sector reforms accompanied by improvements in economic growth and

---

[8]Early examples of this literature include Cameron (1967), Patrick (1966), Goldsmith (1969), McKinnon (1973), and Shaw (1973).

[9]See, for example, Pagano (1993), Roubini and Sala-i-Martin (1992), De Gregorio and Guidotti (1992), and King and Levine (1993a, b).

efficiency, but several other countries, industrial and developing, have faced financial crisis and disruptions to economic growth.

The results of the research reported in Chapter 5 indicate that financial sector reforms can have important structural effects on the transmission of financial variables to the real economy. Where financial reforms are properly managed, they can contribute to strong improvements in economic growth and efficiency. Key elements of successful reforms included increases in real interest rates; management of the credit growth following the reforms, which often allowed for a more gradual increase in credit to the private sector; and improvements in banking efficiency in the postreform period. However, poorly managed reforms that are manifest in financial crisis can damage both economic growth and efficiency. Moreover, expanding the financial sector under conditions of financial repression or poorly managed reforms increases the chances that intermediation will be channeled into unproductive projects, thereby hampering economic efficiency and growth.

Those countries that reformed their financial systems and confronted a financial crisis often encountered a deterioration in economic growth and some decline in output to capital ratios. In these countries, real interest rates declined and credit expansion tended to be more rapid, suggesting that the banking crises may have been partly related to the failure of the authorities to respond to the monetary shocks that accompanied the reforms. The crisis countries also appear to have faced greater problems of banking inefficiency and insolvency. Post-crisis adjustments also imposed heavy real sector costs. In summary, the "quality" of financial reform matters, and the design of reforms is an important determinant of the success of financial reform and of economic performance.

Liberalization of the Capital Account

The issues raised in liberalizing the capital account (Chapter 6) are to a large extent the same as those that confront a country liberalizing its domestic financial system—how to strengthen financial institutions so that they can operate in a market-based system, and how to achieve monetary objectives and maintain macroeconomic stability in such an environment. The liberalization of capital flows can thus be viewed as one aspect of a broader program of financial sector liberalization.

Capital account liberalization also introduces an additional external dimension and urgency to financial sector reforms. Capital inflows will either be channeled through domestic intermediaries or compete with them. In both cases, the intermediaries will need to be strengthened, either to help ensure the efficient use of the capital inflows, or to help domestic financial institutions cope with increased competitive pressure and the need to restructure. Capital account liberalization can also open the way for domestic banks and corporations to take on greater foreign exchange risks than domestic financial liberalizations. Capital account liberalization will also bring more sharply into focus inconsistencies in monetary and exchange rate policies and the weaknesses of direct monetary instruments.

There are a number of reasons for adopting a coordinated and comprehensive approach to financial sector reforms and capital account liberalization. First, from a macroeconomic and balance-of-payments perspective, the stage of development and the stability of domestic financial systems have key influences on the growth and composition of capital movements and on the capacity of the authorities to manage capital flows. Countries with developed financial markets and institutions have been better able to attract portfolio capital flows than countries where such markets are just emerging. Countries with sounder banking systems also have been better able to handle reversals in capital inflows, since under a strong financial system, banking weaknesses do not act as constraints to interest rate and exchange rate policies. The efficiency of the use of capital flows and thus the extent to which such flows contribute to sustained improvements in economic performance will also depend on the stage of development and efficiency of the domestic financial system. This factor in turn may depend on the existence of a well-regulated and supervised financial system, and the elimination of various sources of market failures that may be the legacy of previous financial repression.[10] With greater freedom of capital movements, short-term interest rates will increasingly be determined by the covered interest rate parity condition, which is the consequence of arbitrage between short-term domestic and foreign interest rates and the discount on the currency in the forward exchange market. As a consequence, the capacity to assign monetary and exchange policies

[10]For a discussion of the sources of such market failures and the need for supporting reforms, see Johnston (1997).

to achieve different macroeconomic targets will be increasingly constrained (see Chapters 2 and 6).

Second, the opening of the capital account can have important implications for financial markets and institutions. In many cases, the implications are positive in that the liberalizations help to develop deeper, more competitive, and more diversified financial markets. However, some countries have been confronted with banking crises when faced with sudden inflows and subsequent sharp reversals in capital flows.

Third, the opening of the capital account may involve risks different from those encountered in purely domestic transactions. Such risks include those associated with cross-border lending (including transfer, sovereign, and country risk), the cross-border listing of securities, and the increased exposure to foreign exchange risks (see Johnston, 1998). The Asian currency crises have highlighted the risks associated with the reversibility of short-term capital flows and the importance of having in place appropriate safeguards to prevent large foreign currency open positions, short-term foreign currency maturity mismatches, and excessive reliance on short-term foreign borrowing. As well as prudential measures, such safeguards encompass the regulatory regimes for cross-border capital transactions, and the monetary and exchange rate policy mix (see Chapter 6). The prudent management of short-term capital flows is of critical importance in view of the central role of such flows in international trade finance, the efficient functioning of money and foreign exchange markets, and the international monetary system more generally.

Chapter 6 concludes that capital account liberalization should be integrated with the design of structural and macroeconomic policies. Maximizing the benefits from capital account liberalization while minimizing the risks requires a comprehensive approach to reforms. Although in general it would be advisable to have well-planned and sequenced reforms, this does not necessarily imply a gradualist approach. Rather it calls for coordinated and concurrent reforms irrespective of the pace of the reforms. Faster liberalization of the capital account would require equally rapid progress in the necessary concurrent reforms to domestic financial markets and institutions and in adapting the macroeconomic policy framework. Accelerating these reforms is desirable in any event in view of the limited extent to which countries can insulate themselves from the market.

The experiences of the Asian countries (reviewed in Chapter 6) confirm that it is necessary to approach capital account liberalization as an integral part of a comprehensive program of economic reform, coordinated with appropriate macroeconomic and exchange rate policies—including policies to strengthen financial markets and institutions. The question is not so much one of the capital liberalization having been too fast, since some of the countries in Asia followed a very gradualist approach. Rather, it has more to do with the appropriate sequencing of the reforms and, more specifically, what supporting measures need to be taken.

Conclusion

The literature on sequencing has tended to place financial sector reforms relatively late in the overall order of reforms, favoring a gradualist approach. But if one takes into account the costs of maintaining the controls on the financial sector—in terms of low savings mobilization, capital flight, lack of monetary control, and an inefficient allocation of resources—together with the benefits for stabilization, economic growth, and efficiency of successful reforms, then a strategy of more rapid financial sector reform could be desirable in terms of achieving better economic performance. Such a strategy should anticipate and avoid the risks that poorly sequenced financial sector reforms can pose for macroeconomic stability and the adverse consequences of macroeconomic instability for banking soundness. This two-way interaction between financial sector reforms and macroeconomic control poses special challenges for the orderly sequencing of financial sector reforms.

The experiences with financial sector reforms provide a number of important lessons. First, financial sector reforms require that mutually supporting reforms be undertaken in a number of areas—monetary and exchange, prudential, and structural. Reforms to certain sectors, such as monetary and exchange systems, can perform a critical catalytic function and help to provide momentum to the reform process. However, these reforms need to be concomitant with the strengthening of institutional structure to ensure that the liberalizations induce the appropriate responses in terms of resource mobilization and allocation and help to avoid banking crises. Prolonged periods of financial repression are usually associated with banking sector weakness and private market failures that need to be addressed at an early stage in the reforms through, among other things, implementation of a critical mass of accounting rules, prudential norms, supervisory procedures, and bank restructuring. The parallel development of critical money, exchange, and capital market institutional instruments should facilitate money and exchange system reforms. These institution-building reforms can thus promote more efficient credit and foreign exchange allocation and support macroeconomic adjustment by safeguarding against a financial crisis, and by allowing for a more rapid introduction of indirect and more efficient monetary instruments, as well as external liberalization.

Second, financial sector reforms involve monetary and portfolio shocks. Liberalization of the bank credit market can result in inflationary credit expansions. Similarly, external liberalizations may promote potentially inflationary foreign inflows. The authorities' reaction to these shocks can be critical in the success of financial sector reforms. In particular, real interest rates may need to be increased during the reform period, both to reduce the inflationary impact of the reforms and to help ensure that credit is channeled to more productive uses. The post-liberalization expansion of bank credit may also need to be implemented in phases. Exchange rates may have to be allowed to become more flexible as part of a strategy for addressing increased capital flows. Failure to manage the monetary shocks can contribute to financial crises and result in inflationary finance, which is detrimental to economic growth and efficiency. To facilitate a flexible response to monetary shocks and to the increase in capital flows, indirect instruments of monetary control should be introduced early, and phased in using a mix of instruments that can help ensure adequate monetary control and support financial market development.

Third, the liberalization of the capital account should be approached as an integrated part of comprehensive reform strategies and paced with the implementation of appropriate prudential measures and macroeconomic and exchange rate policies. The management of capital flows depends on the overall incentive structure for such flows, with the configuration of interest rates and exchange rates, as well as the stage of development of the domestic financial system, appearing particularly critical.

Fourth, countries that implemented successful financial sector reforms and avoided financial crisis experienced substantial improvements in economic performance. Real growth rates and the output to capital ratio increased strongly in this group of countries following financial reforms. In countries that faced a financial crisis, however, there has been a deterioration in economic performance. This finding argues forcefully for ensuring that financial reforms, when undertaken, are properly managed and implemented with requisite attention to both stabilization and financial system soundness.

2

Financial Sector Reform and Monetary Instruments and Operations

R. BARRY JOHNSTON AND ODD PER BREKK

Reorienting monetary control to rely increasingly on market-based instruments is not only desirable but also inevitable when countries begin to reform their financial systems. Such reliance increases the scope and flexibility of monetary policy for stabilization purposes, while also facilitating deregulation of interest rates, a removal of direct credit controls, and the development of markets. In financial systems with extensive interest rate and credit controls and subsidies, markets are typically underdeveloped and not competitive. Financial sector reform aims at developing institutional structures and competitive markets that will enhance the mobilization and allocation of resources and support the development of market-based instruments. The development of market-based monetary control instruments need not wait for the full development of market structures, since new instruments could be introduced against the background of underdeveloped financial markets as a means to foster market development.

In the absence of secondary markets in securities and active interbank markets, the main market-oriented instrument used has been pri-

---

Note: This chapter is based on IMF Working Paper 89/48 (1989), "Monetary Control Procedures and Financial Reform: Approaches, Issues, and Recent Experiences in Developing Countries," and has been revised and includes updated statistical and country specific information. We are grateful to Dawit Makonnen for research assistance.

mary issues of government or central bank papers, in addition to repurchase transactions using these papers. These types of instruments are sometimes referred to as "open-market-type operations," to distinguish them from traditional open market operations in developed secondary markets.[1] Open-market-type instruments can help foster the development of money and interbank markets and act as a catalyst to bring about institutional reform and a change in attitude toward interest rate determination, credit control, and competition in the financial system, as well as providing a framework for effective monetary control. The introduction of open-market-type operations is often accompanied by a redesign and adaptation of traditional monetary controls, such as reserve requirements and refinance policy. While the introduction of indirect instruments has helped to foster money and interbank markets, their effective adoption also has required parallel reforms to foster appropriate market institutions, competitive trading arrangements, and payment settlement facilities that will ensure a smooth functioning of these markets.

This chapter examines the background to the development of market-based monetary control and reviews experiences with these instruments in selected developing countries. It first discusses some of the problems with direct controls that have led to a greater reliance on indirect approaches to monetary control. It then reviews the framework for market-based control, with reference to the procedures followed in certain industrial countries. Afterward, this section examines procedures for developing market-based systems of monetary control in financial systems that are initially underdeveloped, and describes the development and experiences with the use of such systems in a sample of developing countries. Finally, it discusses some of the operational implications of the increase in capital flows.

Country experiences confirm that early introduction of indirect instruments can help stimulate money markets and provide a strong support for stabilization policies, thereby facilitating the process of interest rate liberalization. The close technical and operational linkages between monetary operations, money market structures, and features of payment systems suggest that reforms in these areas may have

[1]"Open-market-type operations" also include other market-based instruments, such as credit auctions, deposit auctions, and similar instruments, that do not rely on the existence of developed securities markets.

to be implemented in a well-coordinated manner to support both stabilization and financial liberalization.

Difficulties with Systems of Direct Monetary Control

The systems of direct monetary control used in most countries at one time or another typically involve some if not all of the following elements: direct controls on interest rates (including minimum and maximum interest rates, and preferential rates for certain loan categories); aggregate and individual bank credit ceilings; selective credit controls and preferential central bank refinance facilities to direct credit to priority sectors; and high reserve and liquid asset requirements, designed both to absorb liquidity and to provide government deficit financing.

When properly implemented and monitored, direct instruments of monetary control can be useful in achieving narrowly defined targets, such as maintaining a particular interest rate at a certain level, or keeping a bank's overall credit expansion below a certain ceiling. But the macroeconomic impact of the controls is unpredictable because of the scope for evasion and avoidance, and the controls also distort the allocation of resources. In addition, direct controls are administratively difficult and costly to design and implement efficiently and effectively over a prolonged period of time.

Credit ceilings and other direct controls operate by forcing banks into portfolio positions that they would not voluntarily accept. Hence, banks have incentives to avoid the direct controls. Effective credit ceilings normally involve a buildup of excess liquidity, which discourages deposit taking by regulated institutions, and in turn inhibits savings mobilization or causes disintermediation. In either case, the effectiveness of monetary control may be diminished.[2]

The erosion of effective monetary control that occurs with prolonged use of credit ceilings may not be avoided by mandating positive real interest rates at the regulated institutions. It is generally not pos-

[2]This may occur when savings mobilization is inhibited because a given level of bank credit is associated with higher consumption, and also when disintermediation occurs, because recorded bank credit underestimates the total credit available in the economy through both regulated and unregulated financial institutions.

sible to control both the cost and quantity of credit, although in practice this is what is attempted by the use of a combination of credit and interest rate controls. If the mandated deposit rates are set too high relative to the capacity to use funds under the credit ceilings, regulated institutions may either turn away depositors or find ways of paying lower effective deposit rates—for example, by increasing fees or tightening conditions on withdrawal of funds to discourage deposit mobilization.

The use of direct credit and interest rate controls can also disrupt the efficient allocation and mobilization of financial resources. First, banking system competition is often inhibited by the credit and interest rate controls. Banks will have little incentive to compete on services; and the controls may encourage collusive behavior in setting commissions and charges. Inefficient institutions would lead to higher average transaction margins and lending spreads.

Second, the incentive to price credit according to risk is often lacking when interest rates and credit are subject to direct regulation. As a result, financial resources may not be directed into those activities expected to yield the highest returns, which is detrimental to economic growth, and banks' balance sheets may be weakened by an underpricing of risks. High liquid asset ratios, which create captive markets for government securities, can also result in an inappropriate pricing of credit.

Third, under systems of direct interest rate and credit controls, little attention is often paid to the development of money and capital markets—both critical factors in the efficient mobilization and allocation of financial resources from the private sector, both domestic and international. Within a regulated system, the existence of money and capital markets could undermine the credit and interest rate controls by providing alternative outlets and sources of funds outside the administered system. Commercial bank credit, however, has normally been of a short-term, revolving nature, and not suited for financing longer-term investment projects.[3] As a consequence, the volume of

[3]Within regulated systems without capital markets, the financing of such projects often requires official subsidies through preferential central bank refinance facilities, from the budget, or through development finance institutions. A reliance on central bank refinance interferes with the central bank's capacity to control reserves of the banking system, and undermines its independence, while the experience with development finance institutions in identifying and financing viable projects has not been very positive.

long-term finance may be impaired, while the lack of a range of financial instruments differentiated by maturity, risk, and liquidity may discourage private savings.

Fourth, direct credit and interest rate controls are usually inconsistent with freedom of international capital movements. Such controls may, therefore, interfere with the capacity of the private sector to raise capital abroad, the scope to upgrade the domestic financial system through foreign direct investment, and the liberalization of cross-border trade in financial services. In addition, the low rates of return associated with direct controls, together with uncompetitive financial markets, may encourage capital flight.

Fifth, direct controls create various administrative problems and provide opportunities for "rent seeking" and abuse, such as with the allocation of individual bank credit ceilings. Governments may have difficulty ensuring that credit is used for the productive purposes intended under selective credit and interest rate controls.

The implicit tax imposed on commercial banks, and by default their borrowers and depositors, by credit ceilings, interest rate controls, and high non-interest-bearing reserve requirements, encourages the emergence of other, unregulated, financial intermediaries and instruments that compete with the regulated ones. This weakens monetary control by eroding the effectiveness of the direct controls and may prompt the authorities to bear down even harder on regulated financial institutions to achieve a given restrictive policy stance. Unregulated institutions are by their nature less supervised and more prone to solvency and liquidity problems than regulated institutions and may, therefore, also pose a threat to a financial system's stability.

Alternative Market-Related Monetary Control Framework

A market-based approach to monetary control can be described by distinguishing between the instruments, intermediate targets, and ultimate objectives of monetary policy. The instruments of monetary policy are variables, such as money market interest rates or the level of money market liquidity, which are directly under the control of the monetary authorities, and which influence the path of the intermediate target variables or the final objectives. The intermediate targets are variables, such as various monetary aggregates, that are related in a reasonably predictable manner to ultimate policy objectives—for instance, inflation and nominal GDP. Under an indirect approach to monetary control, the authorities set the instruments consistent with meeting the path for the intermediate targets/objective variables and leave market mechanisms to determine the detailed structure of deposit and lending rates and the allocation of credit.[4] In a liberal system, the main instrument of monetary control would be the central bank's control over interest rates in the money market through its ability to manage its own balance sheet and the stock of reserve money (cash and balances with the central bank). Money market rates, in turn, affect other lending and deposit rates. Such a system does not rely on high or even compulsory reserve or liquid asset requirements, but only on the central bank's ability to manage its balance sheet, particularly the level of bank reserves, and to control the terms at which it is willing to provide assistance to cover reserve shortages.

Market-based procedures have for several years been the main instrument for conducting monetary policy in the industrial countries with developed money and interbank markets. Such procedures have also assumed a larger role in many developing countries with the aim of increasing the flexibility with which monetary policy can be implemented and eliminating impediments to competition and financial market development. These reforms have become more pressing with the increasing volume and freedom of capital movements. Generally, the reforms have involved the redesign of central bank lending facilities and reserve requirements, development of market-based monetary operations, and fostering of supporting money market institutions and payment system arrangements, as needed.

Among the industrial countries, central bank lending facilities aim predominantly at providing credit to meet technical reserve needs, such as clearing short-term payment imbalances and lender-of-last-resort support, but have also included certain specialized lending facilities intended to promote lending to priority sectors. Table 2.1 provides an overview of the main features of the monetary control

[4]An increasing number of central banks target the final objective of low inflation directly and do not rely on an announced intermediate target, although intermediate targets and indicators continue to be used to guide policy implementation. Under direct inflation targeting, the inflation forecast may serve as a form of intermediate target for determining the necessary adjustment in the monetary instruments.

Table 2.1. Monetary Policy Instruments in the Group of Ten Countries, Switzerland, and the European Central Bank

	Belgium	Canada	France	Germany	Italy	Japan	Netherlands	Sweden	Switzerland	United Kingdom	United States	European Central Bank
Central bank lending and deposit facilities												
Ordinary discount facility available	•			•	•	•	•		•		•	•
Loan or advance facility available	•	•	•	•	•	•	•	•	•	•	•	
Access subject to quotas or ceilings	•	•		•	•	•	•	•			•	
Penalty for frequent recourse	•	•			•	•	•					
Key official rate above market rates	•	•	•	•	•				•	•		
Official rate set in relation to treasury bill rate	•	•										
Deposit facilities												•
Market operations												
Outright market transactions												
Purchases of government securities		•			•	•			•	•	•	•
Sales of government securities		•			•						•	•
Purchases of treasury bills	•	•	•		•	•				•	•	•
Sales of treasury bills	•	•	•		•	•					•	•
Purchases of private bills						•				•		•
Sales of private bills						•			•			•
Sales of bills issued by central bank				•		•			•			•
Reversed transactions												
Purchase and resale operations in government securities	•	•	•	•	•	•	•	•		•	•	•
Sale and repurchase operations in government securities	•	•	•					•			•	•

Purchase and resale operations in private bills	•		•	•					•		•
Sale and repurchase operations in private bills			•								•
Foreign currency operations/swaps	•			•	•	•	•	•			•
Transfer of government deposits		•		•				•			
Reserve requirements											
Cash reserve requirements in force		•	•	•	•	•		•		•	•
Averaging provisions for reserve holding		•	•	•	•	•		•		•	•
Carry-over allowed for reserve surplus/deficits			•							•	
Contemporaneous (C), lagged (L) or semi-lagged (SL)	L	SL	SL	L	SL			L		SL	L
Length of reserve holding period (in days)	30	30	30	30	30			30		14	30
Highest reserve ratio for demand deposits	0	1	5	15	1.3			2.5		10	2
Highest reserve ratio for term and saving deposits	0	0.5	2	15	1.2			2.5		0	2
Penalty for reserve deficiencies (percent above discount rate)		3	3	5	3.5						5

Sources: Bank for International Settlements (1989); European Central Bank (1998); and IMF staff estimates.

instruments that have been applied in Group of Ten countries and Switzerland, and proposed for the European Central Bank.[5]

The supply of bank reserves through central bank standing facilities tended to be demand determined at the discretion of commercial banks (or other eligible institutions), with central bank loans extended at a posted interest rate. Many central banks viewed such procedures as cumbersome, however, providing insufficient flexibility in monetary control. Hence, the trend has been toward curbing automatic access to central bank lending by introducing bank-specific ceilings on such access and penalty rates on extended credit, and by adopting market-based procedures. Special credit facilities have generally been reduced in favor of a generalized, lender-of-last-resort window against collateral, with day-to-day liquidity management through market-based operations undertaken at the discretion of the central bank.

Market-based monetary operations include outright transactions in bills and other securities, various types of reversed transactions (such as repurchase agreements in bills and bonds and foreign exchange swaps), and transfers of government deposits between the central bank and commercial banks. Outright transactions in securities in secondary markets have tended to be less important than types of reversed transactions. Reversed transactions consist of a purchase or sale of a security (or foreign exchange) combined with an agreement for its repurchase or resale at a specified price and at a given future date. In the United States, the Federal Reserve has been able to use an already existing private market in repurchase agreements; in other countries, special tender arrangements have been set up by the central bank. Reversed security transactions through tenders generally give the central bank substantial scope for setting the price, amount, and maturity. Transfers of government deposits between the central bank and commercial banks are conceptually one of the simplest procedures for managing bank reserves. The procedure, however, raises practical questions—such as the distribution between banks, remuneration, and

[5]The Group of Ten consists of Belgium, Canada, France, Germany, Italy, Japan, the Netherlands, Sweden, the United Kingdom, and the United States. Effective January 1, 1999, when the exchange rates of the national currencies of the countries participating in EMU became irrevocably locked, a common monetary policy determined by the European Central Bank applies in Belgium, France, Germany, Italy, the Netherlands, and the other members participating in EMU.

collateral requirements. It has long been the major instrument for shorter-term monetary management in Canada.

In recent years, variations in reserve requirements have lost importance in the conduct of monetary policy in industrial countries, being replaced to a large extent by the instruments described above. The need to meet legal reserve requirements, however, has remained the fulcrum of monetary policy. There has been a general tendency toward lower reserve requirements, reflecting a concern that high non-interest-bearing reserve requirements encourage disintermediation. To smooth the functioning of the reserve requirement system, several countries have adopted averaging procedures for meeting reserve requirements, designed to give banks more flexibility in their reserve management and to avoid unintended short-term swings in interest rates.[6] Industrial countries have generally abandoned the use of liquid asset ratios as monetary instruments and modified the design of such ratios as instruments to emphasize prudential aspects.

A Market-Based System for Underdeveloped Financial Markets

Primary Bill Market Operations

A first step in developing market-based instruments of monetary control in countries with underdeveloped financial markets has frequently been primary issues of treasury bills and/or central bank bills, supported by a restructuring of central bank rediscount windows to allow a greater role for market forces. Commercial banks are often already required to hold treasury bills to meet liquid asset requirements, and, therefore, issues of such paper, which involve less risk than longer-term securities, are a convenient starting point. Issues of central bank securities have been considered useful in some circumstances, because of the potentially greater freedom for the central bank to tailor issues of its own papers to achieve monetary objectives. Although the net budgetary and monetary impact from using central bank rather than treasury paper would in principle be similar, the pay-

[6]One or two countries also have carryover provisions for reserve surplus or deficiencies from one reserve holding period to another.

ment of interest by the central bank on its own debt could affect its profit and loss position, and this could have a monetary effect depending upon the legal and technical arrangements to distribute central bank profits and cover losses, if any.[7] In those countries where central bank refinance has been a major source of credit to the banking systems, auctions of the refinance credit have been used to introduce market forces into the allocation procedures. Unlike auctions of bills, however, auctions of credit involve issues of moral hazard and adverse selection, and hence require a careful design to limit these problems as well as measures to reduce the extent of reliance on central bank refinance.[8] It is generally desirable to move quickly away from a situation of significant central bank refinance.

The role of security issues as instruments of monetary control is illustrated in Appendix I, using financial flow and balance sheet equations.[9] Essentially, the technique is to sell a net volume of securities (e.g., treasury bills or central bank bills) outside the central bank in order to meet an objective for banks' excess cash reserves. This objective is the short-run operating target of monetary operations. The net volume to be sold is determined on the basis of monetary policy objectives and a forecast of the supply of reserves, compared with the estimate of the banking systems' demand for reserves. Given these forecasts, the net sales of securities can be targeted to tighten, ease, or maintain the liquidity situation (i.e., raise, lower, or maintain the level of interest rates).

For the central bank to implement the new monetary policy operating framework, a monetary programming procedure must be established to carry out the projections and determine the volume of bills to be sold. The type of operational framework that may need to be developed for determining the regular auction amounts and the volume of money market intervention to be undertaken by the central bank between auctions are illustrated in Table 2.2.

---

[7]See Quintyn (1994) for a discussion of the choice between central bank and treasury securities for monetary control.

[8]In practice, countries need instruments to absorb as well as inject reserves, and hence, use both securities and credit auctions, and over time transform credit auctions into repurchase auctions using treasury or central bank bills.

[9]The same principles apply to the use of other instruments such as credit auctions of a mix of instruments.

Table 2.2. Framework for Regular Forecasting and Daily Monitoring of Cash Positions

Variable	Regular Forecast for Auction	For Money Market Intervention
Commercial banks' required cash balances	Based on projected growth of monetary aggregates developed by central bank as part of macroeconomic policy framework and analysis of seasonal pattern in deposits of commercial banks.	Monitoring unit to prepare assessment of progress under the cash reserve ratios and discuss with banks the level of their desired precautionary cash balances.
Foreign exchange	Based on projections of the balance of payments developed by the central bank and analysis of seasonal pattern in payment flows and intervention by the central bank.	Actual intervention by the central bank to be communicated daily to the monitoring unit. Forecast based on two-day delay in settling international transactions.
Currency outside banks	Based on currency demand estimates; seasonal patterns; and statistical forecasting techniques.	The currency issue to be notified daily to the monitoring unit.
Government accounts	Forecasts of regular receipts and payments, such as customs duties, and wage and social security payments to be prepared by the relevant government departments. General Accountant to notify of large irregular payments expected during forecast period. List of securities outstanding with amounts and maturity dates and notification of new issues with dates and amounts to be made available to the public.	Actual receipts and payments through government accounts to be notified to the monitoring unit. Request forecasts and information from government departments.
Maturing central bank bonds and assistance	Lists of bonds and assistance outstanding with amounts and maturity dates.	Actual repayments to be notified to the monitoring unit.
Central bank current transactions	Central bank staff to prepare weekly forecasts.	Actual payments and receipts to be communicated to the monitoring unit.
Other central bank current accounts	—	Actual balances in accounts to be communicated to the monitoring unit.

Selling techniques for primary bill issues range from "free" auctions to fixed-price tenders. Under "free" auctions, the ministry of finance or, typically, the central bank acting as the agent of the ministry announces the volume of bills to be sold and asks for competitive bids. Interest rates would be allowed to adjust to sell the quantity of bills tendered, and, hence, achieve the targeted stock of reserves. Bills are allocated starting with the highest bid price and moving to the next highest until the tender is fully sold. The auction produces a range of interest rates, with the highest rate determined by the marginal bid that exhausts the tender—known as the "cutoff" or "striking" rate. Bills could be allocated either at the cutoff rate or at the price bid by each successful bidder. Under a fixed-price tender, the central bank sets the interest rate on bills and accepts the volume demanded at that rate, typically during a fixed subscription period. Thus in contrast to the "free auction," the interest rate is determined in the short run, and quantities are allowed to vary. The interest rate in a fixed-price tender may be varied from one tender to the next to exercise the desired quantitative control.

In introducing primary bill auctions, a concern expressed by central banks about a "free" auction is that it may result in excessive volatility in interest rates, while the concern with a fixed-price tender is that it may risk a "bias to delay" in adjusting interest rates. Central banks have thus adopted different selling procedures that seek to avoid excessive interest rate volatility while allowing flexibility in interest rate adjustment. In some cases, bills are auctioned, but no tender volume is announced in advance. Usually the ministry of finance or the central bank exercises its discretion in accepting or rejecting bids, depending on its quantitative or interest rate objectives. The decision not to announce the tender amount can thus give the authorities added flexibility, although at the cost of reducing information to market participants. In some other cases, bills are auctioned and tender volumes announced in advance, and a permissible range is announced for acceptable bids; the range is usually based on the interest rate set at the previous auction. In some countries the central bank or other financial institutions underwrite the bill issue at interest rates indicated by and agreed with the ministry of finance. Another procedure is for the ministry of finance or the central bank to preannounce an initial auction amount, but to vary it once bids are received in order to achieve interest rate objectives. The central bank may also decide to reject all bids if they are not considered satisfactory. The increased flexibility provided by these various techniques can help overcome initial concerns about a loss of control over interest rates when implementing new monetary control and debt management procedures.

Central Bank Facilities

In addition to issuing primary bills, the central bank may need to intervene to manage short-term fluctuations in liquidity.[10] For example, unanticipated deposit withdrawals into cash may be such as to create a reserve shortage and force commercial banks to borrow from the central bank. If not offset by the central bank, the resulting reserve shortages or surpluses could result in excessive volatility in interest rates, complicate banks' compliance with legal reserve requirements, and interfere with the functioning of the payment system.

Under a strict monetary base control system or regimes that allow for period averaging when determining compliance with compulsory reserve requirements, it is conceivable that banks' precautionary reserve holdings would remove the need for frequent money market interventions by the central bank.[11] Nevertheless, most central banks have facilities for day-to-day money market operations, and the arrangements for such facilities have varied depending on local circumstances and the stage of development of the domestic money market.

Central banks have frequently set penalty interest rates (discount or bank rate) at which they are willing to lend to commercial banks, usually against collateral.[12] A loan window provides a facility only to eliminate reserve shortages, and has sometimes been combined with a deposit facility at the central bank to help manage surpluses in liquidity; the European Central Bank has such a facility. The loan window

---

[10]Issues of primary bills could also in principle be held frequently, but because sales of bills to the general public involve administrative costs and delays associated with advertising the sale, receiving and filling bids, and similar operations, primary bill issues have tended to occur no more than once a week.

[11]In some countries where the central bank has been inactive in the money markets, commercial banks have built up large precautionary reserve balances, apparently to meet short-term fluctuations in their liquidity, although this buildup has also often been accompanied by official concerns about "excess liquidity" and the underuse of commercial bank resources. For a theoretical treatment of the optimal holding of precautionary balances in the face of uncertainty see Sprenkle and Miller (1980). The proposed use of reserve requirements with compliance on a period average basis by the European Central Bank has also been justified by the expectation that this would reduce the need for day-to-day money market intervention.

[12]Penalties associated with borrowing from the central bank may reflect quotas that restrict access, rather than specifically posted penal rates.

rate has sometimes come to be viewed as the indicative rate for all interest rates, thus inhibiting their market determination. Some countries have sought to mitigate this concern by providing graduated access to the loan window at progressively higher penalty rates.[13] A few countries with underdeveloped financial markets have found it useful for the central bank to preannounce its willingness to buy or sell bills at posted interest rates close to those determined in the last primary auction. Such procedures, however, can interfere with monetary control objectives and the development of secondary markets. To reduce these risks, central banks have widened the margins between their preannounced buying and selling rates for bills.

In view of the drawbacks of the above-mentioned techniques, the generally preferred procedure for short-term liquidity management is for the central bank to take the initiative on the quantity of intervention and leave the interest rates to the market. The central bank could participate in the interbank market or conduct auctions of its money market intervention instruments, including outright sales and purchases of specified securities, repurchase agreements, foreign exchange swaps, and rediscounts.[14] By restricting these auctions to a few key money market participants, the day-to-day auctions can be implemented more flexibly than the general auctions of primary bills.[15] Various techniques can be used to help identify the need for and the volume of such auctions.[16]

---

[13]Graduated access could be provided in a number of ways, including the use of quotas and credit tranches for accommodation from the central bank.

[14]In principle, direct intervention in the unsecured interbank market, such as the auctioning of deposit placements or other similar devices, is possible for day-to-day control. The choice would depend upon the institutional circumstances.

[15]When shortages are indicated, the central bank would typically announce its willingness to buy bills up to a certain amount, and ask for competitive offers from banks and other money market participants; when surpluses are indicated the central bank would announce its willingness to sell a certain volume of bills, and ask for competitive bids.

[16]Information to be monitored would include: (1) the size of government payments or exchange market intervention by the central bank; (2) interbank rates throughout the day; (3) assistance provided through the loan window (if such a facility existed); (4) the ex post monitoring of developments in the central bank balance sheet components, relative to the forecast used to determine the size of the primary bill issue; and (5) commercial bank progress in meeting cash reserve requirements.

Transitional Considerations in Moving to a Market-Based System

The introduction of more market-based monetary controls raises a number of transitional issues. The transition to full reliance on indirect monetary controls may take time, because experience and confidence in the new system has to be gained by the central bank and the private sector, and new institutional arrangements may have to be established to ensure effective monetary control and competitive market mechanisms. A phased approach to reform may, therefore, be appropriate. If the initial financial system is highly regulated, however, with each regulation supporting the other, it may be difficult to implement a gradual, effective reform. In such cases, a major one-step change in the monetary operations system supported by a critical mass of concomitant reforms of institutions and structures may be unavoidable.

An indirect, market-based approach relies on reasonable efficiency in the monetary transmission mechanism; however, prolonged periods of financial repression usually weaken this mechanism. First, repressed financial systems usually lack competition. While a monopolistic structure may not necessarily interfere with monetary control, it could result in a sluggish response of deposit and lending rates to monetary policy initiatives, inhibit the development of new instruments and markets, and result in an inefficient allocation of resources. The removal of direct controls can itself reduce incentives for monopolistic pricing arrangements by increasing the areas where competition is possible.

Second, repressed financial systems often feature a high incidence of lack of credit discipline and loan delinquency, or arrangements where borrowers or banks expect to have their deficit covered by the government. Such features undermine the role of markets in the allocation of credit. The financial reforms can also bring to the fore weaknesses in bank solvency and in the supervisory arrangements, and can have widespread effects on the viability of borrowers. For example, as the direct controls on interest rates and credit are relaxed, some borrowers that previously had access to directed credit may no longer be viable, and loans will have to be provisioned and written off. Strengthening bankruptcy laws, implementing legal procedures for loan recovery, increasing attention to the quality of bank balance sheets through improved bank supervision, and carrying out bank closures and restructuring may have to accompany the reforms of monetary control procedures. This aspect of reforms is further discussed in Chapter 4.

Third, the effective use of issues of government or central bank securities to manage liquidity will require elimination of captive markets for government securities and the liberalization of interest rates on these securities. These developments could have a direct budgetary impact and call for appropriate institutional arrangements to coordinate monetary and public debt management. But they could also improve the capacity to finance the fiscal deficit, because of the scope for the development of markets in government debt instruments and improved overall savings mobilization. Moreover, under financial repression the actual fiscal burden is often hidden by the below market rates of interest on government debt. These "hidden" deficits still impose a financial burden on the economy, including through low savings mobilization, inefficient allocation of credit, and capital flight.[17]

Fourth, the transition to indirect monetary controls also raises questions about the selection of appropriate monetary target variables and the interpretation of monetary indicators more generally as guides to policy. Relationships between money and credit and final objectives that existed during the prereform phase may become less reliable following financial reform. The introduction of new instruments may shift the interest sensitivity of money demand. A liberalization of interest rates on bank deposits may result in broad money becoming less sensitive to changes in the general level of interest rates. The removal of credit ceilings that constrain portfolio allocation can result in portfolio shifts, and the liberalization of interest rates can reduce cash holdings by the public.

Not only can the monetary relationships shift, but the controllability of certain aggregates may become more difficult following financial reform. In a liberal environment, the impact of a change in interest rates on broad money and credit will depend on the response of financial institutions in adjusting their rates, and on the portfolio responses of individuals and firms. Initially there is likely to be a good deal of uncertainty about these responses. A range of indicators, including the exchange rate, inflation, and asset prices, as well as various monetary and credit aggregates, therefore, may need to be examined to assess monetary conditions. It may also become more difficult to formulate mone-

[17]On the question of sequencing fiscal adjustment with financial sector reform, see Johnston (1997). Issues in the coordination of monetary and public management during financial reform are discussed in Sundararajan, Dattels, and Blommestein (1997).

tary and credit targets that can act as benchmarks in macroeconomic adjustment programs when structural changes are occurring in the financial system. Nevertheless, quantitative monetary or credit targets often remain a central element in macroeconomic policy formulation.[18]

As part of a more gradualist approach to reform, interest rates could be set free in stages, for example, by gradually widening the permissible ranges for deposit and lending rates, or by steadily adjusting minimum deposit rates and maximum lending rates, freeing up commercial bank lending and deposit rates from official interference, or removing credit subceilings. The traditional instruments—reserve requirements and rediscount windows—could be deployed initially to manage bank reserves and thereby the credit-creating capacity of the banking system, while phasing out credit ceilings on banks. Market-based instruments of monetary policy would be introduced as the reforms proceed, to manage interest rates and credit more flexibly. The eventual elimination of direct controls would require that the indirect instruments of monetary policy be already functioning in parallel. By this stage, progress should also have been made on developing a money market and a more competitive financial system.

The particular phasing of reforms would depend upon the institutional circumstances. For example, if reserve requirements are already at high levels, and are nonremunerative, it would be undesirable to increase them further; market-based instruments of greater flexibility should be developed at an early stage in the reform process. If the major source of liquidity and credit creation is preferential refinance credit, the initial focus should be on reducing such credit and applying market interest rates to remaining credit facilities—for example, by auctioning the credit. The parallel development of interbank markets and secondary markets and the supporting payment system may need to be encouraged through appropriate reforms.

Developing Market-Based Procedures of Monetary Control in Nine Developing Countries

This section reviews the use of market-based procedures of monetary control in nine developing countries—Argentina, Brazil, Indonesia,

[18]See Johnston (1993) for a discussion of the design of financial programs with the adoption of indirect monetary controls.

Kenya, Malaysia, Mexico, the Philippines, Sri Lanka, and Thailand—all of which have reduced or abolished the use of direct controls on interest rates and credit, and increased reliance on market-based monetary control. Some of the countries, including Argentina, Brazil, and Indonesia, have for a number of years operated market-based instruments of monetary control, although direct regulations of interest rates and credit have been retained or reintroduced to a certain degree. Other countries have undertaken quite determined reductions in direct controls more recently.

Reforming Monetary Instruments

The approaches to market-based procedures for monetary control followed by these countries are summarized in Table 2.3. Appendix II provides more detailed information on the approaches to monetary control. The main conclusions emerging from the country experiences are:

(1) Market-based approaches to monetary control have usually been adopted in the context of progressive modifications of existing monetary instruments. Most of the countries continued to rely to a greater or lesser extent on reserve requirements, liquid asset ratios, and subsidized refinance facilities while increasing the reliance on market-based procedures for monetary and interest rate control. Also, although interest rate controls were relaxed significantly, they were not eliminated completely in a few cases, partly because of concern over the competitiveness of the banking system.[19] Although specific credit ceilings were eliminated, guidance on lending was retained in some cases. Countries further along in the reform process, however, have been able to abandon the direct forms of control and to rely on indirect procedures.

---

[19]For example, in Thailand, ceilings on savings deposits and loan rates were eliminated in January 1992 and June 1992, respectively, but Thai banks were required to post a minimum lending rate that takes into account the average cost of funds and a minimum retail rate for loans to general customers. There was an understanding that the minimum lending rate would not exceed the average cost of deposits by more than 2 percent, the minimum retail rate would not exceed the minimum lending rate by more than 2 percent, and the maximum loan rates would not exceed the minimum retail rate by more than 2 percent; see Johnston (1991b).

Table 2.3. Development of Market-Based Procedures for Monetary Control in Nine Developing Countries

Country	Primary Issues of Securities and Other Market-Based Instruments	Targets of Security Issues	Instruments of Daily Money Market Management	Other Monetary Instruments and Controls	Intermediate and Short-Term Operating Targets
Argentina (July 85–March 91)	Weekly auctions of participation in government papers in the form of central bank bills.	Volumes sold to meet quantity objectives; however, volume targets overridden to limit volatility in interest rates.	Repurchase/reverse repurchases, foreign exchange swaps at interest rates set by the central bank.	Interest rate regulations. Quotas on non-regulated rate deposits, acceptances and swaps. Subsidized refinance facilities. Reserve requirements varied actively.	*Intermediate*: Monetary aggregates; at times the exchange rate. *Short term*: Interest rates on central bank bills or debt sales.
Brazil	Weekly auctions of central bank bills (and treasury bills, but mainly for budgetary finance).	Volumes preannounced to control money market liquidity; discounts market determined. Prior to 1986, central bank intervened in the treasury bill auctions when bids were unacceptable.	Repurchases/reverse repurchases, and outright sales at interest rates set by the central bank.	Selective credit controls; subsidized facilities.	*Intermediate*: Monetary aggregates; real interest rates. *Short term*: Base money, overnight interest rates.
Indonesia	Auctions of central bank bills. The frequency of auctions has varied between daily and weekly.	Prior to 1987, cutoff interest rate in the auctions determined consistent with exchange rate objective; subsequently a greater focus on liquidity conditions and interest rates increasingly market determined.	Repurchase agreements and daily auctions of central bank bills. Passive central bank accommodation at posted interest rates discontinued, July 1987.	Subsidized refinance facilities. Transfers of government deposits. Limits on borrowing abroad.	*Intermediate*: Monetary aggregates and monetary base. *Short term*: Exchange rate, interest rate.

Table 2.3 (*concluded*)

Country	Primary Issues of Securities and Other Market-Based Instruments	Targets of Security Issues	Instruments of Daily Money Market Management	Other Monetary Instruments and Controls	Intermediate and Short-Term Operating Targets
Kenya	Weekly auction of treasury bills.	Mainly government finance purposes; monetary objectives targeted 1993–mid-1994.	Foreign exchange intervention; open market operations in treasury bills.	Reserve requirements varied actively.	*Intermediate*: Monetary aggregates; at times exchange rate. *Short term*: Reserve money; net domestic assets of the central bank.
Malaysia	Weekly auctions of treasury bills.	Government finance purposes.	Discount window, outright sales and purchases of government securities, repurchase/reverse repurchases, foreign exchange swaps, recycling of government deposits.	Selective credit and interest rate controls; reserve requirements varied actively; subsidized refinance facilities.	*Intermediate*: Broad monetary aggregates. *Short term*: Interbank interest rates.
Mexico	Weekly auctions of treasury certificates.	Budgetary and monetary objectives. Interest rates freely determined, central bank may intervene to moderate interest rate movements.	Outright sales and purchases and repurchase/reverse repurchases. Weekly auctions of fixed deposits and placements from the central bank.	Reserve requirements and liquid asset ratios (credit ceilings removed in 1988/89).	*Intermediate*: Exchange rate; growth of central bank credit. *Short term*: Interest rates.

Philippines	Weekly auctions of treasury bills, issues of central bank bills.	Tender volumes decided based on budgetary needs and increasingly monetary objectives; interest rates determined within a range based on previous auction rate.	Repurchase/reverse repurchases, foreign exchange swaps.	Reserve requirements varied actively.	*Intermediate*: Base money. *Short term*: Money market liquidity, interest rates, exchange rate.
Sri Lanka	Weekly or more frequent auctions of treasury bills; auctions of central bank securities.	Volumes of treasury bills based on budgetary, needs cutoff interest rate set by central bank. Sales of central bank securities based on monetary objectives.	Repurchase/reverse repurchases, foreign exchange swaps. Secondary window for sale and purchase of treasury bills.	Reserve requirements varied actively. Indicative bank by bank credit ceilings. Subsidized refinance facilities.	*Intermediate*: Base money. *Short term*: Central bank net domestic assets.
Thailand	Weekly auctions of treasury bills; central bank bonds.	Sales of treasury bills for budgetary purposes and to meet liquid asset requirements; sales of central bank bonds for monetary purposes.	Repurchase/reverse repurchases, using government bonds; discount window; forward exchange swaps.	Interest rate ceilings gradually eliminated. Subsidized refinance facilities. Guidance on commercial bank lending. Limits on lending spreads.	*Intermediate*: Multiple monetary and credit aggregates. *Short term*: Interest rates, money market liquidity.

(2) Nearly all of the countries surveyed made use of regular auctions—either for central bank or treasury bills—as part of a market-development, debt-management, or monetary-control strategy. Under these auctions, the public submits bids indicating the volume demanded and the bid price to the central bank for treasury/central bank bills on auction. The type of instrument used and the frequency of the auction varied. Typically, the papers used for monetary control through auctions have been short term, with maturities from 7 days to 12 months. In some cases, an inflationary environment has put downward pressure on maturities (Argentina, Mexico, the Philippines, and Sri Lanka). Auctions have normally been held weekly, although the frequency has varied and even daily auctions have been held in one country (Indonesia). Mexico has also held weekly auctions of central bank offers to place or accept deposits to supplement the auctions of treasury bills. Some countries (Mexico and the Philippines) have instituted formal limitations on the cutoff yield in the auctions, in order to promote orderly bidding and to avoid large short-run fluctuations in interest rates. In some countries, participation in the auctions has been formally restricted to financial institutions (Indonesia) or appointed dealers in the papers in question (Mexico and the Philippines). Appointed dealers have sometimes been obliged to make secondary markets in these papers (Philippines).

(3) The objectives and procedures for determining auction volumes and interest rates varied across the countries. In Brazil, Malaysia, Sri Lanka, and Thailand the auction volumes of treasury bills have been determined purely by budgetary considerations. Nevertheless, the central bank has intervened in these auctions, to determine the cutoff rate (Sri Lanka), influence money market liquidity, or moderate the movement in interest rates. In some of the other countries, both budgetary and monetary considerations have been taken into account in determining auction volumes. For example, in the Philippines, the tender volumes of treasury bills have been used to sterilize foreign capital inflows.

Central bank securities have been issued for monetary control purposes, either as a supplement to the issues of treasury bills (Brazil, Philippines, Sri Lanka, and Thailand) or as the primary instrument (Argentina and Indonesia).[20] The central bank accepts or rejects bids

[20]In Argentina, the central bank auctions central bank bills issued against its holdings of government securities (this practice has been named "participations").

on the basis of a cutoff yield determined to be consistent with their desired operating target for monetary policy. The most widely used operating target has been short-term interest rates. Other operating targets have included various measures of liquidity (Argentina, Brazil, and Mexico) and net domestic assets of the central bank (Sri Lanka and Kenya).

(4) Day-to-day money-market operating procedures have varied among the countries, but in most such operations have taken on increasing importance as instruments of liquidity and interest rate management. The most common instrument has been repurchase and reverse repurchase agreements using government papers (Argentina, Brazil, Malaysia, Mexico, the Philippines, Sri Lanka, and Thailand). Some countries, such as Malaysia (initially), Sri Lanka, and Kenya, have operated a secondary window for the purchase and sale of treasury bills with interest rates set based on those determined at the latest auction rate. These interest rate margins have been varied to encourage secondary sales or purchases, which help to achieve objectives for money market liquidity. Several countries have operated a loan or rediscount window carrying varying degrees of penalty (for example, Kenya); and some countries have used foreign exchange swaps (the Philippines and Argentina). Interest rates on most of these facilities are determined by the central bank. Malaysia and Indonesia have supplemented these facilities by the transfer of government or public enterprise deposits between the central bank and commercial banks as a way of managing money market liquidity. Some countries (most notably Indonesia and the Philippines) have also reformed the central bank's refinance facilities for priority sector borrowing to, among other things, restrict the financial institutions' access to central bank credit and to rationalize rediscount facilities.

(5) Countries that have taken the most determined steps toward a market-based monetary control system adopted their intermediate targets for monetary policy sometimes in the context of a modification of their exchange arrangements. Following its financial reform, Indonesia changed from targeting domestic credit of the banking system to targeting base money and broad money. In Malaysia and Sri Lanka, the focus shifted from interest rates to broader monetary aggregates. Also, the Philippines shifted from targeting net domestic assets to targeting base money following the move to a floating exchange rate in late 1984. At different times, the exchange rate has also been used as a

key target in some of these countries, including Kenya. Domestic monetary instruments and exchange market intervention have been used to target the rate. The short-term operating targets have most commonly included money market interest rates. In some cases the exchange rate, money market liquidity, and the net domestic assets of the central bank have been used.

(6) In nearly all the countries surveyed, the introduction of market-based instruments was accompanied by measures to foster money and interbank markets, particularly secondary markets in government securities. Country experiences also revealed the complex two-way interactions between choice of monetary instruments and operating procedures, and the characteristics and pace of development of money and securities markets, including the supporting clearing and settlement system for payments. For example, in both the Philippines and Malaysia, the authorities facilitated money market development by adopting market-based instruments. The effectiveness of the instruments was strengthened in turn by the authorities' efforts to develop money and interbank markets. Their efforts consisted of fostering money market intermediaries, including primary dealer arrangements, rationalizing reserve requirement systems and refinance facilities, and promoting adequate institutional arrangements for coordination of monetary and public debt management.

In some countries, reforms of clearing and settlement systems for payments also helped to strengthen the functioning of money and interbank markets (e.g., Malaysia). Country experiences confirm that aspects of the payment system could play a crucial role in the reform of monetary policy implementation and the pace of development of money markets. For example, lags in the settlement of money and exchange market transactions, accounting rules governing clearing and settlement in central bank books, the level of communications technology, and availability and terms of central bank credit or access to required revenues for settlement purposes are some of the structural elements that influenced the demand for excess reserves and short-term money market conditions.[21]

[21]See Baliño, Johnson, and Sundararajan (1996) for a discussion of linkages between payment systems and monetary policy.

Importance of Market-Based Procedures as Instruments of Monetary Control

The importance of market-based instruments in seven of the sample countries is examined in the tables in Appendix II.[22] These tables attempt to identify the "autonomous sources" of reserve money expansion and the use of market-based and other instruments, including reserve requirements, to offset the expansion.[23] The autonomous sources include the extent to which the domestic financing requirement of the government has to be met by the central bank, the increase in the net foreign assets of the central bank, and central bank autonomous net lending to commercial banks. Instruments used to reduce liquidity include traditional adjustments to reserve requirements or in central bank refinance facilities, and more market-based procedures, including debt sales and money market operations.

Indonesia

In Indonesia, the major monetary disturbances were associated with instability in the balance of payments, and to a somewhat lesser extent domestic financing of the government budget deficit. Indonesia has relied increasingly on market-based instruments to control liquidity since 1983. Up until 1987, the reserve money effects of the changes in net foreign exchange reserves were largely offset by the central bank's net claims on the government. Increasing use of open-market-type operations began in 1986, and operations in central bank certificates subsequently became the most important instrument for offsetting the fluctuations in international reserves. The central bank continued to provide substantial liquidity support to banks through 1990; such assistance, however, was reduced sharply thereafter to counter larger foreign inflows. In spite of the increased use of market-based instruments, reserve money growth has fluctuated substantially, reflecting insufficient flexibility in domestic interest rates. Reserve requirements have not been used actively to manage liquidity, even in the face of substantial foreign inflows.

[22]The available information for Argentina and Brazil was not adequate for the preparation of this type of statistical analysis.

[23]See Appendix I for a theoretical analysis leading to this presentation.

Kenya

In Kenya, the impact of the government's domestic financing needs on reserve money has been moderated through domestic sales of treasury bills and bonds outside the central bank. Before 1990, monetary policy relied largely on direct interest rate controls and bank-specific credit ceilings. In 1990, the Central Bank of Kenya started to pay increased attention to reserve money management and shifted the focus toward indirect monetary policy. The central bank endeavored to counteract autonomous influences on reserve money through open-market-type operations in treasury bills, and in 1992 and 1993 stepped up its sales of treasury bills in the face of a dramatic increase in the government domestic borrowing requirement. This effort led to very high nominal interest rates relative to international levels, which stimulated large capital inflows, and the growth of reserve money was not contained as intended. The government also became increasingly concerned about the domestic interest costs, which undermined the achievements of the budget deficit target. Therefore, the authorities increased the reserve requirement several times during 1993.

Malaysia

Malaysia has employed a wide range of market-based instruments and also relied on changes in reserve requirements since the early 1980s. Initially, reliance was placed on recycling of government deposits in the interbank market, and on foreign exchange swaps. The central bank also posted bid and offer prices for secondary transactions in government securities and bankers' acceptances, but captive markets for these instruments limited the scope of market transactions. In 1987, the central bank began to issue its own certificates in response to the need for large absorption operations arising from foreign exchange inflows. Subsequently, direct operations in the interbank market became the most important market-based instrument. During 1989–91, the central bank also resorted to changes in required reserves. Faced with large capital inflows in 1992–93, however, the central bank relied heavily on a range of money market instruments—including recycling pension fund deposits, central bank certificates, and interbank borrowing—to sterilize the impact on reserve money, and the growth of reserve money was generally contained. Thus, the choice of instruments and markets for monetary control was constrained by the insufficient development of government securities markets, reflecting the continued reliance on captive markets.

Mexico

Monetary policy in Mexico has been implemented against the background of large government domestic financing needs and instability in the external position. The auctions of treasury certificates (*certificados del tesoro* or CETES) have covered only a small percentage of the government's domestic financing needs, and a substantial share of government net domestic borrowing has been provided by the central bank. Changes in the central bank's refinance and discount facilities have offset movements in net foreign assets and, more recently, reliance has been placed on open market operations. Mexico also used liquid asset ratios to limit foreign borrowing and to control the proportion of deposits held in government paper and with the Bank of Mexico. Foreign inflows were only partially sterilized, resulting in declining interest rates and a relatively rapid growth of reserve money.

The Philippines

The Philippines has used a range of market-oriented procedures to meet the targets for the growth of base money since the early 1980s, including weekly auctions of short-term treasury bills, issues of central bank bills, and reverse repurchase agreements. Active use of these money market instruments was facilitated by parallel reforms to foster the money markets and securities trading (i.e., establishment of a system of primary dealers), institutional arrangements to coordinate monetary and public debt management, and a rationalization of central bank credit facilities. A large recourse to required reserve ratios in 1989–90 partly reflected the weak profit position of the central bank; however, the central bank also relied heavily on money market instruments to sterilize the foreign exchange inflows in 1991 and 1992. A subsequent restructuring and recapitalization of the central bank in July 1993 allowed a reduction in the required reserve ratio, and permitted the central bank to focus mainly on open market operations in the conduct of its monetary policy.

Sri Lanka

Sri Lanka's central bank began to auction its own securities in 1984, and such issues were the main instrument of liquidity management until 1987, when a weekly auction of treasury bills became the principal monetary control instrument. The central bank continued to rely on a range of instruments until 1992, when greater emphasis was placed on indirect monetary instruments, including open market operations in treasury bills and central bank securities, in the context of a reserve money program. Monetary policy was complicated by large capital inflows in 1993, which were partly sterilized by the central bank through open market sales of treasury bills and central bank securities, by increases in required reserves, and by reduction in autonomous central bank credit to commercial banks. As a result, growth in reserve money—excluding increases due to required reserves—was contained, while interest rates were maintained at relatively high levels.

Thailand

The primary monetary policy instrument used by Thailand's central bank, the Bank of Thailand, has been double-sided auctions of repurchase agreements in government bonds. The auctions are organized by the central bank, which acts as the principal to all counterparties and intervenes from time to time in response to auction bids and offers. This instrument has been supplemented in recent times by issuance of central bank bonds (because of a shortage of government bonds given fiscal surpluses), a tightening of commercial bank access to refinance facilities, and changes in the central bank's rediscount rate. A surge in capital inflows after 1989 was offset by rising treasury deposits at the central bank, associated with an overall reduction in the government's domestic financing requirement, by issuance of central bank bonds, and by reduction in the Bank of Thailand's refinancing of banks. Reserve money also grew rapidly, however, as interest rates declined. The central bank also increasingly employed foreign exchange swaps to reduce the domestic liquidity consequences of the foreign inflows (see Chapter 6). Increases in required reserves accounted for a significant part of the recorded increase in reserve money.

Implications of the Use of Indirect Instruments for Monetary and Credit Aggregates

This section examines the impact of a greater reliance on indirect approaches to monetary control on the behavior of monetary and credit aggregates, using regression estimates. Error correction models of the following form were estimated for the demand for currency, broad money, and credit to the private sector:

$$\Delta \ln M = a_0 + a_1 \Delta \ln Y + a_2 \Delta \ln P + a_3 r_d + a_4 r_f + a_5 (\ln M_{-1} - \ln Y) + u,$$

when:

- Δ is the first difference operator;
- Y is nominal GDP;
- P is the consumer price index;
- r_d is the domestic deposit rate in the equations for currency and broad money, and the lending rate in the equations for credit to the private sector;
- r_f is the foreign interest rate, the euro-dollar rate in London; and
- u is the stochastic error term.

The regression estimates, reported in the first table in Appendix III, illustrate some of the difficulties of conducting monetary policy in countries with developing financial markets. Although there are some exceptions, the estimated money- and credit-demand equations are generally quite poor. This is particularly the case for the sign and significance of the interest rate responses, with a notable absence of sensitivity of broad money holdings to changes in the domestic interest rate. The response of the demand for currency to interest rates tends to be somewhat more significant. Overall the estimates caution against excessive fine-tuning of monetary operations to meet a specific targeted financial aggregate.

The tests of stability of the aggregates comparing the full sample (1970–92) with those for a prereform subperiod are reported in the second table in Appendix III.[24] In the majority of countries, a greater reliance on indirect approaches to monetary control—and by implication reduced reliance on direct credit and interest rate controls—re-

[24]The prereform periods are Indonesia, 1970–84; Mexico, 1970–88; Philippines, 1970–84; Sri Lanka, 1970–90; and Thailand, 1970–85.

sulted in instability in the determinants of the demand for credit by the private sector. Structural shifts were not seen in either Indonesia or Thailand, and in part this may have reflected these countries' more gradual approach to the liberalization of bank credit markets.[25] Instability in broad money demand was also evident in Malaysia and Kenya following the reforms. Kenya was the only country that showed instability in currency demand. Although caution needs to be exercised in the assessment of all the monetary indicators during the period of financial reform, the tests suggest that the credit aggregates were the most heavily affected by the reforms, and that the demand for broad money was more heavily influenced than the demand for currency. As a consequence, the objectives of monetary policy and the design of financial programs may need to be refocused, and the central bank is likely to have to examine a broader range of financial indicators, including the developments in the central bank's balance sheet, during reform periods.

Capital Flows

In addition to the need to develop market-based monetary controls in the context of financial sector reforms, the growth of international capital flows has added further urgency and importance to the development of such procedures. This section reviews some of the implications of the increase in capital flows for the design of monetary instruments. Capital flows also impose additional constraints on the capacity of a country to conduct independent monetary and exchange rate policies; the latter issues are briefly discussed below and are examined in Chapter 6.

Constraints Imposed by Capital Flows

A simple but powerful way of seeing the impact of free capital movements on monetary and exchange rate policy is through the covered interest rate parity condition, which is the consequence of arbi-

[25]In Indonesia, bank credit continued to be heavily dependent on central bank refinance, while in Thailand the credit markets remained relatively uncompetitive (see Appendix II).

trage between short-term domestic and foreign interest rates and the discount on the currency in the forward exchange market. The covered interest rate parity condition can be written as follows:

$$i_d = i_f + F_d, \tag{1}$$

where

$$F_d = \frac{e^f - e^s}{e^s} \text{ x } 100;$$

i_d is the domestic interest; i_f, the foreign interest rate of the same maturity and F_d, the forward discount for that maturity; e^s is the rate of exchange (units of domestic currency in terms of a foreign currency) in the spot exchange market, and e^f, the forward exchange rate on the date of maturity of the interest rate contracts. Thus, where the foreign interest rate and forward exchange rate are predetermined, a country could determine the domestic interest rate or the spot exchange rate, but not both.[26]

The initial policy response to strong capital inflows with a pegged exchange rate has usually been to conduct sterilized intervention. Such intervention involves quasi fiscal costs, however, and is generally of limited effectiveness since it serves to keep domestic interest rates high, attracting further capital inflows. Pegged exchange rates have also led in some cases to an underestimation of the risks involved in foreign currency borrowing. Thus, as capital account liberalization has progressed, a number of countries have responded to the increase in capital flows by adopting greater exchange rate flexibility, as a way of reducing shorter-term capital inflows that reflect interest rate differentials. In some cases, exchange rate arrangements have evolved in a progressive manner with the degree of flexibility depending on the size of the capital inflow problem. Such arrangements have included exchange rate bands, crawling bands, managed floats, and free floats.

Some countries have followed strong nominal exchange rate anchors, which has required subordinating monetary policy to the maintenance of these anchors and accepting that interest rates be allowed to adjust in

[26]Similar constraints on interest rates and exchange rates would apply in the absence of a formal forward exchange market. For further discussion of the implications of these relationships for monetary and exchange rate policy, see Chapter 4.

response to the capital movements. Such anchors have helped to reduce reversals in capital flows due to uncertainty about the exchange rate. Since the exchange rate instrument is not available to reduce short-term capital inflows, greater attention has been given to the adequacy of prudential standards, including the management of risks associated with potential currency and maturity mismatches in such circumstances.

Some countries have targeted the exchange rate (and hence monetary) policy to maintain competitiveness, and relied on fiscal consolidation to achieve domestic stabilization and to offset the effects of large capital inflows. But because of the limited short-run flexibility of fiscal policy, the authorities have had to rely on other measures to deal with more volatile capital flows, particularly capital controls. Generally, such controls are effective primarily as temporary measures.

Implications for Monetary Instruments

Increased capital mobility will also have a number of operational implications for the design of monetary policy frameworks and the use of different monetary instruments. In the case of fixed or managed floating exchange rate regimes, the external counterpart of money supply may become more volatile, and the demand for domestically defined monetary aggregates may become more sensitive to international interest rate differentials, and may shift as a result of the external liberalization. As a result, it may be more difficult to identify a monetary aggregate with a sufficiently stable behavior that is capable of anticipating the evolution of other nominal variables in the economy. Capital account liberalization, therefore, reinforces the trend toward the adoption of more eclectic monetary frameworks that is frequently a feature of domestic financial sector reforms, and to giving more weight to exchange rates in monetary assessments.[27]

High capital mobility alters the effectiveness of different monetary instruments in achieving the objectives of monetary policy. On the one hand, instruments that impose a high cost or administrative constraint on the banks—as is the case with credit or interest rate ceilings or high

[27]Such frameworks include interest rate targeting in the short-term combined with annual or medium-term frameworks based on inflation targeting; reliance on a wider range of indicators rather than a single monetary aggregate; greater attention to movements in the exchange rate in assessing monetary conditions, including in the context of monetary conditions indicators; and revisions in the targeted definition of money.

nonremunerated reserve requirements—may be circumvented more easily by disintermediation through the capital account and, therefore, become less effective. On the other hand, monetary instruments that operate on the overall cost of money or credit in financial markets may be transmitted more rapidly to credit and exchange markets and allow the central bank to influence the decisions of financial institutions and markets that operate in its domestic currency, both locally and internationally. The characteristics of the major monetary instruments and the effects of capital mobility are reviewed in Table 2.4.

While many countries have reduced, and some have phased out the use of reserve requirements in the context of high capital mobility, some still rely on them to influence the supply and demand in the market for bank reserves (bank deposits with the central bank).[28] Nonremunerated reserve requirements, however, impose a tax on the banks subject to the reserve requirements and thus encourage disintermediation to financial institutions and markets that are not subject to the reserve requirements. A number of countries have responded to this potential problem either by remunerating the reserve requirements at a rate fairly close to market rates or by reducing or eliminating the reserve requirement ratio.[29] However, some countries have retained selected capital controls—for example, on the issue of certificates of deposits locally by nonresident banks to safeguard the effectiveness of their reserve requirements. The expectation is that by limiting foreign banks' access to a particular instrument, the extent of disintermediation would also be limited.[30]

[28]When the central bank adopts a reserves operating framework, it may nevertheless seek to exploit the direct multiplier link between bank reserves and money supply. For a given level of reserve money, reserve requirements can impose an upper limit on the money supply where there is a non-interest-sensitive demand for excess reserves. Reserve requirements may also be used to help ensure that the demand for central bank money is sufficiently stable when the central bank seeks to achieve its monetary objectives by controlling short-term interest rates.

[29]The trend toward a reduction of the ratio of required reserves can be observed in all the industrial countries. Where the level of the ratio is comparatively high, as in Italy, remuneration partly offsets the tax element. In the United Kingdom, reserve requirements are no longer used as a monetary instrument. No reserve requirements are in place in Belgium and Sweden. In Canada, arrangements in place amount to a zero percent ratio.

[30]For example, Germany restricts the sale or issue locally by nonresident banks of deutsche mark-denominated certificates of deposit with a maturity of less than two years. The measure is to preserve the effectiveness of reserve requirements by achieving uniform treatment of resident banks, which are subject to reserve requirements, and nonresident banks, which are not.

Table 2.4. Monetary Instruments and High Capital Mobility

Monetary Instrument	Main Characteristics	Compatibility and Effectiveness with High Capital Mobility
Reserve requirements with no differentiation between residents/nonresidents, domestic/foreign currency	Aims to achieve a combination of different objectives: (1) influence the commercial bank's demand for reserves and, therefore, enhance predictability of reserve money demand, and influence the growth of domestic credit; (2) contribute to the stabilization of short-term interest rates through the effect of averaging provisions; (3) sterilize excess liquidity; (4) increase the seigniorage when reserves are not remunerated.	In the case of nonremunerated required reserves, high capital mobility and the lack of harmonization between regulations may prompt operators to relocate their transactions aboard. In response, some countries reduced or eliminated the ratio. To preserve the effectiveness of the instrument some countries maintain restrictions on the issue of domestic securities abroad by residents and on the issue of securities locally by nonresidents.
Reserve requirements with differentiation between domestic and foreign currency	Used to influence liquidity in domestic and foreign currency and to encourage or discourage deposit taking in local and foreign currency. Impact depends on the level and rate of remuneration of the required reserves. Low or zero reserve requirements in foreign currency deposits are a feature of offshore banking centers.	Applying different ratios on deposits in domestic and foreign currency could serve to influence capital movements. May substitute for reserve requirements differentiated by residency where residents' holdings of foreign currency deposits are restricted.
Reserve requirements with differentiation between residents and nonresidents	With nonremunerated required reserves, which impose a tax on bank intermediation, higher ratio on nonresident deposits compared to resident deposits discourages capital inflows through bank deposits by lowering remuneration for the depositor.	Has been used by a number of countries to influence capital movements. To be effective in limiting short-term inflows, this instrument would need to be applied comprehensively to all short-term capital inflows.
Deposit requirements on certain capital flows	Through its cost effect, a nonremunerated deposit requirement serves to reduce or increase the interest differential between domestic and international rates. In some cases it may be replaced by the payment of a flat fee.	Similar to reserve requirements that differentiate between residents and nonresidents.
Net open position/position limits	Used predominantly as a prudential control when defined as a net foreign currency position.	In some countries open position limits are defined asymmetrically on resident and nonresident transactions and have been changed frequently with the intention of influencing capital flows.

Statutory liquidity ratios	Intended principally as a prudential measure or to influence the allocation of bank assets by imposing the requirement to hold minimum amounts of specified liquid assets as a percentage of specified liabilities. When used as monetary control instrument it affects the allocation of financial assets.	As in prudential measure, helps to manage the risks of short-term capital inflows and potential reversals in such flows.
Minimum (or maximum) portfolio requirements	Intended mainly to affect the allocation of credit rather than overall credit availability. Typically imposes on commercial banks the requirement to hold a minimum or maximum of certain assets (e.g., government securities or loans to priority sectors).	In the case of qualifying assets restricted to domestic assets, it can influence capital flows.
Interest rate controls	Limitation on the ability of commercial banks to determine their lending and for deposit rates. Typically abandoned with the move to indirect monetary controls.	Becomes ineffective with capital account openings because they will be circumvented through capital flows.
Bank-by-bank credit ceilings	Directly limits the domestic counterpart of money supply through a rationing of the total credit provided by commercial banks. Typically abandoned with the move to indirect monetary controls.	Becomes ineffective with capital account openings, because they will be circumvented through capital flows.
Directed credit	Allocates central bank credit to commercial banks mostly to finance priority sectors. Abandoned with move to indirect monetary control.	In the case of qualifying assets restricted to domestic assets, it may influence capital flows.
Bank-by-bank rediscount quotas	Allocates central bank refinance credit among commercial banks, allowing banks to borrow on demand at the central bank. Rediscount quotas usually only available for resident banks.	Increased volatility of money supply due to external factors requires flexibility in central bank's refinancing operations. The importance of rediscount quotas tends to diminish as the main tool for liquidity management.
Standing facilities	Deposit and lending central bank facilities used at the initiative of commercial banks. Standing facilities usually only available for resident banks.	High capital mobility increases volatility of money supply and requires flexibility in the central bank's liquidity management. Role of standing facilities tends to diminish as instrument of liquidity management.

Table 2.4 ***(concluded)***

Monetary Instrument	Main Characteristics	Compatibility and Effectiveness with High Capital Mobility
Public sector deposits	Given magnitude of daily government flows in and out of banking system, reallocation of government deposits between the central bank and the commercial banks can be used to offset impact of such flows on short-term liquidity. Public sector deposits usually only available for resident banks.	Given the need for flexibility in interest rate management, allocation mechanism needs to ensure equitable distribution among the competing commercial banks based on a market mechanism.
Open market operations	Monetary operation at the initiative of the central bank involving one of the following transactions: (1) buying or selling assets outright; (2) buying or selling assets (including foreign exchange) under a repurchase agreement; and (3) lending or borrowing against underlying assets as collateral through an auction mechanism. The central bank typically deals only in its local market and with resident banks.	Becomes the preferred monetary instrument as it allows flexibility for timing and amount of the central bank operations, and for managing interest rates.

Open market operations play a core role for the purpose of steering interest rates, managing the liquidity situation in the market, and signaling the stance of monetary policy with an open capital account. When capital moves freely, the central bank is able to affect the conditions of both the domestic and external markets in its local currency through open market operations. Standing facilities, rediscount quotas, and public sector deposits are frequently used to support open market operations, particularly to guide interest rate movements, and transmit rapidly and clearly the central bank's message to market participants. Movements toward capital account convertibility, therefore, have been supported with the adoption of indirect monetary controls.

Use of Discriminatory Reserve Requirements

Differential reserve requirements on short-term borrowing from nonresidents are frequently used to reduce capital inflows, or change the composition of these inflows. Such measures are sometimes referred to as "Chile-type" measures because of their adoption by the Chilean authorities in 1991, although they have a long history of use in other countries, such as in Germany during the 1970s.

Non-interest-bearing reserve requirements raise the cost of borrowing through the instruments subject to the requirements. If r is the nonremunerated reserve requirement, and i_f the nominal foreign interest rate, then the effective cost of foreign borrowing to a resident after the imposition of the reserve requirement, i_f^e, becomes:[31]

$$i_f^e = \frac{i_f}{(1-r)} \quad . \tag{2}$$

The implementation of the reserve requirements will thus increase the cost of foreign borrowing to residents (or conversely reduce the return on local investments to foreign investors), and therefore, reduce borrowing from abroad.

[31]The impact of the imposition of the reserve requirement can also be examined from the point of view of the foreign investor, where the impact of the reserve requirement will reduce the return to the investor after account is taken of the cost of holding the reserve requirement. If i_d is the nominal domestic interest rate, then the return to the foreign investor after the imposition of the reserve requirements falls to i_d (1 - r). The subsequent discussion would follow whether the analysis is from the point of view of domestic borrower or the foreign investor.

Over time, it would be expected that the interest rate parity condition would be reestablished. Following the imposition of the differential reserve requirement, the domestic interest rate would be determined by the following revised condition:

$$i_d^* = i_f^e + F_d^* \,. \qquad (3)$$

Since $i_f^e > i_f$, the imposition of the differential reserve requirement would require either that the short-term domestic interest rate rise ($i_d^* > i_d$) or the forward discount on the currency fall. A drop in the forward discount could come about through a depreciation of the spot exchange rate.[32]

After the adjustments in the domestic interest rate (or the exchange rate), interest rates would again be constrained by the covered interest rate parity condition (equation 3). The non-interest-bearing reserve requirement on foreign borrowing would introduce a wedge between the domestic and offshore interest rates, and other things being equal, allow the country to have a higher domestic short-term interest rate with a given exchange rate than otherwise. By allowing for higher domestic short-term interest rates, the non-interest-bearing reserve requirement might also encourage a shift to longer-term borrowing by residents, and, in turn, could influence the composition of inflows. The effect on the composition of inflows would depend, however, on the resulting evolution of interest rates along the yield curve.[33]

If the differential reserve requirement is not applied comprehensively to all short-term sources of foreign capital inflows, it may encourage larger short-term inflows through those instruments that are not subject to the requirement. This could result if the general level of short-term domestic interest rates increases with the tightening of monetary policy that accompanies the introduction of the differential reserve requirement, providing, therefore, greater incentives for

---

[32] $F_d = (\frac{e^f}{e^s} - 1) \times 100$. Therefore, for $F_d^* < F_d$, with a given forward rate, the spot exchange rate (e^s) would have to rise, that is, depreciate. If the spot rate is fixed, then the whole adjustment would have to fall on the domestic interest rate.

[33] The implementation of the reserve requirement on shorter flows would have the initial effect of tilting the yield curve to foreign investors by reducing returns on short-term instruments relative to longer-term investments. To the extent that covered interest rate parity is reestablished, however, the effective returns to foreign investors would return to their previous level, and the tilting of the yield curve of returns to foreign investors would only be temporary.

short-term flows through foreign instruments not subject to the discriminatory requirement.

Various empirical studies have sought to examine the impact of such instruments on capital flows and have generally concluded that they have a temporary effect, but one that can be eroded quite quickly depending on the scope of the controls and the stage of development of financial markets and instruments. Financial derivatives that restructure one type of financial transaction into another have now become an important means of circumventing such regulations, in addition to the more traditional channels for circumvention through instruments not covered by the regulations. Over time, Chile found it necessary to extend progressively the instruments covered by its reserve requirement to all short-term capital inflows in an attempt to avoid circumvention. The effectiveness of the measures in Germany in the 1970s appeared to depend on whether they extended to corporate borrowing.[34]

Conclusions

An increasing number of developing countries have begun to operate market-based instruments of monetary policy and use these instruments more actively to achieve macroeconomic policy objectives. The decision to introduce more market-based instruments reflects a number of factors, including: a general desire to liberalize markets and to free them from administrative controls that have tended to inhibit the efficient allocation of resources; the ineffectiveness of direct interest rate and credit controls for macroeconomic management in the face of financial innovations, disintermediation, and large private international capital flows; and the inhibiting effect of direct controls on market development, and, hence, on saving mobilization and investment.

[34]On the effectiveness of the measure in Germany in the 1970s, see Johnston (1983). A recent study on the effectiveness of controls in Chile by Soto (1997) finds that the reserve requirement had an effect on the domestic interest rate and nominal exchange rate that lasts for between a year and a year and a half. The reserve requirement significantly alters capital flow composition, leading to a relative decline in short-term capital flows. This decline is prolonged over time, although no quantitative assessment is provided. Soto concludes that ". . . the impact of the measure is in the expected direction, i.e., it reduces capital inflows, keeps domestic interest rates higher, depreciates the real exchange rate, and changes the composition of capital inflows. However, the economic importance of these effects are minimal."

The developing countries in the sample examined are in a transitional stage of monetary reform; direct controls have been substantially abandoned but full-fledged open market systems of monetary control have not yet been established. Nevertheless, most countries have developed the instruments and an operational capacity to manage money market interest rates or reserve money growth through indirect, market-based procedures and have relied increasingly on these instruments to effect monetary control. The introduction of more market-based monetary control procedures has required a modification of operating procedures, the development of information systems, and the introduction of new instruments.

The increase in capital mobility has posed a particular challenge for monetary operations in recent years, generating huge flows that have strained the capacity of fledgling money markets. It has also provided additional impetus for the introduction of market-based monetary instruments. Countries have also responded to these flows by adjusting more traditional instruments such as reserve requirements.

The financial sector reforms and the increase in capital flows have implications for the behavior of financial aggregates and thus for the design of monetary control frameworks. The trend has generally been toward the adoption of more eclectic monetary frameworks involving an examination of a broader range of monetary indicators.

Appendix I: Security Issues as Instruments of Monetary Control

The role of security issues as instruments of monetary control can be illustrated using the following basic financial flow and balance sheet equations:[35]

Government's total financing requirement, dG,

$$dG = E_G - R_G = dT + dS - dF_G; \qquad (1)$$

Financing of the external current account surplus, CA,

$$CA = dF_G + dF_{CB} + dF_{NB} + dF_B; \qquad (2)$$

[35]This section illustrates the relationship between the treasury bill issue and control of the reserves of the banking system; a similar relationship can be derived for central bank bill issues or other debt issues by the government.

Central bank balance sheet flow,

$$dC_B + dC_{NB} = dL_B + dL_{NB} + dT_{CB} + dS_{CB} + dF_{CB}; \tag{3}$$

Commercial bank balance sheet flow,

$$dD + dL_B = dC_B + dT_B + dS_B + dA + dF_B; \tag{4}$$

Change in net financial wealth of the domestic nonbank private sector, dW,

$$dW = dD + dT_{NB} + dS_{NB} + dF_{NB} + dC_{NB} - dA - dL_{NB}, \tag{5}$$

where the subscripts G, CB, NB, and B refer, respectively, to the government, central bank, nonbank private sector, and commercial banks. E is government expenditure; R, government revenue; dT, the treasury bill issue; dS, other government domestic borrowing; dF, the change in net holdings of foreign assets; dC, the change in holdings of cash and reserves with the central bank; dL, the change in net loans by the central bank; dA, the change in loans by commercial banks to the nonbank private sector; and dD, the deposits of the nonbank private sector with commercial banks.

The financial flows identity also requires that private sector net wealth changes through surpluses with other sectors—the government and the foreign sector,

$$dW = dG + CA \tag{6}$$

The change in the cash reserve holdings of commercial banks, dC_B, can be derived by substituting equations (1) and (2) into (6) and using equations (4) and (5).

$$dC_B = [dG + dF_G] + dF_{CB} - dT_B - dT_{NB} - dS_B - dS_{NB} + dL_{NB} + dL_B - dC_{NB}\ . \tag{7}$$

The change in bank reserves equals the government's domestic financing requirement ($dG + dF_G$), plus central bank net intervention in the foreign exchange market, central bank net lending to banks and nonbanks, less sales of treasury bills and other government debt outside the central bank, plus the change in cash holdings of the nonbank private sector.

Equation (7) provides a framework for using the treasury bill issue, or other central bank or government security issues, to control the reserves of the banking system. The procedure would be to develop forecasts for the relevant reserve holding period of the supply and demand for cash reserves. The forecast of supply would depend on the government's net domestic financing requirement, net foreign exchange market intervention by the central bank (dF_{CB}), net lending by the central bank to the banks and nonbanks ($dL_{NB} + dL_B$), and the change in currency holdings by the nonbank private sector (dC_{NB}). The forecast change in the supply of bank reserves, before a new net issue/net redemption of treasury bills, would be given by:

$$dC_B^s = [dG + dF_G]^* + dF_{CB}{}^* - dS^*{}_B - dS^*{}_{NB} + dL^*{}_{NB} + dL^*{}_B - dC^*{}_{NB}\,, \quad (8)$$

where * indicates a forecast.

This forecast supply can be compared with a forecast of the change in the demand for cash reserves, dC_B^D, to determine the net volume of treasury bills that would need to be issued to control the cash reserves of the financial system.

The change in the demand for reserves by the banking system is given by,

$$dC_B^D = (\alpha + ß)dD^*, \quad (9)$$

where α is the compulsory cash reserve ratio on bank deposits, ß is the estimated precautionary reserve holding ratio of banks, and dD^* is the change in deposits for the relevant reserve holding period.[36] The demand for precautionary reserves would depend on the rules and procedures for reserve holding and interbank clearing, the efficiency of the interbank market and the payment system, the volatility in the reserves of banks due to seasonal and other factors, and the extent to which the central bank stands ready to smooth the reserves of the banking system.[37]

[36]This assumes a uniform reserve ratio is applicable to all bank deposits. With lagged reserve accounting, required reserves would be based on deposits in a previous time period and may be known before deciding on the amount of treasury bills to be issued.

[37]While automatic access by banks to central bank loan or rediscount facilities could reduce precautionary reserve holdings to a low level, the charging of penalty interest rates or uncertainty over the level of interest rates charged by the central bank would still lead to precautionary reserve holdings by banks.

Combining equations (8) and (9) provides a forecast of the banking system's reserve deficiency (if $dC_B^D > dC_B^S$) or excess (if $dC_B^D < dC_B^S$) compared with desired holdings before a net new issue of treasury bills.[38] Given these forecasts, the net new issue of treasury bills can be set to achieve monetary objectives. A neutral monetary policy stance—that is, one that would leave money market rates unchanged—would involve removing the excess reserves of the banking system by selling net a volume of treasury bills outside the central bank equal to the difference between the forecast of the supply of reserves to the banking system and the estimate of the banking system's demand for reserves (or relieving a forecast reserve shortage by not rolling over maturing bills). A restrictive policy stance designed to raise interest rates would involve the creation of a reserve shortage by selling a volume of bills in excess of the forecast reserve surplus. In this case, assuming the forecasts are accurate, banks would find themselves short of reserves and interbank rates would tend to rise. If the sale of treasury bills reduced the aggregate supply of reserves below reserve requirements, banks would have to seek marginal accommodation from the central bank, and the interest rate at which the central bank provides the assistance would become the key determinant of the overall level of interest rates.[39] An expansionary stance would involve selling fewer net bills than the forecast cash surplus. In this case banks would have excess cash reserves that would push interest rates down. Interbank rates would fall, and there would be repayments of the central bank credit. In this framework, the design of rediscount windows is an integral element of reserve and interest rate management.[40]

[38]The following analysis is in terms of the deficiency in desired holdings rather than required holdings. Since desired holdings include a precautionary reserve, the implications for interest rates, etc., are likely to be different when $dC_B^D > dC_B^S > \alpha dD^*$ and $dC_B^S < \alpha dD^*$.

[39]The need to resort to the central bank for marginal accommodation may occur before aggregate shortages emerge in reserves if the interbank system is inefficient.

[40]Sometimes a distinction is made between "defensive" central bank operations, which are designed to offset the impact of autonomous influences on the supply of reserves, and "dynamic" operations, which are designed to bring about changes in the supply of reserves.

Appendix II: The Evolution of Monetary Operations in Nine Developing Countries

Argentina

Prior to July 1985, the Central Bank of Argentina sold government paper through public offering at predetermined interest rates. The central bank also operated a repurchase facility for government paper for commercial banks at a preannounced interest rate set by the central bank. Repurchases were available for periods of 7 to 28 days for a minimum of 25 million pesos. In July 1985, as part of the anti-inflation "austral" plan, the central bank began auctioning central bank bills issued against the central bank's holdings of government paper; these bills have been named "participations" in the bank's holdings of government papers. Bidders at the auction had to bid both a price and quantity, and the central bank decided the cutoff volume so as to achieve its monetary objectives. These objectives involved a target for the volume of sales, but it appears that when the achievement of the quantity objective would have resulted in an excessive movement in interest rates, the authorities would override the volume target so as to stabilize interest rates. The central bank provided a repurchase facility for the "participations" and set interest rates for the new facility, which was used to manage short-term fluctuations in liquidity between auctions.

In April 1991, the Argentine Convertibility Plan was introduced in the context of a broader stabilization effort; the plan effectively established a currency board-type arrangement. The central bank retained the power to change reserve requirements and conduct open market operations. Also, the plan allowed a domestic currency issue to be backed by foreign exchange for up to one-third in the form of U.S. dollar-denominated bonds issued by the Argentine Government (effectively allowing central bank financing of the government).

Brazil

In Brazil, monetary instruments and operating procedures have undergone a number of changes in recent years. Nevertheless, the basic monetary policy implementation framework has remained broadly unchanged, including primary auctions of treasury or central bank bills and intervention by the central bank to determine interest rates in the interbank market. Until 1986, the central bank intervened in the auctions when the treasury bill rate determined by the bids would have been unacceptable. Its intervention in the money market included outright sales and purchases of assets from its portfolio, and overnight repurchases at interest rates set by the central bank.

Following the introduction of the anti-inflation cruzado plan in February 1986, the authorities changed their monetary instruments to make them consistent with an anticipated low-inflationary environment. Between May 1986 and December 1987, a central bank bill (*Letra do Banco Central* or LBC) was issued in maturities of up to one year, at weekly auctions. This bill paid a coupon equal to the average interest rate in the overnight money market in the holding period of the bill, and was sold at a discount determined by competitive bidding at the auction. The amount of bills to be auctioned was preannounced, with the major objective of controlling the trend in the volume of money market liquidity. The overnight rate in the interbank market reflected, among other things, the daily repurchase operations of the central bank. The central bank set its repurchase rate to keep real interest rates in the money market close to zero on average over a month, with the interest rate adjusted to the rate of consumer price inflation recorded in the previous month. The central bank's repurchase operations were, thus, the key influence on overnight rates and, except for the initial discount on new issues at the auctions, which was normally small, also on the yield on LBCs.

In January 1988 a new instrument, the *Letra de Financiamento de Tesoro* (LFT), a treasury liability with the same maturity and yield characteristics as the LBC, was introduced to replace the LBC. LFTs have also been auctioned weekly, but unlike the LBCs, primary issues of the LFT have been largely based on budgetary rather than monetary considerations. The central bank has, however, continued to set interest rates and to exercise monetary control through its repurchases and also through outright sales of LFTs from its own portfolio and purchases of new issues of LFTs at the auction. LFTs and LBCs are traded in secondary markets organized around about 20 money brokers. Repurchases were normally confined to transactions between the commercial banks and the central bank.

Indonesia

In 1983, as part of a broader adjustment effort, Indonesia initiated a comprehensive reform of its monetary control system. Before the reforms, the banking sector in Indonesia had been highly regulated and had lacked effective competition. Monetary policy relied on bank-by-bank credit ceilings and direct interest rate controls. Ready access to central bank refinancing for priority lending led to persistent excess liquidity, and the existence of nonbank financial institutions exempted from the direct regulations resulted in disintermediation and monetary substitution.

Indonesia has taken a gradual approach toward reforming its monetary control system. The first stage of monetary reform in 1983 included the removal of direct controls on interest rates and credit, and some curtailment of the central bank's funding of banks through refinancing of priority sector credits. In 1983–85, new money market instruments—central bank (SBI) and private (SBPU) papers—and an auction system for the SBIs were introduced, and the central bank's refinancing facilities were further restructured. Two new rediscount facilities were introduced in February 1984, to replace the automatic access that all banks had for refinancing priority credits. The access to the new facilities was limited to "sound" banks, and use was discouraged by the maintenance of a high discount rate and the fact that borrowing was seen as damaging to a bank's standing. One of the facilities was designed to smooth short-term liquidity shortages in the banking system, while the other was intended to promote long-term lending and assist banks in addressing maturity mismatches.

When the auctions of SBIs were introduced in March 1984, SBI maturities were for 30 and 90 days, but bills with 7-day and 180-day maturities were introduced later.[41] The frequency of auctions varied from as often as daily to three times a week to once a week. Only banks and nonbank financial institutions have been allowed to participate, but other entities have been permitted to acquire SBIs in the secondary market. The central bank sets the cutoff yield in the auctions. The SBPUs were introduced in February 1985; these instruments were essentially standardized banker's acceptances, promoted by the government. In practice, the interest rates on SBPUs have closely fol-

[41]Bills of 15-day maturity were also issued for a brief period in 1984–85.

lowed those of SBIs. To provide liquidity to the SBPU market, the central bank subsequently started rediscounting of SBPUs.

A state-run securities house, FICORINVEST, was created to facilitate trading in SBIs and SBPUs. Initially, FICORINVEST was the market maker in these instruments (it stood ready to buy and sell SBPUs at posted bid and offer prices), and could automatically rediscount them with the central bank at a profit. Also, it would discount SBIs at the interest rate of the original SBI issue without regard to its remaining maturity, and could automatically rediscount them at the central bank, also at the original issue price. The cutoff rate in the auctions and the posted interest rates through FICORINVEST were initially changed infrequently.

In July 1987, the central bank phased out the automatic rediscounting of SBIs and SBPUs, hence discontinuing its passive accommodation at posted interest rates. The main instruments have since been daily auctions of seven-day SBIs and of seven-day repurchase agreements in SBPUs carried out daily, and interest rates set by the central bank, based on bids or offers received.[42] The central bank began using the cutoff rate at the SBI auctions as the main operational target. In mid-1987, following a deterioration in the external sector, policy shifted to protecting the net international reserves position of the central bank, and the exchange rate as well as interest rates became more flexible.

Another package of reforms to strengthen monetary control and develop money markets was introduced in late 1988. This package (1) refined the daily money market operations of the central bank by, among other moves, channeling the central bank's operations through a group of specifically appointed commercial banks and nonbank financial institutions that acted as primary dealers, brokers, and market makers for SBIs; (2) reduced reserve requirements to 2 percent (excess liquidity created by this operation was absorbed by the issuance of short-term SBIs); (3) eliminated limits on interbank borrowing and promoted the use of SBIs for interbank repurchase transactions and liquidity management. These reforms were complemented by the deregulation of the banking system, including relaxation of barriers to entry, and a strengthening of prudential supervision, through improved on-site and off-site inspections and the introduction of a com-

[42]These auctions—telephone go-around—are conducted through FICORINVEST.

prehensive system of capital adequacy ratios, bad debt provisions, bank ratings, and accounting principles. The use of market-based monetary instruments in Indonesia in 1983–93 is reviewed in Table 2.5.

Kenya

As part of a medium-term structural adjustment program in the late 1980s, the Kenyan authorities began to move toward a market-oriented system of monetary control, to be based on open market operations. While good progress was made initially in making the monetary policy framework more effective and responsive to market forces, the momentum was temporarily lost in the political and economic turmoil that preceded the first multiparty elections in late 1992.

The tendering of treasury bills began in 1985 and of treasury bonds in 1986. The authorities relaxed their direct credit controls in 1986–87; however, concern about the risk of an excessive credit expansion led them to reimpose ceilings on the growth of bank lending to the nongovernment sector in late 1987. Subsequently, the removal of credit ceilings resumed; credit ceilings were fully abolished by December 1994 when marginal ceilings were eliminated.

Open-market-type operations based on the primary issue of treasury bills were introduced in late 1990; market forces were allowed to determine interest rates, and the amount of bills offered was determined by monetary policy considerations. Also, the central bank acquired treasury bills in the auctions on its own account for later use in open-market operations.

The discount window was restructured in support of these operations. Initially, the discount window was available to any holder of eligible securities at a nonpenal rate, with the rediscount rate set at ⅛ of 1 percent above the treasury bill rate. Subsequently, the discount rate was raised to the treasury bill rate plus 1.5 percent. In 1992, the access was further tightened, and a graduated interest rate, increasing with the level of access, was introduced.

The unsettled situation during the democratization process led to a loss of monetary control in 1992 and early 1993, as several banks gained access to central bank credit through irregular means, and the enforcement of the reserve requirement weakened. Monetary expansion accelerated, and a foreign exchange crisis ensued in March 1993. Also, the weak enforcement of prudential regulations undermined the

Table 2.5. Indonesia: Major Factors Affecting Reserve Money

(In billions of Indonesian rupiah unless otherwise noted; ended March)

	1984	1985	1986	1987	1988	1989	1990	1991	1992	1993
Change in central bank net claims on government	–1.475	–2,703	1,051	–1,979	1,780	772	577	–5,367	–479	1,303
Change in net foreign assets of central bank[1]	2,113	1,513	–1,266	–2,630	3,034	–3,009	737	8,970	5,684	10,018
Change in autonomous net domestic assets of central bank[2]	670	1,680	1,724	1,906	555	2,010	4,247	–4,346	842	–319
Of which: liquidity credits	157	2,502	954	1,175	1,320	2,899	4,241	–4,390	708	–335
Change in the use of money market instrument by central bank	–45	7	219	629	–609	–1,243	189	306	–1,037	–12,144
In percent of reserve money at beginning of period	–1.1	0.1	3.8	8.3	–7.6	–13.6	2.1	2.9	–9.4	–83.0
SBIs (central bank certificates)										
Outstanding	–45	–198	–1,151	1,233	–607	–1,602	154	7,198	–1,915	–11,681
Rediscounted	—	—	946	–905	—	—	81	—	—	—
SBPUs (private sector money market papers)										
Rediscounted	—	205	417	313	—	—	—	6,782[3]	–2,586	–1,577
Other facilities	—	—	7	–12	–2	57	–46	162	–162	39
Change in reserve money	1,263	497	1,721	439	1,115	302	1,637	560	3,626	1,075
In percent	31.0	9.3	29.5	5.8	14.0	–3.3	18.6	5.4	33.3	7.3
Memorandum:										
Money market interest rates (in percent)										
Nominal	18.6	10.3	13.0	14.5	15.0	12.6	14.4	15.1	12.1	8.7
Real	9.2	5.8	7.4	6.7	6.7	7.0	3.4	6.8	4.5	2.7

Sources: Data provided by the Indonesian authorities; and IMF staff estimates.

[1]On a transition basis, excluding valuation changes.

[2]Includes refinance and rediscount facilities, loans to private and public enterprises, and other items.

[3]Includes special SBPUs (private sector money market papers) injected to banks amounting to Rp 6.6 trillion to compensate for the withdrawal of state enterprises' deposits.

soundness of the banking system. Subsequently, the authorities took a number of actions to reestablish monetary control and to strengthen the monetary policy framework. These actions included stepped-up issuance of treasury bills, combined with increased flexibility in the interest rates; a series of increases in the reserve requirement; stricter enforcement of the reserve requirement through severe penalties for noncompliance; a streamlining of the settlement procedures for bank clearing to stop unintended access to central bank credit; and further tightening of the access to central bank rediscounting through higher penalty rates and a narrowing of the range of eligible securities. Also, several insolvent banks were closed down.

As the above measures led to very high interest rates, which stimulated capital inflows in late 1993 and in 1994, the authorities relied more on increases in the reserve requirement to sterilize the inflows. This was done to avoid the direct costs to the central government budget of the sterilization operations through treasury bills. The use of market-based instruments in Kenya is reviewed in Table 2.6.

Malaysia

The system of monetary control in Malaysia has evolved over time in response to exogenous developments—notably, the increased international capital mobility and the development of the financial system. Under these circumstances, Malaysia has employed a wide range of monetary policy instruments, with the relative reliance on specific instruments varying over time. Thus, the instruments used by the central bank—the Bank Negara Malaysia—have included reserve requirements; liquidity requirements; shifts of central government deposits between the central bank and commercial banks; money market operations; discount facilities; limits on the commercial bank foreign exchange swap transactions; direct interest rate controls; credit controls and lending guidelines; and moral suasion. Over time the instruments have been adapted gradually in support of a more market-oriented monetary policy, however.

Reserve requirements have continued to play an important role in Malaysia's monetary policy. In particular, in the late 1980s when there was a need for large liquidity withdrawal to neutralize foreign exchange inflows, the central bank raised the reserve ratio several

Table 2.6. Kenya: Major Factors Affecting Reserve Money

(In millions of Kenya shillings; ended December unless otherwise stated)

	1983	1984	1985	1986	1987	1988	1989	1990	1991	1992	1993
Domestic financing of the government deficit[1]	1,577	3,033	3,825	6,783	8,883	3,586	2,274	10,601	6,898	17,381	24,475
Treasury bills	. . .	1,922	2,544	5,310	2,471	–2,162	–132	–2,156	–2,106	3,677	51,383
Other securities	. . .	151	269	724	2,802	5,824	1,584	1,911	6,674	11,392	–14,515
Other[2]		982	812	–251	3,510	–76	822	10,846	2,330	2,312	–12,393
Uptake of government debt by central bank[3]	–784	599	943	955	4,122	790	–1,599	7,821	3,969	–7,752	–3,375
Change in net foreign assets of central bank[4]	884	753	–721	–125	–176	–1,390	707	–3,040	–3,390	202	14,049
Change in autonomous net domestic assets of central bank[5]	204	–234	–44	246	–721	1,013	–1,073	7,010	4,625	3,825	6,568
Change in the use of money market instruments by central bank[6]	. . .	. . .	. . .	. . .	. . .	–2,162	–132	–2,156	–2,106	3,677	51,383
In percent of reserve money at beginning of period[6]	. . .	. . .	. . .	. . .	. . .	–18.6	–1.1	15.6	–13.4	20.4	200.0
Change in reserve money	–120	645	953	2,075	1,961	–231	2,092	3,151	2,756	10,889	16,398
In percent	2.2	11.4	15.1	39.6	19.4	–2.1	17.0	21.8	15.7	53.5	52.5
Change in required reserves	. . .	. . .	. . .	. . .	. . .	325	347	322	639	792	8,313
Memorandum:											
Money market interest rates (in percent)[7]											
Nominal	14.15	13.24	13.90	13.22	12.86	13.48	13.86	14.78	16.59	16.53	49.80
Real	2.5	2.8	0.7	8.1	4.8	2.1	0.8	–0.7	–2.7	–10.0	2.7

Sources: Data provided by Kenyan authorities; and IMF staff estimates.
[1]Fiscal year (July–June) basis.
[2]Residual.
[3]Includes treasury certificates used for monetary control purposes.
[4]Includes valuation changes.
[5]Includes refinance and discount facilities.
[6]± indicates withdrawal/injection of liquidity.
[7]Treasury bill rate.

times.[43] The reserve requirement has been streamlined; the ratio was unified for commercial banks, finance companies, and merchant banks in May 1989; and averaging provisions were introduced in January 1991 to reduce volatility of interbank interest rates.

The liquidity requirement has been used to create captive markets and meet prudential concerns, and the ratio was adjusted only infrequently. But the definition of eligible liquid assets has been changed several times for a variety of reasons, including to direct credit to the government securities and other priority sectors; to influence the financial institutions' scope for credit extension; and to secure demand for new money market instruments and Bank Negara bills.

The central bank operates auctions of treasury bills but solely for government finance purposes.[44] An effort was made in 1986–89 to develop the secondary markets in government securities so as to increase the scope for open-market operations. This effort included modification of the liquidity requirement to reduce the captive market for government securities, introduction of market-based pricing of such papers, and standardization of the issue amounts for treasury bills. It also included increasing the frequency and reducing the maturities of government securities. Primary dealer arrangements were introduced to foster secondary trading in government- and government-guaranteed securities, supported by reforms of the clearing and settlement system for payments. However, the progressive decline in the government's domestic borrowing requirement has made it difficult to develop secondary markets in government debt. Other segments of money and interbank markets have developed sufficient depth to support the effectiveness of market-based instruments.

In the absence of well-developed secondary markets for government securities, Malaysia's central bank has relied on influencing other money market segments, along with shifting government deposits for short-term monetary management—a practice that was intensified in

---

[43]Between January 1989 and January 1994, alone, the required reserve ratio was raised seven times.

[44]The auctions, which were introduced in 1973, have been conducted on a weekly basis, with 91-day bills offered every week, 182-day bills every second week, and 364-day bills every four weeks. The amounts and maturities to be offered are announced in advance of the auction; results regarding, inter alia, amounts tendered, accepted and rejected, and yields are announced after the auction. Given the captive holding requirements, the treasury bill yields do not properly reflect money market conditions.

1990. Faced with considerable excess liquidity as a result of the foreign exchange inflows, government deposits were shifted from commercial banks to the central bank to absorb liquidity. Subsequently, a similar arrangement was put in place for the deposits of the Employees Provident Fund in October 1992. The central bank started issuing bills akin to treasury bills (Bank Negara bills) to absorb liquidity. In addition, the Bank Negara Malaysia has occasionally relied on direct borrowing from and lending to commercial banks in the interbank market. Discount operations traditionally have played only a minor role.[45]

Limits on foreign exchange swap transactions of commercial banks have been used both to contain foreign exchange outflows (in 1988–89) and to restrain foreign inflows (beginning in June 1992). To limit foreign exchange outflows, the central bank fixed a maximum limit on the offer side of swap transactions, while to limit inflows, the limit was set on the bid side. In both cases, trade-related swaps were excluded from the limits.

Interest rate controls were substantially eliminated in February 1991. Earlier, Bank Negara Malaysia, in consultation with the Association of Banks, stipulated minimum lending rates and maximum deposit rates, partly with the aim of limiting competition in the banking system in order to protect domestic banks. In 1983, this system was replaced with a base lending rate influenced by the central bank, to which all banks were required to peg their own interest rates. In February 1991, the base lending rate was freed from administrative influence by the central bank, as were all other interest rates except those for lending to priority sectors, such as small-scale businesses and housing. Loans to these sectors remained subject to the central bank's annual lending guidelines.

Malaysia's central bank has also in some instances maintained direct credit controls to limit lending for certain purposes—notably to curtail consumer spending, particularly for spending financed by credit cards, and for such sundry uses as rental cars. The central bank has also continued to use moral suasion on bank lending policies. These instruments have been aimed at encouraging lending for development

[45]The central bank has operated two categories of discount facilities. First, commercial banks and other eligible institutions (finance companies, merchant banks, discount houses) may discount treasury bills and eligible short-term commercial, industrial, agricultural, and other business bills. Second, eligible institutions may seek a direct advance from the central bank, against collateral of paper eligible for rediscounting. A common discount rate is applied to both windows.

and the avoidance of excessive speculation and risk taking. Malaysia's use of market-based monetary instruments is reviewed in Table 2.7.

Mexico

Since 1978, the Central Bank of Mexico has operated weekly auctions of treasury certificates (CETES). From 1982 to 1985 auction amounts were predetermined and interest rates were allowed to reflect market conditions. This system was temporarily suspended and replaced with a fixed-price tender system in late 1985, because of concern over high interest rates; the market-based auction system was reintroduced in July 1986.[46] The issuance of CETES over a period of several years contributed to the gradual development of financial markets, and in particular government securities markets. This long-term effort provided a solid basis for the liberalization and introduction of an indirect monetary policy framework in 1988.

CETES have been issued in fixed denominations, with maturities between two and seven years. Participation in the auctions was initially restricted to a group of licensed CETES dealers, but others were allowed to acquire CETES by purchasing them from these dealers. Subsequently, the auctions have been opened to all banks and exchange houses. The interest rate on CETES is freely determined, although the central bank has bought CETES in the auction for subsequent use in its money market operations, aimed at moderating transitory swings in interest rates and in money market liquidity. These operations have included outright sales and repurchase/reverse repurchase agreements. The amount of CETES auctioned each week was in principle to be determined by the financing needs of the Treasury and monetary policy considerations. Because of concerns about the budgetary impact of interest costs, however, the weekly auctions of treasury bills have been supplemented by offers from the central bank to place or accept fixed deposits with the commercial banks (*subastas de depósitos*). The deposits have typical maturities ranging from 14 to 91 days, and are also auctioned weekly. Only banks are allowed access to these auctions.

Mexico continued to make active use of direct controls on credit and on longer-term interest rates through 1988, and used reserve

[46]See Leite (1985) for an overview of open-market-type operations in Mexico.

Table 2.7. Malaysia: Major Factors Affecting Reserve Money

(In billions of Malaysian ringgit; ended December unless otherwise stated)

	1984	1985	1986	1987	1988	1989	1990	1991	1992	1993
Domestic financing of the government deficit	1.8	1.8	5.0	8.9	7.0	5.4	4.3	3.2	4.5	2.8
Treasury bills	—	—	0.2	1.0	3.3	—	—	—	—	—
Other securities	3.1	3.6	4.6	7.5	7.0	2.4	3.9	3.2	1.4	–0.6
Other[1]	–1.3	–1.8	0.0	0.4	–3.3	3.0	0.4	0.0	3.1	3.3
Change in net claims on government by central bank[2]	0.9	–0.8	–0.3	–0.4	0.1	–0.6	–3.0	–1.8	–1.1	2.7
Change in net foreign assets of central bank[3]	1.0	2.4	3.5	2.9	–1.2	3.3	5.3	3.4	17.0	29.2
Change in autonomous net domestic assets of central bank[4]	. . .	–3.9	–2.3	2.7	2.4	3.0	–5.4	–0.9	9.0	13.4
Of which: refinance and rediscount facilities	. . .	0.1	–0.1	1.3	. . .	—	0.1	—	—	—
Change in the use of money market instruments by central bank	. . .	1.5	–1.2	–4.7	. . .	–3.0	3.6	1.1	–22.9	–39.7
In percent of reserve money at beginning of period	. . .	16.7	–12.4	–46.4	. . .	–25.2	24.3	6.1	–110.1	–156.9
Foreign exchange swaps	. . .	0.6	0.7	–2.2	. . .	. . .	. . .	. . .	. . .	—
Recycled government EPF deposits	. . .	1.0	–2.6	–1.6	—	—	—	—	–6.7	–6.0
Government securities	. . .	–0.1	0.7	–0.1	. . .	0.7	1.3	–1.1	–1.1	–1.0
Central bank certificates	. . .	—	—	–0.8	—	0.8	—	—	—	–6.1
Interbank borrowing	. . .	—			. . .	–4.5	2.3	2.2	–15.1	–26.6
Change in reserve money	0.4	0.1	0.5	0.5	1.3	3.3	3.5	3.6	2.7	2.9
In percent	3.7	7.6	4.2	5.2	11.8	27.7	22.9	19.0	12.8	11.6
Change in required reserves[5]	0.4	–0.1	–0.02	–0.03	0.2	2.2	2.2	2.6	1.8	1.2
In percent of reserve money at beginning of period	4.2	–1.6	–0.3	0.3	1.7	18.3	14.4	13.9	8.0	4.9
Memorandum										
Money market interest rates (in percent)										
Nominal	9.0	7.6	8.0	2.9	3.2	4.7	6.8	7.8	8.0	3.3
Real	7.9	7.5	7.7	–0.3	1.1	1.7	3.0	3.2	4.5	3.2

Sources: Data provided by Malaysian authorities; and IMF staff estimates.

[1]Residual.

[2]Includes recycled government deposits and government securities used for monetary control purposes.

[3]On a transaction basis, that is, excluding valuation changes.

[4]Includes refinance and discount facilities, loans to private and public enterprises, and other items.

[5]Includes commercial banks, finance companies, and merchant banks.

requirements frequently for monetary control purposes. Under these circumstances, the informal financial sector flourished. But in late 1988, in the context of its broad-based adjustment program, Mexico initiated a series of reforms aimed at altering the financial and monetary control systems in a fundamental manner. Quantitative restrictions on bankers' acceptances were lifted, followed by the deregulation of interest rates and the removal of restrictions on bank lending, as well as the conversion of the reserve requirement to a liquidity requirement in 1989. The liquidity requirement was abolished altogether in 1991. Starting in 1988, the exchange rate policy was aimed at stabilizing the Mexican peso against the U.S. dollar. Foreign exchange controls were eliminated in late 1991. Two new indexed government debt instruments were introduced in 1989: *tesobonos*, indexed to the exchange rate; and *adjustabonos*, indexed to the Consumer Price Index. The above measures were combined with a rapid reprivatization of the banking sector and—to address the problems of insolvent banks—a strengthening of prudential supervision and regulation, including new criteria for rating credit portfolios and capital adequacy.

Following these changes, government securities were the main instrument of monetary policy, both in the primary and the secondary market. As noted above, the Bank of Mexico participates in the weekly CETES auctions, primarily to smooth short-term interest rate movements. The bank intervenes daily in the secondary market, primarily through repurchase agreements and reverse repurchase agreements, rather than through outright sales or purchases. In addition, the Bank of Mexico retains the power to vary reserve requirements and to auction credit, but has generally abstained from making use of these instruments. The bank does not operate a standard discount window, but commercial banks are permitted to run overdrafts on an overnight basis with provisions for next-day settlement.

During the early 1990s, the central bank varied the liquidity coefficient imposed on domestic and foreign currency deposits in order to control the foreign indebtedness of commercial banks, as well as the proportion of deposits that had to be invested in the Bank of Mexico and specific government papers. Subsequently, the Bank of Mexico relied on open-market operations. The importance of market-based monetary instruments in Mexico is reviewed in Table 2.8.

Table 2.8. Mexico: Major Factors Affecting Reserve Money

(In billions of Mexican pesos; ended December unless otherwise stated)

	1983	1984	1985	1986	1987	1988	1989	1990	1991	1992	1993
Domestic financing of the government deficit[1]	824	1,508	4,097	11,120	24,957	46,876	28,943	19,898	–30,200	–45,250	. . .
Treasury certificates (CETES)	12.3	–86	1,149	3,836	8,780	–2,547	8,448	2,867	18,395	–8,525	. . .
Other[2]	701	1,594	2,948	7,284	16,177	49,423	20,495	17,031	–48,595	–36,725	. . .
Change in net claims on government by central bank[3]	1,068	944	2,178	3,935	980	21,442	6,040	2,207	–19,107	–5,819	. . .
Change in net foreign assets of central bank[4] (millions of new pesos)	372	569	–626	382	8,231	–15,278	1,337	9,172	24,609	3,633	8,871
Change in autonomous net domestic assets of central bank[5, 6]	–501	–54	1,419	1,613	2,303	20,598	6,895	–3,487	–16,009	–931	–20,708[7]
Change in the use of money market instruments by central bank[8]	–951	–1,158	–135	–1,100	–1,173	. . .	. . .	. . .	. . .	. . .	. . .
In percent of reserve money at beginning of period	–156.4	–142.3	–10.3	–54.9	32.2	. . .	. . .	. . .	. . .	. . .	. . .
Change in reserve money millions of new pesos	1,157	1,654	827	2,738	5,958	6,472	2,138	8,123	8,662	5,738	4,739
In percent	55.9	51.3	17.0	48.0	70.6	44.9	10.2	35.3	27.8	14.4	10.4
Memorandum:											
Money market interest rates (in percent)											
Nominal	57.5	49.9	62.4	88.4	95.6	69.0	47.4	37.4	25.6	18.9	17.4
Real	17.5	13.3	15.8	31.8	42.3	52.3	26.4	18.7	12.2	9.9	11.9

Sources: Data provided by Mexican authorities; and IMF staff estimates.

[1]Public sector.

[2]Residual.

[3]Includes CETES used for monetary control purposes.

[4]On a transaction basis, that is, excluding valuation changes.

[5]Includes refinance and discount facilities, loans to private enterprises, and other items.

[6]Effective flows.

[7]January–September.

[8]Fixed deposits with or placements by the central bank.

The Philippines

In October 1984, the Philippines authorities reformed their monetary policy framework by floating the Philippine peso and changing the domestic monetary target from the net domestic assets of the monetary authorities to base money.[47] Interest rates had been gradually deregulated in the 1980–83 period and have since been freely determined.

The main instrument of short-term monetary control in the Philippines has been a weekly auction, initially of central bank bills with maturities ranging from 30 to 90 days, and beginning in late 1986, of treasury bills issued at maturities of 91, 182, and 364 days (see Ealdama, 1986, for a description of the auction system). By the end of 1987, treasury bill issues had virtually replaced the issues of central bank bills. A proportion of the proceeds from the sale of treasury bills is held by the government in special fixed deposits with the central bank for the explicit purpose of sterilizing liquidity. The regular auctions of short-term paper have been supplemented by auctions of three-year treasury bills. Participation in the auctions has been limited to a group of commercial banks that have been given status as primary dealers based on their financial soundness; bills are to a large extent sold on to nonbanks. The primary dealers are obliged to participate in the auctions, to have bids regularly accepted, to undertake secondary trading in government securities, to post reasonable two-way prices for these securities, and to submit certain market information to the central bank. An Auction Committee, which includes the top-ranking officials of the Ministry of Finance and the central bank, conducts the auction; the Open Market Committee decides the tender amounts, based on the treasury's financing needs and the monetary policy stance adopted. The cutoff price in the auction usually is linked to the price range accepted in the previous auction, normally so that it deviates by less than 20 to 30 basis points from that auction. At times, this constraint has led to the rejection of all bids. There is also some noncompetitive bidding, limited to 20 percent of the total tender.

For shorter-term monetary control, the auctions have been supplemented by repurchase and reverse repurchase agreements using the bills held in the central banks's own portfolio. The central bank had

[47]Base money is defined as reserve money plus bank holdings of reserve eligible securities and reserve deficiencies.

made extensive use of foreign exchange swaps until late 1984, when it ceased providing new swap agreements, although existing agreements were rolled over. As a result of the depreciating Philippine peso, the central bank has suffered substantial operating losses on its foreign exchange swaps.

The central bank has restructured its refinance facilities, with the aim of reducing use and rationalizing function. By late 1985, the number of refinance facilities had been reduced from five to a single facility, covering a range of purposes (most outstanding credits have been for export refinancing). The interest rate charged under the single facility has been market based, and is adjusted in line with market rates.

During 1991–92, to sterilize the very large capital inflows, the authorities resorted to large issues of short-term treasury securities through the regular weekly auction and the secondary market, and sold central bank bills and conducted reserve repurchase agreements. Reserve requirements were also raised in 1989 and 1990 to their legal maximum of 25 percent. The scope for central bank open market operations had been constrained by the weak financial position of the central bank. The restructuring and recapitalization of the central bank in July 1993 increased the scope for open-market operations and allowed a reduction in the required reserve ratio. The role of market-based instruments of monetary control in the Philippines is reviewed in Table 2.9.

Sri Lanka

Since 1985, the nominal exchange rate for the Sri Lanka rupee has been adjusted regularly to counteract inflation differentials between Sri Lanka and its main trading partners. Within the constraint set by the exchange rate arrangement, the interest rate previously played a major role as the operational target. Since early 1988, the main operational target has been the net domestic assets of the central bank, derived from intermediate targets for monetary and credit aggregates.

Sri Lanka has undertaken several changes in its monetary control system in recent years. The central bank began auctioning its own securities in 1984 and such issues were a main instrument used to manage money market liquidity during 1985 and 1986. Auctions of central bank securities were held about once a month until 1987. Beginning in 1986, many direct credit controls were removed, and the central bank

Table 2.9. Philippines: Major Factors Affecting Reserve Money
(In billions of Philippine pesos; ended December unless otherwise stated)

	1983	1984	1985	1986	1987	1988	1989	1990	1991	1992	1993
Domestic financing of the government deficit (PSBR)	2.0	8.1	11.5	27.7	13.5	19.0	11.4	33.1	19.5	1.6	9.4
Treasury bills	. . .	. . .	. . .	. . .	50.5	36.7	21.7	28.3	20.9	122.5	77.3
Holding by central bank	. . .	. . .	. . .	. . .	. . .	. . .	. . .	–0.8	–0.1	27.4	144.2[7]
Other securities	. . .	. . .	. . .	. . .	3.6	2.7	–1.2	–21.6	24.7	31.3	63.5
Other[1]	. . .	. . .	. . .	. . .	–40.6	20.4	–9.1	26.4	–26.1	–152.2	–131.4
Change in net claims on government by central bank[2]	2.1	–0.6	16.4	–7.9	–36.0	–19.5	6.1	2.1	–15.7	–64.31	273.7[7]
Change in net foreign assets of central bank[3]	–20.9	0.8	–1.8	22.9	–5.1	12.0	8.9	–9.4	53.3	44.5	10.8
Change in autonomous net domestic assets of central bank[4]	16.0	18.9	70.9	23.6	21.0	16.2	22.1	45.1	14.6	7.7	–307.5[7]
Of which: lending to financial institutions and rediscounts	–1.8	1.6	2.7	–1.4	2.4	–0.3	0.6)	2.1	–0.3	–4.0	–7.1
Change in use of money market instruments by central bank[5]	0.2	–9.5	18.3	2.1	19.2	1.0	3.0	0.9	–50.2	–34.6	42.1
In percent of reserve money at beginning of period	1.0	–32.9	–52.9	5.5	37.6	1.7	4.5	1.2	–46.1	–26.7	29.1
Change in reserve money	9.4	5.7	4.6	12.0	6.9	9.6	25.6	15.8	20.7	15.4	26.9
In percent	47.6	20.5	13.8	31.6	13.8	16.6	38.0	17.0	19.0	11.9	18.6
Change in required reserves	4.3	1.7	2.0	0.8	2.0	3.5	13.9	19.9	10.0	9.7	9.4
In percent of reserve money at beginning of period	21.8	5.9	5.8	2.1	3.9	6.1	20.7	20.7	9.2	7.5	6.7
Memorandum:											
Money market interest rates (in percent)[6]											
Nominal	14.2	28.5	26.7	16.1	11.5	14.7	18.6	23.7	21.5	16.0	12.4
Real	–19.3	9.7	26.0	12.5	3.4	3.9	6.2	7.9	13.3	9.0	0.2

Sources: Data provided by Philippine authorities; and IMF staff estimates.
[1]Residual.
[2]Includes the government's fixed deposits with the central bank, associated with the issuance of treasury bills.
[3]On a transaction basis, that is, excluding valuation changes.
[4]Includes refinance and discount facilities, loans to private and public enterprises, and other items.
[5]Repurchases/reverse repurchases, operations in central bank papers and treasury securities.
[6]Treasury bill rate.
[7]Reflects restructuring and recapitalization of the central bank, July 1993.

refrained from strict enforcement of the remaining ceilings. Reserve requirements have continued to be used for monetary control; an important simplification was introduced with the unification of reserve requirements in 1987. The central bank has continued to operate several preferential refinance facilities. The operation of a general discount facility was discontinued in 1984.

Weekly auctions of treasury bills were introduced in early 1987 and since then have become the main monetary control instrument. The auctions have in principle been open to all. Since late 1987, the amount to be auctioned has been determined by a forecasting committee, consisting of central bank and treasury officials, but has been largely based on the amount of bills maturing. The cutoff yield has been determined by a Tendering Committee, chaired by the Senior Deputy Governor of the central bank. Since early 1988 the yield has been set with a view toward the central bank's net domestic assets—thus becoming the main operating target for short-term monetary control.

A lack of depth and competition in money and securities markets hampers monetary management in Sri Lanka. The central bank has been operating a secondary window for the purchase and sale of treasury bills. The prices at this secondary window are linked to those in the most recent auction of treasury bills with a penalty element that has varied over time. There is, however, no active market for government securities with maturities over one year. Although a substantial part of the government's financing requirement has been covered by issuing long-term rupee securities, these have been placed with captive sources. In addition, while short-term interest rates are market-oriented, the primary treasury bill market is not fully operated according to market principles and the secondary market is still very limited.

The central bank has, therefore, used a combination of direct and indirect policy instruments to influence the growth of monetary aggregates in recent years. These have included, among other instruments, statutory reserve requirements, refinance facilities, selective credit controls, and moral suasion. Since 1992, however, greater emphasis has been placed on indirect instruments of monetary control, including open-market operations in treasury bills and central bank securities, within the context of reserve money programming.

The conduct of monetary policy in 1993 was complicated by large unanticipated inflows of interest-sensitive capital, which rendered the system of reserve money management more difficult. The main policy response of the authorities to these inflows was aggressive sterilization by open-market operations through the central bank's secondary window and subsequently by issuing its own securities. However, a relatively passive stance to sterilization resulted in a rapid growth of reserve money in 1993. The role of market-based instruments of monetary control in Sri Lanka is reviewed in Table 2.10.

Thailand

The central bank has used multiple monetary targets as a guide for the conduct of monetary policy, including a monthly monetary base (or reserve money) as an operational target. The primary monetary policy instrument used by the central bank, the Bank of Thailand, has been government bond repurchases in the repurchase market operated by the central bank. This policy has been supplemented at times by the selective use of other monetary policy instruments, including the issuance of central bank bonds, a tightening of commercial bank access to refinancing facilities, and changes in the Bank of Thailand's rediscount rate.

The money market is dominated by the government bond repurchase market established in April 1979. Government bonds, which are issued for maturities of 5, 10, or 15 years on fixed interest rates, are otherwise illiquid. The central bank acts as a principal of the repurchase transactions. It receives daily bids and offers from commercial banks for specified maturities (typically seven days and overnight). Until about May 1986, the central bank's activity largely involved matching the bids and offers for repurchases with limited intervention on its own account. With the emergence of a high level of liquidity in the banking system in 1986, central bank intervention became more active and in May 1987, it introduced a longer-term repurchase contract with maturities up to six months. Also in May 1987, the central bank made the first issue of its own bonds. The treasury bill market is limited and has not been used for active monetary management.[48] The interbank market is also thin and volatile, and a direct repurchase mar-

[48]Bills are auctioned on a weekly basis and are purchased mainly by financial institutions to satisfy statutory requirements. Between auctions, the central bank usually stands ready to sell bills from its portfolio and has occasionally purchased bills before maturity.

Table 2.10. Sri Lanka: Major Factors Affecting Reserve Money
(In millions of Sri Lanka rupees; ended December)

	1983	1984	1985	1986	1987	1988	1989	1990	1991	1992	1993
Domestic financing of the government deficit	6,534	3,991	8,569	9,143	11,355	21,065	15,850	13,509	16,149	15,551	22,258
Treasury bills	80	–2,540	7,420	3,893	3,677	13,850	13,546	10,722	5,000	14,128	10,100
Central bank	664	–3,937	7,301	1,493	174	10,982	828	–3,444	4,378	–9,834	–20,020
Commercial bank	–572	–4	–4	150	3,184	191	2,757	4,322	–1,364	13,520	26,806
Nonbanks	–12	1,401	123	2,250	318	2,678	9,960	9,845	1,987	9,641	3,314
Other securities[1]	3,100	3,073	6,369	3,281	7,078	5,825	5,361	1,344	13,252	2,981	12,757[2]
Other[3]	3,333	3,458	–5,220	1,969	600	1,390	–3,057	1,443	–2,103	–1,558	–599
Change in net claims on government by central bank[4]	577	–3,730	6,735	2,495	786	8,507	466	–2,192	–208	–1,895	–13,663
Change in net foreign asset of central bank[5]	–397	5,969	–3,846	–5,116	–4,936	–182	2,344	5,305	12,938	12,465	36,399
Change in autonomous net domestic assets of central bank[6]	1,579	–1,013	–1,252	1,148	–81	427	1,327	4,039	–4,724	–745	–6,127
Change in the use of money market instruments by central bank	—	–415	–750	–1,439	2,584	—	19.3	–1,251	511	–2,243	–1,236
In percent of reserve money at beginning of period	—	–1.2	–5.5	–8.5	14.3	—	0.1	–4.7	1.6	–5.6	–2.8
Central bank securities	—	–415	–750	–1,439	2,584	—	19.3	—	—	—	–2,155
Outstanding position of treasury bills in secondary market				—	—			1,251	511	2,243	919
Change in reserve money	2,523	2,070	3,184	1,137	1,242	6,292	1,228	4,787	8,477	4,802	11,609
In percent	27.7	17.8	23.3	6.7	6.9	32.6	4.8	17.9	26.8	12.0	25.9)
Change in required reserves	1,177	549	1,944	–357	–786	3,139	886	2,491	1,216	4,098	6,505
In percent of reserve money at beginning of period	12.2	4.5	13.6	–2.0	–4.2	16.3	3.5	9.3	3.9	10.2	14.5)
Memorandum:											
Money market interest rates[7]											
Nominal	12.4	13.1	13.4	10.5	7.3	13.4	14.8	14.1	13.8	16.2	16.5
Real	–1.8	11.7	5.9	3.4	–5.0	3.1	–2.9	3.2	3.6	5.7	14.1

Sources: Data provided by the Sri Lankan authorities; and IMF Staff estimates.
[1]Net of debt sinking fund.
[2]Excludes Rp 24,088 million of bonds issued to recapitalize two state banks.
[3]Residual.
[4]Includes operations in Treasury bills for monetary control purposes.
[5]On a transactions basis,that is, excluding valuation changes.
[6]Includes refinance and discount facilities, loans to private and public enterprises, and other items.
[7]Treasury bill rate

ket among commercial banks has not emerged—partially because of the operating procedures of the Bank of Thailand.

During 1989–91, the substantial consolidation of the fiscal position taking place at the time was reflected in rising treasury deposits at the central bank and served to offset a large part of the impact of large balance of payments surpluses on the growth of reserve money. The decline in net claims on government offset, on average, about 50 percent of the contribution to reserve money growth from net foreign assets during this period. Discretionary monetary policies at this time included the issuance of B 13.4 billion in central bank bonds, a reduction in commercial bank access to refinancing facilities at the central bank, and an increase in the rediscount rate from 8 percent at the end of 1989 to 12 percent at the end of 1990.

The central bank has set maximum interest rates on bank deposits and adjusted it periodically until recently; it has used moral suasion to encourage commercial banks to adjust their interest rates, but has increasingly left interest rates to be determined by market forces. Also since 1980, the authorities removed the usury ceiling of 15 percent in the civil code, and began to adjust lending rate ceilings of banks and finance companies to reflect market conditions and cost developments. Formal interest rate liberalization began only in 1989. During 1990–92 controls on deposit rates were removed initially, then lending rates were lifted progressively. The central bank has resorted on occasion to direct credit controls, most recently in 1984. The authorities have sought to influence the direction of credit by rediscounting on a preferential basis, by imposing lending quotas, and by exempting lending to priority sectors from risk/asset ratios.

Concern over the impact of the oligopolistic structure of the banking system lead the Thai Bankers Association, representing the large commercial banks, to agree with the Bank of Thailand in October 1993 that in addition to the prime lending rate (the minimum lending rate) they would also announce a minimum retail rate to the public, with this rate serving as a benchmark for lending to general customers. The minimum retail rate was introduced to lower the cost of information, increase competition, and reduce the differential between prime and nonprime lending rates. Under this system, the minimum lending rate is announced by each individual commercial bank taking into account their own cost of funds. Banks are required to announce the criteria for qualifying for interest and discounts based on the minimum

Table 2.11. Thailand: Major Factors Affecting Reserve Money

(In billions of Thai baht; ended December)

	1984	1985	1986	1987	1988	1989	1990	1991	1992	1993
Domestic financing of the government deficit	35.9	31.6	50.2	10.6	–28.8	–11.2	–11.9	–46.9	–28.6	–44.3
Of which: Bank of Thailand	–3.3	11.3	–5.9	–8.6	–47.9	–7.9	7.3	5.1	–1.8	–14.1
Treasury Bill	–3.2	4.8	–5.2	5.0	—	—	—	—	—	—
Bonds	–2.2	4.7	0.9	–3.1	–26.8	–8.4	6.3	4.4	–0.6	–11.4
Other	39.1	20.3	56.2	19.3	19.1	–3.3	–19.2	–51.9	–26.8	–30.2
Treasury Bill	5.0	–5.7	4.9	—	—	—	—	—	—	—
Bonds	25.3	17.0	31.0	15.6	5.0	–3.2	–12.5	–48.2	–16.3	–21.8
Change in net claims on government by central bank	–5.2	8.5	–9.4	–7.0	–51.5	–54.6	–36.9	–61.3	–21.9	–23.8
Change in net foreign assets of central bank	10.8	5.6	14.3	18.0	59.1	93.8	90.3	101.5	73.9	97.5
Change in autonomous net domestic assets[1] of central bank	5.1	5.0	13.5	6.7	15.2	–12.3	1.0	–6.5	0.6	–14.0
Change in the use of money market instruments by the central bank	–0.9	1.2	–2.9	0.0	2.0	–2.8	1.4	0.8	4.5	1.2
In percent of reserve money at beginning of period	–11.8	1.5	–3.4	0.0	1.7	–2.1	0.9	0.4	2.1	0.5
Credits for liquidity purposes	–0.9	1.2	–1.0	–0.2	0.3	0.9	–12.0	9.4	1.4	1.4
Bank of Thailand bonds	—	—	—	—[2]	—	—	—	—	—	—
Repurchase agreements in government bonds	—	—	–1.9	0.2	1.7	–3.7	13.4	–8.6	3.1	3.1
Change in reserve money	4.2	6.8	8.8	21.4	17.3	22.7	29.1	24.7	35.5	40.1
In percent	5.3	7.7	9.2	18.3	12.9	14.5	15.7	11.7	15.1	13.9
Change in required reserves	6.1	4.0	5.1	7.1	10.5	16.8	20.8	20.2	21.1	27.0
In percent of reserve money at beginning of period	8.1	5.0	5.9	7.5	9.0	12.5	13.3	10.9	10.0	10.9
Money market interest rates (In percent)										
Nominal	13.6	13.5	8.1	5.9	8.7	9.8	12.7	10.6	7.1	—
Real	11.2	11.7	5.7	2.2	3.6	4.2	7.3	6.6	3.7	—

Sources: IMF, *International Financial Statistics*; data provided by the authorities; and IMF staff estimates.

[1]Includes refinance and rediscount facilities, and loans to private and public enterprise.

[2]Outstanding amount was 2 billion baht in the period June–October 1984.

lending rate, the minimum retail rate, the maximum margin to be added to the minimum retail rate, and the maximum interest rate to be charged in case of a customer's default. Banks are also required to post these rates openly to the public at every branch office. Although commercial banks remain free to determine their deposit and lending rates,[49] the understanding reached with the central bank is that the minimum lending rate would not exceed 2 percentage points above the average cost of deposits and the minimum retail rate would not exceed 2 percentage points above the minimum lending rate. The maximum lending rate would be 2 percentage points above the minimum retail rate. Within these ranges, the actual rate for any individual borrower would depend on the customer's credit rating. The role of market-based instruments of monetary control in Thailand is reviewed in Table 2.11.

[49]The ceiling on all time deposit rates was removed in March 1990, while ceilings were lifted on saving deposits in January 1992 and on loan rates in June 1992.

Appendix III: Estimates of Money and Credit Demand and Tests of Stability

Table 2.12. Determinants of Monetary and Credit Growth
(Dependent variable ΔlnM)

Dependent Variable	Constant	ΔlnY	ΔlnP	r_d	r_f	$\ln(M_{-1}/Y)$	R^2	SEE
Indonesia								
Currency								
1970–84	0.23	0.61	–0.26	0.004	–0.006	0.03	0.21	0.065
	(0.22)	(2.03)	(0.66)	(0.81)	(0.68)	(0.08)		
1970–92	–0.71	0.41	–0.11	–0.004	–0.011	–0.31	0.14	0.078
	(0.78)	(1.26)	(0.24)	(1.01)	(1.34)	(1.01)		
Broad money								
1970–84	–0.17	0.49	–0.12	0.002	–0.003	0.17	0.63	0.052
	(0.98)	(1.76)	(0.37)	(0.41)	(0.58)	(1.64)		
1970–92	–0.06	0.63	–0.28	0.006	0.001	–0.08	0.46	0.062
	(0.58)	(2.43)	(0.79)	(1.98)	(0.10)	(2.37)		
Private sector credit								
1970–84	–0.26	–1.61	2.30	–0.01	–0.03	–0.50	0.44	0.187
	(0.79)	(1.94)	(2.08)	(0.85)	(1.53)	(2.48)		
1970–92	–0.12	–1.20	1.75	0.01	–0.01	–0.18	0.20	0.19
	(0.41)	(1.53)	(1.61)	(1.08)	(0.35)	(2.22)		
Kenya								
Currency								
1970–90	–1.27	0.82	–0.79	–0.003	0.001	–0.47	0.60	0.04
	(2.36)	(2.02)	(2.82)	(0.90)	(0.02)	(2.48)		
1970–92	–0.76	0.56	–0.07	–0.001	–0.009	–0.30	0.29	0.063
	(1.00)	(0.99)	(0.22)	(0.09)	(2.09)	(1.15)		
Broad money								
1970–90	–0.70	0.57	–0.24	–0.005	0.001	–0.61	0.44	0.066
	(2.05)	(0.87	(0.54)	(1.03)	(0.13)	(2.26)		
1970–92	–0.49	0.36	0.37	–0.003	–0.008	–0.48	0.33	0.076
	(1.29)	(0.49)	(0.86)	(0.52)	(1.39)	(1.57		
Private sector credit								
1970–90	–0.76	–0.12	0.30	–0.005	0.008	–0.48	0.51	0.051
	2.48	(0.30)	(0.89)	(1.20)	(1.44)	(3.33		
1970–92	–0.69	–0.39	0.76	–0.004	0.002	–0.46	0.45	0.056
	(2.10)	(0.99)	(2.72)	(1.00)	(0.42)	(2.99		
Malaysia								
Currency								
1970–90	–0.22	0.20	0.51	–0.007	–0.007	–0.16	0.40	0.049
	(0.57)	1.16	1.21	(1.24)	(1.55)	(0.93)		
1970–92	–0.31	0.14	0.24	–0.01	–0.002	(–0.19)	0.35	0.053
	(0.72)	(0.77)	(0.56)	(2.39)	(0.56)	(1.09)		
Broad money								
1970–90	–0.03	0.26	–0.16	0.002	0.005	–0.13	0.44	0.047
	(0.37)	(1.75)	(0.37)	(0.03)	(1.01)	2.57		
1970–92	0.02	0.33	0.28	0.005	–0.002	–0.09	0.28	0.054
	(0.27)	(1.92)	(0.63)	(0.81)	(0.53)	(1.65)		

Table 2.12 (*continued*)

Dependent Variable	Constant	ΔlnY	ΔlnP	r_d	r_f	$\ln(M_{-1}/Y)$	R^2	SEE
Private sector credit								
1970–90	–0.12	0.49	–0.41	0.009	0.01	–0.10	0.45	0.065
	(1.33)	(2.34)	(0.69)	(1.08)	(1.85)	(2.61)		
1970–92	–0.10	0.52	–0.24	0.01	0.009	–0.09	0.44	0.063
	(1.21)	(2.55)	(0.46)	(1.39)	(1.84)	(2.57)		
Mexico								
Currency								
1970–88	–1.72	0.53	–0.48	0.001	0.001	–0.58	0.78	0.098
	(1.76)	(0.90)	(0.10)	(0.28)	(0.15)	(1.79)		
1970–92	–0.74	0.83	–0.50	0.002	0.002	–0.24	0.76	0.093
	(1.18)	(1.64)	(1.15)	(0.87)	(0.33)	(1.23)		
Broad money								
1970–88	0.15	1.11	–0.95	0.004	–0.003	0.01	—	0.26
	(0.16)	(0.78)	(0.75)	(0.69)	(0.09)	(0.03)		
1970–92	–0.16	0.85	–1.13	0.007	0.004	–0.17	0.06	0.243
	(0.34)	(0.63)	(0.97)	(1.39)	(0.22)	(0.75)		
Private sector credit								
1970–88	–0.30	1.85	–0.35	–0.004	–0.01	–0.14	0.17	0.29
	(0.31)	(1.15)	(0.24)	(0.58)	(0.34)	(0.51)		
1970–92	0.37	1.98	–0.81	–0.002	–0.03	0.04	0.11	0.283
	(0.90)	(1.28)	(0.62)	(0.26)	(1.31)	(0.27)		
Philippines								
Currency								
1970–84	1.45	–0.12	–0.12	0.004	–0.01	–0.32	0.14	0.105
	(1.33)	(0.14)	(0.16)	(0.33)	(1.13)	(1.18)		
1970–92	1.22	0.40	–0.54	0.004	–0.007	–0.28	0.01	0.086
	(1.97)	(0.78)	(1.21)	(0.75)	(0.94)	(1.78)		
Broad money								
1970–84	–0.13	0.47	–0.80	0.01	–0.004	0.05	0.08	0.086
	(0.11)	(0.67)	(1.30)	(1.47)	(0.50)	(0.20)		
1970–92	1.04	0.66	–0.73	0.01	0.000	–0.19	0.00	0.004
	(1.33)	(1.35)	(1.73)	(1.79)	(0.03)	(1.29)		
Private Sector credit								
1970–84	–1.55	1.01	–0.19	–0.04	0.01	0.35	0.47	0.73
	(0.89)	(1.68)	(0.29)	(1.96)	(1.17)	(0.99)		
1970–92	0.87	0.93	–0.54	–0.008	0.01	–0.15	0.17	0.13
	(1.22)	(1.20)	(0.81)	(1.09)	(1.21)	(1.08)		
Sri Lanka								
Currency								
1970–90	–1.28	–0.09	0.19	–0.002	–0.01	–0.55	0.22	0.088
	(2.50)	(0.19)	(0.30)	(0.42)	(1.14)	(2.75)		
1970–92	–1.32	–0.15	0.14	–0.004	–0.007	–0.56	0.21	0.086
	(2.69)	(0.33)	(0.23)	(0.81)	(0.78)	(2.89)		
Broad money								
1970–90	–0.40	0.25	–0.57	0.01	0.01	–0.28	0.05	0.092
	(1.12)	(0.37)	(0.80)	(1.52)	(0.66)	(1.28)		
1970–92	–0.39	0.26	–0.57	0.008	0.007	–0.27	0.09	0.087
	(1.21)	(0.42)	(0.85)	(1.79)	(0.77)	(1.38)		

Table 2.12 (*concluded*)

Dependent Variable	Constant	ΔlnY	ΔlnP	r_d	r_f	$\ln(M_{-1}/Y)$	R^2	SEE
Private sector credit								
1970–90	–0.43	0.86	–0.55	0.02	–0.19	–0.19	0.29	0.110
	(1.27)	(1.19)	(0.66)	(2.25)	(0.89)	(1.24)		
1970–92	–0.42	0.87	–0.52	0.02	–0.01	–0.19	0.31	0.104
	(1.33)	(1.30)	(0.68)	(2.51)	(1.32)	(1.30)		
Thailand								
Currency								
1970–85	–0.73	0.16	–0.05	–0.02	0.001	–0.35	0.17	0.048
	(1.22)	(0.40)	(0.14)	(1.65)	(0.20)	(1.40)		
1970–92	–0.79	0.20	–0.11	–0.02	0.002	–0.36	0.36	0.042
	(2.24)	(0.70)	(0.41)	(2.41)	(0.49)	(2.56)		
Broad money								
1970–85	0.15	0.10	0.12	0.001	–0.002	–0.01	0.33	0.40
	(1.02)	(0.26)	(0.35)	(0.15)	(0.37)	(0.12)		
1970–92	0.11	0.41	–0.11	0.005	–0.003	0.007	0.03	0.037
	(1.86)	(1.68)	(0.44)	(0.95)	(0.66)	(0.03)		
Private sector credit								
1970–85	0.18	1.23	–0.36	–0.004	0.00	0.04	0.36	0.60
	(0.39)	(2.57)	(0.78)	(0.20)	(0.01)	(0.31)		
1970–92	0.18	1.23	–0.36	–0.004	0.00	0.04	0.38	0.060
	(0.39)	(2.57)	(0.78)	(0.20)	(0.01)	(0.31)		

Sources: Data provided by the country authorities; IMF, *International Financial Statistics;* and IMF staff estimates.

Note: Data in parentheses indicate t-statistics.

Table 2.13. Test of Homogeneity (F-Statistic)[1]

	Residual sum of squares		
	1970–92 (1) RSS_1	1970[2] (2) RSS_2	Computed F [2,3]
Indonesia			
Currency	.1035	.0385	1.69
Broad money	.0660	.0245	1.70
Credit to private sector	.6198	.3146	0.97
Kenya			
Currency	.0670	.0289	**9.25**
Broad money	.0978	.0656	**3.43**
Credit to private sector	.0367	.0526	**3.03**
Malaysia			
Currency	.0471	.0360	2.16
Broad money	.0500	.0328	**3.67**
Credit to private sector	.0688	.0637	**5.60**
Mexico			
Currency	.1479	.1238	0.59
Broad money	1.0054	.8782	0.43
Credit to private sector	1.3583	1.3972	**4.00**
Philippines			
Currency	.1253	.0993	0.26
Broad money	.0665	.1118	0.68
Credit to private sector	.2696	.0479	**4.63**
Sri Lanka			
Currency	.1242	.1170	0.18
Broad money	.1272	.1271	0.00
Credit to private sector	.1821	.1816	**4.00**
Thailand			
Currency	.0301	.0234	0.37
Broad money	.0232	.0162	0.56
Credit to private sector	.0487	.0361	0.45

[1]Whenever the computed F exceeds the critical F level, one should reject the hypothesis that the results of the individual equations are consistent. In this test, the critical F at 99 percent level of significance is **4.29**; and at 95 percent of significance is **2.74**.

[2]With estimation cut-off period: For Indonesia–1984, Kenya–1990, Malaysia–1990, Mexico–1988, the Philippines–1984, Sri Lanka–1990, and Thailand–1985.

[3] $$F = \frac{(RSS_1 - RSS_2)/(n_1 - n_2)}{RSS_2/(n_2 - K - 1)},$$

where K = 6. Bold type indicates instability in demand following the reform of monetary instruments.

3

Sequencing Financial Reform and Liberalization in Five Developing Countries

AMER BISAT, R. BARRY JOHNSTON, AND V. SUNDARARAJAN

This chapter reviews the experience of five developing countries in liberalizing their financial systems and summarizes the factors that contribute to successful financial liberalizations. Two broad questions are addressed: Are there specific components of financial sector reforms best implemented at specific stages of a broader stabilization-cum-reform program? Is there an appropriate sequencing of various detailed components of financial sector reforms?

The analysis considers several components of financial sector reform, namely: reforms of the interest rate regime; the development of money markets and market-based monetary control procedures; reforms of prudential regulations and supervisory systems; recapitalization and restructuring of weak financial institutions; measures to strengthen competition among banks; reform of selective credit regulations; the development of long-term capital markets; and legislative reforms.

Note: This chapter first appeared in October 1992 as IMF Working Paper 92/82, "Issues in Managing and Sequencing Financial Sector Reform: Lessons from Experiences in Five Developing Countries." The present version updates some of the information in the original paper.

The study examines financial sector reform in Argentina (1976–81), Chile (1974–80), Indonesia (1983–90), Korea (1980–88), and the Philippines (1980–84). Conditions prior to embarking on economic and financial reforms ranged from severe financial repression, distortion in prices, and economic imbalances (for example, in Argentina), to more progressive financial sectors and smaller economic and structural distortions (for example, in some of the Asian economies). In all the countries the activities of financial institutions were tightly controlled prior to the financial reforms, with a high degree of policy-induced segmentation between different types of financial institutions.

In presenting the individual country experiences we have sought to standardize data presentation and to develop some key indicators. Inevitably, with data drawn from many different sources, series are not fully comparable across different countries. The table in Appendix I provides a detailed description of the data. Appendix II provides the statistical tables. The indicators of financial sector development include various measures of private financial assets: currency, M2, M3, and private financial assets. M2 is defined as currency in circulation plus deposit liabilities of the banking system. M3 is defined as M2 plus deposit liabilities with nonbank financial institutions. Private financial assets, the broadest measure of liquidity presented, is defined as M3 plus identified holdings of other financial assets by the private sector, such as treasury bills, and central bank bills where they exist. The relative movements in these aggregates are indicative of portfolio shifts within the financial sector, while their growth rates and the trends in their ratios to GDP are indicative of economic monetization and the development of financial markets.

The amount of credit provided by financial institutions to the private sector—an indicator of the development of financial sector intermediation—and by the central bank to financial institutions—an indicator of the extent of official involvement in the operations of financial institutions—is also analyzed. When the central bank provides a larger part of the funding for credit to the private sector, the credit allocation decisions of the central bank—through its refinancing and rediscount policies—necessarily have a strong influence on private credit allocation decisions regardless of whether there are explicit controls.

The growth of financial institution credit to the private sector relative to the growth of private deposits with financial institutions is an indicator of the change in the use and mobilization of domestic financial resources from the private sector. A more rapid growth of credit to the private sector than of private sector deposits could signify pressures on domestic resources, which would worsen the balance of payments unless offset by a reduction in the fiscal deficit or larger capital inflows.

Other indicators include real interest rates, GDP growth rates, number and types of financial institutions, gross lending margins, international interest rate differentials, and excess bank reserves. For those countries that have faced a financial crisis, selected indicators of these crises are also shown.

Country Experiences with Financial Sector Reform

The presentations for each country describe the prereform financial structure and the broad economic circumstances that were associated with the financial reforms. The financial sector reform measures and their sequencing are then presented. This is followed by an examination of the consequences of reforms using the above-mentioned indicators. Finally, a number of broad conclusions are drawn from each country's experience.

Comparative indicators from the five countries and the lessons from their different liberalization experiences are further examined in the final section. In particular, structural linkages among specific components of financial sector reforms are examined, as is the impact of reforms on key financial variables of macroeconomic significance. Conclusions are drawn about the appropriate sequencing of specific financial sector reforms.

Argentina

Argentina's economic problems had a long history and can be traced to inward-looking economic policies characterized by tariff protection, policy-induced transfers from the agricultural to the industrial sectors, and central control over the allocation of resources that began in the mid-1930s.

Prereform: 1974–76

The Argentinean economy of the mid-1970s was characterized by distortions in relative prices, a highly disorganized and repressed financial system, multiple exchange rates, and restricted international capital flows. GDP growth was negative in 1975 and 1976; inflation increased to as high as 443 percent in 1976; the fiscal deficit reached 12.5 percent of GDP that same year; and balance of payments pressures also increased.

Argentina's financial sector was severely repressed and dominated by commercial banks (see Appendix II, Tables 3.9 and 3.10). The numerous nonbanks were mostly very small. Government ownership—federal, state, and municipal—of banks and other financial institutions was substantial (as measured by the number of branches of government-owned financial institutions) and the financial structure was constrained by strict central bank approval requirements for new banks and for the opening and closing of branches.

The Deposit Nationalization Law of 1973 forced banks to deposit all financial savings with the central bank, in effect creating a 100 percent reserve requirement. Banks could only lend from their capital and reserves, and from access to central bank funds, mainly in the form of selective and subsidized credit to priority sectors. Interest rates on bank deposits and loans were set by the monetary authorities, as were their fees and commissions.

As a result of the controls, real interest rates became increasingly negative between 1974 and 1976 (see Appendix II, Table 3.11), and financial savings through banks and financial institutions declined in real terms, and as a percentage of total financial sector liabilities. An informal money market, based mostly on enterprise promissory notes, expanded rapidly; the size of this market in 1976 was estimated at 40 percent of the interest-bearing deposits of the banking system (Fernández, 1985). The ratio of currency to deposits was very high and the ratios of M2 and M3 to GDP fell sharply. Only about half of the private savings was monetized by commercial banks (see Appendix II, Table 3.10), and credit extended by financial institutions to the private sector fell in real terms (on average by 17 percent a year during 1974–76), reflecting the decline in central bank credit to financial institutions, and declines in the real value of financial institutions' capital.[1] Central bank resources were increasingly directed to finance

[1]The decline in private savings with the banking system also reflected the presence of indexed government bonds that were popular as a hedge against inflation.

public deficits, and between 1974–76 an average of 68 percent of the fiscal deficit was financed by the central bank.

Financial sector reform: 1977–80

In the context of an economic adjustment program aimed at curbing inflation, limiting the economic role of the government, and promoting the international integration of the economy (through the reduction of tariffs and exchange controls), the Argentinean authorities introduced a range of measures to reform the financial system. Table 3.1 summarizes the main measures and the sequencing of the financial reforms.

The liberalization of interest rates commenced in 1976 when interest rates on certificates of deposit (CDs) were freed. This was followed in 1977 by a major financial sector liberalization and reform of monetary control instruments. In 1977, all bank deposit and loan rates were liberalized, the controls on bank credit were removed, the 100 percent reserve requirement was reduced (initially to 45 percent and then lowered progressively to 10 percent by 1980), and interest was paid on required reserves held against time deposits through a newly established Interest Equalization Fund. Selective credit practices were abandoned (except for export-oriented loans), and selective rediscounts were replaced with a single discount window with the discount rate set at a penalty level compared with market rates.[2] Treasury bills, which had been available on tap at predetermined interest rates, were auctioned with the aim of managing financial sector liquidity. Because of the effects on liquidity distribution of the change in the reserve requirement and rediscount policy, transitional arrangements included special temporary rediscount lines for some banks and special deposit requirements with the central bank for some other banks.

Concurrent with the financial liberalization, new prudential regulations were instituted. These included changes in the definition of minimum capital requirements; maximum ratios of assets and liabilities to total capital and reserves; and limits on loans to any single borrower in terms of both the borrower's and the lender's capital and reserves. The minimum requirements for opening new bank branches were eased and the need for prior central bank approval was eliminated. Also, new

[2]As a result, central bank credit to financial institutions fell sharply as a proportion of the total bank credit to the private sector (see Appendix II, Table 3.10).

Table 3.1. Argentina: Sequence of Financial Reform

	1976	1977	1978	1979	1980	1981
Deregulation of the financial sector						
CD rates freed	•					
All interest rate ceilings abolished		•				
Lending autonomy to financial institutions		•				
Reserve requirements of 100 percent eliminated		•				
Approval requirements for new banks eliminated		•				
Branching restrictions eased		•				
Strengthening of regulatory, supervisory and legal systems						
Minimum capital requirements established		•				
Maximum financial liabilities to capital ratios set		•				
Limits on individual borrowing put in place		•				
Deposit insurance of 100 percent eliminated				•		
Supervisory system reformed						•
Reform of monetary control instruments						
Reserve requirements lowered		•	•	•	•	
Treasury bill auctions for monetary control established		•				
Rediscount facilities reformed		•				
Payment of interest on reserve requirements through Interest Equalization Fund established						
Restructuring of financial institutions, including liquidations, mergers, reorganization					•	•
Other reforms and adjustment						
Capital account restrictions eased	•	•	•			
Adjustment program	•					

regulations facilitated the establishment of new financial institutions and the restructuring of old ones. Later, in 1979, the deposit insurance scheme was reformed. Full insurance coverage was removed from all but the smallest deposits, the maximum amount of insured deposits was indexed, insurance premiums were set (previously the central bank sustained the total cost), and foreign exchange deposit insurance was completely eliminated. (The maximum amount was adjusted retroactively following the onset of the financial crisis; see below.) In 1981, financial institution supervision was reorganized through the introduction of new accounting, auditing, and reporting standards, and the responsible department of the central bank was reorganized.

Effects of financial sector reforms: 1977–80

First, the reforms did not have a major effect on financial sector efficiency. Although the reforms were associated with some restructuring in terms of liquidations, mergers, and reorganizations, they resulted in increasing concentration in the financial sector and did not result in significant improvement in financial sector competition or efficiency.[3] Banks' administrative costs remained high, averaging about 8 percent of total loans, and the differential between deposit and lending rates widened following the liberalization. Although the differential narrowed subsequently—partly in response to the progressive reduction in required reserve ratios—it generally remained above its prereform level (see Appendix II, Table 3.11). Also, the capital markets were not developed as part of the reforms, and the number of companies traded, along with their capitalization, on the Buenos Aires stock exchange fell after the reforms (see Appendix II, Table 3.9). In addition to these factors, the government continued to rely on the banking system for financing purposes (see Appendix II, Table 3.12) so that the real stock of government securities outstanding did not increase.

Second, there was a shift in monetary and credit aggregates. The liberalization of bank deposit rates encouraged a shift out of currency into bank deposits, and the currency to deposit ratio fell sharply, as the ratio of broad money to GDP increased (Appendix II, Table 3.10). The growth of bank credit to the private sector increased and was considerably higher than the growth of private sector bank deposits, and the ratio of private savings to GDP fell as a result. The rapid credit expansion and slower increase in deposits in part reflected the negative real interest rates during the initial period of the reforms (the dynamics of deposit and credit growth following liberalization are discussed later in the chapter).

Third, real deposit and lending rates subsequently rose sharply from the highly negative prereform levels (see Appendix II, Table 3.11). Beginning in 1978, the authorities had tried to reduce inflation

[3]While the number of commercial banks nearly doubled, and the total number of bank branches increased by one-third, the number of nonbanks declined, leading to a fall in the total number of financial institutions (see Appendix II, Table 3.9) and an increasing concentration of bank ownership.

by posting a devaluation schedule (*tablita*) for the exchange rate that lagged behind the general price increases. The success of such a policy required credibility and monetary and fiscal discipline, but ambiguities surrounded the *tablita*, weakening its credibility.[4] Fiscal deficits were large and growing, and averaged 12.8 percent of GDP between 1978–82, and monetary financing of the deficits was inconsistent with the preannounced rates of devaluation. The ensuing inflation, which averaged 153 percent in 1977–80, appreciated the real exchange rate by 64 percent between 1977 and 1980, fueled expectations of a breakdown of the *tablita*, and contributed to the sharp rise in real interest rates in 1981. The *tablita* was abandoned in 1982. The real sector's health was damaged by the appreciation in the exchange rate and the sharp increase in real interest rates.

Domestic deposit and loan rates also rose substantially above U.S. dollar interest rates, after adjusting for the actual devaluation of the exchange rate. Although capital movements into and out of Argentina were gradually liberalized, remaining restrictions constrained the scope for international interest rate arbitrage and allowed the domestic–international interest differentials to persist.[5] The remaining exchange controls also protected the inefficient domestic financial system.

Fourth, the initial rapid expansion in bank loan portfolios exposed banks to increasing risks and, combined with the rise in nominal interest rates, resulted in a sharp increase in problem loans (see Appendix II, Table 3.13). Business enterprises' debt to equity ratios also rose with the freer access to bank credit, increasing their vulnerability to a rise in real interest rates. When real interest rates rose in 1981, the result was a sharp increase in distress borrowing.

---

[4]The schedule was sometimes not adhered to; it was frequently changed in mid-course, and was sometimes kept open ended.

[5]Between 1976 and 1978, the previous system of multiple exchange rates was unified, foreign loans were allowed at prevailing foreign exchange rates (with no government insurance), and all foreign exchange transactions up to a determined limit per transaction were permitted. (The limit was gradually increased to $20,000 in September 1978.) Other reasons for the persistence of these interest differentials include a risk premium arising from foreign exchange rate devaluation expectations (Blejer, 1982), and the unequal access to foreign credit between various private borrowers and between private and public borrowers (Petrie and Tybout, 1985).

Financial sector crisis

In March 1980 a major bank failed. The ensuing reshuffling of bank deposits to banks perceived as safer and the drying up of the interbank market placed serious strains on the financial system. By May 1980, the government was forced to intervene in three additional institutions, and by March 1981, it had liquidated a total of 62 financial institutions, holding approximately 20 percent of the country's total deposits.

The financial sector crisis reflected a number of factors. While the prudential regulations instituted in 1977 were fairly comprehensive, their implementation and subsequent bank supervision were inadequate (for a more detailed discussion, see Baliño, 1987). Only in 1981, four years after the financial reforms were initiated, was the supervisory system strengthened. In the interim, bank supervision had weakened. For example, the central bank inspections of financial institutions had fallen to only 10 percent from 23 percent before the financial reforms—and the share of problem loans in bank portfolios had increased fivefold. Comprehensive official deposit guarantees and the associated moral hazard problems further exacerbated the deficiencies in bank supervision. In 1979 the comprehensive deposit guarantees were replaced with partial guarantees.[6] The moral hazard problem became more acute in the early 1980s, since the financial institutions, which eventually failed, had begun offering the highest deposit rates to mobilize resources so as to meet their customers' distressed borrowing requirements and interest payments on deposits.

In the aftermath of the financial crisis, the authorities completely reversed the liberalization measures in 1982, with the aim of redistributing wealth from depositors to borrowers through sharply negative interest rates. Interest rates on most deposits were re-regulated, the 100 percent reserve requirement was reintroduced on most deposits, and the central bank became the major source of funds to the financial

[6]Implicit or explicit deposit guarantees have been emphasized as a source of financial sector instability by many economists. The existence of the guarantees meant that depositors were not responsible for the behavior and losses of the financial institutions, and depositors thus lacked the incentive to impose discipline on the financial institutions. On Argentina, see Diaz-Alejandro (1985) and Fernández (1985).

sector through its rediscount policy.[7] As a result, there was a complete reversal of the financial deepening trends established during financial liberalization, real interest rates became highly negative, and gross margins between deposit and lending rates widened.[8]

Conclusions

The financial reforms in Argentina for the years 1977–80 illustrate the risks of financial sector liberalization when other structural and macroeconomic policies are inadequate to support the liberalization. Unfortunately, the reforms did not sufficiently promote competition within the financial system, and largely resulted in a reshuffling of existing institutions and ownerships rather than a fundamental reorganization. New instruments and markets in securities were not part of the reform. Consequently, the financial system remained uncompetitive and underdeveloped, and borrowers continued to rely mainly on bank borrowing rather than on equity financing. Also, prudential controls were not developed, while at the same time, deposits were guaranteed by the state. As a result, there were problems of moral hazard and credit allocation was ineffective, resulting in an increasingly poor quality of loan portfolios among banks.

Macroeconomic policy also contributed to the failure of the liberalization, where relaxed direct credit controls and initially low real interest rates allowed for a rapid expansion of bank credit. Concurrently, the government deficit was increasing, and gross domestic savings de-

[7]The new law subjected all deposits accepted after June 1982 to 100 percent reserve requirements. Three different types of bank deposits were allowed: short-term deposits that accrued regulated interest payments were government guaranteed, and carried no limits on the amount that each bank could accept; longer term deposits that received free interest rates, but with no guarantees and subject to limits; and one-year indexed deposits that received government guarantees, but were not subject to mobilization limits. On the lending side, the stock of private sector debt was to be refinanced out of a rediscount "basic loan" facility—*préstamo básico*—from the central bank. The central bank also introduced another rediscount window—*préstamo adicional*—to on-lend to banks that required reserves for new loans. The interest rate for refinance and additional loans was equal and was set at negative real levels. In addition, banks could make unregulated interest rate loans using only their capital, foreign exchange resources, and free-interest deposits. Indexed loans could be made only from indexed deposits.

[8]The ratios of money and financial assets to GDP fell, while the ratio of currency to deposits increased as the role of financial institutions in mobilizing deposits declined.

clined as a percent of GDP. In addition, the overvaluation of the exchange rate created by the *tablita* aggravated the external position and weakened the financial position of business enterprises. When monetary policy was eventually tightened in 1981, due to the loss of confidence in the exchange rate, it precipitated a financial crisis because of the weak position of banks and business enterprises.

Chile

Chile's experiences with financial sector reforms between 1974 and 1981 provide another example of the risks of reforms when there is inadequate attention to the weaknesses in financial institutions and regulatory arrangements.

Prereform: 1970–73

The Chilean economy of the early 1970s was characterized by weak GDP growth, domestic and external imbalances, and extensive controls on trade, capital flows, and enterprises. In 1973, GDP fell by 5.6 percent, the fiscal deficit reached 21 percent of GDP, and the inflation rate was approximately 500 percent.

The prereform financial sector consisted of 20 government-owned domestic commercial banks, one foreign-owned commercial bank, and a limited number of nonbank financial intermediaries. The financial sector was highly regulated through interest rate ceilings, quantitative controls on banks, substantial directed credit, and restrictions on operations of financial institutions. Real interest rates were negative.

Reform and stabilization: 1974–81

The Chilean authorities followed programs of stabilization between 1974 and 1981. An initial effort at stabilization through reducing the fiscal deficit and restricting money supply growth coincided with major international shocks, particularly the decline in copper prices, and resulted in GDP contracting by 12.9 percent in 1975. Subsequently, the foreign exchange rate became the main anti-inflationary instrument, the fiscal deficit was gradually reduced until it showed a surplus in 1979, and monetary operations were used mainly for smoothing liquidity.[9] Inflation declined from 212 percent in 1976 to 20 percent in 1981, and real GDP growth recovered; however, the real exchange rate appreciated, which brought into question the sustainability of the policy.[10]

Concurrent with the stabilization program, sweeping liberalization measures were enacted covering the spectrum of economic activities, including an opening of the current account and a gradual liberalization of the capital account between 1976 and 1982.[11] These reforms had as objectives the international integration of the Chilean economy and the improvement of the price mechanism.

The main elements of the financial sector reform and their sequencing are summarized in Table 3.2. First, the measures included financial sector restructuring. In 1974, all but one of the 20 domestically owned commercial banks were privatized. The following year new regulations were introduced allowing the creation of new financial institutions; in 1976, the distinction between banks and nonbanks was removed and liberal rules allowed foreign banks to open numerous branches and purchase Chilean banks. In 1981 the distinction between commercial and development banks was abolished. Finally, during the period 1977–80, banks generally became freer to borrow abroad.[12]

---

[9]The peso was revalued against the U.S. dollar by 10 percent in both 1976 and 1977; then a policy of preannounced devaluations (the *tablita*) was attempted in 1978 only to be replaced in 1979 with a fixed exchange rate.

[10]Between December 1978 and December 1981 the real exchange rate appreciated by approximately 30 percent because of weak inflation. This reflected in part the system of backward wage indexation, which increased real wages at times when inflation was declining. See Edwards (1984) and Corbo (1985).

[11]The order of liberalization of the foreign sector, in which liberalization of the capital account lagged substantially behind that of current account transactions, has been much discussed in the Chilean case. Quantitative controls on current transactions were abolished and tariffs rationalized and lowered by June 1979 to a uniform 10 percent, excepting automobile imports. It has been argued that this was the correct sequence that maximized the chances for adequate macroeconomic control (see McKinnon, 1982; Edwards, 1984; and Calvo, 1983). The sequencing of domestic and external liberalization is examined in detail in Chapter 6.

[12]In September 1977, commercial banks were authorized to use Article 14 of the exchange law for their capital inflows, subject to a quantitative restriction limiting the maximum monthly inflow to 5 percent of the capital and reserves of each bank. In June 1979, the global limits to external borrowing by commercial banks were eliminated and in April 1980, all quantitative restrictions were eliminated. The only restriction on external borrowing was the overall prudential control that limited total bank borrowing to 20 times the capital and reserves of the bank.

Table 3.2. Chile: Sequence of Financial Reforms

	1974	1975	1976	1977	1978	1979	1980
Deregulation of the financial sector							
Short-term money market rates freed	•						
Most commercial banks privatized	•						
Barriers to entry lowered		•					
Subsidized and selective credits reduced		•					
Quantitative credit controls removed		•					
Interest rates liberalized		•					
Saving and dollar deposit rates indexed		•					
Only real interest received is taxable		•					
Easing of restrictions on scope of activities			•				
Foreign bank branches allowed			•				
Commercial banks free to borrow abroad			•	•	•		
Strengthening of supervisory, regulatory, and legal systems							
Disclosure requirements enforced	•						
Capital requirements raised and indexed	•						
Introduction of noncompliance penalties	•						
Limits on concentration of bank ownership	•				[1]		
Jurisdiction of supervisory authorities widened	•	•	•				
Limits on credit to a bank customer rationalized							•
Doubling of maximum firm shares a bank can hold							•
Reform of monetary control instruments							
Foreign exchange rate primary monetary target		•					
Interest paid on reserve requirements		•					
Reserve requirements lowered and unified					•		
Interest payments on reserve requirements phased out					•		
Auctions of central bank credit and treasury bills introduced			•				

[1]Measure rescinded.

Second, several measures were introduced relatively early to strengthen banking supervision and regulation as part of the financial reform. In 1974, minimum capital requirements were raised and penalties imposed for noncompliance, restrictions were placed on the concentration of bank ownership and bank disclosure and reporting requirements were strengthened. Between 1974 and 1976 the jurisdiction of the supervisory authorities was widened to include all financial institutions, but important weaknesses in the supervisory and regulatory framework remained. The restrictions on concentration of bank ownership were difficult to enforce and were removed in 1978. Only in 1980–81, after the financial crisis had developed, were limits imposed on bank lending to interrelated and individual entities (including purchases of shares), and loan classification and provisioning rules established. Further measures to tighten bank supervision were subsequently approved in 1982 and in 1986.

Third, major reforms to monetary and interest rate policy were enacted. Initially, in 1974, interest rates on short-term capital market transactions outside the commercial banking sector were liberalized, followed a year later by the liberalization of commercial bank interest rates. In 1975, quantitative controls on bank credit were abolished and selective credits to priority sectors were greatly reduced. An indirect system of monetary control was implemented, based on auctions of central bank credits and treasury bills, and a reform of the central bank's discount window. In 1976, interest was paid on required reserves. Subsequently, with the lowering of reserve requirements, and their unification across different financial institutions, the payment of interest on reserve requirements was phased out between 1977–80.[13]

Results of the reforms: 1975–81

The financial reforms resulted in an increase in the number of financial institutions (see Appendix II, Table 3.14). The number of commercial banks rose from 21 in 1974 to 41 in 1981; 17 of the new banks were foreign owned. The number of bank branches also increased substantially. The liberalization of short-term capital market interest rates in 1974 also resulted in an initial increase in a new kind of financial entity—*financieras*.

The financial restructuring, however, raised a number of problems. First, the privatization of the domestic banks was controversial. The regulations on the concentration of ownership were not enforced and were abandoned in 1978. As a result, banks were purchased by large conglomerates. The high concentration of ownership, together with the lack of regulation on bank loans to interrelated entities, and the

[13]Reserve requirements on bank time deposits were lowered from 47 percent in March 1977 to 4 percent in December 1980, and that on sight deposits from 75 percent to 10 percent over the same period.

absence of loan classification and provisioning requirements were major factors in the subsequent insolvency of financial institutions. Second, the *financieras* were less stringently supervised and regulated than commercial banks, and, in 1976, *financieras* faced increasing difficulties and eight failed. Only thereafter did the supervisory authorities institute a formal approval procedure for financial institutions or individuals receiving deposits from the public. Accounting procedures for *financieras* were tightened and capital requirements increased to 75 percent of that for commercial banks.

Following the liberalization of bank interest rates in 1975, real interest rates increased sharply (Appendix II, Table 3.15). The gross differential between bank deposit and lending rates fell substantially but remained wide. A subsequent fall in the differential reflected the reduction in reserve requirements and an increase in financial sector competition associated with the entry of foreign banks and the opening of the capital account.[14]

The private sector's holdings of financial assets initially contracted in real terms following the reforms (see Appendix II, Table 3.16). The slow response to the liberalization measures may have reflected the adverse effects on confidence of the severe economic recession in 1975 and the continuing high inflation rate and negative real deposit rates in the immediate postreform period. Once interest rates became positive after 1977, holdings of financial assets increased rapidly in real terms, and money and financial asset to GDP ratios rose. Subsequent to the financial liberalization, the currency to deposit ratio fell steadily.

After the removal of controls on credit and interest rates, the growth of private credit was considerably faster than the growth of private bank deposits and financial assets. In particular, the growth of peso-denominated bank credit occurred far more rapidly than the growth of peso-denominated bank liabilities. By 1980 domestic currency credit issued by financial institutions had exceeded domestic currency deposits, whereas it accounted for only 40 percent of such

[14]Net private capital inflows to Chile rose from $567 million in 1977 to about $4.5 million in 1981. However, the integration of the Chilean financial markets internationally remained weak and a significant ex post interest rate differential remained between Chilean domestic and international dollar rates, reflecting among other things exchange rate uncertainty.

deposits prior to the reforms (see Appendix II, Table 3.17).[15] The initial rapid growth of bank credit was not prevented by highly positive real loan rates in the postreform period, but the growth of credit declined subsequently.

A number of explanations have been provided for the growth in private credit. Initially, the credit growth was associated with borrowing by Chilean conglomerates (*grupos*) that were active in takeovers and in asset price speculation. Facilitated by the ownership structure of the banking sector and inadequate bank supervision, enterprise shares were used as collateral for bank credit, and share and property prices experienced a speculative boom. Later, as the business sector started facing difficulties resulting from the overvalued currency and the high financing costs, there was distressed borrowing by enterprises, and the capitalization of interest payments became common.

Despite the rapid growth of private credit, the ratio of savings to GDP gradually increased between 1977–80, as the growth of private credit was partly offset by a reduction in the government fiscal deficit. Part of the increase in private credit was used for the purchase of publicly owned enterprises that were privatized.

Financial crisis

In the early 1980s, the Chilean authorities faced a financial crisis. By 1981, two years after fixing the exchange rate, the degree of overvaluation of the real exchange rate had become significant and ultimately unsustainable. There was massive speculation against the peso, and interest rates rose sharply because the authorities did not sterilize the capital outflows. The increase in interest rates, combined with the exchange rate overvaluation, led to widespread business bankruptcies, which were subsequently accompanied by a run on a major bank along with government intervention in several smaller financial institutions. The situation was sharply aggravated in 1982 when the stock market

[15]In Chile domestic currency lending differed substantially from total private lending because a major proportion of the increase in private bank credit was foreign currency denominated, and financed by foreign currency borrowing abroad. (Banks were prohibited from taking open foreign exchange positions.) This was encouraged by high domestic interest rates, which were significantly above international interest rates after adjusting for the ex post change in the exchange rate.

crashed, leaving many corporations insolvent, since they had collateralized loans with borrowed shares. This same year, the peso was devalued, further damaging the solvency of the business sector, which was already heavily indebted with foreign loans.

A number of indications of the extent of the financial crisis are provided in Appendix II, Table 3.18. In 1982, 21 percent of total bank loans were judged to be nonperforming; this proportion had increased to 62 percent by 1986. Six commercial banks and eleven *financieras* failed during 1981–83, and the authorities had to intervene in another seven banks and one *financiera*.

Three features of the postreform Chilean financial system facilitated excessive risk-taking and unsound lending practices. First, as noted, the supervisory framework was weak until 1980. Second, the ownership structure contributed to excessive lending to interrelated entities. Third, banks were not subject to discipline by depositors. Although explicit peso deposit guarantees did not exist in Chile until January 1983, there appears to have been a widespread perception that the government would rescue depositors in the event of a bank crash. It has also been argued that firms borrowed excessively because they expected a government bailout (see Arellano, 1983).

The authorities' reaction to the crisis is summarized in Appendix II, Table 3.19.[16] The crisis resulted in a temporary reversal of some of the liberalization measures and in a strengthening of regulations and supervisory arrangements. With the transfer of problem loans to the central bank, the central bank subsequently became a major provider of liquidity to the banking system.[17] In December 1982 the central bank initiated a policy of guiding interest rates through posting suggested deposit rates set on the basis of expected inflation plus a premium.

[16]The main elements of support arrangements include the provision of preferential exchange rates for the nonfinancial sector for the purpose of external debt repayments; subsidized foreign exchange swaps for banks; across-the-board reprogramming of "sound" loans by financial institutions with interest rates and maturities subsidized by the central bank; purchases of portions of the "nonperforming" portfolio loans of the non-intervened institutions by the central bank with the promise that they would be repurchased in a prespecified period of time (by 1986, 31 percent of the total loans of the financial system were owned by the central bank); and the transfer of assets of the intervened banks to a publicly owned entity that recapitalized the banks and resold them to the general public.

[17]In 1984, central bank credit amounted to 110 percent of bank deposits and 45 percent of the deposit and foreign liabilities of financial institutions.

The strengthening of bank supervisory arrangements the same year included a more precise definition of the limit on loans to a single enterprise that took into account the interlocking ownership of firms. Commercial banks were prohibited from investing in equity capital, agricultural land, merchandise, or livestock, and were barred from accepting stock equity as loan collateral. In addition, the Superintendency of Banks began to develop a formal system of rating financial institutions.[18] In 1986, a new banking law further strengthened banking supervision, while permitting banks to establish subsidiaries to engage in new lines of financial business (mutual funds, leasing companies, and credit cards), and related nonfinancial businesses.[19]

Conclusions

The financial liberalization in Chile illustrates the risks in financial reform even with fiscal adjustments and a restrictive monetary policy. In spite of the highly positive real interest rates after the reforms were in place, private credit growth was very rapid—more so than the growth of private sector deposits. This partly reflected the weak prudential regulations that permitted a rapid credit expansion to nonviable projects and subsequent distress borrowing on account of the persistence of high real lending rates. In the meantime, the reduction in the fiscal deficit minimized the impact of the faster growth of credit than deposits on the investment–savings balance. However, the rapid credit growth associated with a high concentration of bank ownership, loans to interrelated entities, and inadequate supervision resulted in a weak allocation of private credit and a serious banking crisis.

[18]For banks classified as unstable or poorly managed, the Superintendency of Banks was empowered to regulate the banks' new lending, rolling over of existing credit, and collateral requirements.

[19]Under the 1986 Banking Law, the government strengthened supervision imposing information disclosure requirements and compelling the supervisory body to publish information on banks; changing supervision regulations into laws; and introducing a precise definition of a bank client as a means of curbing the problem of interrelated borrowing. During the crisis, the deposit guarantees introduced were to be phased out with sight deposits, and small savings became eligible for guarantee. The new banking law also included a more elaborate definition of an insolvent bank, mechanisms for solving bank/creditor disagreements, and new grounds on which a bank could be intervened. It also tightened capital requirements.

Although the authorities in Chile revised the prudential regulations at the beginning of their reforms, the controls were poorly designed, and inadequately implemented, particularly with respect to the concentration of ownership, restrictions on bank loans to interrelated entities, and loan classification and provisioning requirements. There was also little market discipline on the banks, because of implicit deposit guarantees. The weak prudential controls and rapid growth of credit allowed banks and borrowers to become overexposed. A financial crisis resulted when financial conditions tightened in 1981 because of pressure on the overvalued exchange rate.

Indonesia

Indonesian reforms during 1982–90 initially followed a gradual approach; as the reforms accelerated they exposed financial sector weaknesses.

Prereform: 1978–82

Indonesia achieved high rates of growth during the 1970s, mainly because of oil exports. For the period 1978–82, real GDP growth averaged 7 percent, and gross domestic savings averaged 28 percent of GDP. Savings were generated largely through the oil revenues accruing to the government, and the resources were redistributed to the economy by way of government policies affecting resource allocation, production, price setting, and financial sector decisions. The efficiency of investment, however, was declining and private savings were low.[20] In 1982, as a result of the decline in the prices of oil, real GDP growth slowed to 2.2 percent and the current account registered a deficit.

The structure of the Indonesian financial sector is summarized in Appendix II, Table 3.20. The five state commercial banks dominated the financial sector, accounting for an average of 76 percent of total financial sector assets, followed by private and foreign banks, accounting for 7–9 percent each; nonbanks accounted for only about 4 percent of the total. The Indonesian stock market, established in 1977, re-

[20]Investment efficiency deteriorated, with the incremental capital output ratio increasing from 5.27 in 1978 to 9.73 in 1982.

vealed only limited activity.[21] Indonesia had a convertible currency, the rupiah, and a managed floating exchange rate indexed to a basket of currencies. It also had eliminated most controls on capital outflows while retaining controls on capital inflows.[22]

The financial sector was highly, and asymmetrically, regulated, which resulted in a high degree of policy-induced segmentation. State banks were subject to ceilings on most deposit and lending interest rates, but had a number of advantages over other financial institutions. State bank interest revenues were tax exempt. State banks also had larger and easier access to liquidity credits, their deposits were guaranteed, and they had a virtual monopoly over government and other public sector banking activities. Foreign and private domestic banks and nonbanks were free to set their rates. The central bank automatically rediscounted priority loans (liquidity credit) at highly subsidized rates, and in 1982 the liquidity credits amounted to 27 percent of total bank credit. Detailed credit ceilings applied to all individual banks based on the category of bank, category of assets, previous performance, and aggregate monetary targets. The permissible activity of each type of financial institution was restricted and regulations on licenses and branch openings differed according to the type of institution.[23] Nonbanks in contrast were subject to neither interest rate nor credit ceilings, and development banks, while restricted in the scope of their operations, had generous access to liquidity credit. The interbank market was thin and segmented.

Prudential regulations and banking supervision were weak in the prereform period. Banks supervised by the central bank were categorized according to four levels of "soundness," based on capital, liquidity, and compliance with credit regulations. Reliable information was

[21]Although equity issues provided the enterprise with tax advantages, they also involved complex disclosure requirements, minimum dividend rates (equal to bank deposit rates), and a maximum trading range for most stocks. Bond trading was allowed in 1977 though no trading occurred until 1983. In 1982, the value of stocks issued reached Rp 60 billion ($90 million). Trading volume was weak.

[22]See Chapter 6 for a detailed discussion of the regulatory framework for external transactions in Indonesia.

[23]For example, only 10 of the private national banks were allowed to engage in foreign exchange transactions, and only selected private national banks had access to liquidity credits. Foreign banks were only allowed to extend credit to customers in the Jakarta area, development banks specialized in priority sectors and regions, and state banks were prohibited from extending credit to joint ventures.

lacking, however, and basic regulations on capital adequacy, loan concentration and provisioning, and interest accrual rules were inadequate. Nonbanks were under the jurisdiction of the Ministry of Finance.

Monetary policy was based on interest rate controls, credit ceilings, and access to central bank liquidity credits. The effectiveness of the central bank refinance policy as a monetary instrument was weakened by its development-oriented objective, and the automatic availability of credit for this purpose. Moreover, because of the liberal supply of liquidity credits and binding credit ceilings, the state banks at times accumulated excess reserves.

The implication for interest rates and financial assets of the asymmetrical financial regulation and system of direct monetary controls are summarized in Appendix II, Tables 3.21 and 3.22. The administratively fixed state bank deposit rates were negative in real terms, and considerably below the corresponding private national bank rates. As a result, the share of domestic currency deposits accounted for by state banks fell from 82 percent to 56 percent between 1978 and 1982. The rigid structure of interest rates was at times inconsistent with banks' liquidity and with free capital mobility.[24] International interest rate differentials resulted in large swings in bank liquidity and a volatile call money market rate. Foreign currency deposits, which were not subject to interest rate controls, grew rapidly, and by 1982 accounted for 17 percent of total bank deposits.

Adjustment and financial sector reform: 1982–90

After 1982, the Indonesian authorities adopted programs of adjustment that included exchange rate devaluations in 1983 and 1986, fiscal retrenchment (especially in public investments), progressive deregulation of trade and industry, and financial sector reform. These measures enabled the economy to maintain growth in GDP, private investment, and nonoil exports, while achieving a significant reduction in external and domestic imbalances.

[24]The deposit rate yield curve of the state banks was rigidly fixed and sloping upward. This represented a distortion in that state banks could not flexibly react to recurrent liquidity movements caused by capital flows. For example, between 1978 and 1981, when banks had huge amounts of excess liquidity, the spread between short- and long-term interest rates should have been much lower than in 1982 when banks experienced a liquidity crunch caused by exchange rate devaluation expectations and capital outflows.

The main financial sector reforms and their sequencing are illustrated in Table 3.3. The financial sector reforms began in June 1983 with the elimination of credit ceilings and interest rate controls on most categories of deposits and all but priority loans, and with an extensive modification of the liquidity credit facility. Indirect instruments of monetary control were introduced and discount window policy was reformed beginning in February 1984. Open market operations using regular auctions of central bank certificates (SBIs) became the main monetary instrument. In February 1985, new money market instruments (SBPUs—essentially banker's acceptances) were introduced, and a publicly owned investment company was also established as a market maker in money market papers.[25]

Despite these reforms, Bank Indonesia continued as a major supplier of credit to the financial system and the share of central bank credit in total financial institution credit to the private sector increased on average following the reforms (see Appendix II, Tables 3.22 and 3.23). This factor inhibited financial sector competition and the development of the money and interbank markets. Thus, while the capital and money markets, in particular, expanded with the issue of short central bank and private papers, these markets remained small compared to credit provided through financial institutions (see Appendix II, Table 3.24).[26] Moreover, the initial reforms did not ease barriers to entry, and the total number of financial institutions remained largely unchanged between 1983 and 1988.

A second phase of reforms began in 1987–88. Commencing in mid-1987, following a deterioration in the external sector, monetary policy shifted to protecting the exchange rate, and as a result the interest rates became more flexible. In 1988 the Indonesian authorities relaxed restrictions on the ability of banks and nonbank financial institutions to establish new branches and on the creation of new private and joint-venture banks. The measures included the following: (1) all domestic commercial banks were permitted freely to open new branches throughout the country; (2) nonbank financial intermediaries and for-

[25]For a detailed discussion of the reforms to the monetary instruments, see Appendix II of Chapter 2.

[26]Subsequently, in early 1990, the central bank announced the end of most subsidized refinance facilities with the objectives of encouraging a more efficient banking system and of improving monetary control.

Table 3.3. Indonesia: Sequence of Financial Reform

	1983	1984	1985	1986	1987	1988	1989	1990	1991	1992
Deregulation of the financial sector										
Credit ceilings abolished	•									
State banks free to set interest rate structure	•									
Reform of liquidity credit facility	•									
Limited easing of restrictions on scope of financial institutions' activities				•	•	•				
Substantial reduction of liquidity requirement						•				
Public enterprises allowed limited dealings with non-state banks						•				
Relaxation of licensing and branching requirements						•				
Equalizing tax treatment of time deposits, CDs, and equity						•				
Financial institutions allowed to raise capital through equity						•				
New private stock exchanges licensed						•				
Strengthening of regulatory, supervisory, and legal systems										
Setting lending limits to single borrowers/companies						•				
Responsibility for supervising rural banks shifted to Bank Indonesia						•				
Improved supervisory monitoring system						•				
Strengthened capital adequacy and loan processing									•	•
New banking law						•				•
Strengthened regulatory structure for capital markets						•		•	•	
Reform of monetary control instruments and money markets										
Establishment of two new rediscount windows		•								
Introduction of auctions of central bank bills (SBIs) for monetary control		•								
Development of banker's acceptances (SBPUs)			•							
Investment house established to intermediate the money market[1]			•							
Active interventions through repurchase agreements and daily SBI auctions and other measures to activate money markets[1]					•	•	•			

[1]In January 1989, the role of the investment house was replaced by establishing a network of 15 dealers in SBIs and SBPUs through whom interventions were implemented.

eign banks were permitted to open one branch in each of seven cities; (3) joint-venture banks could be established by foreign banks already operating in Indonesia; and (4) new private banks became eligible for licenses. Rural banks could also upgrade their status to private bank—outside main cities and municipalities—conditional on a certain operational history.

Reserve requirements were also unified among various classes of banks and reduced from 15 percent to 2 percent.[27] Public enterprises were permitted to deposit up to 50 percent of their deposits with nonstate banks, and prudential regulations were strengthened by limiting the concentration of bank lending, extending central bank supervision to the rural banks and nonbanks, and developing a comprehensive supervisory monitoring system.

Several measures were also enacted to strengthen the money and capital markets. Interest income from bank deposits became subject to withholding taxes, thus, equalizing the tax treatment with other debt and equity instruments. In January 1989, Bank Indonesia organized a syndicate of 15 private banks and nonbanks to act as dealers and agents for the issuance of SBIs in regular weekly auctions and as market makers in the secondary market. All money market operations of Bank Indonesia began to be implemented through this dealer network. Limits on interbank borrowing were removed, and an active campaign was mounted to encourage the use of SBIs in liquidity management.[28] In addition, in January 1990, wide-ranging reforms of institutional and regulatory aspects of capital markets were initiated, including privatization of the stock exchange.

Results of the reforms

The removal of the credit ceilings, interest rate controls, and discriminatory regulations on different financial institutions benefited

[27]The large reduction in the reserve requirement was used in part to compensate for the effect of introducing 15 percent tax on interest incomes on time deposits and certificates of deposits. In addition 80 percent of the surplus reserves following the reduction in required reserves were to be invested in three- and six-month SBIs at fixed interest rates and banks were to agree to use the SBIs for liquidity management.

[28]See Cole and Slade (1996), who provide evidence that secondary trading in SBIs rose sharply following these measures.

the more efficient private banks, and their balance sheets grew more rapidly than those of the state banks in the postreform period (see Appendix II, Table 3.24).[29] The pressures of competition led to a narrowing of interest margins and led the national commercial banks to adopt modernization programs in order to compete more effectively with the private banks.[30]

Real lending rates did not rise initially because the increase in bank deposit rates to positive real levels was absorbed through a reduction in lending margins. Concurrently, the growth of bank deposits fell, reflecting a sharp increase in capital outflows in response to expectations of rupiah devaluation. The loss of bank liquidity was financed through a large expansion in central bank credit to the banking system and nominal interest rates were maintained broadly unchanged.[31] A rapid growth of bank credit in 1984 initially followed the removal of credit ceilings, but credit growth fell in 1985 in response to a slowdown in the economy and a sharp rise in real lending rates to historically high levels. Credit growth increased sharply again following the 1988 reforms.

The ratios of private financial assets, M2, and private bank credit to GDP all increased substantially, while the ratio of currency to deposits fell steadily in the postreform period. Commercial bank holdings of excess reserves, which had averaged 7 percent of deposits in 1978–82, fell to about 2 percent in 1983–88, reflecting both the rapid growth of bank credit and the development of short-term markets that facilitated banks' day-to-day cash reserve management.

The first phase of financial reforms in Indonesia did not involve banking system instability. In part, this seemed to reflect the gradual nature of the reforms, the continued large role of subsidized liquidity

[29]In the prereform period the growth of total assets of the state-owned and national private banks had been broadly similar, since both had previously been limited by credit ceilings. The greater interest rate freedom of national private banks had meant that they had a more rapidly growing deposit base, but the state banks were compensated through greater access to liquidity credit from the central bank.

[30]The deposit rates of state banks increased immediately after the reform. The gap between state banks' 12-month deposit rates and those of private banks declined from 16 percent in 1983 to 1.25 percent in 1984, increasing thereafter to remain in the 2–4 percent range. Such a gap is explained by the tax advantages accorded to deposits held with state banks.

[31]This episode can be contrasted with the experience in Chile in 1981, when real interest rates were allowed to rise sharply in response to a similar loss of confidence in the value of the exchange rate.

credits, and a tighter management of interest rate levels during the liberalization.[32] Competition-enhancing policies were also adopted only at a later stage in the reform process. Real GDP continued to expand during and after the financial reforms, and serious problems of industrial reorganization and bankruptcy did not arise; however, the weaknesses in bank supervision and regulation and in banking solvency were highlighted by the subsequent developments. Soon after the announcement of the 1988 reforms, two private banks faced short-lived bank runs and liquidity problems that were contained through lender-of-last-resort support from Bank Indonesia. The rapid expansion of money and credit following the second phase of financial liberalization in 1988, and the 1989–90 investment boom, resulted in a deterioration in the quality of many banks' assets. The reforms in 1988 also reduced the regulatory segmentation between different financial institutions, leading to a substantial increase in financial sector competition. To enhance the soundness and stability of the banking system, new prudential regulations for capital adequacy, liquidity, and mandatory provisioning for nonperforming assets were introduced in early 1991, and the supervisory authority of Bank Indonesia was further enhanced by a new banking law enacted in March 1992.

Conclusions

Indonesia's phased and gradual approach to reforms appeared to mitigate some of the major risks of financial sector reforms. The first phase of the financial reforms in Indonesia involved removal of direct credit and interest rate controls, and a shift toward a more market-oriented system of credit allocation and monetary control. The central bank continued to refinance a very large proportion of commercial bank credit, however, and many portfolio and entry regulations limiting competition remained. Market-based instruments of monetary control and capital markets evolved relatively slowly, partly reflecting the heavy involvement of Bank Indonesia in credit allocation and the limited interest rate flexibility.

---

[32]Sharp increases in the average real lending rate did not occur, in part, because of continued availability of subsidized liquidity credit, and the authorities' focus on targeting interest rates in the immediate postreform period. Only following significant pressures in the exchange market in 1986–87 did greater interest rate flexibility occur.

The second phase of deregulation, which began in October 1988, significantly altered the financial system structure, with a substantial reduction in directed credit and a major increase in the number of financial institutions. It also included measures aimed at further developing the money and capital markets, reducing the central bank's role in credit allocation, and streamlining the operating procedures of monetary policy and banking supervision. The second phase of reforms highlighted the weaknesses in prudential regulation and supervision.[33]

The sequencing also illustrated the essential complementarily of financial sector reform and macroeconomic and monetary management. On the one hand, the challenges of dealing with capital inflows and outflows complicated domestic monetary management and speeded up the need for the introduction of indirect monetary controls; the increased flexibility of interest rates allowed the authorities to manage more effectively the volatile capital flows. On the other hand, the expansionary impact of the initial surge in private sector credit following the liberalization was offset by a fiscal surplus, and the potentially destabilizing macroeconomic consequences of the rapid credit expansion were avoided. The increase in real interest rates to substantially positive levels following the reforms also appeared to be an important factor that contributed to an increase in deposit mobilization and helped to mitigate the rapid growth of bank credit. The reforms resulted in a rapid growth of financial intermediation, with sharp increases in both the money to GDP and credit to GDP ratios, and a decline in the currency to deposit ratio.

Korea

Korea followed a very gradual and managed process of financial sector reforms from 1980 to 1988.

Prereform: before 1980

Korea's average annual growth during the 1960s and 1970s was more than 8 percent. This strong increase depended on heavy gov-

[33]The number of standard commercial banks increased by 21, insurance companies by 11, and other credit institutions by almost 1,700 in the 12 months following the October 1988 reforms.

ernment intervention that directed the economy according to detailed five-year plans. By the second half of the 1970s, however, the economy became too large and sophisticated to be efficiently directed by central controls. In the period 1975–80, GDP growth slowed and was negative in 1980.[34] Fiscal and current account balance of payments deficits averaged 1.7 percent and 4.5 percent of GDP, respectively, during this time; the ratio of gross external debt to GDP rose from 40.5 percent to 44.7 percent; and inflation increased, reaching 29 percent in 1980.

The financial system consisted of nationwide, local, and specialized banks; branches of foreign banks; various nonbanks; a capital market; and an active informal credit or curb market.[35] There were high barriers to entry for new banks and the number of domestic banks hardly changed between 1975 and 1980. The number of bank branches increased by 46 percent and the number of foreign banks rose from 9 in 1975 to 33 in 1980 (see Appendix II, Table 3.25).[36] Meanwhile, the government used banks to finance investment and to guarantee foreign investment in heavy industry.

The government relaxed restrictions on entry of nonbanks in the mid-1970s as part of its efforts to restrict the curb market.[37] Together with the less stringent restrictions on their activities, including higher interest rate ceilings, the number and magnitude of nonbanks' operations grew rapidly, and their share of total deposits increased from 8.5 percent to 11.8 percent between 1976 and 1980 (see Appendix II, Table 3.26). The size of Korea's capital market declined during

[34]The negative GDP growth for the first time in Korea's modern history reflected a political crisis, a disastrous harvest, unfavorable external developments, and adjustment policies aimed at correcting the current account deficit.

[35]The nationwide commercial banks had extensive networks throughout the country, while the local commercial banks had their branches confined to the province in which their head office was located. The commercial banks were engaged in long-term financing in addition to short-term banking operations. Each of the specialized banks was established under its special law with a specific mandate to complement the functions of the commercial banks.

[36]Such an expansion was encouraged by the Korean authorities as a way to import banking technologies and facilitate the introduction of foreign capital.

[37]Nonbank financial intermediaries comprised development banks, investment and savings companies, mutual savings and finance companies, and security investment trust companies.

1977–80 and the curb market remained active despite efforts to absorb it into the formal sector.[38]

The financial sector was highly regulated. Monetary policy was conducted through direct instruments, of which the most important were interest rate and individual bank credit ceilings, the central direction of credit to specific sectors, a varied reserve requirement ratio, and subsidized central bank rediscount operations. The Bank of Korea's lending and rediscounting operations were also used as development instruments, resulting at times in inconsistencies between monetary control and development objectives, with the latter taking priority. Strict exchange controls facilitated monetary control through direct instruments. The monetary authorities were also closely involved in the personnel budgeting decisions of financial institutions, including privately owned banks but less so in the nonbanks, and the introduction of new financial instruments required a lengthy approval process. Prudential regulations on banks were reasonably strict, but less so for nonbanks.[39]

The main characteristics of the prereform interest rate structure are shown in Appendix II, Table 3.27. Ceilings on deposit and loan interest rates were changed in response to inflation; nevertheless, real interest rates fluctuated by large amounts and were significantly negative in 1980–81. During the high inflationary period of 1978–81, nonpreferential loan rates were raised by less than the corresponding increase in deposit rates, leading to a considerable decline in banks' gross lending spreads. Preferential lending rates were 8 to 10 percentage points

---

[38]Although little is known about the curb market's operations its size was estimated to have reached 1 trillion won in 1980, or 6 percent of the economy's total liquidity (Kwack and Chung, 1986). The informal market was completely unregulated; it operated through mobilizing deposits of small savers and transferring them to large corporations mostly for working capital purposes. In 1972, an emergency presidential decree froze and attempted to rearrange all the loans in the market. The measure to establish nonbanks was also ineffective because of the simultaneous policy of low interest rates and the persistence of government intervention in the formal sector.

[39]Supervision of commercial banks is conducted by the Office of Bank Supervision and Examination of the central bank. The Ministry of Finance has responsibility for the supervision of nonbanks but has delegated this function to the Office of Bank Supervision and Examination. Prudential regulations of banks include a minimum capital requirement, provisioning for doubtful debts according to Office of Bank Supervision and Examination instructions, and limits on the concentration of lending to a single customer of 25 percent of the financial institution's net worth.

below the nonpreferential rates. The interest rate ceilings on nonbank financial intermediaries' operations were higher than the corresponding ceilings on bank rates, and nonbank financial intermediaries were better able to circumvent the interest rate ceilings through charging fees and commissions. The spread between the curb market rate and bank deposit rate remained wide throughout the period 1975–80.

The combination of interest rate and credit ceilings, segmentation between the activities of different financial institutions, and directed credit led to an inefficient pricing and allocation of credit. The priority sectors (export, heavy chemical, and large manufacturing industries) had preferential access to bank credit and faced lower borrowing costs than nonpriority sectors. However, the average rate of return on the capital invested in these sectors was 1–3 percent below that in the nonpriority sectors in the prereform period (see Cho and Cole, 1986). The debt/equity ratio of the manufacturing sector increased considerably during the 1970s, in part reflecting the subsidized cost of bank borrowing.

Financial deepening as measured by increases in financial assets relative to GDP was not significant during 1975–80 (see Appendix II, Table 3.28). The increase in the financial sector's activity was mostly accounted for by the less regulated nonbanks. The ratio of M2 to GDP was broadly flat in this period, while the ratio of M3 to GDP increased, reflecting the faster growth of nonbanks' deposits. The ratio of currency to deposits was sensitive to nominal interest rates and fluctuated without any strong trend. At the same time, the growth of financial sector credit to the private sector was faster than the growth of private claims on financial institutions, and the ratio of private credit to GDP rose sharply. The proportion of total bank credit to the private sector financed through central bank credit to financial institutions also increased.

Financial reform: 1980–88

The financial reforms in Korea were part of a broader economic adjustment program that included currency devaluation, tight monetary policy, contractionary fiscal policy, strict wage guidelines, and increases in administered prices. Simultaneous with the stabilization and financial reform programs, the Korean authorities also liberalized international trade and rationalized public investments. The Korean economy, assisted by an improving world economy, responded well to the adjustment program. Export-led GDP growth averaged 8 percent and inflation averaged 6 percent a year during 1981–88. The current account registered a surplus starting in 1986, which permitted a substantial improvement in the external debt situation.

The decision to liberalize the financial markets reflected concern that imbalances in the economy were aggravated by the misallocation of financial resources. The objectives of the reforms were to develop financial management systems that would promote more effectively free enterprise and private initiative. Officials proceeded slowly with financial liberalization for a number of reasons. They were concerned that if interest rates were liberalized too quickly persisting expectations of inflation would raise interest rates sharply and damage the highly leveraged industrial sector. They were also concerned that too liberal a financial system could result in interrelated ownership of banks and a concentration of lending to large industrial conglomerates.[40] The financial reform measures included institutional reform to improve financial sector competition, limited liberalization of interest rates and credit allocation, and some shift toward indirect monetary control procedures. The reforms and their sequencing are summarized in Table 3.4.

Between 1981 and 1983, all five nationwide government-owned commercial banks were privatized.[41] Simultaneously, approvals were given for the establishment of two new nationwide commercial banks and one specialized bank. In addition, especially after 1982, a large number of foreign bank branches and nonbanks were allowed to be established and some regulations limiting competition among various types of financial institutions were eased, mostly by allowing all institutions to deal in the newly introduced financial instruments.[42] In 1980, rules regulating bond transactions and repurchase agreements were instituted. Between 1981 and 1984, several measures were taken to integrate and activate money markets, such as measures to widen participation in the interbank call market and to liberalize the discount

[40]For a fuller account of official objectives behind the financial reform, see Choi (1984) and Lee (1986).

[41]The "de-nationalization" law limited the percentage of a bank's share that individuals or enterprises could hold. Nevertheless, it is believed that ownership concentration by large industrial conglomerates, called "Chaebul," occurred (Cho and Cole, 1986).

[42]Examples of these instruments were corporate bonds, commercial papers, CDs, cash management accounts, bond management funds, trust accounts, beneficiary certificates, and bond repurchase agreements.

Table 3.4. Korea: Sequence of Financial Reform

	1980	1981	1982	1983	1984	1985	1986	1987	1988	1989	1990	1991	1992
Deregulation of the financial sector													
Formalizing transactions in bonds and repos	•												
Privatization of state-owned commercial banks		•	•	•									
Restrictions on scope of activities eased		•	•	•									
Permitting the introduction of many financial instruments		•	•	•	•	•							
Indirect portfolio investment by foreigners allowed		•	•	•	•	•							
Entry of new institutions allowed			•	•	•	•				•			
Credit ceilings abolished			•										
Reduced use of credit and management directives			•	•	•	•	•	•	•				
Preferential interest rates abolished			•										
Min./max. interest rate ranges introduced[1]					•								
CD rates set at higher than time deposits							•						
Interest rates liberalization[2]									•	2	2	•	•
Over the counter market established for small and medium-sized firms								•					
Capital market laws revised								•					
Strengthening of regulatory, supervisory and legal systems													
Reform of supervisory procedures and focus			•	•	•	•	•	•	•				
Regulatory and support measures for the stock exchange										•	•	•	•
Reform of monetary control instruments and money markets													
Lower and unified reserve ratios		•								•			
Reduced reliance on directed credit			•	•	•	•	•	•	•				
Increased use of stabilization bonds							•	•		•			
Increased use of repurchase agreements to control reserve money												•	
Integration and strengthening of interbank call money markets and other measures to liberalize money markets										•	•	•	•
Rescheduling of bank debts and financial assistance to banks to support industrial restructuring					•	•	•	•	•				
Exchange systems reforms													
New exchange rate arrangement allowing for greater role of market forces.											•		

[1]Interbank call rates and corporate bond rates were freed.
[2]Interest rate control is reintroduced in 89–90, and gradual deregulation reinstated in 91–92.

rate of commercial paper. In 1987, an over-the-counter market for shares of small- and medium-sized firms was established, and laws governing the capital market were revised. The emphasis of bank supervision shifted from monitoring routine operations to monitoring procedures of credit analysis, bank portfolios, and the enforcement of prudential ratios. In addition, each financial institution became subject to both annual and unannounced visits by regulators.

Between 1980 and 1986, rediscount mechanisms, directed credit, and interest rate ceilings remained the major tools of monetary control, to be supplemented by sales of stabilization bonds later on. In 1981 the central bank substantially reduced reserve requirement ratios to 3.5 percent and unified them for different financial institutions and types of deposits. Until 1986, reserve requirements were changed only once after their reduction and unification in 1981. In 1982, individual credit ceilings on nationwide commercial banks were abolished, directives influencing the daily operations of financial institutions were discontinued, and beginning in 1982 directed credit to priority sectors was progressively reduced. Overall ceilings on credit established by the Monetary Board remained in effect, however, and the authorities continued to exercise window guidance on the allocation and overall growth of credits. Moreover, a large part of the central bank's loans to commercial banks carried low interest rates and supported the financial assistance schemes for ailing industries.[43] After 1986 the rediscount mechanisms and directed credit policies became insufficient for monetary control because the accumulation of net foreign assets threatened monetary stability. In 1986 and 1987, the central bank sold stabilization bonds (equivalent to 108 percent and 76 percent of the increases in net foreign assets in each year, respectively), increased reserve requirements, and tightened its rediscount mechanisms to manage the foreign inflow. Also, since 1989 repurchase operations have been used to influence money market rates.[44]

The interest rate liberalization measures included the following: In 1982, the interest rate differential between general and preferential

[43]This was part of a government imposed industry restructuring of enterprises in shipping and the overseas construction sector and of more than 50 other enterprises that were designated for rationalization and financial restructuring during 1984–88.

[44]However, only since 1993 have market-based operating procedures been adopted, with auctions of stabilization bonds and repurchase agreements, supported by a tightening of rediscount windows and reforms of the interbank payment systems.

loans was reduced and some preferential rates were eliminated. In 1984, to allow banks to better differentiate credit risk, loan interest rate ceilings were replaced by an allowable range for interest rates. (The range between the maximum and minimum rates varied from 1.5 percent to 3 percent during the period 1984–88.) In 1986, interest rates on CDs were raised to higher levels than those on ordinary time deposits. In December 1988, the authorities announced an interest rate liberalization package, which included the liberalization of most bank and nonbank lending rates, long-term deposit rates, money instruments, and trust accounts. Most of the reforms were not implemented, however, because of unfavorable economic and financial conditions that had developed in early 1989. In August 1991, the government announced a new four-phased program for the full liberalization of interest rates, commencing with the deregulation of interest rates for most money market instruments and banks' large-denomination CDs. Subsequently, interest rates on loans were liberalized first, before proceeding to a step-by-step liberalization of deposit rates—with long-term rates and those on larger deposits being freed before rates on short-term and smaller deposits.

Consequences of liberalization

The size of the formal financial sector expanded, with the addition of two nationwide commercial banks, a sharp increase in total bank branches, and the opening of other financial institutions (see Appendix II, Table 3.25). Financial intermediation in the formal sector grew sharply, although because of more restrictive controls on banks, the expansion continued to favor nonbanks (see Appendix II, Table 3.26). The ratio of M2 to GDP increased from 33 percent in 1981 to 36 percent in 1987, while the ratio of private financial assets to GDP increased from 39 percent to 48 percent in the same period (see Appendix II, Table 3.28). A major part of the increase in both ratios occurred in 1982 as a reaction to the problems in the curb market.[45] In addition, the size of the Korean capital market grew rapidly, especially after the

[45]Although no data are available, it is believed that the curb market's size diminished, reflecting higher official interest rates, smaller direct intervention in the formal market, and increased corporate reliance on self-financing, as well as the loss of confidence associated with an incident of fraud in 1982.

capital market reforms of 1987. By 1988, the ratio of the total value of stocks and bonds traded on the Korean Securities Market to private financial assets had reached 85 percent (see Appendix II, Table 3.26).

The increasing depth of the financial system was reflected in greater financial sector competition. The allocative efficiency of financial resources, as measured by the uniformity in the rates of return on capital in different sectors, showed considerable improvements over the period 1981–88. The structure of interest rates also became more uniform following the interest rate reforms, with a narrowing in differentials between nonbank and bank deposit rates, between curb and official market rates, and between interest rates on credits to priority sectors and maximum loan rates (see Appendix II, Table 3.27). Nevertheless, the interest rate structure remained closely controlled, continuing to limit banks' ability to differentiate among maturities and risks when setting interest rates. With successful disinflation, the whole interest rate structure turned positive by 1982 and remained so through 1988.

Various legislative barriers between banks and nonbanks precluded the complete elimination of segmentation. Nonbank financial intermediaries continued to be subject to higher interest rate ceilings, and the burden of directed credit was heavier on the banks than on the nonbanks. Following the reforms, central bank domestic currency credits to financial institutions rose initially, reaching 22 percent of total bank credit to the private sector in 1985, compared with 18 percent in 1980, as the authorities used this to support their directed credit policies (see Appendix II, Table 3.28).

Conclusions

Financial sector reform in Korea was a gradual and managed process. Overall, financial sector intermediation increased sharply following the financial reforms, and there was an improvement in the efficiency of credit allocation in the context of a successful stabilization program, supported by interest rates that were maintained substantially positive in real terms. The authorities did not allow a complete liberalization of interest rates, and they continued to direct credit, to provide substantial refinance to the banking system in support of the industrial sector, and to differentiate between different types of financial institutions. The banks remained under tighter control compared to nonbanks and increasingly lost market share to these nonbanks. As a result, traditional instruments of monetary policy that relied on control through the banks became less effective, and, with a sharp increase in net foreign assets, the Bank of Korea had to resort increasingly to indirect monetary control instruments for effective monetary control. Major issues of financial institution stability did not arise, partly because the regulation and control of credits and interest rates generally remained significant.

The Philippines

The Philippines' experience with financial sector reform between 1980 and 1984 illustrates the interrelationship between financial sector reforms, financial sector weakness, and macroeconomic management.

Prereform: 1975–81

Between 1975–81, GDP growth averaged 5.5 percent a year, reflecting expansionary domestic policies. Gross domestic investment averaged about 30 percent of GDP, compared with gross domestic savings of 25 percent of GDP. Private investment constituted the major component of total investment and was financed by subsidized and directed credit. The peso followed a managed float since 1973, and its rate to the U.S. dollar was kept stable between 1975 and 1980.

The financial sector included several types of banks—commercial, thrift, rural, and specialized—and nonbank financial institutions (see Appendix II, Table 3.29).[46] As a result of strict barriers to entry, the total number of commercial banks remained essentially unchanged between 1975 and 1980.[47] By 1980, there were 28 domestic commercial

[46]These institutions included investment houses that engaged in underwriting, portfolio management, and stockbroking, as well as quasi-banking functions. The latter largely consist of borrowing funds through the issuance of debt instruments. Such deposit substitutes, which were also issued by commercial banks, largely took the form of banker's acceptances, promissory notes, certificates of assignment, and trust certificates. Other financial institutions included insurance companies (both private and public), trust companies, and the government social security system.

[47]In the early 1970s, a prohibition was instituted on the entry of new commercial banks, with the objective of consolidating and improving the efficiency of the already existing financial institutions. Consistent with this prohibition was the relaxing of banks' branching activities. An exception to this rule allowed a number of foreign banks, offshore banking units, thrifts, and rural banks to enter. Due to the perceived need for more financial activities, the prohibition did not include nonbanks.

banks and four foreign banks. The domestic commercial banks were free to pursue an aggressive branching policy, and their total number of offices increased by 50 percent between 1975 and 1980. Barriers to entry were lower for thrift banks and rural banks, which mostly serviced small customers and farmers, and between 1975–80 their number grew rapidly. Nevertheless, their share in total assets remained small.

Commercial banks were the largest component of the financial sector, accounting for around 45 percent of total assets (see Appendix II, Table 3.30). Within the commercial banks, the importance of government-owned banks' was declining, and their share of financial sector assets fell from 14.6 percent in 1975 to 11.3 percent in 1981. The specialized banks' share of total assets increased from 9.7 percent to 11.9 percent between 1975–81, while the share of financial assets accounted for by nonbank financial intermediaries declined by about 4 percent over this period.[48]

The activities of different financial institutions were closely defined by law. Rural banks had to limit their activities to "small" clients, while the operations of thrift banks and specialized banks were strictly defined in terms of purpose, collateral, and maturity. A strict separation existed between investment and regular banking activities, with only investment houses allowed to underwrite government and corporate securities. With few exceptions, commercial banks were the only entities allowed to accept and manage demand and checking accounts.

All interest rates—deposit, lending, and interbank rates, including those of nonbanks—were subject to ceilings, which together with the central bank discount rate, were altered in response to shifts in inflationary pressures. Rates were lowered in 1978 as inflation abated, and increased in 1979 with the resurgence of inflation (see Appendix II, Table 3.31). In 1979 and 1980, interest rate adjustments were not sufficient to compensate for increasing inflation, and real interest rates became highly negative as a result. Interest rate determination became more flexible after 1980, when the usury laws, which mandated a maximum of one interest rate change per year, were abolished.

The Central Bank of the Philippines issued a number of directives to influence bank lending activities, and its rediscounts were used primar-

[48]Three were in operation during the period. Two were active in implementing the industrial and agricultural policies of the government. The third operated according to Islamic principles and was intended to service a predominantly Muslim region.

ily to execute selective credit policies at highly subsidized rates. Financial activity was also directed through minimum loan ratios to selected sectors—mostly agriculture and agroindustries—and involved high degrees of government influence in the credit program of state-owned commercial and specialized banks. Liquidity was controlled mainly through operations in central bank certificates of indebtedness, beginning in the mid-1970s.[49] These certificates had a final maturity of seven years and were issued through a monthly auction. The central bank also entered into repurchase agreements in these certificates. Treasury bills existed but were not used extensively for monetary control. Reserve requirements were not varied for monetary control. (Reserve requirements for the banking sector against the peso-denominated demand, time, and savings deposits were 20 percent.)

The central bank performed bank supervision, but the Securities and Exchange Commission supervised some nonbanks. Supervision efforts focused on ensuring that each financial institution was operating within its prescribed domain of activities. Prudential regulations included a high minimum capital requirement for commercial banks, capital to risk asset ratios for all institutions, limits on equity investments in enterprises as a ratio of a financial institution's capital and reserves, and limits on borrowing by directors, officers, stockholders, and their related interests (known as "DOSRI" requirements). Limited deposit protection was provided with an insurance limit of ₱10,000 per depositor (equal to $1,300 in 1980). However, during the 1970s, supervisory regulations were relaxed. Capital to risk asset ratios were lowered from 15 percent in 1972 to 10 percent in 1973, and after 1980 ratios as low as 6 percent became permissible as the authorities sought to provide banks with greater leverage to expand their asset portfolios. The rules regarding maximum credit to DOSRIs—set in 1973 equal to a bank's total capital—were also relaxed.

Certain indicators point to financial deepening during the prereform period. Between 1976 and 1981 the ratio of currency to deposits declined from 13.5 percent to 10 percent; the ratio of M2 to GDP increased from 21.5 percent to 28.8 percent; and the ratio of M3 to GDP increased from 35.2 percent to 39.9 percent. The ratio of private credit to GDP also rose (see Appendix II, Table 3.32).

[49]Foreign exchange swaps with commercial banks became an active instrument in 1982.

The segmented financial sector, interest rate controls, and directed credit all restricted financial sector efficiency and competition. The main objectives of financial sector reform were to improve competition and to rationalize financial decisions by making them sensitive to market forces. These would be pursued through liberalizing interest rates and reducing operationally restrictive policies.

Financial reform: 1980–84

During the period 1980–84, financial reform measures included a breakdown of the segmentation of the activities of different financial institutions, a gradual liberalization of interest rates, and the move toward an indirect system of monetary control. The main elements and the sequencing are summarized in Table 3.5.

A number of functional distinctions between the different financial institutions were removed in July 1980. A commercial bank with a minimum capital of ₱500 million could become a universal bank (unibank), thereby becoming authorized to engage in a greatly expanded range of financial services, most important of which was to invest in the equity of nonfinancial enterprises. Smaller commercial banks were also permitted to engage in equity financing through the creation of venture capital subsidiaries. Rural banks were granted access to the central bank rediscount facility in certain circumstances.

A phased liberalization of interest rates began in 1980, with the removal of interest rate ceilings on deposits with maturities greater than two years. Over the next few years, ceilings on interest rates were removed from loan rates with a maturity greater than two years (1981), from remaining deposit rates (1982), and from remaining loan rates (1983). In 1982, a prime rate monitoring system was instituted and the compilation of a deposit reference rate (the Manila Reference Rate) was initiated.[50] In 1983, the central bank rediscount rate was brought into line with the 90-day Manila Reference Rate.

The reform of monetary policy instruments began in 1981 with a decision to phase out certificates of indebtedness—a move designed to

[50]The prime rate refers to rates charged to borrowers with the highest credit ratings on 90-day loans greater than ₱0.5 million. The Manila Reference Rate was designed to indicate rates available for deposits of various maturities. The Manila Reference Rate has been used increasingly for establishing lending rates.

Table 3.5. Philippines: Sequence of Financial Reform

	1980	1981	1982	1983	1984
Deregulation of the financial sector					
Large commercial banks can become "unibanks"	•				
Smaller commercial banks could acquire equity	•				
Thrift, rural and private development banks can engage in limited "commercial banking operations"	•				
Investment houses can engage in trust functions, foreign exchange operations and have access to CBP rediscount	•				
Long-term deposit rates freed	•				
Long-term loan rates freed		•			
Short-term deposit rates freed			•		
Prime rate monitoring system introduced and MRR system expanded			•		
Short-term loan rates freed				•	
Strengthening regulatory, supervision and legal systems					
Reform of monetary control instruments					
More active variation of interest rate ceilings	•				
Attempt to give primacy to treasury bills in monetary operations		•			
Reduction of reserve requirements			•		[1]
Adjustment of rediscount rate in line with market rates				•	
Access to CBP rediscounts rationalized			•		
New liquidity window for "normal" needs				•	
New central bank bills issued					•
Shift to base money as intermediate target					•
Dealership network for government securities introduced			•		
Financial restructuring to assist distressed financial & non-financial firms	•	•	•	•	•

[1]Rescinded.

rationalize the government securities market and to give primacy to treasury bills as the monetary control instrument. This was not initially successful and, in 1984, two new central bank bills were issued. In 1982, a plan was instituted to reduce reserve requirements on peso deposits by 1 percent every six months to 16 percent by 1985. Due to the financial crisis, however, the plan was frozen in 1983 and reserve ratios were raised in 1984 to 24 percent to contain liquidity pressures. In 1983, limits on financial institution access to central bank rediscounts were introduced; the number of rediscount facilities was substantially reduced; and a new liquidity window was designed to meet the day-to-day liquidity needs of financial institutions. In 1984, and following the adoption of a floating exchange rate regime, base money replaced net domestic assets of the central bank as the principal intermediate target of monetary policy.

Consequences of reforms and financial crisis

The immediate results of the financial liberalization were sharp increases in the number of financial institutions and in financial sector credit to the private sector. In the period 1981–83, the growth of credit far outstripped the growth of deposits in the financial system, despite the increase in interest rates to positive real levels (see Appendix II, Table 3.31). The more rapid growth of credit than deposits was associated with a fall in gross domestic savings to GDP and an increase in banks' gross lending margins (see Appendix II, Table 3.32). Combined with weaknesses in the postreform supervisory framework, the rapid credit expansion contributed to the subsequent financial crisis. Concurrently, the ratios of financial assets, M2, and M3 to GDP increased and a larger proportion of private savings was intermediated through the financial system (see Appendix II, Table 3.33).

During 1981–86, the Philippines faced a major financial sector crisis (see Appendix II, Table 3.34).[51] The difficulties began in 1981 as a crisis of confidence when fraud in the commercial paper market resulted in large-scale defaults by borrowers in this market and in bankruptcies among a number of nonbank financial intermediaries and their holding companies. This crisis spread to rural and thrift banks as

[51]See Nascimento (1990) for a detailed analysis of the financial sector crisis in the Philippines.

investors shifted their funds into higher quality assets, and caused a number of these institutions to fail.[52] These failures were followed in 1982 and 1983 by intensified government assistance to financial and nonfinancial institutions, including emergency lending and equity contributions to public financial institutions and the takeover of troubled private financial and nonfinancial institutions by government financial institutions.

In 1984 a sharp deepening of the crisis occurred. An unstable political environment in the first half of 1983 was followed by a balance of payments crisis and a government-announced moratorium on external debt payments to foreign commercial banks. A financial panic followed that resulted in runs on financial institutions, including commercial banks, a flight to currency, large-scale capital outflows, and a contraction in financial intermediation. Between September 1983 and September 1986, private sector credit fell in real terms by 53 percent. A further contraction of banking system credit occurred when some 30 percent of the banking system's total assets, representing the nonperforming loans of two government-owned commercial and development banks, were transferred to a government agency, the Asset Privatization Trust. In all, three commercial banks, 128 rural banks, and 32 thrift institutions failed during the crisis, while two large government-owned financial institutions were declared insolvent, requiring restructuring supported by the transfer of nonperforming assets. Thus, the increase in the number of financial institutions following the reforms was reversed (see Appendix II, Table 3.29).[53] The fiscal and real sector consequences of the crisis were substantial.

Following the crisis, the central bank increased its credit to financial institutions. The amount provided by the central bank rose from about 19 percent of total credit to the private sector in 1981–82 to 32

[52]Capital markets were also hurt by the crisis and the ensuing recession. The value of trading on the stock markets plunged from ₱4.65 billion in 1980 to ₱1.3 billion in 1981 and the trading value remained low until the end of 1986.

[53]Following the 1980 bank reform, the number of commercial bank offices surged ahead by 15 percent in one year. During the crisis, three commercial banks closed, and the total number of offices declined from the 1981 level. Between 1980 and 1981, both the number of rural bank headquarters and offices substantially increased, but by 1986, failures and merger activities resulted in a 16 percent decline in the number of these banks. Despite the failures in both rural and thrift banks, liberal branching policies during the crisis resulted in their total number of offices rising between 1981–86. Finally, a major publicly owned specialized bank failed during the crisis.

percent in 1985. This proportion fell back to 19 percent in 1986 as nonperforming assets of banks were transferred to the Asset Privatization Trust, a government agency. Despite the increase in central bank assistance, the growth of reserve money was kept under control through money market operations in central bank and treasury securities.

The extensiveness of the crisis can be traced partly to a failure to enforce supervisory rules on credit meeting DOSRI requirements; inadequacies in the rules on provisioning for overdue loans; various banking irregularities exacerbated by the political environment; and excessive risk taking by bank holding companies through newly created and inexperienced subsidiaries. The central bank did not establish firm provisioning rules, and practices regarding the accrual of interest on overdue loans varied greatly between banks. There was asymmetry in the supervision of various categories of financial institutions: banks were supervised by the central bank, while many nonbank subsidiaries were afforded weaker monitoring by the Securities and Exchange Commission. The liberal entry policies for rural and thrift banks created a vulnerable component of the banking sector. Lending rules to customers associated with banks were effectively ignored and excessive interrelated and risky lending occurred. Accounting and operating rules, including those for the provisioning for bad debt, were not codified or transparent. Troubled banks exploited this weakness by accruing interest on nonperforming loans and distributing book profits.

Following the financial crisis there was a dramatic fall in the ratio of bank credit to the private sector—from 51 percent of GDP in 1983 to 25 percent in 1985. Explanations for the fall—that bank runs caused a drop in the supply of deposits or that demand for bank loans fell because of the economic recession—leave a large part of this decline unexplained (see Appendix II, Table 3.35). For example, the decline in the supply of loanable funds available to banks that can be attributed to deposit withdrawals and a reduction in central bank credit amounts only to one-third of the decline in banking system credit during 1984–85. Similarly, while the ratio of banking system credit to GDP fell by 26 percent during 1984–85, the ratio of total investment to GDP fell by only 11 percent, while private consumption did not fall as a percent of GDP.

The dramatic fall in private credit from financial institutions seems even more surprising given the estimated size of overdue bank loans, which amounted to 13 percent of total loans in 1981, and rose to 19 percent by 1986 (see Appendix II, Table 3.34). This amount is not high compared with other countries that have faced financial crises and does not imply severe insolvency of the banking system.[54] Moreover, real lending rates became negative in 1984 and 1985.

The "unexplained" portion of the decline may reflect voluntary credit rationing by financial institutions. The interest rate developments in the period seem to substantiate this hypothesis. Even though between 1984 and 1985 nominal loan rates rose sharply, the spread with the rate on the treasury bills was negative in 1984 (see Appendix II, Table 3.31). For prudential reasons, banks seemed to prefer to invest in safer government securities and to ration credit to the private sector rather than raise their loan rates—an apparent case of concern about "adverse selection."[55] By 1986, the growth of credit to the private sector had begun to recover (after taking account of the transfer of bad loans to the Asset Privatization Trust) and banks' gross interest margins, which had risen sharply during the crisis, began to fall.

Conclusions

The postreform developments in the Philippines reflect a complex set of circumstances. Initially, the liberalization was associated with a sharp increase in financial intermediation and in the number of financial intermediaries, and with an expansion in credit to the private sector. Considering the weak supervisory arrangements that accompanied the liberalization, these developments increased the vulnerability of the financial system to a shock in confidence. The subsequent financial crisis resulted in substantial portfolio shifts between assets and a severe interruption to financial sector development.

Perhaps the most striking feature of the Philippines' experience was the drastic reduction in banking system credit following the crisis. The drop was much more dramatic than in either Argentina or Chile, both

[54]Nevertheless, pervasive misallocation of credit and the true magnitude of banking distress became evident subsequently when two large government financial institutions were restructured.

[55]The financial viability of enterprises in the midst of a recession was unclear and further increases in loan rates could have exacerbated the financial position of firms and attracted riskier forms of lending (e.g., distressed borrowing and riskier borrowers), thus reducing the expected future returns to banks and inducing the banks to ration credit.

of which appeared to face a more severe situation with problem loans than did the Philippines. Following the financial crisis banks in the Philippines appeared to become very cautious about extending new credits. At the same time, the central bank's capacity to moderate this by easing monetary policy appeared limited by the immediate domestic stabilization and external adjustment objectives. The excessive contraction in credit eventually caused the real economy to undershoot. The Philippines' experience, therefore, again illustrated the dynamic interrelationships between financial sector reform, financial sector weaknesses, and macroeconomic management.

Lessons in Managing Financial Liberalization

This section seeks to draw out the major lessons for managing and sequencing financial sector liberalization from the experiences in the five countries examined in the previous section. It examines the implications of financial liberalization for the various financial aggregates and indicators of the financial sector, and presents a stylized model of the dynamic adjustments following financial liberalization and the implications for managing the macroeconomic risks following liberalization.

Monetary Dynamics of Financial Reforms

Financial indicators and aggregates

Table 3.6 presents the differences between the average values of indicators of financial sector development for the three years before and after the initiation of major financial sector reforms. Table 3.7 shows the average values of the indicators for the three years after the reforms were introduced. In all of the countries for which a comparison is possible, financial reform was accompanied by increases in real interest rates and in the ratios of money, financial assets, and credit to the private sector to GDP, and a fall in the ratio of currency to deposits (prereform data are not available for Chile). The first conclusion is that policy design has to anticipate and allow for the shifts in financial aggregates that accompany financial sector reforms. For example, a failure to allow for the increased financial intermediation following financial liberalization could result in a policy that is tighter than an-

Table 3.6. Change in Financial Indicators Between Pre- and Postreform Periods

(Differences in averages for three years before and after reforms, in percent)

	Argentina 1977	Chile[1] 1974	Indonesia 1983	Korea 1981	Philippines 1980
Growth of:					
Private financial assets[2]	20.0	. . .	2.6	3.3	–4.7
Credit to private sector[2]	31.3	. . .	–5.9	–2.8	0.8
Difference between growth of private deposits and credit to the private sector[2]	–9.5	. . .	6.9	5.6	–7.0
Private financial assets/GDP	5.4	. . .	6.0	3.0	1.6
M2/GDP	3.6	. . .	6.5	3.1	1.1
Currency/Deposits	–20.0	. . .	–11.4	–3.6	–1.7
Credit to private sector/GDP	10.0	. . .	7.4	17.23	8.0
Proportion of financial institutions' credit financed by central bank	–108.0	. . .	11.4	–1	5.8
Gross domestic savings/GDP	–1.9	. . .	–1.2	1.1	–0.6
Real GDP growth	—	. . .	–1.6	4.4	2.9
Real deposit rate	30.6	. . .	13.9	5.2	3.1
Gross interest margin	11.9	. . .	1.1	1.7	–0.8

Sources: Various country authorities; IMF, *International Financial Statistics.*

[1]Prereform data are not available for Chile.

[2]In real terms, that is, after deflation by CPI.

ticipated when targets are set at the level of the banking or financial system. Another approach—setting targets at the level of the central bank—carries its own risk, however, because it does not allow for a possible shift out of currency into bank deposits, and a change in the behavior of excess reserves could result in a looser than anticipated policy.

In all of the countries studied, financial liberalization was followed by a period in which credit growth exceeded the growth of deposits with financial institutions (see Table 3.7). In two of the countries (Argentina and the Philippines), the difference between the growth of credit and the growth of bank deposits increased following the reforms.[56] A second conclusion is that financial reform may initially reduce net private savings and increase the pressure on resources. Maintaining macroeconomic balance during financial sector reforms may, therefore, require a reduction in the fiscal deficit, and/or an initial attraction of foreign resources to cover the balance of payments deficit.

[56]Prereform data are not available for Chile. However, the magnitude of the growth of credit in the postreform period in Chile suggests that it would also be included in this group of countries.

Table 3.7. Development of Financial Indicators in the Postreform Period
(Averages for three years following the reforms, in percent)

	Argentina 1977	Chile 1974	Indonesia 1983	Korea 1981	Philippines 1980
Growth of:					
Private financial assets[1]	2.8	–16.4	15.3	11.2	4.6
Credit to private sector[1]	13.6	46.5	19.3	20.5	13.8
Difference between growth of private deposits and credit to the private sector[1]	–8.9	–40.0	–2.4	–9.0	–10.2
Private financial assets/GDP	33.5	27.4	23.9	40.6	36.4
M2/GDP	29.2	17.5	23.6	35.5	22.6
Currency/deposits	25.7	11.6	24.2	12.4	12.7
Credit to private sector/GDP	34.0	17.4	18.2	68.0	43.8
Proportion of financial institutions' credit financed by central bank	5.4	13.5	49.5	18.4	20.5
Gross domestic savings/GDP	23.5	13.6	28.9	28.1	23.4
Real GDP growth	1.8	0.2	5.1	9.5	2.2
Real deposit rate	–14.1	–8.7	10.3	4.3	0.5
Gross interest margin	25.4	89.7	1.1	2.1	3.4

Source: Various country authorities; IMF, *International Financial Statistics*.
[1]In real terms, that is, after deflation by CPI.

The rapid growth of credit is perhaps not surprising following the removal of interest rate and credit controls that had previously restricted credit growth, with the extent of adjustment reflecting the speed of the reforms. In Korea and Indonesia, the growth of private credit relative to deposits slowed in the postreform period compared to the prereform period, and the reforms therefore appear to have reduced the private resource imbalances compared to the prereform situation. Financial reform in Korea was a much more gradual process than in other countries in the sample and the authorities continued to maintain extensive control over credit through the national commercial banks. Also, in Indonesia the central bank continued to exercise significant influence on overall credit growth through selective refinance and other policies that initially limited the extent of competition in the banking system.

A third conclusion is that financial liberalization can have important effects on the cost of funds to borrowers (see Table 3.6). Generally, real interest rates increased and banks' gross lending margins widened initially following the reforms. These margins reflected a number of influences. The removal of interest rate controls allowed banks to price credits and risks more appropriately, possibly serving to raise margins, since controlled lending rates were usually set too low. Against this, reserve requirements were normally lowered as part of the reforms—reducing the cost wedge between deposit and lending rates. In addition, the reforms generally sought to increase financial sector competition through the reduction of barriers to entry and segmentation between different types of financial institutions; in some cases, however, the improvements in competition did not materialize owing to greater concentrations of ownership.

The speed of adjustment of financial indicators following the liberalization is examined in Table 3.8. This table compares the average value of the indicators for the first and three postreform years. The maintenance of real interest rates was quite critical in the reform dynamics. In the three countries that maintained positive deposit interest rates on average in the postreform period, credit growth slowed down after the first postreform year; whereas in Argentina, where real deposit and lending rates were negative on average, credit growth accelerated following the reforms. Credit growth also accelerated in Chile, despite very high and positive real lending rates that coincided with negative deposit rates.[57] High real interest rates also helped countries to attract capital inflows, and thus to finance the balance of payment implications of the more rapid credit expansions following the financial liberalizations.

Dynamics of deposit and credit growth with financial liberalization

Country experiences suggest some stylized dynamics for the growth of deposits and credit following financial liberalization. These are illustrated in Figure 3.1. In the prereform period, deposit growth declines because of the negative real deposit rates and the overall repressed nature of the financial system at this time. Credit growth is usually maintained through increasing liquidity support from the central bank. The lower deposit than credit growth is associated with increasing resource pressures in the prereform period.

After financial liberalization, both credit and deposit growth tend to increase. The response of credit growth is initially more rapid than deposit growth. The decline in the real value of deposits that generally

[57]Real rates, however, turned strongly positive in Chile during 1978–83.

Table 3.8. Difference in Financial Indicators Between Three-Year Averages After the Reforms and One Year After the Reforms
(In percent)

	Argentina 1977	Chile 1974	Indonesia 1983	Korea 1981	Philippines 1980
Growth of:					
Private financial assets[1]	0.4	13.4	5.4	4.2	4.6
Credit to private sector[1]	9.3	27.6	2.4	0.5	–8.8
Difference between growth of private deposits and credit to the private sector[1]	–7.5	–3.7	5.0	–3.0	12.5
Gross interest margin	–16.8	—	1.6	0.1	1.8
Memorandum item:					
Average real deposit rate	–14.2	–3.8	10.3	4.3	0.5

Sources: Various country authorities; IMF, *International Financial Statistics*.
[1]In real terms, that is, after deflation by CPI.

occurs in the prereform period reflects a voluntary portfolio response to financial repression rather than a reaction to specific controls. In the postreform period, however, there is usually a gradual portfolio adjustment by depositors to the new liberal financial situation. Credit growth, in contrast, is likely to be limited by direct controls with an excess demand for credit in the prereform period. Once the direct controls are removed, however, financial institutions respond by meeting the excess demand for credit—usually by running down excess reserves that have built up under the direct credit controls or by attracting capital inflows—with the result that credit expands rapidly.

The subsequent development in deposit and credit growth depends on the structure of real interest rates. If real interest rates are maintained at a positive level by the authorities, the growth of credit slows down compared to the initial postreform credit boom. The growth of credit may still remain higher than in the prereform period because of the general increased role of the financial sector in mobilizing and allocating resources following financial liberalization. The growth of deposits usually continues to increase, reflecting the lagged portfolio adjustment to the financial liberalization measures, the development of new financial instruments and institutions, and the reduction in central bank liquidity support of financial institutions, which are therefore forced to mobilize deposits to meet credit demand. After some point, the growth of deposits and credit tend to converge, al-

Figure 3.1 Dynamics of Credit and Deposit Growth with Financial Liberalization

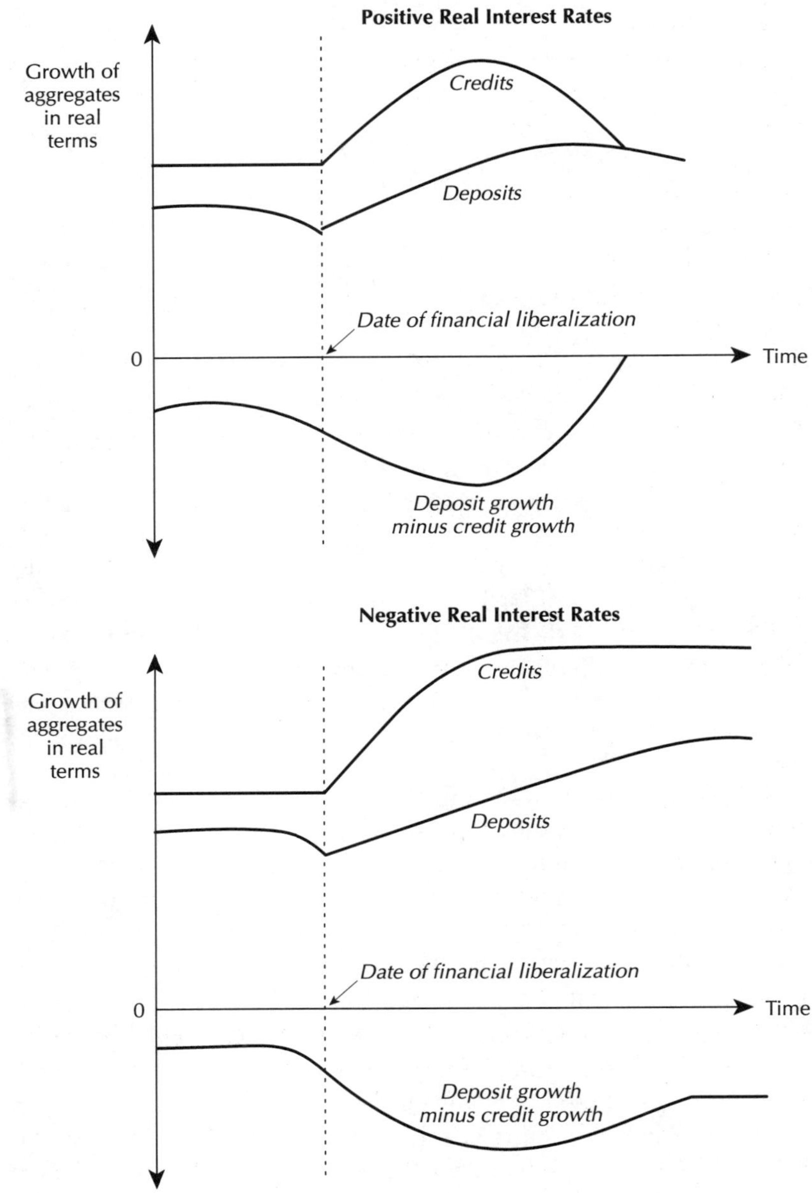

lowing for balanced growth with a higher level of overall resource mobilization than in the prereform period.

If real interest rates are kept negative by the authorities in the postreform period, this most often encourages a more rapid growth of credit and slower growth of deposits. The maintenance of negative real rates then requires expansionary central bank policies that finance the faster growth of credit than deposits. As a result, the growth of deposits generally does not catch up with the growth of credit, and resource imbalances remain—sometimes expanding from the level of the preliberalization period.

Even with the maintenance of positive real interest rates, there is likely to be an initial postliberalization credit boom. The management of the credit boom is a critical element of successful financial liberalization. To the extent that the initial credit growth reflects a one-time stock adjustment to a new equilibrium position—or reflects low or perverse interest elasticity of credit demand on account of distress borrowing and loans to related interests—an attempt to limit credit demand solely through interest rates could result in very high real interest rates with attendant risks for the real economic growth and stability of the financial sector. Chile's experience in 1981 illustrates these risks. Therefore, other options may need to be considered to manage the credit expansion. As already noted, these could include a reduction in the fiscal deficit, thus reducing the need to raise interest rates to maintain overall macroeconomic stability, or an accommodation of the credit expansion by attracting capital inflows. The latter approach, however, carries its own risks if the financial sector is weak so that the capital is not invested efficiently and in ways that can cover the debt service costs (see Chapter 6 for an analysis of the relationship between capital account liberalization and financial sector reform).

Another option, therefore, would be to constrain the credit growth through the temporary continuation of some types of credit controls. While the postliberalization stock adjustment in credit probably cannot be avoided, it could be phased in using direct controls to be more closely aligned with the otherwise lagging growth of bank deposits. Credit ceilings that allow banks to increase credit only in response to increases in deposits might achieve the desired gradual approach, while reducing disincentives to deposit mobilization. To be effective, these ceilings would have to be supported by positive real interest rates, an adjustment in the indirect instruments of monetary policy, the development of suitable intermediate targets of monetary policy, and a strengthening of financial institutions and their capacity to assess and manage risks.

Financial Reform and Financial Sector Stability

In three of the countries, financial liberalization was followed by a financial crisis that seriously disrupted the financial sector and was accompanied by a sharp contraction in real GDP. These crises reversed the financial deepening that had followed the initial financial liberalization and resulted in a complete reversal of the reforms in one country (Argentina).

The timing and intensity of the crises, the timing and scope of financial sector reform, and the linkages between reform and these crises differed considerably in the cases examined in this chapter. In Argentina and Chile, the deregulation of interest rates had been completed and branching restrictions relaxed by the mid- to late 1970s. The financial crises were concentrated in the early 1980s, coinciding with major shifts in macroeconomic adjustment policies and external shocks. In the Philippines, entry regulations had been eased in the mid- to late 1970s, and the deregulation of interest rates began in 1981, just preceding the first episodes of the financial crisis. The weaknesses of problem banks that surfaced during the crisis, however, had originated much earlier, but it took some time for the problems to be discovered because of the normal tendency of banks to reduce the transparency of their accounts in situations of distress, and because of regulatory forbearance by the supervisory authorities.

The connection between financial sector reform and financial crisis is complex. The crises derived from an unstable macroeconomic environment; the development of unsound liability structures of nonfinancial firms prior to reform (due to subsidized credit and, following reform, due to insider loans, loans to related interests, and similar causes); changes in relative prices that influence the viability of borrowers; and weaknesses in the institutional structure of banking (a bank ownership structure that facilitated risk taking, weak prudential regulations, and banking supervision that condoned excessive risk taking).

The financial crises have features in common, particularly the insolvency of a number of financial institutions that were involved in lending to interrelated entities and the rapid growth of bank credit following the liberalization. Rapid credit growth itself strains the credit approval process and often results in an increase in lending to more high-risk projects. When this was combined with extensive lending to interrelated entities and the lack of rules regarding classification and provisioning for bad debts and interest capitalization, the result was banking insolvency. With a proper sequencing of financial sector reforms—including an early and timely attention to developing vigilant bank supervision and well-designed prudential regulations—the buildup of financial fragility might have been detected and contained. Concomitantly, the addressing of bank portfolio problems and the prevention of the growth of banking distress, supported by sound financial policies (timely and adequate fiscal adjustment, maintenance of real interest rates, and relative price adjustments), would have helped to reduce the vulnerability of the financial system to the vagaries of the macroenvironment.

In two countries—Argentina and Chile—financial reform was, in fact, accompanied by a strengthening in prudential regulations, but implementation was ineffective and some critical regulations did not even exist, such as lending to interrelated entities, loan classification and provisions, and accounting rules on interest accruals. Other regulations were rescinded because of the inability to implement them. This situation underlines the importance of having not only adequate regulations but also an implementing capacity. (Such capacity is in part technical, but also requires the absence of political interferences.) The achievement of this ability takes time and often involves the strengthening of key public institutions, particularly the central bank. In Argentina and Chile, financial liberalization was essentially a one-time change that did not permit the ongoing development of an implementing capacity. Moreover, the large number of other modifications that were occurring in the financial systems may have distracted attention from monitoring financial institutions' detailed operations—for example, the frequency of on-site inspections declined in Argentina following the reforms. The abruptness of the financial liberalization also did not give the private financial institutions themselves the time to develop internal monitoring, credit appraisal, and risk management processes that would have been necessary safeguards in the more liberal financial environment, nor did banking supervision ensure that bank management had the appropriate capacity for such monitoring and appraisal.

There was also evidence of "market failures." In practice, financial liberalization was not always associated with a reallocation of credit to new and more productive sectors. In some cases, existing borrowers, who already had access to preferential credit, were granted even larger facilities. In Argentina, explicit deposit guarantees existed, and in Chile, there appears to have been a general perception that deposits were implicitly guaranteed. Because of the guarantees, depositors did not take account of the riskiness of banks when placing their deposits. At the same time, financial disclosure rules and markets in bank equity were poorly developed so that there was no adequate market signal of the risk level of different financial institutions. This was a problem especially in those countries where ownership concentration was high and there was lending to interrelated entities, since owners had little incentive to disclose the true valuation of their institutions.

The situation in the Philippines may have differed from that in Argentina and Chile insofar as deposit guarantees and the settlement of deposit insurance claims were inadequate. In the Philippines, the banks were initially perceived as less risky than nonbank financial intermediaries, and deposits were shifted toward the banks during the initial phase of the crisis. However, once confidence was lost in the banks, the inadequacy of deposit guarantees may have resulted in more severe deposit withdrawals and contraction in bank credit than in either Argentina or Chile. As discussed in the second section of this chapter, "adverse selection" may have played a role in the Philippines, with banks voluntarily rationing credit and maintaining loan rates at low levels relative to market rates in the expectation that this would improve the quality of their loan portfolio.

Financial System Soundness and Financial Sector Reforms

The soundness of financial institutions carries significant implications for the effectiveness of macroeconomic policies and the sequencing of reforms. The existence of weak banks—and the resulting contingent liabilities of the government due to implicit insurance of deposit liabilities—has two major policy implications. Interest rate policies and real sector reforms face difficult constraints and lose their effectiveness if a significant group of financial institutions has sizable nonperforming loans and faces persistent cash flow problems. This is because a weak banking system, burdened with rolling over the loans of weak firms or otherwise supporting them, cannot readily shift lending priorities to new activities and investments; higher interest rates on deposits will compound the cash flow problems, with higher lending rates merely worsening the bad debt problem. Insofar as banks are free to compete for deposits, weak banks will be pushed into borrowing to pay interest on deposits. Weak institutions also become a greater source of pressure on central bank credit or on money market funds, thereby affecting monetary control. In such an environment, a restructuring of weak institutions—through recapitalization, mergers, liquidation, provision of interest subsidies, and similar measures—and a concomitant strengthening of key prudential regulations are needed simultaneously with, or even prior to, monetary control and money market reforms, the timing depending upon the seriousness of the bank's condition. Fiscal reforms have to be expedited to make room for the budgetary or monetary effects of various recapitalization and restructuring schemes that might be needed; and flexible monetary policy instruments should be developed—if not already in place—to absorb the excess liquidity that might be generated by the recapitalization measures.

In any event, a minimal set of prudential reforms—including proper accounting rules for suspension of interest on nonperforming loans, a good loan classification system and associated provisioning rules, capital adequacy guidelines, and limits on loan concentration—are very desirable, if not essential, to support real sector liberalization, to improve the allocative effects of interest rate policy, and to maximize the growth content of stabilization policies. This is because such prudential rules and guidelines have significant side effects on credit allocation and credit expansion and, therefore, could be utilized to support both expenditure reduction and switching policies that typically accompany adjustment programs. For example, it is easier to implement tight credit policies—and minimize any output loss associated with such policies—if nonperforming loans are written off promptly, and poor loans are recognized quickly, thereby improving the mobility of credit. Fairly tight regulations on provisioning and interest accounting, based on loan performance and other appropriate criteria, could thus contribute both to a strengthening of the banking system and to ensuring greater efficiency and flexibility in credit allocation. Also, appropriate capital adequacy rules can complement stabilization policies by limiting asset expansion by banks in line with the availability of capital funds. These arguments suggest that certain key prudential reforms should accompany any move to liberalize or otherwise raise interest rates, and should ideally precede major real sector reforms.

Prudential regulations and banking supervision objectives could interact with monetary policy goals, an aspect that could influence the sequencing of reforms. The strengthening of capital adequacy ratios, implementing limits on loans to single borrowers, and, more generally, any tightening of supervision of loan quality could slow down growth in bank credit. This strategy could complement monetary policy goals at times, but could counteract monetary policy intentions at other times. A properly phased introduction of reforms to tighten banking supervision and subsequent maintenance of a steady-as-you-go approach to banking supervision would help to minimize conflicts with monetary policy. The timing of interventions in problem banks could be constrained by the macroeconomic situation and could conflict with the objectives of monetary policy reforms. Any large injection of bank reserves in the course of interventions in problem banks could weaken monetary policy and slow the pace of reform in monetary policy instruments. Prudential rules on liquidity management by commercial banks typically have an impact on the demand for liquid assets (treasury bills and other short-term paper) and interbank funds, and such rules could well be designed to complement the reforms of money markets. Rules to limit foreign exchange exposure of commercial banks could act to limit capital flows and influence the extent to which domestic short-term interest rates could be set independently of foreign rates.

Interest Rate Liberalization and Reform of Monetary Instruments

The experience of countries reviewed here suggests that reforms of monetary control procedures and the measures to develop money and interbank markets should be pursued together and be implemented fairly early in the reform sequence. First, the development of indirect instruments of monetary policy to replace direct credit controls contributes to efficiency and strengthens the adjustment effort. Second, interest rate liberalization—defined as the management and control of interest rates through indirect and market-oriented instruments of monetary policy rather than through direct administrative fixing of a wide range of interest rates—also calls for reforms of monetary control procedures. Third, the development of indirect monetary instruments becomes critical for effective monetary control once countries become more open to capital flows (see Chapter 6 for a discussion of the links between monetary policy instruments and capital flows).

The development of a money market in any case requires an active involvement of the central bank because only the central bank can ensure that there is a two-way market in bank reserves and short-term funds by avoiding situations of protracted excess reserves and alleviating shortages of reserves. In doing so, the central bank should learn to switch gradually from being the market to creating and supporting a market. That is, the central bank should not simply react to the initiatives of individual institutions to obtain funds or invest their excess reserves, but should anticipate the surpluses and deficits developing in the market and provide reserves at its own initiative, leaving the market participants to seek each other out for funds during normal times. Since such reforms of operating procedures take time, certain initial steps should be in place early in the reform sequence—such as the development of new monetary instruments (treasury bills or central bank bills), selling procedures for the instruments, changes in rules of access to central bank credit, reforms of the reserve requirements system, and liquid asset ratios (these reforms are discussed in detail in Chapter 2).

The introduction of indirect instruments typically stimulates the volume of transactions in money and interbank markets, and makes it opportune to carry out technical reforms to foster money market institutions and trading arrangements. For example, operations at market-related rates, the choice of securities that are eligible as collateral for refinance of repurchase operations, the specification of eligible liquid assets, the structure of the reserve requirement system, and the choice of instrument mix (particularly the mix between liquidity absorption by security sales and liquidity injection by refinance) are factors that influenced the demand and supply of securities, the growth of interbank markets, and the relative depth of various segments of the market. This is well illustrated by the country cases, and suggests that an early start in the interactive reforms of monetary operations and money market structures would be highly effective in supporting both stabilization and financial liberalization.

The feasibility of interest rate liberalization depends not only on the existence of an adequate set of monetary policy instruments and the development of appropriate operating procedures, but also on the broader institutions and regulatory environment. The country experiences suggest that the macroeconomic effects of interest rates and the ability to control rates following the liberalization will be affected by (1) the degree of competition in the financial system, particularly in banking markets; (2) the degree of openness of the economy to capital flows; (3) the soundness of financial institutions; and (4) the financial structure of nonfinancial firms.

With the oligopolistic banking systems found in all of the sample countries, the speed of adjustment of deposit and lending rates to monetary policy was often slow, as was the adjustment of the margin between deposit and lending rates. This was probably because the banks tended to price their loans based on average cost of funds, which adjusted to changes in the marginal cost of funds with a considerable lag. Typically, competition-enhancing policies based on changes in entry regulations, unification of regulations, mergers, and divestitures can be pursued over time. Indeed, the liberalization of interest rates and the absence of direct credit controls are likely to provide an environment most conducive to an increase in financial sector competition and innovation. There is no pressing need to alter the banking industry structure as a precondition for initiating interest rate liberalization, although it is probably desirable that it occur simultaneously with the liberalization to reinforce competition in interest rate setting and financial services. In such situations, moral suasion or regulatory limits might be useful initially to guide developments in banks' spreads, while competition is strengthened over time through other policies.

Nevertheless, the speed and nature of interest rate liberalization—and the phasing in of various prudential regulations—may have to be adjusted, taking into account the financial structure of nonfinancial firms and the pace with which problem banks and their borrowers could be restructured. If the nonfinancial firms are highly leveraged, any sharp increase in real interest rates, or a sluggish fall in nominal rates while inflation falls, could further weaken the repayment capacity of these firms and aggravate the bank's condition. Under such circumstances, and if the resources are not available to recapitalize the banks and restructure their portfolios (which would be the preferable option), the ability to control interest rates may become a critical issue. It may then be desirable to liberalize bank interest rates only gradually, while encouraging greater competition and more rapid liberalization in other segments of financial markets.

Country practices show wide variations in terms of speed and sequencing of interest rate liberalizations. The Philippines preferred to liberalize long-term rates first, before moving on to short-term rates.[58] Indonesia and Korea, in contrast, liberalized interest rates of one group of intermediaries before proceeding to more complete liberalization. Korea proceeded gradually, liberalizing loan rates first before embarking on a gradual freeing of deposit rates; long-term deposit rates and larger deposits were freed, before moving on to shorter rates and smaller deposits, in hopes that this would prevent sudden portfolio shifts. Other countries (see Chapter 2) have preferred to liberalize both loan and deposit rates simultaneously. A gradual approach to interest rate liberalization involves continuing the inefficiency in resource allocation over a short period of time, but this appears to offer a better opportunity to put in place the range of supporting reforms that would ensure the longer-term effectiveness of interest rate liberalization. Most countries have liberalized money market rates first, even while pursuing a more gradual approach to liberalization of bank deposit and lending rates.

As regards reforms of selective credit policies, generally, it is better to shift interest rate subsidies offered through the central bank to the budget, and to reduce the range of refinance facilities to a minimum needed for monetary control purposes. Instruments and markets to facilitate maturity transformation—longer-term capital markets in particular—may have to be developed to avoid major disruptions in investment finance due to withdrawal of central bank support. In the meantime, if banks are to be induced to continue to lend to certain high-risk sectors that are supported by central bank refinance policies, it may be necessary to increase the interest rate flexibility offered to banks, and reduce the costs of information and debt recovery. The timing of Indonesian reforms of refinance policies illustrates these approaches. In Indonesia, central bank support for term lending by commercial banks was only withdrawn gradually while alternative policies to increase the supply of long-term capital were put in place. Insofar as the existence of such selective refinance policies cause significant ex-

[58]Such a policy may not work best if the general level of interest rates is expected to fall during the reform period. This is because banks that carry long-term liabilities, previously contracted at high interest rates, may be reluctant to reduce loan rates following the fall in liability rates.

pansion in the reserve base, the authorities would have to strengthen the instruments to absorb excess reserves and make sure that interest rates on selective refinance facilities are promptly adjusted in line with market rates. Moreover, policies to improve the allocation of selective refinance between financial institutions, such as through auctions, can help mitigate the allocative efficiencies and institutional distortions of the refinance.

Some countries have first developed money markets for short-term instruments before developing ones for long-term securities. This is because money markets provide a more convenient vehicle to implement monetary policy in a market-oriented way.[59] Also, the development of well-capitalized dealers in securities is easier in short-term instruments, such as treasury bills and bankers' acceptances, where the price risks are lower in comparison with long-term instruments. The dealership skills developed through short-term instruments can then be translated to long-term instruments over time. In any case, central banks should play a major role in developing money and capital market intermediaries (brokers, dealers, and market makers) through liquidity and regulatory support—Indonesia and the Philippines are examples—and through fostering efficient clearing and settlement systems for payments (e.g., Malaysia, as discussed in Chapter 2).

[59]In some other countries, such as Japan and Germany, capital markets have been developed first to provide long-term finance, and money markets have evolved with the switch to indirect monetary controls.

Appendix I: Definition of Data Measures Used for Each Country

Statistical Measures	Argentina	Chile	Indonesia	Korea	Philippines
M2	Currency + deposit money bank's demand, time, savings and foreign exchange deposits	Currency + commercial banks' demand, time, savings and foreign exchange deposits	Currency + deposit money banks' demand, time, savings, foreign exchange, and other deposits	Currency + deposit money banks' demand, time, savings, and foreign exchange deposits	Currency + demand, time, savings and foreign exchange deposits
Private financial assets	M2 + deposits of other financial institutions	M2 + forward sales of foreign exchange + liabilities held by CEPAC (national savings institution) + central bank and mortgage bonds (1979–87)	M2 + deposit money bank import deposits + other financial institutions' savings deposits	M2 + deposit money bank import deposits + time and savings deposits of other financial institutions	M2 + deposit money bank import deposits + deposit substitutes + other deposits (= M3) + nonbank holdings of government securities
Currency to deposit ratio	Currency outside banks to deposits of all financial institutions	Currency outside banks to commercial bank deposits	Currency outside banks to deposits of all financial institutions	Currency outside banks to deposits of all financial institutions	Currency outside banks to deposits of all financial institutions
Credit to private sector	By all financial institutions	By commercial banks	By all financial institutions	By deposit money banks and nonbank financial institutions	By deposit money banks and other banking institutions
Proportion of credit financed by central bank	Proportion of private sector credit financed by central bank credit to all financial institutions	Proportion of total commercial bank credit financed by central bank credit to commercial banks	Proportion of total credit financed by central bank credit to all institutions	Proportion of total credit financed by central bank domestic currency credit to Deposit Money Banks	Proportion of total credit financed by central bank credit to all institutions
Gross domestic savings	GDP - Private consumption - Public consumption	GDP - Private consumption - Public consumption	GDP - Private consumption - Public consumption	GDP - Private consumption - Public consumption	GDP - Private consumption - Public consumption
Deflating index	Annual average change in CPI (1985 = 100) (for GDP growth: GDP deflator	Annual average change in CPI (1985 = 100) (for GDP growth: GDP deflator)	Annual average change in CPI (1985 = 100) (for GDP growth: GDP deflator)	Annual average change in CPI (1985 = 100) (for GDP growth: GDP deflator)	Annual average change in CPI (1985 = 100) (for GDP growth: GDP deflator)

Appendix II: Country Tables
Table 3.9. Argentina: Structure of Financial System

	1976		1977		1978	
	Head offices	Branches	Head offices	Branches	Head offices	Branches
Total number of financial institutions	692	3,171	723	3,298	721	3,621
Commercial banks (total)	111	2,906	112	2,951	150	3,101
Government	29	1,580	30	1,617	30	1,637
Private domestic	64	1,100	65	1,132	102	1,250
Foreign owned	18	226	17	202	18	204
Investment banks (total)	4	—	4	—	3	—
Government	—	—	1	—	1	—
Private domestic	4	—	3	—	2	—
Foreign owned	—	—	—	—	—	—
Development banks	2	33	2	33	2	33
Other government-owned financial institutions						
Mortgage banks	1	51	1	52	1	52
Credit cooperatives	1	40	1	40	1	39
Other private financial institutions						
Credit cooperatives	424	13	423	34	377	173
Finance companies	80	40	80	58	138	147
Savings and loan associations	—	—	35	52	35	56
Consumer credit association	69	88	65	78	14	20
Number of firms traded on the Buenos Aires Stock Exchange	309		303		296	
Stock market capital/ GDP (%)	. . .		. . .		. . .	
Government paper in circulation[1]						
Treasury bills	1.11		1.36		2.09	
Government bonds (indexed)	1.62		1.21		1.45	
Other[2]	0.88		0.45		0.27	

Sources: World Bank (1984); International Finance Corporation (1989); Central Bank of Argentina, *Memoria Annua*

[1]Quarterly averages; in millions of 1985 australs. On June 14, 1985, the austral replaced the peso at the rate of 1 aus to 1,000 pesos. On January 1, 1992, the peso replaced the austral at the rate of 10,000 australes to one peso.

[2]Between 1978–80, includes variable interest rate and fund mobilization bonds. Between 1981–83, includes monetary absorption and consolidation bonds.

1979		1980		1981		1982		1983	
Head offices	Branches	Head offices	Branches	Head offices	Branches	Head offices	Branches	Head offices	Branches
496	4,106	469	4,119	449	4,199	413	4,364	402	4,641
211	3,720	207	3,714	199	3,787	197	3,957	203	4,336
30	1,688	30	1,715	30	1,741	31	1,742	31	17
161	1,814	151	1,784	137	1,705	133	1,369	140	2,140
20	218	26	215	32	341	33	346	32	341
4	—	3	—	3	—	3	—	3	—
1	—	1	–	1	—	1	—	1	—
2	—	1	–	1	—	1	—	1	—
1	—	1	–	1	—	1	—	1	—
2	33	2	33	2	33	2	32	2	33
1	52	1	52	1	53	1	53	1	53
1	40	1	40	1	49	1	50	1	51
104	13	92	24	92	26	76	23	71	24
142	205	135	216	126	218	111	214	102	208
31	43	28	40	25	33	22	35	19	36
—	—	—	–	—	—	—	—	—	—
287		278		263		248		238	
. . .		2.50		3.70		4.10		6.00	
1.66		2.11		1.08		1.43		. . .	
1.43		1.19		1.15		0.14		. . .	
0.32		0.33		0.19		0.79		0.91	

Table 3.10. Argentina: Selected Financial Indicators

	1974	1975	1976	1977	1978	1979	1980	1981	1982	1983	1984	1985	1986
	(In millions of australs; 1985 prices)[1]												
Total financial assets	13,567	11,156	9,313	11,692	11,980	13,375	12,709	13,496	12,002	13,475	12,918	8,587	9,534
Currency	3,531	3,581	2,184	2,049	2,302	2,108	2,188	1,992	2,150	2,554	2,397	2,015	2,093
Deposits	8,103	6,156	5,563	7,500	7,715	9,503	8,596	8,544	8,099	9,562	8,848	5,818	6,663
Financial sector credit to private sector	11,425	10,229	7,726	10,308	10,742	12,792	15,090	21,003	25,959	29,309	29,902	9,770	10,272
Central bank credit to financial institutions	11,583	11,018	8,451	1,179	444	265	1,594	2,762	11,914	7,822	7,338	4,551	6,890
	(In percent)												
Private financial assets/GDP	34.39	26.88	22.96	28.86	32.58	34.67	33.26	37.38	32.65	35.18	31.68	21.69	24.39
M2/GDP	30.79	25.17	20.91	24.73	27.99	30.53	29.03	31.96	31.12	33.72	31.08	21.29	23.89
Currency/deposits	40.97	56.36	38.77	27.37	30.08	22.16	24.98	20.95	24.38	25.91	23.89	31.63	29.01
Credit to private sector/GDP	28.47	24.32	19.04	25.46	29.23	33.16	39.49	58.17	74.46	88.34	81.75	24.81	26.28
Proportion of private sector credit financed by the central bank	105.78	114.17	122.45	12.31	4.05	1.94	10.16	11.21	37.10	21.32	18.06	43.17	56.13
Change M2/gross domestic savings	. . .	60.66	51.34	56.61	65.15	89.74	66.52	94.98	95.52	121.57	. . .	. . .	. . .
Gross domestic savings/GDP	20.76	24.41	31.49	30.29	27.78	22.57	20.55	17.83	20.17	22.21	. . .	. . .	. . .
Real GDP growth rate	6.25	–0.74	–0.23	6.39	–3.22	7.02	1.49	–6.66	–4.95	3.00	2.56	–4.54	5.46
Real deposit rate	–5.45	–57.40	–71.26	–1.44	–16.30	–15.43	–10.65	23.98	–15.04	–15.91	–33.70	–49.00	–15.78
Gross interest rate margin	5.94	20.65	13.89	65.45	42.14	15.00	18.90	54.57	26.29	42.17	76.00	77.95	27.87
Average required reserves	100.00	100.00	100.00	45.00	39.70	24.75	11.83	13.38	57.50	100.00	. . .	. . .	. . .
Total number of financial institutions	. . .	. . .	692	723	721	496	469	449	413	402	. . .	. . .	. . .

Sources: Central Bank of Argentina; IMF, *International Financial Statistics*; and IMF staff estimates.

[1]On June 14, 1985, the austral replaced the peso at the rate of 1 austral to 1,000 pesos. On January 1, 1992, the peso replaced the austral at the rate of 10,000 australes to one peso.

Table 3.11. Argentina: Interest Rate Structure

(Annual percent)[1]

	1976	1977[2]	1978	1979	1980	1981	1982[3]	1983	1984	1985	1986	1987[4,5]	1988[5]
Nominal													
Deposit rates[6]	56.09	172.12	130.58	119.48	79.38	153.50	124.97	273.22	381.79	293.79	60.10	143.55	386.89
Loan rates[6]	69.98	237.57	172.72	134.48	98.28	208.07	151.26	315.39	457.79	371.74	87.97	162.95	. . .
Gross margin	13.89	65.45	42.14	15.00	18.90	54.57	26.29	42.17	76.00	77.95	27.87	19.40	. . .
Real[7]													
Deposit rates	–71.26	–1.44	–16.30	–15.43	–10.65	23.98	–15.04	–15.91	–33.70	–49.00	–15.78	5.28	9.97
Loan rates	–68.71	22.27	–1.01	–9.65	–1.24	50.66	–5.11	–6.40	–23.25	–38.90	–1.12	13.67	. . .
Differential with devaluation adjusted dollar interest rates[8]													
Deposit minus LIBOR	1,142.59	38.67	44.93	38.94	38.64	–600.23	–509.21	–69.11	–230.52	–569.71	–7.47	0.26	46.83
Loan minus U.S. prime	1,148.69	102.03	85.95	52.52	55.92	–560.87	–495.33	–32.03	–163.54	–506.89	18.19	16.89	. . .
CPI inflation	443.17	176.09	175.49	159.51	100.76	104.48	164.78	343.82	626.72	672.15	90.10	131.33	342.73

Sources: IMF, *International Financial Statistics*; Central Bank of Argentina.

[1]For 1976–82, quarterly average. For 1983–88, monthly average.

[2]Quarterly average of second half of 1977.

[3]From July 1982–November 1987, rates reported are the regulated rates.

[4]Loan rates: monthly average of January–October 1987.

[5]From November 1987–December 1988, deposit rates are the average paid on interest free deposits of various maturities.

[6]Data for 1976 are from Gaba (1981) as reported by Baliño (1987).

[7]Deflated by average annual CPI inflation. Real=(1 + nominal) / (1 + inflation) – 1

[8]Adjustment formula used: (1 + LIBOR) * (1 + actual devaluation) – 1.

Table 3.12. Argentina: Summary of Financial Sector Operations
(In millions of australes valued at 1985 prices)[1]

	1974	1975	1976	1977	1978	1979	1980	1981	1982	1983	1984	1985	1986
Domestic liabilities													
Central bank													
currency	3,531	3,581	2,184	2,049	2,302	2,108	2,188	1,992	2,150	2,554	2,397	2,015	2,093
Commercial banks	9,610	8,234	7,112	9,682	10,465	12,510	11,933	13,798	10,128	11,178	13,519	6,874	7,807
Deposits	8,103	6,156	5,563	7,500	7,715	9,503	8,596	8,544	8,099	9,562	8,848	5,818	6,663
Demand	3,736	3,959	2,755	1,957	1,617	1,613	1,474	1,048	1,526	1,325	937	992	841
Savings	3,425	1,837	1,286	623	733	688	846	. . .	742	1,731	1,855	1,468	1,348
Time[2]	942	360	1,521	4,919	5,366	7,202	6,276	7,496	5,831	6,506	6,056	3,358	4,474
Foreign exchange	—	—	—	—	—	124	586	1,377	1,789	1,375	4,219	667	976
Other financial institutions	1,540	795	922	1,815	1,843	1,735	1,762	2,199	658	684	348	162	200
Deposits	1,065	621	750	1,518	1,666	1,584	1,513	1,865	545	551	243	154	193
Sight	180	215	134	102	91	. . .	. . .	. . .	. . .	. . .	. . .	. . .	. . .
Savings	655	264	162	139	30	8	8	. . .	26	68	54	41	25
Time[2]	229	142	454	1,277	1,546	1,576	1,506	1,865	518	483	189	113	168
Domestic credit	15,583	14,032	9,050	11,994	13,336	15,986	18,976	28,133	38,565	63,804	82,164	22,370	27,784
Central bank credit	16,192	16,056	11,218	3,710	2,267	1,257	2,986	4,224	20,111	35,321	46,789	16,643	19,347
Public sector[3]	4,400	5,215	2,481	2,065	899	350	1,545	2,854	7,911	14,898	19,089	6,602	8,187
Credit to financial sector	11,583	11,018	8,451	1,179	444	265	1,594	2,762	11,914	7,822	7,338	4,551	6,890
Commercial banks	9,958	9,068	7,056	644	403	221	1,363	2,417	10,377	6,906	6,607	. . .	. . .
Rest of financial sector	1,625	1,950	1,395	535	41	44	231	345	1,537	915	731	. . .	. . .
Commercial bank credit	8,658	7,159	4,609	7,480	10,169	13,481	15,393	23,487	27,513	32,507	43,312	9,732	12,441
Public sector[3]	–475	–226	–565	–568	180	852	588	3,566	6,061	7,320	10,697	763	1,994
Private sector	9,292	7,915	5,649	7,775	9,109	11,064	13,192	19,101	24,548	28,351	29,321	9,539	10,069
Domestic currency	. . .	. . .	. . .	. . .	. . .	. . .	. . .	. . .	10,863	10,012	8,501	5,829	6,704
Foreign currency	. . .	. . .	. . .	. . .	. . .	. . .	. . .	. . .	13,686	18,339	20,820	3,711	3,365

Other financial institution credit	1,900	1,888	1,532	1,909	1,520	1,530	1,768	2,142	1,474	651	888	368	584
Public sector[3]	. . .	–353	–260	–158	29	30	15	65	94	60	38	8	8
Private sector	2,133	2,315	2,077	2,533	1,633	1,728	1,898	1,902	1,410	958	581	231	203

Sources: IMF, *International Financial Statistics*; and IMF staff estimates.

[1]On June 14, 1985, the austral replaced the peso at the rate of 1 austral to 1,000 pesos. On January 1, 1992, the peso replaced the austral at the rate of 10,000 australes to one peso.

[2]For 1981, data for time deposits include savings deposits. After 1982 includes accrued interest payments.

[3]Includes net credit to central government and to the rest of the public sector. For commercial banks (after 1979), includes foreign exchange loans to official sector.

Table 3.13. Argentina: Manifestations of the Financial Crisis

	1977	1978	1979	1980	1981
Real exchange rate (1975 = 100)	95	65	50	32	53
Debt/equity (normal firms)[1]	85	90	85	128	162
Liabilities of bankrupt firms (deflated by wholesale price index)	3,985	10,099	16,452	20,024	35,800
Problem loans/banks' portfolio[1]	1.52	2.22	2.62	9.13	—

Sources: IMF, *International Financial Statistics*; Fernández (1985); World Bank (1984); and Baliño (1987).

[1]In percent.

Table 3.14. Chile: Structure of the Financial Sector

	1974	1975	1976	1977	1978	1979	1980	1981	1982	1983	1984
Numbers of institutions	...	...	46	39	47	54	56	54	49	45	45
Commercial banks	21	21	20	21	26	36	38	41	40	38	38
Domestic owned[1]	20	20	18	18	22	24	25	23	21	19	19
Foreign owned	1	1	2	3	4	12	13	18	19	19	19
Financiaries	...	...	26	18	21	18	18	13	9	7	7
Capital Market											
Volume of traded stocks (in millions of 1985 pesos)	3,400	3,410	3,827	10,142	19,728	26,287	56,115	32,016	16,531	8,009	6,638
Index of stock prices (Valued at 1980 prices)	...	...	2	7	21	34	92	76	60	69	85

Sources: Velasco (1991); Chile, Superintendencia de Valores y Seguros, *Revista de Valores*; and IMF, *International Financial Statistics*.

[1]Only one domestic bank was state owned after 1975.

Table 3.15. Chile: Interest Rate Structure

(In percent per year; monthly average[1])

	1975	1976	1977	1978	1979	1980	1981	1982	1983	1984	1985	1986	1987
Nominal													
Loan rate	484	351	142	85	61	47	55	63	43	37	40	26	27
Deposit rate	. . .	136	89	63	46	38	42	47	28	26	32	19	25
Gross spread	. . .	215	54	22	16	9	12	16	15	11	9	7	2
Real[2]													
Loan rate	153	45	26	32	21	9	29	48	12	14	7	6	6
Deposit rate	. . .	–24	–2	16	9	2	19	34	1	5	1	–0	4
Differential with devaluation adjusted U.S. prime rate[3]	94	232	71	53	32	32	36	–53	11	–27	–17	6	2
Inflation rate	216	212	92	40	33	35	20	10	27	20	31	19	20

Sources: Central Bank of Chile; IMF, *International Financial Statistics.*

[1]Interest rates refer to those on short-term credit transactions and time deposits of commercial banks.

[2]Real = (1 – nominal) / (1 – inflation) – 1.

[3]Difference between the devaluation-adjusted U.S. prime rate and the domestic loan rate.

Adjustment formula: (1 + prime rate) * (1 + devaluation) – 1.

Table 3.16. Chile: Selected Financial Indicators

	1974	1975	1976	1977	1978	1979	1980	1981	1982	1983	1984	1985	1986
						(In billions of 1985 pesos)							
Private financial assets													
Currency	70	54	57	62	77	88	93	98	86	81	84	80	91
Deposits	225	186	230	273	373	481	572	648	697	550	624	. . .	. . .
Commercial banks' credit to private sector	100	119	163	315	503	684	978	1,155	1,533	1,283	1,420	1,448	1,419
Central bank credit to financial institutions	40	36	20	40	38	22	32	69	149	655	964	1,749	1,615
							(In percent)						
M2/GDP	16.04	17.10	17.54	17.55	19.52	20.79	23.58	26.71	31.67	25.87	28.59	. . .	. . .
Currency/deposits	30.87	28.96	24.76	22.68	20.67	18.35	16.31	15.06	12.31	14.78	13.43	. . .	. . .
Credit to private sector/GDP	5.43	8.46	9.96	16.51	21.81	24.98	34.67	41.40	62.05	52.56	57.40	83.39	111.70
Total financial sector credit financed by central bank	25.00	20.45	9.36	10.56	7.05	3.04	3.21	5.84	8.88	46.14	60.61	. . .	. . .
Change in M2/Gross domestic savings	78.05	139.11	56.62	71.52	59.17	51.27	46.50	50.94	69.79	9.87	61.16	37.82	. . .
Gross domestic savings/GDP	22.28	11.14	17.11	12.62	14.47	14.96	16.82	12.37	9.39	12.53	12.56	16.47	18.42
Real GDP growth rate	0.97	–12.91	3.52	9.86	8.22	8.28	7.78	5.53	–14.09	–0.71	6.34	2.45	5.66
Annual real deposit rate	. . .	. . .	–24.46	–1.79	16.48	9.40	1.96	19.02	33.78	0.51	5.21	0.69	–0.40
Gross interest rate margin	. . .	. . .	215.50	53.69	22.10	15.51	9.03	12.11	15.81	14.80	11.10	8.80	7.20
Reserve requirement[1]	. . .	. . .	47[2]	20	20	. . .	4	4	4	4	4	4	4

Sources: Central Bank of Chile; and IMF, *International Financial Statistics*.

[1]Reserve requirement on one- to three-month time deposits applicable at the end of December of year.

[2]Applicable since March 1977.

Table 3.17. Chile: Summary of Financial Sector's Operations
(In billions of 1985 pesos)

	1974	1975	1976	1977	1978	1979	1980	1981	1982	1983	1984	1985	1986
Domestic liabilities													
Currency	70	54	57	62	77	88	93	98	86	81	84	80	91
Deposits of financial institutions	225	186	230	273	373	481	572	648	697	550	624	. . .	. . .
Demand	101	67	57	64	74	92	115	61	76	80	68	. . .	. . .
Time[1]	5	24	64	103	185	285	305	459	482	440	507	. . .	. . .
Savings and other deposits	76	52	75	74	87	83	128	108	96	. . .	. . .	. . .	. . .
Foreign currency deposits	43	44	33	32	27	21	24	19	43	30	49	. . .	. . .
Other deposits[2]	429	268	102	88	82	127	227	240	348	167	194	992	1,122
M2	295	240	287	335	450	569	665	745	782	631	708	1,061	1,112
Money	171	121	114	126	151	180	208	159	162	161	152	200	240
Quasi-money	124	119	173	209	299	389	457	587	621	470	556	861	872
Domestic credit													
Central bank credit													
Public sector	740	741	552	582	522	508	375	201	184	160	547	1,131	1,272
Commercial banks	40	36	20	40	38	22	32	69	149	655	964	1,749	1,615
Commercial banks' credit	160	174	217	383	537	722	1,006	1,182	1,673	1,419	1,590	. . .	. . .
Public sector	60	56	54	68	34	39	28	27	140	137	169	. . .	. . .
Private sector	100	119	163	315	503	684	978	1,155	1,533	1,283	1,420	1,448	1,419
Domestic currency credit[3]	. . .	. . .	107	199	288	405	600	727	894	. . .	. . .	. . .	. . .

Sources: Central Bank of Chile; IMF, *International Financial Statistics*; and IMF staff estimates.

[1]For 1983 and 1984, includes savings deposits.

[2]Includes forward sales of foreign exchange, liabilities held by CEPAC (national savings institution), and private capital and surplus. For 1979–87, also includes central bank and mortgage bonds. After 1985, includes deposits.

[3]Staff estimates.

Table 3.18. Chile: Indicators of Financial Crisis

	1974	1975	1976	1977	1978	1979	1980	1981	1982	1983	1986
Number of bankrupt institutions											
Commercial banks	. . .	. . .	2	. . .	. . .	. . .	. . .	2	2	2	. . .
Finance companies	. . .	. . .	. . .	8	. . .	3	5	. . .	. . .	. . .	. . .
Companies	. . .	. . .	. . .	. . .	2	4	15	29	75	. . .	. . .
						(In percent)					
Loans defaulted/Total loans[1]											
Commercial banks	1.40	2.80	1.70	1.40	1.20	1.10	0.90	2.40	8.20	18.70	. . .
Finance companies	. . .	. . .	. . .	. . .	. . .	. . .	. . .	2.10	8.10	18.50	. . .
Proportion of total loans judged as problematic[2]	. . .	. . .	. . .	. . .	. . .	. . .		16.00	21.00	54.00	62.00
GDP growth	0.01	–12.90	3.50	9.80	8.20	8.30	7.80	5.70	–14.30	–0.70	. . .

Sources: Velasco (1991); World Bank Data; Central Bank of Chile; IMF, *International Financial Statistics.*

[1]For 1981–83, loans defaulted include "high-risk portfolio" loans sold to central bank.

[2]Calculated as the ratio of the sum of loans sold to the central bank, reprogrammed loans, and overdue loans to total commercial bank loans less loan provisions.

Table 3.19. Chile: Major Elements of the Financial Sector Rescue Program

Measure	Year(s)	Details
Sale of bad loan portfolio to the Central Bank of Chile	June 1982–1986	In June 1982, the central bank bought problem bank loans in exchange for zero-interest bills. From February 1984, banks could sell loans to the central bank up to 2.5 times their November 1983 capital, and in a worst-case-scenario up to 3.5 times their November 1983 capital. Portions of payments made in interest-bearing bills and in repurchase of bills were to come out of shareholders' dividends.
Preferential exchange rates	Sept. 1982–Feb. 1987	These rates were provided to troubled nonfinancial private sector firms to service their foreign liabilities.
Foreign exchange swaps	Jan. 1984–June 1985	Subsidized foreign exchange swaps were provided by the central bank to commercial banks.
Loan reprogramming	April 1983–June 1984	"Productive" loans to the private sector were reprogrammed at subsidized rates with the central bank providing the interest subsidy and the liquidity to the bank.
Recapitalization	Jan. 1985	Assets of intervened banks were transferred to a publicly owned holding company and the banks subsequently recapitalized. Shares of recapitalized banks were then sold to the public at favorable prices.

Source: Information provided by the authorities.

Table 3.20. Indonesia: Structure of Financial Sector

	March 1979		March 1982		March 1985		March 1987		December 1988		March 1991		March 1992	
	Head offices	Branches	Head offices	Branches	Head offices	Branches	Head offices	Branches	Head offices	Branches	Head offices	Branches	Head offices	Branches
Total number of financial institutions	. . .	1,149	215	1,240	214	1,397	238	1,559	237	. . .	325	3,715	353	4,286
Deposit money banks	127	1,149	118	1,240	116	1,397	113	1,559	117	. . .	176	3,715	196	4,286
Commercial banks	94	981	87	1,029	85	1,160	81	1,265	86	. . .	144	3,173	164	3,687
State owned	5	687	5	712	5	749	5	780	5	. . .	5	957	5	961
National privately owned	78	274	71	297	69	390	65	464	70	. . .	111	2,168	130	2,672
Foreign owned	11	20	11	20	11	21	11	21	11	. . .	28	48	29	54
Development banks	28	156	28	197	29	224	29	251	28	. . .	29	420	29	472
State owned	1	11	1	19	1	22	1	22	. . .	. . .	1	30	1	41
Regional	26	144	26	177	27	201	27	228	. . .	. . .	27	376	27	412
Private	1	1	1	1	1	1	1	1	. . .	. . .	1	14	1	19
Savings banks	5	12	3	14	2	13	3	43	3	. . .	3	122	3	127
State owned	1	8	1	12	1	12	1	15	1	. . .	1	43	. . .	43
Private	4	4	2	2	1	1	2	28	2	. . .	2	79	2	84
Nonbank financial intermediaries	. . .	. . .	97	. . .	98	. . .	115	. . .	120	. . .	149	. . .	157	. . .
Investment finance company	9	. . .	11	. . .	11	. . .	11	. . .	11	. . .	9	. . .	9	. . .
Development finance company	3	. . .	3	. . .	3	. . .	3	. . .	3	. . .	3		3	. . .
Insurance company	. . .	. . .	83[1]	. . .	84[2]	. . .	101[3]	. . .	106	. . .	137[4]	. . .	145[5]	. . .

Source: Bank Indonesia, *Report for the Financial Year,* several issues.
Note: Information refers to March of each year, except for 1988, when it refers to December.
[1]Figure for 1981.
[2]Figure for 1984.
[3]Figure for 1986.
[4]Figure for December 1991.
[5]Figure for December 1992.

Table 3.21. Indonesia: Interest Rate Structure
(In percent per year)

	1978	1979	1980	1981	1982	1983	1984	1985	1986	1987	1988	1989	1990
Nominal rates													
One-year time deposit[1]													
State banks	9.0	9.0	9.0	9.0	9.0	9.0	18.7	20.0	15.0	15.0	17.6	18.2	17.2
Private national banks	. . .	15.0	18.0	24.0	24.0	25.0	20.0	24.0	18.0	17.0	19.7	20.6	19.0
Foreign banks	. . .	. . .	. . .	. . .	. . .	17.0	18.5	22.0	16.5	18.0	18.0	18.8	18.0
Average loan[2]													
State banks	. . .	. . .	. . .	. . .	. . .	17.7	18.2	19.9	19.0	18.4	19.7	20.5	19.0
Private national banks[3]	. . .	. . .	. . .	. . .	. . .	27.3	24.9	28.2	25.5	24.1	23.5	23.5	20.7
Foreign banks	. . .	. . .	. . .	. . .	. . .	22.2	21.3	26.4	22.2	22.2	23.1	22.8	18.8
Money market													
Call money[4]	5.9	12.7	14.7	15.9	17.1	17.8	16.4	13.2	13.3	14.8	15.4	13.5	10.0
SBI cutoff rate[5]	. . .	. . .	. . .	. . .	. . .	. . .	15.0	16.0	14.0	14.0	. . .	16.9	13.3
BI discount[6]	. . .	. . .	. . .	. . .	. . .	. . .	17.5	21.0	18.5	18.5	18.5	16.0	16.0
SBPU discount[7]	. . .	. . .	. . .	. . .	. . .	. . .	. . .	20.5	17.0	17.1	17.0	16.0	13.4
Real rates[8]													
12-month time deposit[1]													
State banks	0.8	–7.8	–7.6	–2.8	–0.4	–2.4	7.5	14.5	8.6	5.2	8.8	11.0	8.7
Private national banks	. . .	–2.8	–0.0	10.4	13.2	11.8	8.6	18.4	11.5	7.0	10.7	13.3	10.3
Foreign banks	. . .	. . .	. . .	. . .	. . .	4.6	7.2	16.4	10.0	7.9	9.2	11.6	9.4
Average loan[2]													
State banks	. . .	. . .	. . .	. . .	. . .	5.2	7.0	14.4	12.4	8.3	10.7	13.2	10.3
Private national banks[3]	. . .	. . .	. . .	. . .	. . .	13.8	13.0	22.4	18.5	13.6	15.2	16.0	11.9
Foreign banks	. . .	. . .	. . .	. . .	. . .	9.3	9.8	20.6	15.4	11.83	13.9	15.4	10.2
Money market													
Call money[4]	–1.9	–4.6	–2.7	3.3	6.9	5.4	5.3	8.0	7.0	5.0	6.5	6.6	2.0
SBI cutoff rate[5]	. . .	. . .	. . .	. . .	. . .	. . .	4.1	10.7	7.7	4.3	–7.4	9.8	5.1
BI discount[6]	. . .	. . .	. . .	. . .	. . .	. . .	6.3	15.5	11.9	8.4	8.2	9.0	7.6
SBPU discount[7]	. . .	. . .	. . .	. . .	. . .	. . .	. . .	15.0	10.5	7.1	–7.4	9.0	5.1
CPI inflation	8.1	18.3	18.0	12.2	9.5	11.7	10.4	4.7	5.8	9.2	8.0	6.4	7.8

Spreads													
State bank—private national bank deposit	. . .	–6.0	–9.0	–15.0	–15.0	–16.0	–1.2	–4.0	–3.0	–2.0	–2.1	–2.4	–1.8
State bank—foreign bank deposit	. . .	. . .	. . .	. . .	. . .	–8.0	0.2	–2.0	–1.5	–3.0	–0.4	–0.6	–0.8
Call money—state bank deposit	–3.0	3.7	5.7	6.9	8.1	8.8	–2.3	–6.8	–1.7	–0.2	–2.5	–4.7	–7.2
State bank loan—State bank deposit	. . .	. . .	. . .	. . .	. . .	8.7	–0.5	–0.1	4.0	3.4	2.1	2.3	1.8
Private national bank loan—private national bank deposit	. . .	. . .	. . .	. . .	. . .	2.3	4.9	4.2	7.5	7.1	4.8	2.9	1.7
Foreign bank loan—foreign bank deposit	. . .	. . .	. . .	. . .	. . .	5.2	2.8	4.4	5.7	4.2	5.1	4.0	0.8
Deposit yield curve[9]	3–3	3–3	3–3	3–3	3–3	3–3	0.75–0	1–1	0.5–0	0.5–0	0.3–0.1	0.1–0.7	0.9–0.8
Call money—LIBOR[10]	–60.0	–1.8	–1.7	–6.1	–3.9	–39.0	–2.8	0.03	–42.7	7.5	5.3	9.4	6.1

Sources: Bank Indonesia, *Report for Financial Year,* several issues; IMF, *International Financial Statistics*, Bank Indonesia, *National Financial Statistics;* data provided by the Indonesian authorities.

[1]For each category of banks, the rate reported is the maximum rate offered for March of year.

[2]Average rate charged for working capital loans to nonpriority sectors.

[3]Simple average of rates for foreign and nonforeign exchange private national banks.

[4]Weighted average of rate for the first quarter of year.

[5]Rediscount rate of 30-day SBI bill prevailing at end of March of year.

[6]Rate prevailing at end of March of year.

[7]Rate of Bank Indonesia rediscount rate of SBPUs prevailing at the end of March of year.

[8]Real = (1 + nominal) / (1 + inflation) – 1.

[9]Difference between state banks' time deposit rates of maturities: (12 months–6 months) – (24 months–12 months).

[10]Difference between call money rate and the devaluation adjusted overnight dollar LIBOR rate. Adjustment formula used: (1 + LIBOR) * (1 + devaluation) – 1.

Table 3.22. Indonesia: Selected Financial Indicators

	1978	1979	1980	1981	1982	1983	1984	1985	1986	1987	1988	1989	1990
							(In millions of 1985 rupiahs)						
Private financial assets	8,911	10,418	13,017	14,351	14,768	17,335	19,048	23,469	26,497	29,706	34,240	44,511	59,786
Currency	2,704	2,898	3,448	3,604	3,794	3,864	3,888	4,460	5,044	5,017	4,999	5,947	6,344
Deposits	6,208	7,520	9,569	10,748	10,973	13,471	15,160	19,008	21,453	24,689	29,242	38,564	53,442
Financial sector credit to private sector	4,750	5,377	6,829	8,585	10,759	12,585	15,300	18,014	21,367	25,242	31,822	45,299	68,753
Central bank credit to financial institutions	1,859	2,139	2,805	3,772	6,809	7,209	10,514	10,769	12,690	13,438	17,068	12,205	15,334
							(In percent)						
Private financial assets/GDP	17.97	17.35	18.02	17.44	18.28	19.31	20.23	24.20	27.31	27.52	30.11	35.40	43.82
M2/GDP	16.74	16.29	16.96	16.70	17.72	18.90	19.96	23.89	26.89	27.16	29.67	35.01	43.27
Currency/deposits	45.90	41.50	37.08	34.79	35.00	29.10	25.67	23.54	23.57	20.40	17.00	15.40	11.79
Credit to private sector/GDP	9.55	8.92	9.36	10.22	12.97	13.51	15.67	17.82	21.16	22.46	27.31	34.93	49.67
Proportion of financial institutions' credit financed by central bank	28.87	29.50	31.19	34.04	49.25	45.82	52.62	47.17	48.80	45.67	46.02	24.10	20.86
Excess rupiah liquidity/total deposits	9.08	10.11	8.72	6.02	1.27	3.31	2.47	–0.02	0.49	0.56	6.1	7.47	—
Change in M2/Gross domestic savings	. . .	16.04	18.79	10.31	7.9	15.99	12.24	18.13	15.85	15.32	16.91	26.23	36.4
Gross domestic savings/GDP	27.42	27.41	29.17	33.34	27.73	28.96	29.7	29.8	27.27	32.9	33.99	37.52	36.66
Real GDP growth rates	7.84	6.26	9.88	7.93	2.25	4.19	6.97	2.46	5.88	4.93	5.78	7.46	7.24
State banks' real deposit rate	0.82	–7.88	–7.64	–2.89	–0.44	–2.49	7.51	14.58	8.67	5.24	8.85	10.99	8.72
Gross interest rate margin	. . .	. . .	. . .	. . .	. . .	8.7	–0.55	–0.01	4.00	3.40	2.10	2.30	4.80
Total number of financial institutions	. . .	. . .	. . .	. . .	215	. . .	. . .	214	. . .	228	237	325	353

Sources: IMF, *International Financial Statistics*; and Bank Indonesia, *Report for the Financial Year*, various issues.

Table 3.23. Indonesia: Summary of Financial Sector Operations
(In millions of 1985 rupiah)

	1978	1979	1980	1981	1982	1983	1984	1985	1986	1987	1988	1989	1990
Domestic monetary liabilities													
Currency	2,704	2,898	3,448	3,604	3,794	3,864	3,888	4,460	5,044	5,017	4,999	5,947	6,344
Deposits	5,890	6,983	9,298	10,359	10,842	13,276	15,148	18,947	21,399	24,596	29,411	38,623	53,793
Deposit money bank	5,853	6,946	9,241	10,295	10,772	13,190	15,045	18,813	21,191	24,295	29,017	38,405	53,277
Demand	2,601	3,140	4,442	5,446	5,345	4,832	5,045	5,560	5,747	5,859	6,429	9,383	10,137
Time and savings	2,300	2,150	2,353	2,877	3,222	5,430	6,689	9,607	10,730	14,034	16,819	22,484	32,194
Foreign currency	574	1,256	1,866	1,549	1,818	2,648	3,083	3,378	4,334	4,034	5,221	6,063	10,215
Imports	379	400	581	422	388	280	228	268	380	367	548	475	731
Other financial institutions	36	38	57	65	70	86	103	134	208	301	394	217	516
Private financial assets	8,911	10,418	13,017	14,351	14,768	17,335	19,048	23,469	26,497	29,706	34,240	44,511	59,786
M2	8,303	9,782	12,247	13,740	14,320	16,970	18,785	23,177	26,094	29,318	33,673	44,017	59,037
Money	5.425	6,337	7,963	9,166	9,207	8,764	8,987	10,124	10,990	10,986	11,518	15,462	16,616
Quasi-money	2,878	3,445	4,283	4,574	5,113	8,206	9,798	13,054	15,104	18,332	22,155	28,555	42,421
Domestic credit													
Central bank	7,586	7,511	7,711	8,575	11,472	11,124	12,475	12,039	15,647	16,510	20,657	16,280	19,506
Public sector	5,727	5,372	4,905	4,802	4,663	3,915	1,962	1,270	2,957	3,073	3,589	4,075	4,171
Financial sector	1,859	2,139	2,805	3,772	6,809	7,209	10,514	10,769	12,690	13,438	17,068	12,205	15,334
Deposit money bank	1,845	2,118	2,736	3,607	6,530	6,786	9,971	10,041	11,861	12,592	16,307	11,462	14,643
Other financial institutions	13	21	70	165	278	423	542	729	829	846	760	743	692
Deposit money banks	6,218	7,128	8,964	11,044	13,799	15,703	19,911	22,791	25,980	29,322	36,957	50,460	73,266
Public sector	1,481	1,773	2,204	2,633	3,317	3,568	5,189	5,510	5,446	5,080	5,891	6,535	5,499
Private sector	4,737	5,355	6,760	8,412	10,482	12,135	14,752	17,281	20,534	24,242	31,061	43,925	67,767
Domestic currency	. . .	5,291	6,574	8,219	10,054	11,305	14,038	16,443	19,105	23,163	29,429	. . .	. . .
Foreign currency	. . .	64	186	193	428	830	714	838	1,429	1,079	1,32	. . .	. . .
Other financial institutions	13	21	70	173	286	450	548	734	833	1,000	761	1,374	985

Source: IMF, *International Financial Statistics.*

Table 3.24. Indonesia: Development of the Financial Sector

(In millions of 1985 rupiah; end of March of each year)

	1979	1980	1981	1982	1983	1984	1985	1986	1987	1988	1989	Average Rate of Growth (in percent) 1979–82	1983–87	1988–90
Gross assets of financial sector[1]	10,352	12,684	15,391	18,425	22,435	24,384	30,469	35,137	37,505	52,898	95,576	21	15	37
Commercial banks	9,655	11,794	14,169	17,004	20,799	22,359	27,844	31,841	34,753	46,609	85,797	20	16	35
State owned[2]	7,860	9,650	11,758	14,040	16,540	17,326	21,184	23,745	25,548	44,036	78,994	211	3	47
National privately owned	928	1,093	1,392	1,754	2,405	3,221	4,402	5,810	6,970	...	...	21	32	...
Foreign owned	866	1,050	1,019	1,210	1,854	1,811	2,258	2,285	2,235	2,573	6,803	11	15	47
Development banks	326	423	569	631	681	805	1,004	1,109	1,083	4,038	6,488	25	12	109
Nonbank financial intermediaries	371	467	653	790	954	1,200	1,621	2,188	1,670	2,451	3,291	27	19	26
Investment and finance companies	...	381	532	652	777	952	1,299	1,841	1,252	...	...	16	16	...
Development finance companies	...	86	110	138	177	248	322	347	383	...	...	13	23	...
Money and capital markets														
Central bank paper[3]	...	...	...	...	...	108	389	1,443	811	1,337	1,332	...	...	21
Money market paper (SBPU)[3]	...	...	...	...	...	...	182	546	...	...	...	...	...	...
Stocks[4]	32	27	12	78	41	...	...	...	...	122	5,574	...	...	...
Bonds[4]	...	...	...	...	179	73	130	47	113	749	1,454	...	...	213

Source: Bank Indonesia, *Report for the Financial Year,* several issues.

[1]Excludes savings banks and insurance companies.

[2]For 1988–90, includes national privately owned banks.

[3] Figures represent (monthly) average outstanding value of instruments. SBIs and SBPUs were introduced in 1984 and 1985, respectively.

[4]Figures represent value of year's issues. No stock was issued in 1978. Bonds were introduced in 1983.

Table 3.25. Korea: Structure of Financial Sector
(Number of institutions)

	1970		1975		1980		1982		1985[1]	
	Head offices	Branches	Head offices	Branches	Head offices	Branches	Head offices	Branches	Head offices	Branches
Banking sector	27	85	31	503	54	713	67	925	77	1,238
Nationwide	6	32	6	361	5	475	6	599	7	840
Local	9	53	10	142	10	238	10	326	10	398
Specialized	6	...	6	...	6	...	7	...	7	840
Foreign branches	6	...	9	...	33	...	44	...	53	...
Nonbank financial intermediaries										
Investment and Finance Company	...	10	...	18	...	26	...	32	...	...
Mutual Savings and Finance Company	...	223	...	193	...	200	...	332	...	...
Securities Investment Trust Company	1	1	...	3	...	3	...	3	...	...
Merchant banks	...	...	...	...	...	...	...	6		
Insurance	...	...	...	...	...	...	...	6	...	...
Credit unions	...	...	...	...	...	...	...	1,292	...	...

Sources: Kwack and Chung (1986); Bank of Korea, *Financial System in Korea.*
[1]As of July 1988, the number of bank head offices remains unchanged from its July 1985 level, except for one new foreign bank branch.

Table 3.26. Korea: Summary of Financial Sector Operations
(In millions of 1985 won)

	1978	1979	1980	1981	1982	1983	1984	1985	1986	1987	1988	1989	1990
Domestic liabilities													
Currency	2,928	2,911	2,618	2,354	2,790	3,013	3,186	3,286	3,580	4,196	4,525	5,120	5,385
Deposits	16,536	17,682	18,519	19,002	21,843	24,248	26,172	31,518	37,363	46,050	54,659	66,989	75,566
Deposit money banks	15,111	16,072	16,329	16,610	19,277	21,501	22,693	25,879	30,236	35,256	40,249	45,705	49,617
Demand	2,844	2,991	2,707	2,288	3,584	4,059	3,870	4,302	5,083	5,505	6,269	7,021	7,080
Time, savings and foreign exchange	11,183	11,983	12,306	13,582	15,291	16,933	18,324	21,001	24,354	28,495	32,425	36,949	40,552
Imports	706	672	870	688	304	320	294	359	706	1,233	1,493	1,073	808
Other	378	427	445	52	98	189	205	218	93	23	62	662	1,177
Other financial institutions	1,425	1,610	2,190	2,392	2,566	2,747	3,479	5,638	7,128	10,794	14,411	21,284	25,949
Private financial assets	19,464	20,593	21,136	21,355	24,633	27,261	29,358	34,803	40,944	50,246	59,184	72,109	80,951
M2	17,016	17,925	17,674	18,210	21,578	24,044	25,313	28,565	32,928	38,041	43,137	48,898	52,770
Money	5,824	5,942	5,368	4,628	6,287	7,110	6,988	7,558	8,573	9,546	10,711	11,948	12,216
Quasi-money	11,192	11,983	12,306	13,583	15,291	16,934	18,325	21,007	24,354	28,496	32,426	36,950	40,554
Domestic credit													
Central bank credit	6,235	6,778	6,110	6,596	7,096	8,376	10,036	11,778	13,183	16,714	17,008	16,284	17,107
Public sector	3,031	2,532	1,997	2,382	2,551	2,878	2,766	2,700	2,625	2,651	2,941	2,821	2,090
Deposit money banks[1]	3,205	4,245	4,112	4,214	4,545	5,497	7,270	9,078	10,558	14,063	14,066	13,463	15,017
Deposit money banks	18,705	21,879	23,924	25,008	29,788	33,635	37,749	43,344	48,729	54,250	57,157	66,751	76,953
Public sector	1,112	1,147	1,452	1,635	2,416	2,510	2,968	2,968	3,499	4,180	4,513	4,109	3,941
Private sector	17,594	20,732	22,472	23,373	27,372	31,124	34,781	40,376	45,230	50,070	52,644	62,642	73,012
Nonbank financial intermediaries	5,966	7,402	8,808	9,872	11,953	14,430	17,306	22,025	26,802	33,850	42,680	54,928	63,095
Public sector	94	94	102	131	165	180	258	286	207	129	19	53	83
Private sector	5,872	7,308	8,706	9,741	11,788	14,249	17,048	21,739	26,594	33,721	42,661	54,876	63,012
Money and capital markets													
Government bonds[2]	915	966	817	2,249	2,752	3,917	5,790	8,418	9,414	12,878	18,050	15,497	14,134
Traded stocks and bonds	9,825	6,476	4,281	5,648	10,053	5,668	5,637	7,142	11,768	23,803	49,836	67,893	41,043

Sources: IMF, *International Financial Statistics*; Bank of Korea, *Monthly Statistical Bulletin*.
[1]Loans to deposit money banks in domestic currency.
[2]Includes the monetary stabilization account, monetary stabilization bonds issued, and foreign exchange stabilization bonds issued.

Table 3.27. Korea: Interest Rate Structure

(In percent, end of year data)

	1978	1979	1980	1981	1982	1983	1984	1985	1986	1987	1988	1989	1990
Nominal													
Deposits[1]	18.6	18.6	19.5	16.2	8.0	8.0	9.2	10.0	10.0	10.0	10.0	10.0	10.0
Loans[2]	19.0	19.0	20.0	17.0	10.0	10.0	10.0	10.0	10.0	10.0	11.0	10.0	10.0
Loan (maximum)	. . .	. . .	. . .	. . .	. . .	. . .	11.5	13.0	12.0	12.0	13.0	13.0	13.0
Export loans[3]	9.0	9.0	15.0	15.0	10.5	10.0	10.0	10.0	10.0	10.0	10.1	12.0	12.0
Money market	19.3	18.8	22.8	18.1	14.1	13.0	11.3	9.3	9.7	8.9	9.6	13.7	15.0
Commercial paper[4]	. . .	. . .	. . .	39.7	14.0	13.0	12.5	12.0	12.1	11.9	10.0	. . .	. . .
CDs	. . .	. . .	. . .	. . .	. . .	. . .	11.0	11.7	11.0	10.7	11.0	11.0	13.0
Curb market	41.2	42.4	44.9	35.3	32.9	25.8	24.8	24.0	23.10	. . .	. . .	. . .	. . .
Real[5]													
Deposits[1]	4.0	0.5	–7.3	–3.9	0.9	4.8	7.0	7.8	6.8	6.8	2.8	4.0	1.3
Loans[2]	4.3	0.8	–6.9	–3.3	2.8	6.8	7.8	7.8	6.8	6.8	3.7	4.0	1.3
Curb market	23.8	20.6	12.3	11.8	24.2	22.1	22.3	21.5	19.5	. . .	. . .	. . .	. . .
Inflation (CPI)	14.0	18.0	29.0	21.0	7.0	3.0	2.0	2.0	3.0	3.0	7.0	5.7	8.5
Spreads													
Loan-deposit[6]	0.4	0.4	0.5	0.8	2.0	2.0	2.3	3.0	2.0	2.0	3.0	3.0	3.0
Curb market-deposit	22.6	23.8	25.4	19.1	24.9	17.8	15.6	14.0	13.1	. . .	. . .	. . .	. . .
Deposit maturities[7]	4.1	0.0	–1.8	1.4	–1.9	0.4	3.2	4.0	4.0	4.0	4.0	4.0	4.0
Loan maturities[8]	. . .	1 – 1	1 – 1	1 – 1	. . .	0 – 0	0 –1.5	0 – 1	0 – 0	0 – 0	0 – 0	. . .	. . .
Deposit-LIBOR[9]	9.7	6.5	–23.8	–14.8	–13.6	–8.4	–6.0	–7.0	1.7	5.0	11.4	9.0	–7.25

Sources: IMF, *International Financial Statistics*; Bank of Korea, *Monthly Statistical Bulletin*; for curb market rates, Cho and Cole (1986).

[1]Ceiling rate on one-year term deposits.

[2]Rate for one-year loans extended to "other than superior enterprises." After 1984, data represent minimum loan rate.

[3]Subsidized rate on export-related investments.

[4]Interest rate of Grade (A) CDs. Rates reported are those effective at the date of the last central bank directive for year. As of December 1988, CDs have been merged with investment and finance companies' bills sold without recourse.

[5]Real rate = (1 + nominal) / (1 + inflation – 1).

[6]Between 1984–90, loan rate used is the maximum loan rate.

[7]Difference between long-term (more than one year) and short-term (6–12 months) deposit rates.

[8]Difference between loan rates of maturities: (3 to 8 and 1 to 3 years)-(8 to 10 and 3 to 8 years).

[9]Three-months dollar LIBOR rate adjusted for actual devaluation. Adjustment formula: (1 + LIBOR) * (1 + devaluation) – 1.

Table 3.28. Korea: Selected Financial Indicators

	1976	1978	1980	1981	1982	1983	1984	1985	1986	1987	1988	1989	1990
	(In millions of 1985 won)												
Private financial assets	13,471	19,464	21,136	21,355	24,633	27,261	29,358	34,803	40,944	50,246	59,184	72,109	80,951
Currency	1,832	2,928	2,618	2,354	2,790	3,013	3,186	3,286	3,580	4,196	4,525	5,120	5,385
Deposits	11,640	16,536	18,519	19,002	21,843	24,248	26,172	31,518	37,363	46,050	54,659	66,989	75,566
Financial sector credit to private sector	15,537	23,465	31,178	33,113	39,160	45,374	51,829	62,116	71,825	83,791	95,305	117,518	136,024
Central bank credit to deposit money banks	1,858	3,205	4,112	4,214	4,545	5,497	7,270	9,078	10,558	14,063	14,066	13,463	15,017
	(In percent)												
Private financial assets/GDP	35.57	37.28	39.41	38.70	41.74	40.74	39.44	42.41	43.94	47.45	50.43	57.97	58.71
M2/GDP	30.04	32.59	32.95	33.00	36.56	35.93	34.01	34.81	35.34	35.92	36.76	39.31	38.27
Currency/deposits	15.74	17.71	14.13	12.39	12.77	12.43	12.17	10.42	9.58	9.11	8.28	7.64	7.13
Credit to private sector/GDP	40.49	44.94	58.13	60.01	66.35	67.81	69.63	75.69	77.09	79.12	81.21	94.47	98.65
Proportion of deposit money bank credit financed by central bank	15.52	18.22	18.30	18.03	16.61	17.66	20.90	22.48	23.34	28.09	26.72	21.49	20.57
Change in M2/Gross domestic savings	32.55	29.30	29.29	27.67	31.05	16.62	7.97	15.00	15.80	15.26	16.49	17.47	15.04
Gross domestic savings/GDP	23.15	28.82	23.84	23.87	25.04	28.59	30.53	31.35	34.82	37.68	39.44	37.21	37.30
Real GDP growth rates	12.89	9.71	–2.16	6.72	7.30	11.78	9.41	6.93	11.55	11.52	11.27	6.38	9.51
Real deposit rates (in percent)	1.04	4.04	–7.36	–3.97	0.93	4.85	7.06	7.84	6.80	6.80	2.80	4.07	1.31
Gross interest rate margin (in percent)	1.80	0.40	0.50	0.80	2.00	2.00	2.30	3.00	2.00	2.00	3.08	3.00	3.00
Total number of banking institutions	534[1]	. . .	767	. . .	992	. . .	. . .	1,315	. . .	. . .	1,695	2,056	. . .

Sources: IMF, *International Financial Statistics*; and Bank of Korea, *Annual Report*.

[1]Figure for 1975.

Table 3.29. Philippines: Structure of Deposit Money Banks
(Number of institutions)

	1975		1980		1981		1986	
	Head offices	Total offices	Head offices	Total offices	Head offices	Total offices	Head offices	Total offices
Total banks	92	2,156	1,164	3,364	1,216	3,652	1,025	5,359
Commercial banks	33	996	32	1,503	33	1,732	301	1,765
Domestic owned[1]	33	996	28	1,499	29	1,728	26	1,712
Foreign owned	. . .	. . .	4	4	4	4	4	4
Thrifts	88	259	144	673	140	631	116	661
Rural banks	768	834	985	1,096	1,040	1,167	877	1,117
Specialized banks	3	67	3	92	3	122	2	100
Nonbanks[2]	. . .	. . .	. . .	. . .	. . .	. . .	1,820[3]	2,494

Source: Central Bank of the Philippines, *Annual Report*.
[1]Includes nine "unibanks" in 1986.
[2]Includes nonstock savings and loans associations, mutual building and loan associations, and private insurance companies.
[3]Figure for 1982.

Table 3.30. Philippines: Development of the Financial Sector

(In billions of pesos; end of year)

										Annual Average Growth Rate (in percent)	
	1975	1980	1981	1982	1983	1984	1985	1986	1987[1]	1975–81[2]	1982–86
Gross assets of the financial sector	123	315	362	432	554	694	755	731	743	18	16
Central bank	26	65	72	92	131	206	252	314	316	15	35
Commercial banks	53	138	164	191	248	289	283	249	254	20	10
Privately owned	35	85	103	111	142	161	168	167	178	20	11
Government owned	18	35	41	53	65	80	70	35	29	16	2
Foreign owned	. . .	19	21	27	41	48	45	47	47	. . .	19
Thrifts	2	11	12	13	16	15	15	18	17	24	8
Rural banks	3	6	7	8	10	9	9	9	10	16	7
Specialized banks	12	34	43	53	65	79	88	29	27	25	2
Nonbank financial intermediaries	27	60	64	75	93	96	108	113	119	12	12
Insurance	12	30	33	41	45	50	61	71	75	15	17
Investment companies	10	26	24	26	25	20	24	23	24	7	—
Trust banks	3	2	1	1	2	1	2	1	2	–29	20
Other	2	2	6	7	21	25	21	18	18	100	41
Money and financial markets											
Total value of money market transactions	. . .	. . .	. . .	942	1,111	. . .	506	520	. . .	. . .	. . .
Total value of stock market transactions	. . .	. . .	. . .	2	10	. . .	12	58	. . .	. . .	. . .

Sources: World Bank (1988); Central Bank of the Philippines, *Annual Report.*

[1]June 1987.

[2]A constant annual rate of growth was assumed for 1975–80.

Table 3.31. Philippines: Interest Rate Structure
(Percent per year)

	1976	1977	1978	1979	1980	1981	1982	1983	1984	1985	1986	1987	1988
Nominal													
Time deposit (2–3 months)	8.5	8.5	8.5	8.6	12.2	13.7	13.7	13.5	21.1	18.9	11.2	8.2	11.3
Loan[1]	12.0	12.0	12.0	14.0	14.0	15.3	18.1	19.2	28.2	28.6	17.5	13.3	15.9
CBP discount rate	6.0	6.0	4.0	11.0	4.5	6.6	6.3	8.0	12.1	11.5	9.6	9.0	8.9
Call money rate	. . .	12.0	10.5	13.6	11.9	15.5	12.3	16.6	28.3	16.9	12.2	11.8	14.2
Treasury bill (3 months)	0.2	10.9	10.9	12.3	12.2	12.5	13.8	14.2	28.6	26.7	16.1	11.6	14.7
Real[2]													
Time deposit (2–3 months)	–0.6	–1.2	1.0	–7.5	–5.0	0.5	3.1	3.2	–19.4	–3.4	10.4	4.2	2.3
Loan[1]	2.5	1.9	4.3	–3.0	–3.5	1.9	7.1	8.3	–14.7	4.4	16.6	9.2	6.5
CBP discount rate	–2.9	–3.5	–3.1	–5.5	–11.5	–5.6	–3.5	–1.8	–25.4	–9.4	8.8	5.1	0.1
Call money rate	1.9	2.9	–3.3	–5.3	2.1	1.8	5.9	–14.6	–5.0	11.3	7.7	5.0	. . .
Treasury bill (3 months)	0.9	0.9	3.3	–4.4	–5.0	–0.5	3.2	3.7	–14.4	2.9	15.2	7.5	5.4
Inflation (CPI)	9.2	9.9	7.3	17.5	18.2	13.0	10.2	10.0	50.3	23.1	0.7	3.7	8.7
Spreads													
Loan—Call money	. . .	. . .	1.5	0.4	2.1	–0.1	5.8	2.6	–0.1	11.7	5.3	1.5	1.7
Loan—Time deposit	3.5	3.5	3.5	5.3	1.7	1.6	4.3	5.6	7.0	9.7	6.2	5.1	4.6
Loan—Discount	6.0	6.0	8.0	3.0	9.4	8.6	11.8	11.1	16.0	17.1	7.9	4.2	6.9
Loan—Treasury bill	1.8	1.1	1.1	1.7	1.8	2.8	4.3	5.0	–0.4	1.9	1.4	1.7	1.2
Deposit yield curve[3]	. . .	. . .	. . .	. . .	5.0/NA	5.0/NA	4.3/2.8	4.0/2.3	13.3/3.0	11/0.0	3.7/3.3	. . .	. . .
Deposit—LIBOR[4]	0.1	2.9	0.1	3.6	4.0	–9.1	–8.7	–29.1	–45.5	–1.8	–5.8	0.0	0.5

Source: IMF, *International Financial Statistics*; IMF/IBRD (1980); World Bank (1986).

[1]Average loan rates for all maturities charged by deposit money banks.

[2]Deflated by CPI inflation using: real = (1 + nominal) / (1 + inflation) – 1.

[3]Difference between deposit rates of maturities: (Savings – 1-year deposit) / (2-year deposit – 1–year deposit).

[4]Three-month dollar LIBOR adjusted for actual devaluation. Adjustment formula: (1 + LIBOR) * (1 + devaluation) – 1.

Table 3.32. Philippines: Selected Financial Indicators

	1976	1978	1980	1981	1982	1983	1984	1985	1986	1987	1988
					(In millions of 1985 pesos)						
Total financial assets[1]	. . .	. . .	. . .	. . .	316,879	337,733	238,929	240,828	270,887	320,114	. . .
M3	197,897	252,704	272,404	273,432	281,242	302,569	212,955	184,528	178,482	195,223	220,536
Currency	23,509	28,685	25,833	26,092	25,821	36,287	26,834	24,072	29,093	33,902	35,807
Deposits	174,389	224,019	246,571	247,340	255,422	266,282	186,121	160,456	149,388	161,321	184,729
Financial sector credit to private sector	172,767	225,387	243,561	298,579	310,276	359,164	240,884	154,700	104,053	121,892	132,074
Central bank credit to financial institutions[2]	27,240	34,157	53,209	60,716	62,770	70,166	58,377	51,476	22,678	22,295	20,887
						(In percent)					
Private financial assets/GDP	. . .	. . .	. . .	. . .	45.69	47.51	35.91	39.31	43.52	47.26	. . .
M3/GDP	35.17	40.34	40.55	39.91	40.55	42.56	32.01	30.12	28.67	28.82	30.31
M2/GDP	21.54	27.82	30.03	28.77	30.17	33.58	27.67	26.11	25.30	25.62	27.23
Currency/deposits	13.48	12.80	10.48	10.55	10.11	13.63	14.42	15.00	19.47	21.02	19.38
Credit to private sector/GDP	30.71	35.98	36.26	43.58	44.74	50.53	36.21	25.25	16.72	17.99	18.15
Proportion of financial institution credit financed by the central bank	12.82	12.62	18.62	17.91	17.47	16.98	20.49	25.31	14.41	13.68	11.50
Excess reserves (avg.)/required reserves	. . .	. . .	5.00	2.30	3.78	–1.43	–1.50	–7.52	–11.41	0.82	. . .
Change in M2/Gross domestic savings	. . .	26.12	28.43	11.35	19.58	30.28	20.15	10.45	–1.25	18.41	29.63
Gross domestic savings/GDP	25.86	23.94	24.73	24.07	22.43	22.55	18.85	16.26	16.53	17.49	17.88
Real GDP growth rates	7.92	7.33	2.92	2.00	1.23	2.49	–6.40	–7.91	1.59	8.83	7.39
Real deposit rate	–0.64	1.09	–5.03	0.56	3.19	3.23	–19.40	–3.40	10.42	4.25	2.35
Gross interest rate margin	3.50	3.50	1.75	1.62	4.38	5.66	7.02	9.70	6.28	5.14	4.61

Sources: IMF, *International Financial Statistics*; IMF/IBRD (1980); World Bank (1986); Central Bank of Philippines, *Annual Report;* Nascimento (1990).

[1]Includes nonbank holding of government and central bank securities.

[2]For 1983–86, includes financial institutions' reserve deficiencies.

Table 3.33. Philippines: Summary of Financial Sector Operations
(In millions of 1985 pesos)

	1976	1978	1980	1981	1982	1983	1984	1985	1986	1987	1988
Currency	23,509	28,685	25,833	26,092	25,821	36,287	26,834	24,072	29,093	33,902	35,807
Deposits of: money banks	151,259	196,135	215,210	214,932	222,757	239,457	174,079	146,895	136,168	146,510	167,044
Demand	26,715	31,068	31,379	26,707	22,023	23,841	14,570	11,710	13,247	16,190	16,551
Time and savings	53,863	82,503	83,489	94,526	112,422	117,275	94,048	88,405	93,159	99,249	117,267
Foreign currency	17,087	32,031	61,009	49,758	48,990	61,320	48,617	35,755	21,964	24,186	28,455
Deposit substitutes	45,225	40,529	31,399	36,926	33,734	31,658	12,769	8,609	4,839	3,821	2,228
Import	8,369	10,003	7,934	7,014	5,588	5,363	4,073	2,416	2,959	3,065	2,543
Other financial institutions											
Time and savings deposits	23,130	27,884	31,361	32,408	32,665	26,824	12,042	13,561	13,221	14,810	17,685
Private financial assets[1]	...	...	...	316,879	337,733	238,929	240,020	270,007	320,114	...	...
M3	197,897	252,704	272,404	273,432	281,242	302,569	212,955	184,528	178,482	195,223	220,536
M2	121,174	174,287	201,709	197,084	209,256	238,722	184,070	159,942	157,464	173,527	198,080
Money	50,224	59,753	57,212	52,799	47,844	60,128	41,404	35,782	42,341	50,092	52,358
Quasi-money	70,950	114,534	144,498	144,284	161,412	178,594	142,665	115,123	123,434	145,722	
Domestic credit											
Central bank credit	46,185	57,863	74,395	89,932	102,550	128,214	102,520	87,741	79,770	68,646	57,680
Public sector[2]	18,946	23,706	21,186	29,216	39,780	58,468	44,482	37,790	59,376	46,351	36,793
Financial sector	27,240	34,157	53,209	60,716	62,770	69,746	58,038	49,951	20,395	22,295	20,887
Commercial banks	17,798	20,656	35,757	39,779	37,265	32,475	23,792	21,901	10,960	13,804	13,955
Other financial institutions	9,442	13,501	17,452	20,937	25,505	37,272	34,246	28,050	9,435	8,491	6,932
Deposit money banks credit	161,815	206,343	237,720	250,980	267,027	303,707	210,362	151,135	123,259	141,251	150,226
Public sector[2]	31,436	36,530	35,364	33,265	42,869	46,871	38,803	35,795	34,719	36,277	44,928
Private sector	130,379	169,813	202,357	217,715	224,158	258,916	171,559	115,340	88,540	104,974	113,298
Other financial institutions	50,719	64,397	48,024	88,033	92,203	104,949	72,932	46,209	18,272	21,754	23,419
Public sector[2]	8,331	8,822	6,820	7,169	6,085	4,701	3,607	6,849	2,758	4,836	4,643
Private sector	42,388	55,575	41,204	80,864	86,119	100,248	69,326	39,360	15,513	16,918	18,775

Source: IMF, *International Financial Statistics.*
[1]Total financial assets include M3 and the nonbank holdings of government securities.
[2]Includes holdings of government securities.

Table 3.34. Philippines: Indicators of the Financial Crisis

	1970	1975	1980	1981	1982[1]	1983	1984	1985	1986	1987
Number of bank failures[2]	6	7	24	30	8	7	26	44	26	22
Commercial banks	3	1	—	—	—	—	—	2	—	1
Thrift banks	. . .	. . .	—	4	2	1	16	6	—	3
Failed bank assets/total assets (in percent)										
Commercial banks	1.9	1.0	—	—	—	—	—	1.2	—	4.0
Thrift banks	5.2	—	—	0.4	0.3	1.3	10.8	35.4	—	5.0
Rural banks	0.3	0.3	1.1	1.2	0.2	0.2	0.4	1.9	1.4	1.0
Past due loans (in percent of total)										
All financial institutions	16.7	19.2	11.5	13.2	13.0	8.9	12.7	16.7	19.3	. . .
Commercial banks	. . .	. . .	11.9	13.1	11.5	7.5	11.0	15.6	18.4	. . .
Capital/outstanding loans (in percent)[3]	. . .	. . .	12.1	13.6	14.4	12.9	16.7	16.1	17.7	. . .
Number of bank deposit accounts (in millions)	. . .	5.3	21.0	22.6	24.9	25.6	23.7	20.2	19.5	18.6
Commercial banks	. . .	. . .	10.1	13.3	15.1	15.2	14.0	12.6	12.4	11.8
Thrift banks	. . .	3.3	7.2	5.1	5.5	5.8	5.0	3.1	2.7	2.5

Source: Nascimento (1990).

[1]Data are from the month of June.

[2]For 1970 and 1975, data refer to cumulative amounts during 1970–74 and 1975–79, respectively. Data on bank failures exclude the five commercial banks in distress that have been acquired by government financial institutions.

[3]Capital defined as "net worth" or unimpaired capital plus free reserves.

Table 3.35. Philippines: Determinants of Financial Sector Credit
(Annual changes in ratios to GDP; in percent)

	1984	1985	Total 1984–85
Total financial sector credit	–15.20	–10.43	–25.63
Public credit	–0.88	0.53	–0.35
Private credit	–14.32	–10.96	–25.28
Supply of loanable funds	–7.30	–1.09	–8.39
Domestic currency deposits	–6.20	–0.72	–6.92
Central bank credit to the financial sector	–1.10	–0.37	–1.47
Total investment	–9.75	–1.56	–11.30
Private fixed investment	–3.21	–0.78	–3.99
Public fixed investment	–3.20	–1.46	–4.66
Changes in stocks	–3.34	0.68	2.65
Contraction of financial sector credit relative to:			
Supply of loanable funds	–7.90	–9.34	–17.24
Total investment	–5.45	–8.87	–14.33
Memorandum:			
Private financial assets	–9.64	2.99	–6.65

Source: IMF, *International Financial Statistics.*

4

Prudential Supervision, Bank Restructuring, and Financial Sector Refom

V. SUNDARARAJAN

Recent debates on the appropriate pace of financial sector liberalization have highlighted the issue of how best to sequence the reforms of prudential supervision and bank restructuring policies (see Sundararajan, 1992; and Alexander, Baliño, and Enoch, 1995). In addition, the growing globalization of financial markets has underscored the importance of strengthening prudential supervision and related information systems to deal effectively with interest rate and exchange rate risks, and other banking risks, particularly in the context of capital account liberalization.[1] It is by now widely recognized that weak and inefficient banking systems are more vulnerable to contagion, less able to cope with volatile capital flows and exchange market pressures, and more likely to propagate and magnify the effects of financial crises on other economies. This recognition has highlighted the need for global adoption of strengthened standards for banking

Note: An earlier version of this chapter was issued in 1996 as IMF Working Paper 96/128, "The Role of Prudential Supervision and Financial Restructuring of Banks During Transition to Indirect Instruments of Monetary Control."

[1]See "Benefits of Capital Flows Tied to Strong Risk Management" in the June 19, 1995 issue of *IMF Survey*.

supervision.[2] The appropriate sequencing of banking restructuring and supervision policies has also become a pressing issue in many developing countries and economies in transition, where a large part of the banking system is undercapitalized or insolvent, in part reflecting major macroeconomic shocks, large structural changes, and weak banking supervision. The resulting distress in the banking system has, in turn, complicated monetary management and affected the effectiveness of stabilization policies.[3]

In this context, it has been suggested that the development of a sound banking system and of well-functioning prudential supervision arrangements should precede the adoption of market-based monetary arrangements (see Villanueva and Mirakhor, 1990; and Mathieson and Haas, 1994). The rationale for this argument is that in insolvent banking systems, adverse selection and moral hazards could distort the impact of market-based instruments—such as the treasury bill auctions and credit auctions—and exacerbate instability. This chapter argues that except in extreme cases of systematic bank insolvencies and widespread fragility of the nonfinancial sector, the moral hazard and adverse selection risks are best handled by appropriate and timely sequencing of specific supervisory policies and bank restructuring schemes and by the appropriate design of market-based monetary instruments and money market development policies. The design and sequencing of these monetary and prudential measures should take into account the technical interlinkages among these measures, as well as their impact on stabilization and market development goals. With the appropriate sequencing of banking supervision policies and financial restructuring measures, indirect instruments of monetary policy could be adopted rapidly to support stabilization objectives.

In practice, however, proper sequencing of prudential and bank restructuring policies has proven difficult to implement. For example, actions to restructure bank portfolios or close weak banks tend to get delayed in most countries, because of high fiscal costs, likely monetary

[2]See "All Countries Share in Effects of Globalization" in the July 15, 1996 issue of *IMF Survey*.

[3]For a discussion of macroeconomic consequences of financial distress, see World Bank (1989) and Sheng (1991). For a more specific discussion of bank and enterprise restructuring in transitional economies, see Borish, Long, and Noël (1995), Long and Rutkowska (1995).

or systemic consequences, inadequate regulatory framework, captive connections between banks and their borrowers, and, in many instances, inadequate information on the magnitude of loan losses. Often, regulators lack incentives for prompt action and might suppress information so as to postpone or lessen pressures from the market, as noted by Kane (1987 and 1992). Also, the presence and persistence of large weaknesses in banks' balance sheets have also affected the effective and uniform enforcement of prudential norms, further delaying the process of strengthening banking supervision. The delays have magnified loan losses, raised the vulnerability of the financial system to macroeconomic and structural shocks, and required different degrees of government intervention to prevent systemic crises.

Such a process and the close two-way interaction between the soundness of the banking system and macroeconomic stability are discussed in Sundararajan and Baliño (1991), where several banking crisis episodes of the mid-eighties are analyzed. Worldwide experience with financial fragility, examined in Lindgren, Garcia, and Saal (1996), also confirms the earlier lessons, and highlights the importance of a sound banking sector for macroeconomic stability and of the efficient implementation of stabilization programs.

In light of these findings, this chapter considers whether a mix of financial restructuring and supervisory policies could be devised that could be rapidly implemented with available information systems at modest fiscal cost, consistent with medium-term restructuring needs. The rationale is that by avoiding costly delays in initiating a bank-restructuring process, the scope for effective implementation of both prudential supervision and market-based monetary management improves, and major risks to macroeconomic stability are avoided, while gaining time to institute medium-term restructuring measures and spread over time the budgetary costs of restructuring.

Sequencing of Banking Restructuring and Prudential Supervision Policies

Various components of financial sector reforms and the issues in the appropriate sequencing of these reforms are discussed in Chapters 3 and 6. This section focuses on the sequencing of specific measures to restructure banks, strengthen prudential supervision, and contain systemic risk during the transition to market-based instruments and fully liberalized interest rates.

Moving toward greater flexibility in interest rates and eventual liberalization requires parallel or prior reforms of the financial sector, including reforms in many central banking functions. In general, successful interest rate liberalization—that is, successful management of interest rates through indirect instruments—is associated with several factors: a relatively stable macroeconomic environment; an interest rate structure that is not in serious disequilibrium prior to liberalization; adequate competition in the banking sector; reasonable financial strength in the banking sector; an active and well-functioning money market supported by a sound payment system; monetary policy instruments that are flexible and effective in influencing the marginal cost of fund to banks; and sufficiently strong banking supervision policies and instruments.[4]

The various groups of policies and reforms mentioned above have to be implemented in an orderly sequence—some measures simultaneously and others sequentially to reflect various technical and operational linkages among specific reform measures and to sustain stabilization efforts. In particular, the transition from direct controls on interest rates and credit toward indirect instruments involves a simultaneous pursuit of measures to develop market-based instruments and foster money and government securities markets. Effective implementation of this transition process requires supporting reforms in banking supervision and banking restructuring.

Country Experiences

The importance of early attention to prudential supervision of banks in the course of the stabilization-cum-reform process, as well as the crucial role of timely intervention in problem banks, has again been underscored by the episodes of financial distress and crises in the 1990s in several countries (see Table 4.1). In particular, the large magnitude of loan losses recorded in these countries suggest that potential gains from a more orderly sequencing of policy implementation are significant. In some of the countries, despite seemingly sound banking

[4]See Leite and Sundararajan (1990) for a discussion of concomitant reforms in support of interest rate liberalization.

Table 4.1. Features of Recent Banking Crises: An Overview

Country and Crisis Period	Magnitude of Losses	Resolution Methods	Financial Sector Reforms	Macroeconomic Factors
Indonesia, 1992–93	Nonperforming loans estimated at 26 percent of total loans by the end of 1993, about $18.4 billion or 13 percent of GNP. One private bank closed; 26 private banks considered insolvent; major weaknesses discovered in state bank loan portfolio.[1]	Restructured and recapitalized state-owned banks with borrowed funds. Closed or merged private banks with some central bank financial support. No formal deposit insurance was enacted, resulting in some losses to depositors. Made special efforts to recover loans from large borrowers. Held special audits of private banks and special supervision teams to monitor problem . loans	Interest rates liberalized and indirect instruments adopted in 1983. Entry eased and selective credit abolished in 1988. Measures to strengthen banking supervision increased in 1991–92. Weaknesses have been addressed in bank liquidation rules and loan recovery arrangement through new regulations in 1995. Prudential controls eased in May 1993 to encourage bank lending.	Boom in investment and credit growth following 1988 financial sector and investment liberalization. Major tightening of monetary policy andhigh real interest rates in 1992–93.
Nordic countries, 1990–92	The state absorbed loan losses of between 5 percent and 7 percent of GNP by recapitalization and liquidity support. Large number of banks faced liquidity crisis; depletion of capital and loss of public confidence occurred.	Public guarantee of all deposits. Government takeover of failed banks. Formation of "bad banks"—asset management companies—to deal with . problem loans	Credit control and interest rates liberalized in mid-1980s. Insufficient attention to strengthening capital adequacy and prudential supervision.	Major expansion in credit/GNP ratio following deregulation. Major shifts in real interest rates and real exchange rates, and asset price inflation. High debt equity ratio of nonfinancial firms.
Turkey, 1994	Large short positions in foreign exchange and excessive depreciation of domestic currency led to losses and runs. Losses in government securities portfolio occurred	Expanded coverage of savings deposit insurance to 100 percent of deposits. Increased limits on central bank credit to individual banks.	Interest rates liberalized and indirect instruments adopted in mid-1980s, and competition strengthened.	Major macroeconomic factors during 1994 included instability, high and growing fiscal deficit, accelerating inflation, high real interest

	as interest rates rose. Three mid-sized banks closed down. While financial distress was reportedly widespread and bank profitability weak, the magnitude of losses is unclear.	Arranged for temporary administrators to oversee pay-off to eligible depositors. Deposit insurance fund to initiate bankruptcy procedures Established weaknesses in problem bank resolution options.	Some initial bank restructuring and measures to strengthen banking supervision implemented in mid-1980s. Sophisticated off-site analysis and early warning system established. Limited reforms of state-owned banks that provided subsidized credit. Inadequate bank accounting standards revised.	rates, and foreign exchange crisis.
Venezuela, 1994	Loan losses absorbed by the state through recapitalization and liquidity support totaled $9 billion in 1994, 13 percent of GNP. Three waves of bank runs, involving nearly 50 percent of the banking system in terms of deposits, triggered massive government intervention.	Government took over several failed banks. Provided large, unconditional liquidity assistance to some. Closed some banks after paying off insured depositors. Management control altered so as to work out a restructuring plan.	Interest rates liberalized and indirect instruments adopted in 1989. Major portfolio weaknesses, which developed prior to 1989 when direct controls severely distorted credit allocation, were allowed to continue. New laws to strengthen banking supervision became effective in late 1993. Prior to their establishment, enforcement of banking supervision had been weak, with significant weaknesses in accounting standards, coordination among supervisory agencies, and supervisory practices.	Significant stabilization efforts during 1989–90 were reversed in 1990–91. The lax financial policies contributed to boom in asset prices and periodic capital flights, and exchange crisis in October 1992. Fiscal deficit remained unsustainably high in 1993; monetary policy erratic; very high real interest rates in 1992–93.

Sources: Drees and Pazarbaşıoğlu (1995); Garcia (1995); and Lindgren, Garcia, and Saal (1996).

[1]Following the 1997 currency and banking crisis, the extent of the losses and the magnitude of banking insolvency were estimated to be considerably larger. For example, Moody's estimated nonperforming loans at 30–75 percent of total loans (see Moody's Investors Service, 1998).

supervision systems, significant weaknesses in the enforcement or in the design of specific regulations contributed to or exacerbated the crises (e.g., Indonesia, Turkey, and Venezuela).[5] In many countries, no significant efforts were made to address the weak balance sheets of banks at the start of the financial liberalization process, a factor that magnified subsequent losses and complicated stabilization efforts (e.g., Indonesia and Venezuela). Also, as noted in Lindgren, Garcia, and Saal (1996), nearly two-thirds of IMF member countries have experienced significant banking problems since 1980. While banking crises pose a threat to stability, owing to their fiscal and monetary impact, they also reduce real economic growth significantly (Chapter 5).

The experience of economies in transition also illustrates the significant impact of the pace and sequencing of bank restructuring and supervision policies on macroeconomic performance and financial market development. In Eastern and Central Europe, bank restructuring policies—recapitalization with government funds (Hungary, Czechoslovakia, and Poland), the carving out of bad loans (Poland and Czech Republic), and conversion of enterprise debt to equity (Bulgaria and Croatia)—have been implemented in varying degrees since 1991 (Dittus, 1994). The restructuring policies were not always initiated at the outset of reform and in some countries they were not comprehensively implemented. Nevertheless, in many countries these efforts have helped over time to foster institutional development of banks and greater efficiency in credit allocation, and have generally helped to avoid major systemic crises so far.[6] The process of bank and enterprise restructuring has only just begun in the Baltics, Russia, and other states of the former Soviet Union in response to the impact of stabilization policies and privatization initiatives (Borish, Long, and Noël, 1995; and Long and Rutkowska, 1995). While two Baltic countries have already faced major banking crises, states of the former Soviet Union are experiencing significant distress in the banking system, requiring prompt restructuring actions and supervisory reforms to avoid risks to sustained economic recovery and stabilization.

[5]See de Juan (1995) for a discussion of pitfalls in the enforcement of prudential supervision and bank restructuring schemes. In many countries, international standards are adopted without adjusting these standards to specific economic circumstances—see Dziobek, Frécaut, and Nieto (1995); and Kane (1995).

[6]There were, of course, many individual bank failures, and widespread bank insolvencies have surfaced in some countries (e.g., Bulgaria).

These experiences with banking fragility continue to reinforce the lesson that the connection, if any, between financial sector reform and financial crises derives from an unstable macroeconomic environment where large changes in relative prices and in macroeconomic policies can influence the viability of borrowers. The connection between reform and crises stems from several common deficiencies in the financial structure, including unsound liability structures of nonfinancial firms prior to reform; a flawed institutional structure of banking that facilitated risk taking; and defective prudential regulation and banking supervision that condoned excessive risk taking. (Unsound liability structures resulted from subsidized credit, a lack of equity markets, tax policies favoring debt, and similar issues, and, following reform, from insider loans, interest capitalization, excessive workout lending, and the like.) Thus, inadequate prudential policies and enforcement procedures interacted with macroeconomic and relative price imbalances in the course of financial reform, and this combination contributed to excessive increases in interest rates in some cases, partially reflecting excessive risk taking by banks. These factors further weakened credit quality, contributed to an increasing volume of loan losses, and threatened the sustainability of stabilization efforts by creating excessive demand on central bank credit from banks that faced solvency and liquidity problems. Thus, the effectiveness of financial liberalization has required sustained efforts toward stabilization, while the simultaneous pursuit of both liberalization and stabilization has required the proper design and enforcement of bank restructuring and prudential supervision policies in order to avoid major disruptions to growth and stability.

The recent currency crisis in Asia has, once again, highlighted the linkages between financial sector weaknesses and macroeconomic performance. A distinguishing aspect of these recent experiences was the finding that weak banking systems can threaten macroeconomic stability, even in the context of macroeconomic policies that were generally considered sound. In Asia, underlying structural weaknesses in the financial sector went undetected, in part because of the interlinkages between the banks and their borrowers and in part because of explicit and implicit guarantees, which meant that depositors and lenders were not vigilant with regard to the banking risks. These underlying weaknesses were exposed and exacerbated by a weakening external situation—initially the widening of current account deficits, followed by a surge in private capital outflows—that resulted in sharp adjustments in interest rates and exchange rates, which had significant effects on the value of real and financial assets and on banking soundness. As in other country experiences reviewed here, attention to appropriate risk management procedures, the strengthening of capital standards, and enforcement of basic supervisory arrangements could have helped to reduce the financial frigidity and improve the capacity of the financial system and the economy more generally to deal with the external shocks.

Sequencing of Banking Supervision and Restructuring

In light of this conclusion, Box 4.1 provides a three-stage stylized sequencing of prudential supervision and banking restructuring policies during the transition process.[7] It emphasizes that, to ensure successful transition toward full interest rate flexibility, specific groups of reforms of prudential regulations and supervision systems should be implemented early in the process (see Stages 1 and 2 of Box 4.1), and should be coordinated with monetary and exchange management and market development policies. Thus, the scope and content of prudential supervision would continuously evolve along with the development of markets and internal governance of financial market participants. In addition, financial restructuring policies to deal with problem loans and enterprises should also be phased in appropriately to support interest rate liberalization, beginning with some initial restructuring measures in Stage 1.[8] Specific configuration of measures in

[7]This three-stage categorization is based on Sundararajan (1994) and Alexander, Baliño, and Enoch (1995). Stages are used for analytical convenience and do not signify that the steps listed in different stages cannot be implemented simultaneously if technically feasible, or that reforms should be gradual rather than rapid.

[8]The role of deposit insurance reforms is not addressed in this chapter, since it poses a difficult dilemma in sequencing. Arguably, the introduction of deposit insurance in the presence of widespread insolvencies in the banking system is not desirable. Yet in cases of crises, deposit insurance becomes desirable to prevent contagion. This raises complex issues in the appropriate design and sequencing of deposit insurance in relation to bank restructuring and bank supervision policies. It could be argued that deposit insurance should be limited in coverage to small depositors and should be introduced only in late stages of financial reform when banks have been restructured and supervision has been strengthened. For a discussion of these issues, see "All Countries Share in Effects of Globalization" in the July 15, 1996 issue of *IMF Survey*.

various stages, particularly at the initial stage, would depend upon a variety of country specific factors, such as the extent of disintermediation, extent of state ownership of banking, degree of openness, adequacy of laws on collateral, bankruptcy, and strength of the court system. The challenge is to ensure that regulatory reforms and restructuring measures support market development and do not stifle market initiatives and well-managed risk taking.

Preparatory Stage

The task of strengthening banking supervision and cleaning up bank balance sheets is an extended process that requires considerable resources as well as technical preparations. Therefore, only key elements of banking supervision can be effectively introduced in the initial stage. Similarly, only a minimal program of financial restructuring to address the most pressing impediments to interest rate flexibility is feasible—possibly even desirable—in the preparatory stage. At this stage, prompt attention to the legal and organizational basis of banking and banking supervision is likely to set the stage for a more competitive banking environment and more comprehensive reforms of prudential supervision in the subsequent phases of financial liberalization. In particular, close attention should be paid to the adequacy of licensing policies, as well as to the framework for orderly liquidation or intervention in banks. Weaknesses in bank liquidation procedures—including loan recovery arrangements—have been a source of costly delays in many countries and hence such procedures should be in place early in the reform process. Indeed, policies that liberalize entry and streamline exit are best addressed jointly, in order to encourage financial discipline.

Avoiding excessive risk taking and ensuring adequate competition during financial liberalization require, in addition to setting up adequate banking supervision, appropriate measures to recapitalize and restructure banks or to liquidate those banks as needed.[9] Experience shows that a core program of financial restructuring should be initi-

[9]The importance of dealing with problem loans in the course of the move to market-based systems in economies in transition is stressed in Brainard (1990).

Box 4.1. Banking Supervision and Financial Restructuring During Various Stages of Financial Sector Reform

The sequencing of prudential supervision and banking restructuring reforms during the transition to indirect instruments can be divided into three stages. (Stages are used for analytical convenience and do not imply that the steps listed in different stages cannot be implemented simultaneously, if technically feasible.)

Stage 1: Preparatory

Preparatory stage for interest rate liberalization; direct controls on credit and interest rates dominate; limited liberalization of interest rates—for example, interbank rates—is initiated and the beginning stages of impediments to broader interest rate flexibility are dealt with.

- A minimal program of financial restructuring policies is introduced to deal with fixed-rate loans, selected nonperforming loans, capital adequacy, and subsidized selective credit.
- Legal and organizational arrangements for banking supervision are reviewed and adjusted.
- Licensing and entry regulations are strengthened. A framework for orderly intervention and liquidation of banks is put in place or streamlined.

Stage 2: Initiating market development

Direct controls on credit begin to be phased out; simple market-based instruments of monetary and exchange policy—for example, open-market-type operations based on treasury bill and credit auctions—begin to be used. Discount window and Lombard credit provide liquidity to money markets; efforts are made so that policy interest rates will be sufficiently flexible.

- Reform of commercial bank accounting and bank reporting systems are phased in to help enforce prudential norms and facilitate monetary analysis.
- Prudential regulations, particularly loan classification and provisioning, credit concentration limits, credit appraisal guidelines, and foreign exchange exposure rules begin to be phased in based on new accounting standards.
- Capital adequacy norms are strengthened and phased in, in line with bank restructuring strategy.

ated as part of the preparatory phase and a more comprehensive bank and enterprise restructuring should be continued subsequently. The design and phased implementation of financial restructuring poli-

- A strategy to combine off-site, on-site, and external audits is introduced, the balance among the components initially dictated by the availability of resources and technical assistance.
- Institutional development of banks is pursued actively; portfolio audits of major banks initiated.
- A comprehensive program of bank restructuring, bank liquidations, and loan recovery and loan workout arrangements is formulated. As part of this program, simple financial restructuring policies for banks—supported by enterprise financial restructuring—are implemented (e.g., policies to reduce the debt-equity ratio of nonfinancial firms and recapitalize banks through portfolio restructuring).

Stage 3: Strengthening financial markets

Money markets and secondary markets in government securities are strengthened through supporting reforms of institutional arrangements and payment systems; open-market operations become more active; foreign exchange markets are fostered. Central bank manages money market liquidity at its own initiative, and interest rates are fully flexible.

- Comprehensive reforms to foster bank and enterprise restructuring are continued systematically, in line with the program designed in Stage 2.
- Well-capitalized and well-supervised dealers in government securities (and money market instruments) are promoted as part of strengthening security market regulations and supervision.
- Reforms of bank accounting and prudential standards are completed.
- Financial risk management in payment systems is further strengthened.
- Reinforcement of supervision of asset-liability management (interest rate risks, liquidity management), internal controls, and management systems of banks is continued.
- Appropriate balance between off-site supervision, on-site inspection, and external audit is achieved through technical assistance and training.
- Risk implications of financial innovations and internationalization are monitored closely.

cies—measures that seek to influence and strengthen the balance sheet structure of banks and the debt-equity mix of enterprises—are two factors that are likely to greatly facilitate adjustments by borrowers and banks to the effects of higher interest rates and other stabilization measures.[10]

A minimal program of financial restructuring at the outset of reforms—or during the preparatory stage—would facilitate stabilization efforts. This is illustrated by the experience of several countries in Eastern Europe. These countries implemented policies to deal with the sizable share of low fixed-rate loans and some nonperforming loans at the outset of the transformation process so as to permit more active interest rate policies and more efficient credit allocation.[11] For example, in late 1989, the National Bank of Poland made major adjustments in the low fixed-rate loans inherited by banks from the previous monobank system to facilitate the liberalization of interest rates as part of a stabilization program. Interest rates on various fixed-rate loans for housing, agriculture, environmental projects, and the like were raised to ensure bank profitability (in the face of increases in market-determined deposit rates), but only part of the increase was to be serviced by the debtors, and the remainder was covered in part as a subsidy from the budget and in part as government-mandated loans to capitalize part of the higher interest due. In the Czech Republic, banks were assisted in 1991 by shifting some low-interest "inventory loans" into a separate consolidation bank (funded by banks themselves) and by injecting capital through a government agency. In Hungary, low-interest housing loans were replaced in 1989 by government securities, to help recapitalize the Savings Bank (part of the housing loans were written off in due course). In addition, in both Poland and the former state of Czechoslovakia, a large part of central bank credit to banks was rescheduled and converted to medium-term loans at the outset of the

[10]Financial restructuring should accompany or be linked to "real" or operational restructuring in terms of changes in management, physical assets, product mix, and other similar bank operation considerations. Discussion of real restructuring, including privatization that combines, in effect, real with financial restructuring, is beyond the scope of this chapter. The scope for phasing in financial restructuring policies early in the reform process and the relationship of such policies to real restructuring, which takes time to design and implement, are covered at greater length later in this chapter.

[11]Only debt restructuring and recapitalization initiated at the beginning of the stabilization-cum-reform program (1989–91) are dealt with in this section. Major financial restructuring programs implemented later on (1993–95) and alluded to in the previous section on country experiences are not discussed in detail in this chapter. For details, see Dittus (1994) and Borish, Long, and Noël (1995).

reforms so as to streamline central bank credit policies and facilitate monetary management.[12] Subsequent to the initial restructuring policies, more comprehensive policy packages were introduced to restructure banks and enterprises, partly in the context of privatization schemes.

Prudential Reforms to Support Stabilization and Market Development

As market-based instruments of monetary policy are introduced as part of stabilization policies (Stage 2), high priority should be given to the implementation of key prudential regulations supported by phasing in complementary accounting reforms. These norms should be phased in, taking into account the feasibility of compliance under the country-specific operational circumstances. At the same time, a graduated spectrum of enforcement procedures to ensure compliance should also be put in place. The balance between off-site supervision, on-site inspections, and external audits that would be appropriate at this stage of reform would have to be flexible, sometimes determined by the availability of technical assistance and trained resources. Since on-site inspections are resource-intensive, greater attention to off-site analysis and simple early warning systems, with selective and well-targeted on-site follow-up, could be a possible alternative at this point. Such a strategy could be implemented fairly rapidly, and, if well executed, should adequately contain excessive risk-taking, if any, during this period of interest rate liberalization, when many policy interest rates are not yet fully flexible and market development is still in its infancy. To establish greater interest flexibility and further market development, however, a comprehensive framework of bank restructuring, bank liquidation, loan recovery, and loan workouts should be formulated. As part of this framework, a core program of financial restructuring of *both* banks and enterprises should be initiated as described in the final section of this chapter.[13]

[12]See Sundararajan (1994) for a discussion of the rationale for such restructuring of central bank credit to commercial banks.

[13]This program of financial restructuring is distinct from any minimal balance sheet restructuring that might have been implemented in the preparatory stage to facilitate initial interest rate and exchange rate adjustments.

Implementation of key prudential regulations could be phased in, taking into account their impact on monetary policy goals. The strengthening of capital adequacy ratios, implementing limits on loans to single borrowers and to "insiders," and, more generally, any tightening of supervision of loan quality—say, through loan classification and provisioning—could retard credit growth.[14] This could prove, however, to be a suitable counterforce to offset partially the rapid credit expansion that could follow a liberalization of direct controls on credit and interest. For example, measures to strengthen banking supervision and phase in capital adequacy norms in Indonesia during 1991/92 reinforced monetary policy for some time and helped slow down credit growth. Prudential controls were eased in May 1993 to encourage bank lending. Thus, while key prudential regulations would complement monetary policy goals when implementing anti-inflationary policies, these regulations could counteract monetary policy intentions at other times. Therefore, a properly phased introduction of reforms to tighten prudential regulations and the subsequent maintenance of a steady-as-you-go approach to the stance of banking supervision would help to minimize conflicts with monetary policy.

Appropriate design and enforcement of prudential regulations and early warning systems would require a good reporting system based on proper accounting standards. Early attention to developing accounting standards is therefore necessary—an action justified because of the long lead time needed to implement bank accounting norms in a comprehensive manner.[15] In addition, experience shows that accounting reforms can be carefully phased in to ensure that the needs of off-site analysis, prudential monitoring, and monetary analysis are promptly met in the short run through timely and rapid adaptations to the exist-

[14]The impact of capital adequacy rules on the effectiveness of monetary policy is discussed in Kashyap and Stein (1994), which reviews the influences on aggregate demand arising from changes in bank lending induced by monetary policy and by accounting and regulatory decisions. The literature on the lending channel of monetary policy is part of a broader literature that links the financial structure of banks and nonbanks to macroeconomic outcomes. See Bernanke and Gertler (1987), Bernanke and Blinder (1988), Gertler (1988), and Gertler and Rose (1991).

[15]While such attention would justify initiating accounting reforms as part of the preparatory stage, these reforms are included in Stage 2 in light of the practical convenience in combining accounting reforms with modernization of prudential norms and reporting systems in that stage.

ing accounting system, even while a more comprehensive overhaul of accounting and reporting framework are implemented over the medium term.[16] Early attention to reforms of accounting standards also remains critical to obtain timely and reliable information on the condition of banks. This information is needed for financial restructuring decisions.

Loan classification and provisioning rules play a critical role in identifying and limiting loan losses, and should be implemented in conjunction with risk-based capital adequacy norms in Stage 2. Tax treatment of loan-loss provisions should be adjusted to encourage adequate and timely provisioning. A bank's capital adequacy ratios are directly related to its decisions on loan-loss provisions, and hence the capital adequacy regulations for banks have an important effect on this aspect of limiting loan losses. These provisions are also influenced by tax laws, management strategy, and general economic conditions. In particular, provisioning rules might act to increase loan-loss reserves and interest spreads during recessions when bad loans rise, and reduce reserves and lower interest spreads during expansionary periods. This procyclical behavior could exacerbate the business cycle.[17]

Several aspects of interaction between supervisory actions on the one hand, and monetary policy and money-market development on the other, are important to consider in the course of implementation. The timing of interventions in problem banks could be limited by the macroeconomic situation and by conflict with monetary policy objectives. Any large injection of reserves—even if temporary—in the course of interventions in problem banks could weaken monetary policy. Prudential rules on liquidity management by commercial banks typically have an impact on the demand for liquid assets (treasury bills and other short-term paper) and interbank funds, and such prudential rules should be designed to complement the reform of money markets.[18]

---

[16]For example, in Poland, the initial reform of the commercial bank chart of accounts was completed in about 15 months beginning in late 1989, leading to an integrated reporting system for banks covering both prudential and monetary analysis needs. Full-scale reforms of the commercial bank chart of accounts continued alongside and were completed over the next three years.

[17]See Beattie and others (1995) for a discussion of accounting and macroeconomic aspects of loan-loss provisions.

[18]See "Benefits of Capital Flows Tied to Strong Risk Management" in the June 19, 1995 issue of *IMF Survey*. For a discussion of liquid asset ratios as a tool of monetary, public debt, and prudential policies, see Gulde and Zamalloa (1997).

Prudential rules that limit interbank credit exposures in correspondent banking and in payment-netting arrangements could influence the depth of money and interbank markets. Prudential rules to limit foreign exchange exposure of commercial banks could limit capital flows, depending upon the design of these rules, and influence the extent to which domestic short-term interest rates could be set independently of foreign rates.

The design of monetary policy instruments and money market arrangements should also take into account prudential concerns, particularly the need to contain systemic risks. The technical aspects of market-based instruments—such as access rules and collateral—are typically chosen so as to minimize adverse selection, moral hazard, and collusion.[19] In general, bank capital serves as the basis to limit access to standing credit facilities (e.g., Lombard credit), and to set bilateral and multilateral exposure limits in interbank dealings. Moreover, close consultations and exchanges of information with bank supervisors on bank conditions are essential for the effective operation of lender-of-last-resort functions. Finally, insofar as the regulatory stance and financial structure of banks and nonbanks inhibit or encourage the ability of banks to finance growth, those making monetary policy decisions should be cognizant of these additional influences on the macroeconomy.

Risk Management to Consolidate Market Development

In Stage 3, when markets become more liquid and interest rates become fully flexible, the range of prudential supervision issues to be addressed becomes necessarily more complex. In particular, the authorities should strengthen the supervision of security market activities of banks, complete the reforms of accounting and disclosure rules, foster well-capitalized—and well supervised—government securities dealers, and support adequate financial risk management in the payment system. For example, issues of managing market and liquidity risks arising from interest rate and exchange rate fluctuations would become important. This poses complex questions in measuring and

[19]Mathieson and Haas (1994) raise concerns regarding moral hazard and adverse selection in using market-based instruments. Saal and Zamalloa (1994) discuss how the design of credit auctions could take into account such prudential concerns.

containing market and liquidity risks and in assessing the adequacy of internal controls in banks to manage such risks (see Basle Committee on Banking Supervision, 1996). Also, coordinating banking supervision with the regulatory framework for capital markets becomes a key issue. The tasks of enhancing market discipline on banks and of allowing banks to raise additional capital at market-related terms are also important considerations in Stage 3

With an increase in the turnover in money and foreign exchange markets, policies to manage the size and distribution of credit and liquidity risks in the payment system would also become pressing in Stage 3. Such policies include: rules and practices on intervals between settlements in clearing arrangements; risk controls and loss-sharing provisions in netting arrangements; and arrangements to establish a large-value-payment system based on real-time gross settlements and on rules to manage intra-day liquidity in such systems. The range of instruments and institutions with access to the systems and the practices on the timing of debit and credit entries in bank accounts at the central bank and in customer accounts at commercial banks may need to be clarified. Thus, while banking supervision should be concerned with risk exposures of individual banks on account of their participation in payment systems, the regulation of risks in payment systems themselves poses new challenges as market turnover grows.

Significance and Sequencing of Financial Restructuring Policies

As noted in the last section and in Box 4.1, a comprehensive framework for bank restructuring, bank liquidation, and loan recovery and loan workout arrangements should be developed, and its implementation initiated in Stage 2. This section examines the components of such restructuring policies designed to deal with financial fragility and distress, a typical situation in many emerging markets, and highlights their linkages with banking supervision and monetary management. Some issues in the appropriate sequencing of financial restructuring of banks and enterprises are also highlighted.

This section addresses the following issues by identifying: (1) the major components of financial and real (operational) restructuring policies; (2) whether the authorities pursue transitional measures that can be implemented more readily at possibly lower cost if comprehensive restructuring policies cannot be quickly implemented for technical reasons and for reasons of costs; (3) the desirable features of such transitional measures; and (4) the relationship between prudential bank supervision and financial restructuring policies.

Components of Bank and Enterprise Restructuring

While individual bank insolvencies typically should be handled in the framework of well-designed bank liquidation and other bank resolution strategies grounded in banking/deposit insurance laws, the procedures to deal with systemic insolvencies raise macroeconomic issues. Policy mechanisms to redress financial distress—such as banks with a large volume of nonperforming loans and perhaps with low or negative capital—should serve to contain interest rate and credit risks for banks and the liquidity and bankruptcy risks for enterprises, and thereby facilitate necessary adjustments by borrowers and banks to the effects of higher interest rates and other stabilization measures. Thus, a key objective of bank restructuring is to allow the smooth implementation of monetary policies (and other stabilization measures).

Policies to deal with financial distress generally include the following components:

- subsidies and resource transfers assumed by the government or a government agency (e.g., interest subsidies to borrowers, tax policies to foster recapitalization, capital infusion by the government, either in cash or by replacement of value-impaired assets of banks with government or government-guaranteed securities at market rates);
- subsidies and resource transfers maintained by the central bank, often coupled with changes in lender-of-last-resort policies;[20]
- debt reduction or partial loan write-offs for potentially viable enterprises, with the remainder of their loans being renegotiated and rescheduled;

[20]Subsidies and resource transfers could also be shifted to other institutions, such as special funds or a deposit insurance agency, with the view to distribute the financial burden to other parties besides the taxpayers in the nonfinancial sector.

- capitalization of part or all of interest payments, either voluntarily negotiated between bank and borrowers within the constraints of accounting rules, or involuntarily based on laws and regulations;
- programs to recapitalize banks and firms, in the context of policies governing direct investment from abroad, foreign borrowing, and privatization;
- introduction of or a strengthening of prudential regulations on capital adequacy, liquidity, loan classification, credit limits, and similar areas;
- real sector programs to facilitate restructuring of enterprise assets (including operational restructuring in the framework of privatization and in the context of institutional arrangements for loan recovery, loan workouts, loan liquidation, and asset management);[21] and
- intervention, reorganization, and liquidation of banks—including mergers, changes in organization and management, nationalization, privatization, and changes in the range of financial services offered, and similar actions designed to improve profitability and risk management.

A comprehensive program for restructuring banks and enterprises will encompass some or all of the above components. Financial restructuring policies can be defined as those that seek to influence and strengthen the balance sheet structure of banks and the financial structure of enterprises. Such policies typically incorporate the first five components listed above, and also include general economic policies that influence the interest rate structure, interest subsidies, and aggregate debt. Although prudential regulations also strengthen bank balance sheets, and could be regarded as a component of financial restructuring, prudential policies will be discussed separately.

Financial restructuring and prudential supervision policies should be closely coordinated with "real" restructuring policies—the last two components listed above that influence the products, services, owner-

[21]The issue of whether a centralized agency (e.g., Resolution Trust Corporation) should handle loan recovery and loan workouts or if it should be dealt with in a decentralized fashion by banks themselves, or through competing smaller units ("bad banks"), is a controversial one (see Sheng, 1991). Gray and Holle (1996) analyze experience with decentralized arrangements in Poland based on bank-led loan recovery and enterprise restructuring programs.

ship, and management of both banks and enterprises. Such close coordination is crucial to avoid the moral hazard arising from subsidies and resource transfers, which could establish adverse incentives to continue excessive risk taking. In addition, details of loan recovery arrangements could result in adverse incentives to banks.[22] Therefore, financial restructuring should be combined with a tightening of prudential supervision and well-designed real restructuring policies to establish an appropriate balance of incentives. It is generally recognized that efficient restructuring of nonfinancial enterprises requires parallel and well-sequenced implementation of financial sector reforms.[23] Moreover, effective enforcement of prudential norms and supervisory systems can by itself strengthen internal governance of banks and contribute to operational restructuring of banks.

The design and implementation of such a comprehensive restructuring package—and the associated institutional and regulatory details—require thorough technical preparations, including several rounds of diagnostic studies and audits of banks and businesses, development of appropriate accounting standards, confirmation of accounting treatment of restructuring transactions, and a strengthening of the legal framework for supervisory sanctions, liquidations, and asset recovery.

The specific mix of financial restructuring policies, and particularly their sequencing, will depend upon the magnitude and urgency of the problems to be tackled, the speed and size of macroeconomic adjustments that are needed or feasible, and the legal and institutional constraints affecting the absorption of loan losses (and their distribution among various interest groups).[24] The magnitude of financial distress as

[22]Institutional arrangements for loan recovery and loan workouts comprise a number of factors, among them, laws on collateral and debt collection, court systems and judicial processes for commercial cases, bankruptcy procedures for nonfinancial firms, and aspects of bank exit procedures. If these arrangements have not been adequately designed, the monitoring and enforcement capacity of creditors (including banks) will likely be weakened, risk premiums in credit markets will rise (including possible withdrawal of banks from credit markets), and debtors will be induced to assume excessive risk. Under these circumstances, risks of moral hazard and adverse selection will be magnified and the task of bank supervision will become highly complicated, raising the eventual cost of bank restructuring.

[23]See Demirgüç-Kunt and Levine (1994) for case studies on the relationship between financial sector reform and public enterprise reform.

[24]For discussion of the scope of financial restructuring policies in several countries and the factors governing the choice of such policies, see Sundararajan and Baliño (1991), and Sheng (1991).

revealed by the classification of borrowers according to creditworthiness and the speed and size of macroeconomic adjustments that are incorporated in the stabilization strategy together dictate the speed with which financial restructuring needs to be accomplished. Therefore, they influence the specific restructuring components that are chosen for implementation (see Sundararajan and Baliño, 1991; and Sheng, 1991).

As regards the choice of restructuring policies, the experience of some countries demonstrates that a shifting of losses or interest subsidies to the central bank has undesirable effects on monetary control. Experience also shows that widespread capitalization of interest will raise financial fragility and magnify future losses if real interest rates rise. For these reasons, it seems appropriate to focus on the components of financial restructuring policies that rely on debt reduction and debt rescheduling, with the needed resource transfers organized through the budget. Such an approach can be more efficient and provide greater stability than alternative approaches.

Sequencing of Financial Restructuring Policies: Need for Transitional Measures

If comprehensive restructuring policies cannot be quickly implemented for technical reasons, should the authorities pursue transitional measures? The answer depends upon the desired speed and size of macroeconomic (particularly fiscal) adjustments and the feasibility of designing transitional measures that will be consistent with the comprehensive restructuring strategies to be implemented in the medium term. If the stabilization program calls for significant interest rate flexibility and a rapid reduction in inflation, then the sustainability of such a program will be threatened if the existence of significant financial distress leads to sizeable losses or a financial crisis. Thus, some degree of financial restructuring of banks and enterprises could become essential to the sustainability and credibility of the program, and hence would need to be implemented quickly. Several impediments, however, could easily prevent such rapid implementation: (1) the lead time needed for technical preparations (audits of banks and enterprises, adjustments in legal and accounting framework, setting up of institutions for asset disposition and bank and enterprise restructuring, and the like); (2) uncertainties governing the classification of enterprises by creditworthiness owing to major ongoing relative price changes and the high level of indebtedness of enterprises in some countries; and (3) the need to phase in the required fiscal adjustments to cover the loan losses, which, if large, could only be absorbed by the public in stages.[25] For these reasons, there is significant merit in devising transitional policies for financial restructuring that can be implemented quickly, while simultaneously preparing the technical grounds for comprehensive restructuring policies, which may take from three to five years to design and implement.

Debt Reduction and Debt-to-Equity Conversion as a Transitional Measure

What are the desirable features of transitional measures that can be implemented quickly? These measures should facilitate the adjustments by borrowers to relative price changes and real interest rate increases by reducing their excessive debt or debt-service burden—if that is a problem—and at the same time facilitate the capitalization and credit decisions of banks by reducing the volume of below-market rate and nonperforming assets, including removing loans to nonviable debtors from the banks' balance sheets. Such simultaneous restructuring of both enterprise and bank balance sheets often requires the government to recapitalize the bank (e.g., by providing government securities to finance debt reduction), while at the same time raising the equity in the enterprise (e.g., by converting enterprise debt owed to banks into government or bank-owned equity). Such debt-reduction and debt-equity conversion (or debt write-off) operations should be based on specific and yet readily applicable guidelines so that they can be rapidly implemented. These operations should also be put in place so as not to create adverse incentives and not to limit future restructuring options—including privatization—that should be designed based on comprehensive technical analysis.[26]

Institutional and policy approaches to bring about enterprise debt-reduction and debt rescheduling and the associated resource transfers would be different depending upon whether enterprises are mainly

[25]With high indebtedness, even sound firms will be facing cash-flow and debt-servicing problems, causing difficulties in classifying firms for the purposes of implementing restructuring policies.

[26]Some prior financial restructuring is often essential to facilitate subsequent privatization, particularly of banks.

state or privately owned. Debt reduction operations in free-enterprise economies raise complex questions on the redistribution of private wealth, but in systems with state-owned banks and enterprises, redistribution of assets and transfers are far easier to implement. While bank restructuring can be established based on the supervisory authority deriving from banking laws and regulations, enterprise restructuring, including debt rescheduling would require setting up appropriate incentive systems and institutional arrangements tailored to the ownership structure of enterprises and the existing legal framework for insolvencies. In the case of state-owned enterprises, the government could more readily set up guidelines for enterprise debt reduction and debt rescheduling in coordination with supervisory authority.[27] In the case of private enterprises (and household debtors), however, special arrangements—laws, institutions, or incentives—may be needed to encourage debt rescheduling agreements between banks and debtors and at the same time ensure orderly management of the assets of viable enterprises (and the seized collateral from nonviable ones). These institutional arrangements should ensure that initial financial restructuring of enterprises and banks would be followed up by agreed-upon real restructuring actions. Thus, financial restructuring should be accompanied by an action plan for real restructuring, even if the latter will take time to implement for technical reasons.

Financial restructuring of enterprises would be more efficient if it brings about debt reduction, rather than debt service reduction, based on subsidized interest. The rationale for debt reduction derives from the macroeconomic significance of aggregate debt of nonfinancial firms in relation to equity. In particular, relief to an enterprise through interest subsidy is arguably inferior from the perspective of efficiency and stabilization than relief through equivalent debt reduction, with the remaining loans carrying market rates.[28] Debt reduction deals with both

[27]For example, in Poland, the Enterprise and Bank Restructuring Program, adopted in parliament in 1993, created a decentralized arrangement enabling commercial banks to take concrete steps to resolve their problem loans, while recapitalizing the banks on a "one-time-only" basis.

[28]For example, an interest subsidy of 20 percent of interest payments is equivalent, in terms of immediate cash impact on firms, to 20 percent debt reduction. Also, since the stream of cash payments differs over time under the two options, the present value of debt reduction would differ from that of debt service reduction by the discounted value of debt forgiven. In terms of overall economic impact, however, the two policies can be quite different.

the stock and the flow problem of the debtor, whereas debt service reduction deals only with the cash-flow problem. With high debt-equity ratios, even sound firms are vulnerable to insolvency if real interest rates rise sharply. By reducing the risks of insolvency, debt reduction can raise the value of the enterprise, and thereby facilitate privatization and new investments in the business enterprise.[29] Debt reduction can enhance the quality of remaining bank debt, and this contributes to stability by raising the interest elasticity of credit demand (in part by reducing distress borrowing). Debt reduction also facilitates the rescheduling of remaining debt at market rates, with freely negotiated maturity and risk premiums, thereby enhancing efficiency and avoiding the need for explicit interest subsidies, which are often difficult to remove once established. Debt reduction and the associated strengthening of the bank balance sheet can naturally improve credit allocation (by releasing funds tied up in rolling over bad loans or capitalizing interest on such loans), in addition to rationalizing the interest structure of banks (by reducing the costs of provisioning and improving cash flows).

On the basis of these considerations, it seems appropriate in some circumstances to replace part of bank debt to potentially viable borrowers—and all of the debt to nonviable borrowers—with government securities at market rates. The government could then either convert these debts into its own equity or quasi-equity in potentially viable enterprises or set up arrangements for banks or other agents to assume additional equity claims, as part of an enterprise restructuring plan and as the counterpart to bank restructuring.[30] The choice, as noted ear-

[29]See Markelew (1995) for evidence of major adjustments in debt-equity ratios and in the structure of equity as part of industrial restructuring in France, Germany, and the United Kingdom.

[30]Even if the state already owns the enterprises, the additional buildup of the government's equity claims on them has some operational and budgetary implications. Nonviable enterprises would have to be liquidated; however, as already noted, resource transfers to viable enterprises (or banks) through financial restructuring should be accompanied by changes in management and operations to prevent moral hazard. Such restructuring will increase the value of the state's direct investment. This could have budgetary implications insofar as the cost of capitalizing the banks is not offset over time by the increased budgetary contributions from viable restructured enterprises and loan recoveries from nonviable ones. Therefore, the size of such restructuring operations will have to be phased in over time depending upon the extent of fiscal adjustments that is considered feasible at a given point in time. Also, uncertainties in loan classification might warrant a phasing in of restructuring operations until classification can be progressively refined.

lier, would depend upon the ownership structure of enterprises and the details of insolvency laws. In any case, some limited amount of debt-equity swaps for viable borrowers by banks themselves could be considered as part of the debt reduction process, but within prudential limits on equity investments by banks.

These simultaneous bank restructuring and enterprise debt reduction (or debt-equity conversion) operations should be based on readily available information. These moves could be regarded as the first step in a more comprehensive restructuring plan involving both operational restructuring as well as phasing in of financial restructuring measures. The phasing in of financial restructuring operations would take into account budgetary considerations (spreading the fiscal costs over time), and the progressive availability of additional diagnostic information (as loan classification is progressively refined and diagnostic audits are completed). The initial debt-equity conversion for potentially viable firms could be based on norms for debt-equity ratios (or some other generally applicable guidelines), which could be derived as part of the financial analysis of firms used for loan classification. The debt-equity conversion for potentially viable firms could permit a reduction in interest subsidies to such firms, or improve their profitability—with attendant revenue effects on the budget—thereby containing the overall fiscal cost of the restructuring plan. More generally, a combination of tax and regulatory policies that serve to reduce debt-equity ratios of firms would also permit a reduction in interest subsidies and an increase in enterprise profitability.

The criteria used to classify bank credits as nonviable (doubtful or loss) or potentially viable (good, substandard) could be built up from the loan classification procedures already in place, based on prudential regulations for provisioning. Loan classification, supported by financial analysis of firms, would assist the authorities in devising appropriate financial restructuring policies, in addition to helping the banks in renegotiating and provisioning their loans.[31] The criteria for classification should combine information on debt-service performance of enterprises, as well as other indicators of their financial condition, in order to assess creditworthiness and viability.[32] The loan classification

[31]For a technical discussion of valuing and classifying loans in the course of handling a systemic crisis, see Berggren (1996).

[32]For a detailed description and analysis of loan classification and valuation techniques, see Beattie and others (1995) and the references contained therein.

process could be complemented by a closer analysis of the relationship between solvency and profitability ratios of firms, in order to further refine the classification and to assess the changes needed in the financial structure of enterprises.[33]

Summary

It is by now well-recognized that the timely implementation of bank restructuring and banking supervision policies, in addition to adequate stabilization procedures, is essential to avoid major disruptions to growth and stability in the course of financial liberalization. This has led some economists to suggest a delay in interest rate liberalization and external financial liberalization until banking supervision is adequate and banks are sufficiently sound.

In practice, however, policies to restructure banks (and enterprises) and strengthen prudential supervision can, and should, be phased in appropriately to support the interest rate liberalization process, and thereby avoid undue delays or abrupt interruptions in liberalization due to a financial crisis. Appropriate sequencing of bank restructuring and supervision policies requires attention to technical linkages among these policies, their macroeconomic effects, and the scope for market discipline and internal governance. To illustrate the feasibility of such sequencing, the phasing in of bank supervision and financial restructuring measures are classified into three progressive stages of implementation. The preparatory stage focuses on the legal basis of bank supervision restructuring together with a minimal program of financial restructuring to initiate stabilization and prepare the ground for financial market development. As market-based instruments of monetary policy are introduced to initiate financial liberalization in Stage 2, a critical mass of reforms in prudential supervision and in bank and enterprise balance sheets are implemented in parallel. This initial group of reforms helps accelerate the adoption of indirect instruments, improve their effectiveness, and set the stage for more comprehensive reforms of prudential supervision and bank restructuring over the medium term. As markets develop, prudential norms, supervisory

[33]Such an analysis could provide guidance on the desirability and magnitude of debt-equity conversions.

procedures, and restructuring actions are progressively refined and modified in line with the state of market development and of internal governance of financial institutions, thereby helping to consolidate financial market development in Stage 3.

Some of the specific principles that govern the proposed sequencing of prudential supervision and bank restructuring policies include:

- Policies to strengthen prudential supervision—including the phasing in of prudential regulations, the development of a balanced application of off-site analysis, on-site inspections, and external audits, and the enforcement of firm exit policies—should be combined with policies to restructure banks and to establish institutional arrangements for loan recovery and enterprise restructuring. Such a comprehensive package encompassing both supervision systems and restructuring options is necessary to avoid adverse incentives toward excessive risk taking by banks and debtors.
- Phasing in of reforms of the commercial bank accounting system, together with the properly phased implementation of prudential standards for capital adequacy, foreign exchange exposures, loan concentration, loan classification and provisioning, and early warning systems, can support stabilization objectives and also facilitate financial restructuring of banks. Therefore, these aspects of banking supervision should be part of the critical mass of reforms that is introduced at the outset of financial liberalization.
- A package of financial restructuring policies to strengthen bank asset portfolio and profitability, reduce the debt-equity ratio of nonfinancial firms, and eliminate interest subsidies (and related directed credit) should also be implemented early in the process as part of the critical mass of reforms. This approach has the advantage of financing the fiscal costs of bank restructuring in part through reduced interest subsidies to enterprises, thereby containing the overall fiscal burden of bank restructuring in the initial stages. Such a financial restructuring program should be a component of, and be accompanied by, an action plan for comprehensive restructuring of both banks and enterprises that would be phased in over the medium term. The action plan should include steps to develop supporting institutional arrangements that would ensure that operational restructuring (including privatization) would be carried out as the counterpart to financial restructuring.

5

Financial Sector Reform and the Real Sector

R. BARRY JOHNSTON AND CEYLA PAZARBAŞIOĞLU

The experience of various countries in the aftermath of financial sector reform has been diverse. Many countries have improved economic growth and efficiency, but several others, including both industrial and developing, have faced financial crisis and disruptions in economic growth. Many economists share a concern that financial sector reforms may involve transitional costs stemming from real sector restructuring, which accompanies reform. This chapter examines some of the channels through which financial sector reform can affect real economic growth and the efficiency of capital using panel data (pooled cross-country and time-series data) from a sample of countries that have liberalized their financial system.

A large body of theoretical literature has analyzed the extent of financial intermediation in an economy as an important determinant of its real growth rate, identifying the channels of transmission from financial intermediation to growth. Early examples of this literature include Cameron (1967), Patrick (1966), Goldsmith (1969), McKin-

Note: The chapter was first issued in 1995 as "Linkages Between Financial Variables, Financial Sector Reform, and Economic Growth and Efficiency," IMF Working Paper 95/103. The authors are grateful to Dawit Makonnen and Kiran Sastry for research assistance.

non (1973), and Shaw (1973). These papers emphasized the role of financial intermediaries in the credit supply process, and concluded that there is a strong positive correlation between the extent of financial development and economic growth. McKinnon and Shaw emphasized the role played by financial liberalization in increasing savings and, hence, investment, while Goldsmith focused primarily on the relationship between financial development and the efficiency of investment. A survey article on financial structure and aggregate economic activity by Gertler (1988) describes these and subsequent models.

Some of the more recent studies, such as Greenwood and Jovanovic (1989) and Bencivenga and Smith (1991), argue that to the extent that financial intermediaries tend to alter the composition of savings in a way that is favorable to capital accumulation, they will tend to promote growth. Similarly, Levine (1992) concludes that financial structures enhance growth by promoting the efficient allocation of investment through various channels.

Empirical tests of the impact of financial intermediation on growth conducted in the context of a large sample of countries by Jappelli and Pagano (1992), Roubini and Sala-i-Martin (1992), De Gregorio and Guidotti (1992), and King and Levine (1993a, b), have concluded that financial variables have an important impact on economic growth. Most of these studies use a similar methodology and follow the strategy of adding variables of financial development to Barro's (1991) basic cross-country regression to analyze their impact on growth. An alternative approach used by Agarwala (1983), Anderson (1987), Khatekhate (1988), Gelb (1989), Gallagher (1991), Odedokun (1992), and Sundararajan (1985 and 1987) is to model the effects of financial variables on economic efficiency. These studies use the real interest rate and various monetary aggregates as a proxy for financial intermediation.

Although these studies allow inferences to be made about the impact of financial reform on economic growth and efficiency, to the best of our knowledge, none of the studies has sought to examine the role of financial reforms directly on economic growth and efficiency. Moreover, the studies have tended to proxy financial sector development by a single financial indicator—the ratio of either money or credit to GDP or the real interest rate. This approach, however, has its limitations given that financial development and reform have many dimensions. The need to examine the relationships between financial sector variables and the real sector at a more complex level becomes especially important in designing financial sector reforms, and in understanding the reasons why some countries have had more successful financial sector reform experiences than others. As noted by Galbis (1994) and Johnston (1997), the transition from repressed to more market-oriented financial systems involves shocks to interest rates, the exchange rate, and financial flows. Naturally, the authorities' reactions to these shocks can effect economic performance and the transitional costs of financial sector reform.

To help shed some light on these latter issues, this chapter examines the impact of financial sector variables on economic growth and efficiency using panel data for 40 countries. The financial sector is hypothesized to affect economic growth and efficiency through different channels, which are proxied by the real interest rate, the volume of intermediation, and a measure of financial sector efficiency. To separate their effects, proxies for these channels are entered simultaneously into the estimation equations. The impact of financial sector reform is explored by examining prereform, reform, and postreform periods. A sample of countries that faced financial crisis is compared to a sample of countries that did not face a financial crisis.

The results confirm earlier findings on the importance of financial variables in equations for economic growth and efficiency. Average economic growth and output to capital ratios in countries that reformed their financial systems and avoided financial crises improved strongly following the reforms. The results indicate that financial reforms have structural implications for the way financial variables affect the real economy. Moreover, the results demonstrated that it is important to take account of the different dimensions of the financial reform, in terms of their effect on the interest cost of capital and on the volume and efficiency of intermediation, in explaining the impact of financial variables on economic performance. In addition, the conclusions show that financial variables had quite different effects in countries where financial crises were avoided and in those where they were not. The different results can be attributed partly to the failure of crisis countries to adjust real interest rates and to prevent the inflationary credit and monetary expansion that accompanied the financial sector reforms, and partly to the greater inefficiencies in the banking systems in the crisis countries.

Research Methodology and Linkages Between Financial Sector Variables and the Real Sector

Financial sector reforms typically involve the liberalization of interest rates; the liberalization of quantitative restrictions, including credit and exchange controls; and measures to improve the allocative efficiency and soundness of the financial sector, particularly the banking system. The financial system has its effect on the real sector through a number of channels, including: the cost of capital; the volume of savings and investment funds; and the distribution of funds and project selection.

The channels through which the financial sector affects the real sector are not all readily observable, and therefore, it is necessary to rely on a number of observable indicators or proxies of financial development. In this study we focus on the impact of three proxies of financial development: (1) the level of the real interest rate; (2) the volume of intermediation; and (3) a measure of financial sector efficiency. Each of the above mentioned financial sector reform measures is likely to impact all three proxies. For example, the liberalization of interest rates could affect the real interest rate, the volume of intermediation, and banking sector efficiency by permitting greater competition. There is also no necessary strict one-to-one relationship between these proxies and the channels through which the financial system affects the real sector. For example, the level of the real interest rate would have an impact on the interest cost of capital, the volume of savings, and possibly the distribution of funds through adverse selection incentives. By entering all three proxies simultaneously, however, into the equations for economic growth and efficiency, it should be possible to distinguish somewhat better the importance of the different channels. Thus, including the volume of intermediation and a measure of banking efficiency along with the real interest rate in the estimation equations should allow the real interest rate term primarily to proxy the impact of the financial system on the interest cost of capital, while the savings/investment effect would be reflected in the volume of intermediation, and the allocative efficiency effect in the financial sector efficiency proxy.

The impact of financial sector reform would be observed partly through the movements in the proxies. Financial sector reform, however, is also a process encompassing structural and institutional changes spread over time, which are likely to have effects on the transmission of financial sector variables on the real sector. Therefore, the approach followed here is to split the sample into separate periods—prereform, reform, and postreform—with the period of reform embracing the five years following the introduction of certain discrete financial reforms, usually the elimination of interest rate or quantitative controls. This approach allows us to study the impact of the different channels through which the financial sector affects the real sector under conditions of financial repression and during the reform and postreform periods. This approach also allows analysis of the transitional effects of financial sector reforms.

The transitional impact of the financial reforms on economic growth would depend partly on the starting conditions, including how far unproductive sectors had been supported previously, the extent to which subsidization of unproductive sectors continued, and how quickly the financial system could respond to the demands for new credit from viable sectors that previously had limited access to finance. The restructuring of formerly unprofitable sectors may have an initial adverse effect on growth, but this would be offset by the higher productivity of new investments.

As a measure of economic efficiency, two real sector variables are examined: the rate of real GDP growth and the output to capital ratio. There has been some discussion of whether the financial sector impacts mainly on economic efficiency or more directly on growth, and use of these two proxies allows us to study the importance of the different channels. We follow the methodology adopted in previous empirical tests of the impact of financial sector reform on growth and efficiency, by using the approach in the endogenous growth literature. The use of this approach helps to control, among other things, for the importance of commonly used policy indicators and structural determinants of growth that otherwise might explain the observed correlations between the financial variables and growth and efficiency.

As first developed by Barro (1991), the endogenous growth approach examines the determinants of growth by regressing average per capita growth on a set of relevant variables using cross-section data over an extended period of time.[1] These variables include proxies for

[1]The basic growth equations estimated by Barro include a cross-section study of about 100 countries during the 1960–85 period.

capital accumulation (human and physical), the macroeconomic environment, government spending, degree of openness, and the terms of trade.[2] This approach has been helpful in highlighting the factors that affect growth, although the estimation of semi-reduced forms may present problems of an endogenous nature and hamper the interpretation of coefficient estimates.[3]

Among the earlier studies that have added variables of financial development to Barro's basic cross-country regressions, Roubini and Sala-i-Martin (1992) include a dummy variable for financial repression.[4] They find that this variable has a negative and significant coefficient implying that a higher degree of financial repression leads to lower economic growth. De Gregorio and Guidotti (1992) add the ratio of domestic credit granted to the private sector by the central bank and commercial banks to GDP (*CREDIT*) as a proxy for the degree of financial intermediation; they find a significantly positive effect of this variable on long-run growth of real per capita GDP.[5] However, when De Gregorio and Guidotti use a panel data set for 12 Latin American countries for the period 1950–85, they find a significant negative correlation between *CREDIT* and economic growth. They interpret this result as evidence that more financial intermediation may be associated with lower efficiency of investment where the financial liberalization was unsustainable due to inadequate regulation.

King and Levine (1993a) conduct both a cross-country analysis using data averaged over the 1960–89 period and a pooled cross-country time-series study (panel data) using data averaged over the

---

[2]The average growth in per capita income is regressed on the following explanatory variables: the initial value of GDP, the initial amount of human capital as proxied by initial values of primary and secondary school enrollment rates, the rate of physical capital accumulation, the ratio of government spending to GDP, the openness of trade policies, the rate of inflation, the rate of foreign direct investment, and an index for political tensions.

[3]See Levine and Renelt (1992) for a detailed study of the sensitivity of cross-country regressions of growth.

[4]The variable takes the value 1 when real interest rates are positive; 2 when real interest rates are negative but above –5 percent; and 3 when real interest rates are below –5 percent. As an alternative approach, they use the reserve requirement ratio as a proxy for financial repression and conclude that high required reserves lead to a lowering of economic growth.

[5]The effect is particularly strong in low- and middle-income countries, and stronger in the 1960s than in the 1970s and 1980s.

1960s, 1970s, and 1980s. They use four indicators of the level of financial sector development:

- the ratio of liquid liabilities of the financial system to GDP;[6]
- the ratio of deposit money bank domestic assets to deposit money bank domestic assets plus central bank domestic assets;
- the ratio of claims on the nonfinancial private sector to total domestic credit; and
- a variable similar to *CREDIT* used by De Gregorio and Guidotti.

Including the indicators one at a time in the regressions, they conclude that higher levels of financial development are positively associated with faster rates of economic growth, physical capital accumulation, and economic efficiency improvements.[7]

Sundararajan (1987) examines the impact of real interest rates on savings, investment, and efficiency of capital, taking into account the effect of interest rates on the share of debt and equity in non-financial firms (and their cost of capital) and finds that the efficiency effects of interest rates depend upon the size of debt equity ratios.

Odedokun (1992) examines the effect of selected policies on economic efficiency measured by the incremental output-capital ratio (the ratio of the change in GDP to investment) in 81 developing countries using panel data over various periods between 1961–90.[8] He concludes that the stock of credit to private sector to GDP ratio is a better proxy for financial depth than the stock of liquid liabilities to GDP, and that in general increases in the real interest rate have a positive effect on the efficiency of resource use.

---

[6]Liquid liabilities are currency held outside the banking system plus demand and interest-bearing liabilities of banks and nonbank financial intermediaries (a measure of M3).

[7]The dependent variables used are the real per capita GDP growth rate, average growth rate of the real per capita capital stock, the ratio of investment to GDP, and the residual of real per capita GDP growth after accounting for the rate of physical capital accumulation (a proxy for economic efficiency).

[8]Odedokun emphasizes that ideally the actual output to capital ratio (as opposed to the incremental ratio) should be used as the appropriate index. However, due to lack of data on capital stock for developing countries he uses the IFS data on investment. The variables included in the regression are export orientation, size of the public sector, inflation rate, real exchange rate distortion; and the financial variables examined are the real interest rate, directed credit program through development bank lendings, and financial depth (measured as the ratio of the stock of liquid liabilities of the banking system to GDP).

The empirical work reported here differs from earlier work in a number of respects. The earlier studies have tended to proxy financial sector development by a single financial indicator at a time, and have not distinguished between pre- and post-financial reform experience. The approach, however, does not take into consideration the many channels through which the financial sector can affect the real sector. This study examines the simultaneous impact of the three main proxies for the channels of financial sector development on economic growth and efficiency. Another difference between this study and earlier work is the use of the output to capital ratio as the measure of economic efficiency. The output to capital ratio is a better indicator of economic efficiency than the incremental output capital ratio, both qualitatively and quantitatively. Private capital stock data compiled by the World Bank is used in calculating the output to capital ratio. This study also seeks to differentiate the effects of financial variables before, during, and after the reform, and distinguish between the experiences of countries that faced financial crisis following reforms and those that did not face such crises. The study examines panel data from 40 countries that have introduced financial sector reforms.

Relationship Between the Proxies and Economic Growth and Efficiency

The real interest rate

The real rate of interest affects financial sector development through its influence on financial savings and on the cost of capital (see McKinnon, 1973; Shaw, 1973; Fry, 1988; and Leite and Sundararajan, 1990). The real rate of interest is determined by real factors over the longer term. In the short run, however, the real rate of interest is determined by both monetary policy actions, as well as by structural and environmental factors that influence inflation expectations and the pace of adjustment of nominal rates in the market to policy actions. Thus, monetary policy actions can affect real rates and real sector performance in the short run. For example, maintenance of a low or negative real interest rate on monetary financing could result in the support and expansion of unproductive, nonviable projects, and the channeling of funds into consumption rather than investment, which would be detrimental to economic growth and efficiency. Sufficiently positive real rates can improve the efficiency of investment, while very high real rates can affect the soundness of the banking system and adversely affect allocative efficiency.

Under repressed financial systems, the real interest rate may be maintained at a low level through directed credits and central bank refinancing of certain projects at subsidized interest rates. In contrast, the real rate of interest may be extremely high for other projects that do not meet the criteria for central bank refinance, and must rely on the curb markets for their funds.

Financial sector reform would thereby involve an upward adjustment in the real rate of interest on subsidized projects, and a decline for other projects. This might require some restructuring of the capital stock with a retiring of capital from previously subsidized firms that are no longer viable. The reforms, however, would in all likelihood increase the opportunities for new and more productive activities.

In theory, higher equilibrium real interest rates should be associated with more efficient investment and higher rates of return on capital, in addition to higher savings and growth. Unusually high real interest rates, however, may also be associated with adverse selection and the channeling of funds into more high-risk projects. Such high real interest rates may also reflect other factors, such as a lack of credibility, a country risk premium, or fragility of the banking system (see Calvo, 1988; Calvo and Guidotti, 1991; and Persson and Tabellini, 1990).

The calculation of the real interest rate is problematic since it depends on inflation expectations and can vary depending on the agents involved and the tax system. At this point, we substitute the average deposit rate less the concurrent annual rate of change of consumer prices for the real interest rate (*RIR*). Except for the caveats mentioned above, we would expect a positive relationship between *RIR* and economic growth and efficiency.

The volume of intermediation

McKinnon (1973) and Shaw (1973), among others, have emphasized the role played by financial intermediaries in increasing savings and hence investment. Liberalization of interest rates and the introduction of new financial instruments as part of financial sector reform encourage the holdings of financial assets and financial deepening. Various monetary indicators of financial development (deposit/currency and broad money/GDP ratios) generally improve with financial sector reforms.

Two main factors, however, are likely to determine whether the observed increase in intermediation will improve economic growth: the sources and uses of credit expansion. First, to result in higher growth, the increase in financial intermediation should involve a savings rather than a purely inflation component. Inflationary increases in money and credit would at most have a temporary effect in increasing economic growth, and subsequently higher inflation would have detrimental longer-term effects.

Based on various country experiences, financial sector reforms may involve shocks to the volume of intermediation. Rapid credit expansions most often follow the liberalization of controls on the banking system.[9] Domestic liberalization can also lead to a reflow of capital flight and improvements in capital accounts, especially if accompanied by external sector liberalization (see Calvo, Leiderman, and Reinhart, 1993; Johnston and Ryan, 1994; and Schadler and others, 1993). Nonsterilized foreign exchange inflows would add to the supply of free reserves in the banking system and fuel the credit boom.

Financial sector reforms will also have structural effects. Liberalization of the financial system resulting in higher financial savings may mean that the authorities will be able to tolerate a somewhat more rapid growth of money and credit in the postreform period without increasing inflationary pressures. A higher foreign demand for the country's financial assets following external liberalization could take a considerable time to work through and may allow the country to sustain a somewhat large current account deficit in the balance of payments and, therefore, to accept some loss of competitiveness and real exchange rate appreciation. Hence, the authorities may be able to accommodate some of the initial credit and external shocks without affecting long-term growth prospects. Beyond allowance for these structural shifts, however, the resulting monetary and credit expansion will be inflationary and will, therefore, need to be offset by the central bank if the credit expansion is not to have an adverse effect on economic performance.

[9]See Chapter 3, also Sundararajan and Baliño (1990), and Drees and Pazarbaşıoğlu (1995).

How the increase in credit is used will also determine whether a rise in intermediation will stimulate economic growth and efficiency. As already noted, this increase may be channeled to consumption rather than investment or into unproductive activities. The level of the real interest rate and the proxy for the efficiency of the financial system should control for these factors. Hence, we anticipate that the volume of intermediation variable will mainly play the role in the financial system of promoting savings and hence positively contribute to growth and efficiency. Insofar as the volume of intermediation rises due to inflationary growth in money and credit, the impact on growth and efficiency would be negative.

We use two alternative proxies for the volume of financial intermediation through the banking system: the share of credit to the private sector by banks in GDP (denoted as *CRED*), and the share of M2 in GDP (denoted as *M2GDP*). These variables represent the two main functions of financial markets: the credit allocation role and the deposit mobilization role. *CRED* is a more appropriate indicator of the volume of intermediation through the banking system than the *CREDIT* variable used by De Gregorio and Guidotti (1992) and King Levine (1993 a,b) because it excludes the credit granted to the private sector by the central bank, which is often high during financial repression.

Efficiency of intermediation

The channeling of finance through organized financial intermediaries can improve investment and growth for a number of well-known reasons, including the benefits of economies of scale in savings mobilization and allocation and the role of intermediaries in project selection. It also must be recognized, however, that efficiency in intermediation is not something that is necessarily automatic, particularly after prolonged periods of financial repression, and that it has to be promoted as part of the process of financial sector reform.

Appropriate management of banking soundness and efficiency is an important issue in the course of financial sector reforms (see Leite and Sundararajan, 1990). Insolvent banks have incentives to allocate credit to high risk/high return projects without due regard to the prospects for loan recovery. At the same time, the ability of sound banks to compete with insolvent banks is constrained. In some financial reform occurrences ownership interrelationships have resulted in the concentration of lending to connected enterprises, thereby magnifying risk exposures and reducing the supply of credit to new borrowers. Large and inefficient financial institutions may seek to exploit their monopoly power following financial liberalization. Weaknesses in financial intermediation may also be created by poorly designed legislative frameworks that are not attuned to enforce financial contracts and financial discipline among borrowers. These systems are often beset by inadequate accounting and information systems that delay recognition of unsoundness, and inadequate institutional capabilities, knowledge, and skills that perpetuate risk taking. Rapid credit expansion in the wake of financial liberalization can also strain credit approval procedures and result in increased lending to risky projects. Thus, efficiency in credit allocation following financial liberalization requires appropriate policies to foster banking soundness (see Chapter 4).

It is difficult to measure directly the efficiency of the banking system in the allocation of credit. Generally, the efficiency of banks in credit allocation is likely to be reflected in other aspects of their activity. For example, inefficiency in the banking industry may be associated with wide lending margins reflecting, say, lack of competition between banks and attempts by insolvent banks to recoup loan losses. It may also be reflected in the management of bank assets, for example, in the tendency of inefficient banks to hold larger nonremunerated excess reserves, or revealed by the portfolio behavior of nonbanks in their willingness to hold and use bank deposits rather than cash.

Two different variables are used to represent the efficiency of intermediation. One is the gross spread between the average lending and deposit rates (denoted as *SPREAD*) and the other is the ratio of reserve money to deposits (denoted as *RMDEP*). The spread variable is calculated as the difference between the average lending and deposit rates. Some caveats, though, are in order. The spread may not be a good measure of efficiency before financial reform when interest controls are in place or after financial reform if the spread reflects different regulations on the banking industry. The spread may also vary with the level of nominal interest rates and inflation, although it will be partly accounted for by the estimates that include a separate inflation term in the regression equations.

Reserve money is defined as the currency in circulation plus the required and excess reserves of the banking system. The variable

RMDEP, therefore, includes: the currency to deposit ratio, which is a measure of the efficiency of the banks in mobilizing deposits; the excess reserves, which represent the efficiency of banks in the use of funds; and required reserves, which tend to be higher under financial repression. *RMDEP* would also reflect the effect of an unsound banking system, if such weakness leads to a run on deposits and shift to cash. A negative relationship is expected between the efficiency proxies and economic growth.

Estimation and Results

Our sample includes 40 industrial and developing countries that undertook financial sector reforms, and is divided according to the stages of the financial reform process: prereform, reform, and postreform. For analytical purposes, the start of reforms is identified with the elimination of credit ceilings and/or elimination of interest rate controls, while the reform period covers the five-year period following the start date of the reforms. The five-year period preceding the start of financial sector reforms is identified as the prereform period, and the five-year period following the reform period as the postreform period. The use of five-year data periods is somewhat arbitrary, but country experience also indicates that many countries have implemented financial reform programs over three to five-year periods. The sample was further divided into two subsamples—namely, the noncrisis and crisis countries, based on whether the country experienced a financial crisis. The cases of financial crisis were identified from a review of country case studies.[10] Appendix I provides a list of the sample countries, the subsamples of crisis and noncrisis countries, and the subperiods for each country in the sample.

The dependent variables are:

RGDPGR the growth rate of real GDP as a proxy for economic growth,

and

[10]See Chapter 3; see also Sundararajan and Baliño (1990), and Drees and Pazarbaşıoğlu (1995).

OCR the output to capital ratio as a proxy for economic efficiency;

whereas the explanatory variables include:

INF the rate of inflation; or alternatively;

GDPDEF the GDP deflator;

GEGDP the ratio of government spending to GDP.

XMGDP the openness of trade as proxied by the share of total exports plus imports in GDP;

INVGDP the share of investment in GDP;

DIGDP the share of foreign direct investment in GDP; as well as the financial reform variables discussed in the previous section.

Because of the endogenous nature of the problem of using the ratio of investment to GDP as an explanatory variable, this variable was instrumented in the regressions.[11] Appendix II provides a list of the variables and data sources.

The estimation equations are of the following form:

$$y_{it} = \alpha_i + \beta x_{it} + u_{it} \ , \qquad (1)$$

where i denotes a country and t a time period (prereform, reform, and postreform periods), α_i is a country specific parameter, y represents *RGDPGR* or *OCR*, x is a matrix of explanatory variables as described in the previous paragraph, and β is the vector of regression coefficients.

In estimating equation (1) we use the panel data "random effects" method, which considers each country-specific parameter as a random variable and includes its stochastic component in the error term of the regression (see Hsiao, 1986). Hausman test statistics were used to check for correlated effects. In all cases, the hypothesis that the intercepts are drawn from a common distribution with mean α and variance σ_α^2 was rejected, implying that the use of the random effects model would provide inconsistent estimates and thus the equation has to be estimated by generalized least squares.

[11]The current level of investment was regressed on its own lagged values, and the fitted values were included in the regression.

Average Performance During Financial Reforms

The mean values for rates of growth, the output to capital ratios, and the financial explanatory variables for the prereform, reform, and postreform periods for the crisis and noncrisis countries are shown in Table 5.1. For the noncrisis countries, the financial reforms are associated with strong improvements in average economic growth rates and output to capital ratios. The crisis countries, however, encountered, on average, a deterioration in economic growth and a decline in output to capital ratios.

Concerning the behavior of the financial variables, the noncrisis countries dramatically increased the average real interest rate to positive real levels in the reform period. Real interest rates increased further on average in the postreform period, suggesting that while the real interest rate adjustment during the reform was significant, it may have involved some modest undershooting.

The volume of financial intermediation expanded following the reforms, with the ratio of credit to the private sector to GDP increasing on average by a larger amount than the ratio of broad money to GDP. This result is consistent with earlier observations that credit grows more rapidly than money immediately following financial reforms. In the noncrisis countries, it is interesting to note that the credit to the private sector to GDP ratio in the postreform period continued to be much lower than the ratio of M2 to GDP, suggesting that the credit expansion was limited. This constraint may have been because a significant percentage of banking sector assets continued to be subject to portfolio constraints during the reform period, or because the banks were risk averse. Only in the postreform period did the ratio of credit to the private sector to GDP increase to the level of M2 to GDP.

During the reform period, the ratio of reserve money to deposits fell substantially while the average spread between bank loan and deposit rates widened until the postreform period, when it declined. This widening of the spreads has been observed in other studies and attributed to several factors, including the greater freedom to price credit according to risks, to delays in improvements in banking competition, and to a greater reliance on noninterest-bearing reserve requirements during the reform period.[12]

[12]See Chapter 3; see also King and Levine (1993a).

Table 5.1. Mean Values for Selected Variables

	Noncrisis Countries			Crisis Countries		
	Prereform	Reform	Postreform	Prereform	Reform	Postreform
Dependent variables						
RGDPGR	2.64	4.18	4.36	4.18	3.51	2.16
OCR	0.35	0.36	0.39	0.34	0.33	0.31
Financial variables						
RIR	–5.79	1.43	2.51	–3.20	–6.56	6.14
CRED	0.32	0.42	0.53	0.34	0.48	0.43
RMDEP	0.35	0.30	0.26	0.37	0.27	0.39
M2GDP	0.48	0.54	0.56	0.39	0.50	0.38
SPREAD	4.08	4.61	4.07	5.86	8.27	11.05

Notes: The variables are defined as follows: *RGDPGR,* the growth rate of GDP as a proxy for economic growth; *OCR,* the output to capital ratio as a proxy for economic efficiency; *RIR,* real interest rate; *CRED,* claims on private sector by deposit money banks divided by nominal GDP; *RMDEP,* reserve money divided by nominal GDP; *M2GDP;* the sum of money and quasimoney divided by nominal GDP; *SPREAD,* lending rate minus deposit rate.

One can see some important differences in the behavior of the financial variables of the crisis countries compared with the noncrisis countries in the prereform and reform periods. In the crisis countries, the real interest rates, negative to begin with, dropped during the reform period rather than becoming positive; the volume of intermediation expanded much more rapidly with the ratio of credit to the private sector to GDP, reaching a level close to that of M2 to GDP; and the spread between deposit and lending rates widened sharply. While these results are only indicative, they suggest that during the reform period, the crisis countries permitted a much more rapid monetary and credit expansion in the context of a relatively inefficient financial system.[13]

The mean values for the crisis countries for the postreform period indicate the magnitude of subsequent policy adjustments as real interest rates were raised on average to high positive levels. In addition, the financial crises were associated with a reversal of financial deepening, as measured by the ratio of credit to the private sector and M2 to GDP. The fact that the ratio of credit to GDP exceeded the ratio of M2 to GDP in the postreform period may reflect official support operations in the wake of financial crisis. The indicators of financial in-

[13]See also Drees and Pazarbaşıoğlu (1995) for a discussion of the expansionary impact of financial deregulation and subsequent financial crises in the case of Nordic countries.

termediation efficiency deteriorated during the postreform period in response to the banking crisis. The crisis countries experienced a sharp reduction in real economic growth in the postreform period.

Estimation Results

In this section we examine the direction of the effect of each explanatory variable. First, we provide a brief discussion of the effects of the macroeconomic variables that are commonly used in the literature, and subsequently we discuss in more detail the effects of the financial reform variables. Appendix II provides the estimation results for the real rate of growth for the crisis and noncrisis countries for the entire period, including the prereform, reform, and postreform periods and for each separate period. Appendix II also provides the results in a similar format for the output to capital ratio.

The effect of the macroeconomic variables are as follows:

The size of the public sector proxied by the share of government expenditure in GDP (*GEGDP*) has a significantly negative effect on both economic growth and efficiency in the reform and postreform periods and for both noncrisis and crisis countries, indicating that the expansion of the public sector may be detrimental to economic growth and efficiency.

The inflation rate (*INF*) has a significant and negative effect across all subperiods and in both noncrisis and crisis countries, implying that inflation hampers both growth and efficiency of resource allocation through channels other than the impact of financial variables. (Similar results are obtained when the GDP deflation is used to measure inflation.)

The openness of trade, proxied by the ratio of the sum of exports and imports over GDP (*XMGDP*), has the expected positive sign during the reform period, implying that trade liberalization is generally beneficial to economic growth and efficiency. However, for the crisis countries the impact of the openness of trade on growth and efficiency becomes negative in the postreform period. This unexpected result may be explained by the greater vulnerability of the more open economies to a loss of international confidence following the onset of a banking crisis, resulting in withdrawals of foreign capital, and possibly in greater recourse in these countries to trade and exchange restrictions in the aftermath of the crisis.

The ratio of investment to GDP (*INVGDP*) has the anticipated positive effect on growth, whereas the ratio of foreign direct investment to GDP (*DIGDP*) has a positive effect in the noncrisis countries on growth and on efficiency of resource utilization during the postreform period. For the crisis countries, the variable is negative in the growth equations in the prereform period, which is an unexpected result.

Regarding the impact of financial reform variables in the noncrisis countries, all three financial channel proxies enter with the correct sign in the real growth and efficiency equations for the entire period, and are significant in the growth equations where efficiency is represented by the spread. Hence, the results show the importance of financial variables on the real sector, even after controlling for commonly used policy indicators and structural determinants of growth. They also indicate the importance of taking account of the different dimensions of financial reform in explaining economic growth over a relatively long data period and across countries.

Some important differences in the results, however, occur when comparing the prereform periods with the reform and postreform periods, and between the crisis and noncrisis countries. These are discussed in the following section.

The real interest rate

The real interest rate (*RIR*) has an insignificant effect on real growth and a significantly negative impact on economic efficiency in the prereform period. This result suggests that the measured real interest rate was not a good indicator of the real cost of capital during this period, perhaps reflecting the impact of credit rationing and the importance of directed finance under financial repression.

Following financial reforms, the impact of the real interest rate on economic growth and efficiency becomes a significant and positive factor. Upward adjustments in real interest rates, which are observed to accompany financial sector reforms, therefore, do not appear to have negative effects on growth. The failure of the crisis countries to raise their real interest rates during the reform process may also partly explain the weaker economic growth and efficiency performances.

In the postreform period, the real interest term becomes highly positive for the crisis countries. The sharp increases in real interest rates, which generally accompany financial crises, therefore, appear to have had quite adverse real sector effects as interest costs rise significantly. These effects may also be magnified given the potential for "adverse selection," namely the allocation of credit to more high-risk borrowers under conditions of high real interest rates. The real interest rate continues to have a significant positive effect on growth and efficiency in the noncrisis countries in the postreform period.

The volume of intermediation

The volume of financial intermediation (represented by *CRED* or *M2GDP*) is not a significant determinant of economic growth and has a significant negative effect on efficiency during the prereform period. This result would be consistent with the weakness of the banking sector in mobilizing savings, with expansions in intermediation involving inflation rather than savings components, and with the allocation of credit into low productivity uses under financial repression.

Following financial reforms, the volume of financial intermediation has a generally positive and significant effect on growth and efficiency for the noncrisis countries. This is the expected effect to the extent that the banking system contributes to enhancing savings mobilization. This positive effect continues in the postreform period. For the crisis countries, the volume of intermediation has a significantly negative effect on growth and efficiency following financial reforms. Hence, under conditions that are conducive to financial crisis—which may involve factors such as banking insolvency, lending to interrelated institutions, and similar issues—expansions of financial intermediation do not appear to improve growth and efficiency. As noted in the discussion of mean values, credit expansion is considerably more rapid in the crisis than noncrisis countries during the reform period. Thus, the negative impact of intermediation on growth and efficiency may reflect the much larger inflationary component in intermediation in the crisis countries compared with the noncrisis countries during financial reforms.

During the postreform period, the size of the financial system continues to be negatively related to growth and efficiency in the crisis countries. The latter result may reflect the burden on growth imposed by financial sector restructuring in the wake of financial crises, and the continuing weak role of the banking systems in savings mobilization

(De Gregorio and Guidotti, 1992, provide similar results). It also suggests that countries that downsized their financial systems more rapidly in the wake of a banking crisis may improve growth and efficiency.

Efficiency of intermediation

The proxies of the efficiency of financial intermediation, *RMDEP* or *SPREAD*, have the correct sign. The variables are insignificant in the growth equations and significant in the efficiency equations for the noncrisis countries. These results indicate that the efficiency of the financial system mainly affects the efficiency of investment, while the impact on growth is indirect. The results are similar for the crisis countries, but the efficiency proxies are insignificant during the reform period, which may again underline the weakness of the banking systems in these countries and the trouble banks have with the efficient mobilization and allocation of resources.

Conclusions

The results reported in the previous section lead to three broad conclusions. First, financial sector reforms can have important structural implications for the way financial sector variables affect the real economy. In particular, the expected effects of financial variables on economic growth and efficiency based on deductive reasoning become evident only after countries reform their financial systems. Under conditions of financial repression, expansions of financial intermediation can have limited or even perverse effects on economic performance. Also, policies to raise interest rates are likely to be ineffective under financial repression, unless they are accompanied by reforms intended to make the banking systems more responsive to financial variables.

Second, it is important to take into account the different dimensions of financial sector reform in explaining the impact of the reforms on economic performance. Earlier research has tended to represent financial development with a single variable. Our results from the entire sample, as well as the subsamples, though, suggest that separate effects on the interest cost of capital, the volume of intermediation, and the efficiency of intermediation can be identified. It is these effects that are important in understanding how financial reforms influence the real sector. For example, the positive effects on growth and efficiency of interest rate liberalization can be blunted by inefficiencies in the banking system, thus illustrating the importance of having a balanced and comprehensive approach to financial sector reform that includes a range of concomitant reforms to foster sound banking and institution building in support of financial liberalization.

Third, whether countries do or do not face financial crisis is an important determinant of the response of the real sector to financial sector reform and financial variables in general. The noncrisis countries usually experience strong improvements in economic growth and efficiency following the financial reforms. Crisis countries, however, tend to experience expansions in financial intermediation with negative effects on economic growth and efficiency. Moreover, according to our findings the wide fluctuations in real interest rates and the volume of intermediation in these countries harm economic performance. The timing and intensity of the banking crisis and the timing and size of the financial sector reforms differ considerably between the sample of countries. Nevertheless, analysis of the data suggests that the banking crises may in part have been related to the failure of the authorities to respond to the monetary shock, which can accompany financial reform, and the failure to adjust real interest rates during the reforms. In addition, a crisis may also have reflected the greater inefficiency and possibly solvency problems in the banking systems before reform.

These results underscore the importance of managing the monetary shocks that accompany financial sector reforms and that may lead to temporary inflationary financing. They also emphasize the significance of addressing institutional and banking sector weaknesses at a very early stage in financial sector reforms. (Specific issues in addressing banking sector weaknesses in the course of financial sector reforms are discussed in the previous chapter.) In summary, the "quality" of reform matters and the design of reforms is an important determinant of their success and of their impact on economic performance.

Appendix I: Financial Sector Reform Dates

Countries[1]	Date of Financial Reforms	Prereform Period	Postreform Period
United Kingdom	1971–75	1966–70	1976–80
Chile and Uruguay	1974–78	1969–73	1979–83
Argentina	1977–81	1972–76	1982–86
Japan	1978–82	1973–77	1983–87
Australia, Korea, and Philippines	1981–85	1976–80	1986–90
Indonesia and Italy	1983–87	1978–82	1988–92
France, Israel, Morocco, New Zealand, Norway, Spain, Sri Lanka, and Turkey	1985–89	1980–84	1989–93
Brazil, Costa Rica, Finland, Greece, Ireland, Jamaica, Malaysia, Mexico, Portugal, and Thailand	1986–90	1981–85	1990–93
Guatemala, Mauritius, and Venezuela	1989–93	1984–88	—
Ghana, Honduras, Kenya, Malawi, Paraguay, Peru, and Tanzania	1990–93	1986–90	—
El Salvador and Zambia	1991–93	1987–91	—

[1]Countries that encountered banking crises after the reform process include Argentina, Chile, Finland, Ghana, Israel, Norway, the Philippines, Thailand, Turkey, Uruguay, and Venezuela.

Appendix II: Description of the Data and Estimation Results

This table provides the description of the annual data used in the empirical analyses.

RGDPGR:	First difference of real GDP (line 99b.p of IFS).
OCR:	Output-capital ratio, calculated as output at 1987 prices divided by capital stock at 1987 prices (World Bank Database).
GEGDP:	Central government expenditure (line 82 of IFS) divided by nominal GDP (line 99b of IFS).
GDPDEF:	GDP deflator, calculated as nominal GDP divided by real GDP.
INF:	Percentage change in consumer price index (line 64 of IFS).
XMGDP:	Sum of exports (line 77aad of IFS) and imports (line 77abd of IFS) divided by nominal GDP.
DIGDP:	Foreign direct investment (line 77bad of IFS) times the exchange rate (line rf of IFS) divided by nominal GDP.
EDUCP:	Primary school enrollment rate (World Bank Social Indicators Database).
RIR:	Real interest rates, calculated as the nominal deposit interest rate (line 60l of IFS) minus the inflation rate.
CRED:	Claims on private sector by deposit money banks (line 32d of IFS) divided by nominal GDP.
M2GDP:	The sum of money (line 34 of IFS) and quasimoney (line 35 of IFS) divided by nominal GDP.
RMDEP:	Reserve money (line 14 of IFS) divided by nominal GDP.
SPREAD:	Lending rate (line 60p of IFS) minus deposit rate (line 60l of IFS).

Table 5.2 Estimation Results for the Noncrisis Countries: Growth Equations

Constant	GEGDP	INF	XMGDP	INVGDP	DIGDP	EDUCP	RIR	CRED	M2GDP	RMDEP	SPREAD	R^2
					Entire Period							
6.677**	–11.638**	–0.114**	0.422	0.132**	22.995	0.218*	0.049*	1.024*	—	–0.407	—	0.48
(5.38)	(–5.02)	(–4.11)	(1.37)	(11.93)	(1.40)	(1.72)	(1.84)	(1.95)	—	(–0.34)	—	
6.996**	–11.229**	–0.114**	0.360	0.132**	23.540	0.220*	0.050*	—	1.574*	–0.297	—	0.48
(5.41)	(–4.84)	(–4.09)	(0.32)	(10.15)	(1.44)	(1.74)	(1.77)	—	(1.83)	(–0.45)	—	
7.156**	–11.859**	–0.106**	0.217	0.136**	23.540	0.228*	0.044*	1.215*	—	—	–0.060*	0.49
(7.70)	(–5.30)	(–3.80)	(0.18)	(12.11)	(1.35)	(1.77)	(1.78)	(1.94)	—	—	(–1.80)	
7.423**	–11.307**	–0.105**	0.176	0.137**	22.497	0.231*	0.045*	—	1.789*	—	–0.062*	0.48
(7.73)	(–4.97)	(–3.78)	(0.15)	(12.18)	(1.38)	(1.88)	(1.72)	—	(1.80)	—	(–1.74)	
					Prereform							
4.361*	–3.995	–0.065	0.027	0.101**	6.388*	—	0.007	–1.241	—	–0.924	—	0.52
(1.86)	(–1.02)	(–1.26)	(1.013)	(3.89)	(1.76)	—	(0.12)	(–0.55)	—	(–0.31)	—	
3.791	–3.777	–0.063	0.209	0.103**	6.225*	—	0.008	—	–0.384	–0.282	—	0.52
(1.68)	(–0.979)	(–1.24)	(0.107)	(4.01)	(1.74)	—	(0.14)	—	(–0.19)	(–0.09)	—	
3.720**	–3.006	–0.073	0.062	0.096**	6.887*	—	0.009	–0.815	—	—	–0.036	0.53
(2.30)	(–1.01)	(–1.58)	(0.031)	(3.53)	(1.84)	—	(0.18)	(–0.45)	—	—	(–0.48)	
3.504*	–3.787	–0.067	0.247	0.098**	6.777*	—	0.007	—	–0.254	—	–0.038	0.53
(2.16)	(–0.99)	(–1.53)	(0.13)	(3.60)	(1.83)	—	(0.17)	—	(–0.14)	—	(–0.51)	
					Reform							
5.275**	–7.558**	–0.115*	3.537**	0.136**	19.298	—	0.041*	0.215*	—	–0.197		0.64
(2.93)	(–2.99)	(–1.72)	(3.49)	(6.41)	(0.94)	—	(1.68)	(1.87)	—	(–1.16)	—	
5.601**	–7.155**	–0.117*	3.549**	0.136**	18.872	—	0.036*	—	0.761*	–0.078	—	0.64
(3.46)	(–2.71)	(–2.04)	(3.52)	(6.51)	(0.93)	—	(1.69)		(1.75)	(–0.66)	—	
5.412**	–7.735**	–0.118*	3.522**	0.136**	16.694	—	0.043*	0.322*	—	—	–0.016	0.65
(3.28)	(–3.18)	(–1.69)	(3.54)	(6.35)	(0.79)	—	(1.72)	(1.77)	—	—	(–1.32)	
5.720**	–7.207**	–0.125*	3.559**	0.136**	15.982	—	0.034*	—	0.912*	—	–0.022	0.65
(3.83)	(–2.78)	(–2.13)	(3.57)	(6.47)	(0.77)	—	(1.68)	—	(1.79)	—	(–1.45)	

Table 5.2 (concluded)

Constant	GEGDP	INF	XMGDP	INVGDP	DIGDP	EDUCP	RIR	CRED	M2GDP	RMDEP	SPREAD	R^2
					Postreform							
14.613**	–19.043**	–0.129*	2.227	0.172**	15.260	—	0.070*	5.958**	—	–2.119	—	0.78
(3.84)	(–4.48)	(–1.76)	(1.17)	(5.81)	(0.61)	—	(1.89)	(2.82)	—	(–1.10)	—	
8.856**	–13.606**	–0.065*	2.888	0.173**	10.579	—	0.050**	—	2.981*	–0.144	—	0.74
(2.73)	(–3.24)	(–1.84)	(1.18)	(5.70)	(0.05)	—	(2.60)	—	(2.13)	(–0.76)	—	
13.028**	–17.555**	–0.149*	2.309	0.166**	10.854	—	0.093*	5.036**	—	—	–0.012	0.76
(3.84)	(–4.21)	(–2.03)	(0.95)	(5.95)	(0.41)	—	(1.76)	(2.47)	—	—	(–0.16)	
18.818**	–13.630**	–0.065*	14.373	0.169**	39.536	—	0.068*	—	2.338*	—	–0.054	0.73
(2.89)	(–3.27)	(–1.92)	(1.51)	(5.97)	(0.30)	—	(1.85)	—	(1.86)	—	(–0.69)	

Note: * = significant at 95 percent confidence level.
** = significant at 99 percent confidence level.

Table 5.3 Estimation Results for the Crisis Countries: Growth Equations

Constant	GEGDP	INF	XMGDP	INVGDP	DIGDP	EDUCP	RIR	CRED	M2GDP	RMDEP	SPREAD	R^2
					Entire Period							
1.705	–3.764	–0.502*	1.592**	0.152**	29.767	0.597**	0.004	–2.41*	—	–0.871	—	0.53
(0.54)	(–0.83)	(–1.82)	(3.62)	(8.34)	(0.97)	(1.84)	(1.28)	(–1.82)	—	(–1.11)	—	
2.236	–4.891	–0.478*	1.691**	0.153**	40.279	0.845**	0.004	—	–0.601*	–0.918	—	0.53
(0.80)	(–1.01)	(–1.84)	(3.90)	(8.28)	(1.33)	(1.74)	(1.29)	—	(1.76)	(–1.22)	—	
0.544	–3.618	–0.434*	1.562**	0.147**	21.763	0.369	0.004	–3.134*	—	—	–0.009	0.52
(0.18)	(–0.79)	(–1.93)	(3.35)	(8.16)	(0.72)	(1.52)	(1.28)	(–1.89)	—	—	(–1.97)	
1.116	–6.172	–0.415*	1.689**	0.149**	31.787	0.704	0.005	—	0.237*	—	0.006*	0.53
(0.42)	(–1.30)	(–1.98)	(3.70)	(8.08)	(1.07)	(1.69)	(1.29)	—	(1.73)	—	(–1.98)	
					Prereform							
13.175*	–1.617	–0.018	–1.146	0.086*	–14.914**	—	0.032	–3.424	—	–3.438	—	0.51
(2.16)	(–0.25)	(–1.23)	(–1.49)	(2.22)	(–2.51)	—	(0.74)	(–0.53)	—	(–1.30)	—	
16.757*	–1.492	–0.034	–5.500	0.108**	–14.578**	—	0.052	—	–1.441*	–4.131*	—	0.56
(2.87)	(1.28)	(–1.21)	(–0.68)	(2.66)	(–2.58)	—	(0.81)	—	(–1.72)	(–1.85)	—	
12.874*	–1.437	–0.179*	–1.624*	0.063*	–14.221**		0.249*	6.206	—	—	–0.185	0.61
(3.50)	(–1.66)	(–2.56)	(–2.27)	(1.73)	(–2.76)	—	(2.92)	(–1.24)	—	—	(–1.58)	
12.402*	–2.420*	–0.161*	–1.439*	0.086*	–15.664**	—	0.155**	—	–6.228	—	–0.158	0.61
(3.38)	(–2.00)	(–2.36)	(–1.95)	(2.33)	(–3.11)	—	(1.70)	—	(–0.88)	—	(–1.53)	
					Reform							
5.493	–7.160	–0.355*	3.087**	0.172**	50.630	—	0.103*	–7.024*	—	–0.120	—	0.78
(0.55)	(–0.88)	(–1.69)	(3.08)	(5.10)	(–0.94)	—	(2.05)	(–1.68)	—	(–1.15)	—	
–12.272	–24.691*	–0.203	16.329*	0.168**	48.535	—	0.081**	—	–19.177*	–8.211	—	0.80
(–0.95)	(–2.06)	(–0.87)	(2.11)	(5.86)	(–1.03)	—	(1.76)	—	(–2.25)	(1.25)	—	
12.452	–2.732	–0.217	20.064**	0.168**	–53.641	—	0.082**	–1.830*	—	—	–0.052	0.77
(1.55)	(–1.408)	(–0.47)	(2.82)	(5.79)	(–1.16)	—	(1.71)	(–1.74)	—	—	(–1.52)	
13.486*	–0.927	–0.045	23.897**	0.159**	–45.405	—	0.068*	—	–6.001*	—	–0.071*	0.77
(1.72)	(–0.13)	(–0.08)	(2.86)	(5.39)	(–0.97)	—	(1.73)	—	(–1.83)	—	(–1.68)	

Table 5.3 (*concluded*)

Constant	GEGDP	INF	XMGDP	INVGDP	DIGDP	EDUCP	RIR	CRED	M2GDP	RMDEP	SPREAD	R^2
					Postreform							
–6.297*	–4.062*	–0.085*	–3.508**	0.196**	–48.090	—	–0.044**	–3.581**	—	–0.533	—	0.78
(–3.27)	(–4.27)	(–2.09)	(–3.50)	(4.85)	(–1.02)	—	(–1.79)	(–7.59)	—	(–1.39)	—	
19.066	–3.476*	–0.599*	–3.566	0.121*	–53.224	—	–0.031*	—	–4.591**	–0.469	—	0.72
(0.78)	(–2.06)	(–1.94)	(–1.62)	(1.99)	(–1.30)	—	(–2.35)	—	(–3.53)	(–1.61)	—	
–3.307	–2.822*	–0.489	–2.146*	0.129**	–48.531	—	–0.115*	–3.067**	—	—	–0.019	0.73
(–1.63)	(–2.47)	(–1.62)	(–1.72)	(3.48)	(–1.45)	—	(–2.51)	(–6.71)	—	—	(–0.20)	
5.397	–3.704*	–0.411*	–1.768	0.165**	–59.874	—	–0.237*	—	–4.265**	—	–0.158	0.70
(0.24)	(–2.14)	(–1.91)	(–1.55)	(3.25)	(–1.07)	—	(3.38)	—	(–3.56)	—	(–0.67)	

Note: * = significant at 95 percent confidence level.
** = significant at 99 percent confidence level.

Table 5.4 Estimation Results for the Noncrisis Countries: Efficiency Equations

Constant	GEGDP	INF	XMGDP	DIGDP	EDUCP	RIR	CRED	M2GDP	RMDEP	SPREAD	R^2
					Entire Period						
0.364**	−0.288**	−0.014*	0.025	0.693*	0.020**	0.009*	0.091**	—	−0.030	—	0.58
(9.02)	(−5.13)	(−2.40)	(0.80)	(1.93)	(3.84)	(1.74)	(4.64)	—	(−1.09)	—	
0.386**	−0.265**	−0.013*	0.028	0.784*	0.021**	0.010	—	0.126**	−0.021	—	0.59
(9.26)	(−4.73)	(−2.33)	(0.89)	(2.19)	(3.94)	(1.58)	—	(4.66)	(−1.46)	—	
0.387**	−0.304**	−0.014*	0.034	0.711*	0.020**	0.009*	0.098**	—	—	−0.004*	0.57
(11.42)	(−5.63)	(−2.41)	(1.09)	(1.98)	(3.84)	(1.75)	(5.45)	—	—	(−1.72)	
0.404**	−0.274**	−0.013*	0.035	0.805*	0.020**	0.010	—	0.134**	—	−0.003*	0.56
(11.85)	(−5.04)	(−2.34)	(1.11)	(2.26)	(3.97)	(1.68)	—	(5.50)	—	(−1.78)	
					Prereform						
0.320**	−0.025	−0.002**	0.036	1.155**	—	−0.002**	−0.046*	—	−0.048	—	0.58
(6.87)	(−0.43)	(−3.21)	(1.25)	(3.41)	—	(−2.90)	(−1.91)	—	(−1.30)	—	
0.302**	−0.027	−0.002**	0.033	1.122**	—	0.002**	—	−0.065	−0.057	—	0.49
(6.36)	(−0.48)	(−3.34)	(1.13)	(3.46)	—	(−3.00)	—	(−1.56)	(−1.56)	—	
0.341**	−0.029	−0.018**	0.022	1.121**	—	−0.001**	−0.033*	—	—	−0.002*	0.51
(8.54)	(−0.50)	(−2.89)	(0.73)	(3.35)	—	(−2.53)	(−1.68)	—	—	(−1.86)	
0.332**	−0.032	−0.017**	0.018	1.099**	—	−0.001**	—	−0.047	—	−0.002*	0.50
(8.25)	(−0.56)	(−2.91)	(0.61)	(3.40)	—	(−2.52)	—	(−1.21)	—	(−1.91)	
					Reform						
0.462**	−0.217**	−0.006	0.038*	0.299	—	0.003*	−0.039		−0.147**	—	0.43
(8.22)	(−3.98)	(−0.94)	(1.76)	(1.20)	—	(1.73)	(−1.17)	—	(−3.87)		
0.506**	−0.203**	−0.004	0.029*	0.282	—	0.004*	—	0.096*	−0.178**	—	0.46
(8.38)	(−3.78)	(−0.53)	(1.77)	(1.14)	—	(1.76)	—	(1.98)	(−4.41)	—	
0.359**	−0.175**	−0.005	0.052*	0.023	—	0.005*	−0.010	—	—	−0.004*	0.53
(6.42)	(−3.22)	(−1.66)	(1.70)	(1.11)	—	(1.73)	(−0.917)	—	—	(−1.79)	
0.358**	−0.173**	−0.004	0.051*	0.022	—	0.006*	—	0.065*	—	−0.004*	0.55
(6.21)	(−3.16)	(−0.61)	(1.78)	(0.86)	—	(1.80)	—	(1.94)	—	(−1.74)	

Table 5.4 (*concluded*)

Constant	GEGDP	INF	XMGDP	DIGDP	EDUCP	RIR	CRED	M2GDP	RMDEP	SPREAD	R^2
					Postreform						
0.011	–0.062*	–0.021**	0.147**	0.211*	—	0.006*	0.036*	—	–0.067*	—	0.65
(0.11)	(–1.75)	(–3.29)	(3.70)	(1.94)	—	(1.75)	(1.76)	—	(–2.06)	—	
0.009	–0.012*	–0.023**	0.159**	0.260*	—	0.006*	—	0.027*	–0.046*	—	0.64
(0.09)	(–1.81)	(–3.21)	(3.68)	(1.83)	—	(1.84)	—	(1.77)	(–1.95)	—	
0.072	–0.061*	–0.022**	0.170**	0.144	—	0.004	0.028*	—	—	–0.001*	0.67
(0.57)	(–1.92)	(–3.02)	(4.03)	(1.57)	—	(1.63)	(1.91)	—	—	(–1.71)	
0.087	–0.024*	–0.024**	0.176**	0.201*	—	0.004**	—	0.034*	—	–0.002*	0.65
(0.68)	(–1.88)	(–2.94)	(3.91)	(1.77)	—	(2.58)	—	(1.75)	—	(–1.732)	

Note: * = significant at 95 percent confidence level.
** = significant at 99 percent confidence level.

Table 5.5 Estimation Results for the Crisis Countries: Efficiency Equations

Constant	GEGDP	INF	XMGDP	DIGDP	EDUCP	RIR	CRED	M2GDP	RMDEP	SPREAD	R^2
					Entire Period						
0.791**	–0.118*	–0.010*	0.226**	0.554*	0.093**	–0.005*	0.049*	—	–0.001	—	0.43
(12.23)	(–1.72)	(–1.62)	(4.23)	(1.61)	(6.92)	(–1.73)	(1.77)	—	(–1.11)	—	
0.755**	–0.075	–0.009*	0.206**	0.429	0.083**	0.006	—	–0.015	–0.005	—	0.45
(10.99)	(–1.04)	(–1.85)	(3.87)	(1.25)	(5.71)	(1.58)	—	(–1.33)	(–1.58)	—	
0.790**	–0.109*	–0.023*	0.219**	0.570*	0.093**	–0.006*	–0.049*	—	—	–0.001*	0.44
(12.46)	(–1.70)	(–1.91)	(4.03)	(1.67)	(6.98)	(–1.75)	(–1.83)	—	—	(–1.70)	
0.756**	–0.064*	–0.023	0.199**	0.467	0.082**	–0.005*	—	–0.013	—	–0.001*	0.42
(11.35)	(–1.89)	(–1.59)	(3.67)	(1.36)	(5.82)	(–1.67)	—	(–1.29)	—	(–1.73)	
					Prereform						
0.715**	–0.009*	–0.033*	–0.098	0.339	—	–0.009*	–0.046*	—	–0.025	—	0.53
(4.81)	(–2.09)	(–2.08)	(–1.24)	(0.63)	—	(–2.09)	(–1.61)	—	(–1.45)	—	
0.719**	–0.048*	–0.027*	–0.075	0.410	—	–0.006*	—	–0.087	0.028	—	0.57
(4.99)	(–2.38)	(–1.65)	(–0.91)	(0.82)	—	(–2.16)	—	(–1.11)	(–1.52)	—	
0.683**	–0.296*	–0.025**	0.043	0.531	—	–0.005**	–0.070*	—	—	–0.002**	0.62
(6.66)	(–2.07)	(–2.48)	(–0.67)	(0.51)	—	(–3.70)	(–2.13)	—	—	(–2.84)	
0.695**	–0.274*	–0.022*	–0.031	0.232	—	–0.004**	—	–0.066	—	–0.002**	0.61
(7.24)	(–2.01)	(–2.32)	(–0.48)	(0.58)	—	(–2.92)	—	(–1.05)	—	(–2.64)	
					Reform						
0.864**	–0.042	–0.011*	0.238**	–0.417	—	0.008*	–0.159**		0.070	—	0.69
(5.60)	(–0.45)	(–2.05)	(3.63)	(–0.96)	—	(1.85)	(–3.63)	—	(–0.92)	—	
0.884**	–0.086	0.020*	0.237**	–0.257	—	0.005*	—	–0.042*	–0.038	—	0.58
(5.27)	(–0.71)	(–1.74)	(3.05)	(–0.54)	—	(1.98)	—	(–1.73)	(–0.38)	—	
0.917**	–0.059	–0.047*	0.203**	–0.468	—	0.004*	–0.135**	—	—	–0.002	0.68
(9.15)	(–0.73)	(–1.82)	(3.07)	(–1.10)	—	(1.75)	(–3.29)	—	—	(–1.64)	
0.811**	–0.022	–0.038*	0.169**	0.255	—	0.005*	—	–0.054*	—	–0.001*	0.67
(8.84)	(–0.38)	(–1.75)	(2.29)	(1.32)	—	(2.26)	—	(–1.76)	—	(–2.17)	

Table 5.5 (*concluded*)

Constant	GEGDP	INF	XMGDP	DIGDP	EDUCP	RIR	CRED	M2GDP	RMDEP	SPREAD	R^2
					Postreform						
0.868**	0.386**	–0.066*	–0.116*	0.363	—	–0.002**	–0.060*	—	–0.058**	—	0.64
(5.12)	(2.61)	(–1.70)	(–1.71)	(1.57)	—	(–3.47)	(–2.30)	—	(–3.38)	—	
1.024**	0.607**	–0.095**	–0.104*	0.478	—	–0.001**	—	–0.312**	–0.036**	—	0.66
(9.92)	(5.45)	(–2.72)	(–1.78)	(1.46)	—	(–4.13)	—	(–4.30)	(–2.55)	—	
0.827**	0.485**	–0.054*	–0.126*	0.874*	—	–0.001*	–0.144**	—	—	–0.002*	0.62
(3.58)	(2.63)	(–1.81)	(–1.93)	(1.68)	—	(–2.01)	(–2.71)	—	—	(–1.78)	
1.030**	0.590**	–0.098*	–0.134*	0.801*	—	–0.001*	—	–0.296**	—	–0.003*	0.69
(13.22)	(10.58)	(–1.94)	(–1.67)	(1.78)	—	(–1.88)	—	(–7.61)	—	(–2.14)	

Note: * = significant at 95 percent confidence level.
** = significant at 99 percent confidence level.

6

Sequencing Capital Account Liberalization: Lessons from Chile, Indonesia, Korea, and Thailand

R. BARRY JOHNSTON, SALIM M. DARBAR, AND CLAUDIA ECHEVERRIA

Capital account liberalization can have significant benefits for economic growth and welfare. It can improve a country's ability to tap global savings (at a lower cost than using only domestic savings); allow domestic economic agents the freedom to choose how and where to borrow, invest, or exchange assets; improve resource allocation through increased competition for financial resources; and increase the availability of resources to support investment, finance trade, and boost other significant economic sectors. At the same time, however, the opening of the capital account entails certain risks, if not accompanied by the necessary structural reforms and macroeconomic policies.

Against this background, one needs to consider sequencing capital account liberalization with structural measures, especially in the monetary and financial sector, and pacing liberalization in conjunction

Note: This chapter was first issued as IMF Working Paper 97/157, "Sequencing Capital Account Liberalization: Lessons from the Experiences in Chile, Indonesia, Korea, and Thailand," in November 1997. It has been expanded here to include a section examining the relationship between the nature of capital account liberalization and the events leading up to the Asian currency crisis.

with the development of appropriate macroeconomic policies. This chapter examines some of the general issues involved in the sequencing and pacing of capital account liberalization and draws lessons from emerging market economies that have liberalized their capital accounts and at the same time have received large capital inflows: Chile, Indonesia, Korea, and Thailand. These countries were chosen in order to illustrate the diversity as well as some of the similarities of approaches toward capital account liberalization. The information reviewed is for the period 1985–96, but has been extended to 1997 in the case of Thailand to include the period leading up to the 1997 crisis.

A complete analysis of the role of capital account liberalization would require a comprehensive assessment of structural and macroeconomic policies. This study focuses on key variables and certain interrelationships that are considered critical—specifically, (1) the development of domestic financial markets, instruments, and institutions; (2) reforms to foreign exchange and trade systems; (3) the development in countries' balance of payments; and (4) the role of monetary and exchange rate policy.

A Conceptual Framework for Orderly Capital Account Liberalization

The conventional view on liberalizing the capital account is that it should follow the opening of the current account and the domestic financial system (see, for example, McKinnon, 1973 and 1982; Frenkel, 1982; and Edwards, 1984). Others have argued for simultaneous liberalization of the current and capital accounts (see, for example, Little, Scitovsky, and Scott, 1970; Michaely, 1986; and Krueger, 1984). Hanson (1994) suggests that a stable macroeconomy and domestic financial liberalization to a significant degree are preconditions to international financial liberalization. Our own assessment suggests that such stylized prescriptions are misleading, because the results of the survey indicate that undertaking the liberalization of the capital account and other aspects of economic and financial sector reform is a good deal more complex and requires attention to linkages among specific components of broader reform areas. In each country, different components and aspects of the capital account were liberalized at various stages, along with specific aspects of the current account and domestic financial sector, in line with each respective country's overall macroeconomic objectives. In some instances liberalizing, or easing of restrictions, occurred in response to adverse macroeconomic developments. The survey does, however, lead to broad conclusions about the conceptual framework for an orderly liberalization of the capital account.

The Need for an Integrated Approach

The first broad conclusion from this survey is that there is a fundamental need for an integrated approach to capital account liberalization and financial sector reform. It is erroneous to draw sharp distinctions between the public policy approach to the deregulation of the capital account on the one hand, and the approach to the regulation and development of financial markets on the other. Rather, capital account liberalization should be treated as an integral part of economic reform programs.

More specifically, the liberalization of direct investment is often a significant part of real sector reforms, while the liberalization of portfolio investment flows is often coordinated with financial sector reforms and the development of financial markets and instruments.

Liberalizations of *direct investment* inflows have often gone hand-in-hand with reforms aimed at strengthening the real sector and export potential of the economy, including reforms to the trade and investment regimes, adjustments to the exchange rate to improve competitiveness, and liberalization of exchange controls on current international transactions. Such loosening of capital account controls have aimed, for example, at supporting the development and restructuring of selective industries and sectors, through management and technology transfers, injections of foreign capital, and improved access to trade finance.

Liberalizations of *portfolio capital flows* have tended to be coordinated with domestic financial sector liberalization and reforms—liberalization of interest rates, development of indirect monetary control procedures, and the strengthening of banks and capital markets.

There are a number of reasons for adopting a coordinated and comprehensive approach to financial sector reforms and capital account liberalization. First, from a macroeconomic and balance of payments perspective, the stage of development and the stability of domestic financial systems are critical to the growth and composition of capital movements. Such factors are often as important, if not more so, in explaining the volume and nature of the capital flows than the particular regulatory framework for such movements. Countries with developed financial markets and institutions have been better able to attract portfolio capital flows than countries where such markets are just emerging. In some circumstances, concerns about banking solvency or inadequate regulatory frameworks have discouraged foreign investment or encouraged capital flight regardless of the capital control framework. Financial sector weakness may also contribute to currency crises to the extent the weaknesses are seen as limiting the scope or the willingness of authorities to use interest rates to defend the currency; or cast doubts on the prospects of the economy in general (e.g., recognition that addressing financial sector weakness may have significant budgetary costs); or cast doubts on the political autonomy and the integrity and governance of financial institutions.

Second, and conversely, the opening of the capital account can have important implications for financial markets and institutions. In many cases, the implications are positive in that the liberalizations help to develop deeper, more competitive, and more diversified financial markets. The sophistication of domestic financial markets can also be improved if foreign financial institutions are allowed to operate directly in the country. The greater volume of intermediation and increased competition that may accompany capital account liberalizations, however, may also increase pressure on previously protected domestic financial institutions and bring weaknesses to the fore in such institutions. Some countries have experienced banking crises when confronted with sudden inflows and subsequent sharp reversals in capital flows. The banking sector problems may be exacerbated by significant open positions of banks, or their borrowers. In such cases, adjustments in interest rates and exchange rates can reduce the net worth of financial institutions that have not developed adequate mechanisms to manage interest and exchange rate risks. Countries with sound banking systems have been better able to handle reversals in capital inflows since in a strong financial system, banking weaknesses do not constrain interest rate and exchange rate policies.

Third, the efficient use of capital flows and, thus, the extent to which such flows contribute to sustained improvements in economic performance depend on the stage of development and efficiency of the domestic financial system. The strength of the domestic system in turn may depend on the existence of a well-regulated and supervised financial system, and on the elimination of various sources of market failures that may be the legacy of previous financial repression. Consequently, there is a need for opening the capital account in step with the reforms of domestic financial markets and institutions.[1]

Fourth, successful and sustained opening of the capital account requires the existence of a minimum set of instruments, institutions, and markets for the effective management of monetary and exchange rate policy with an open capital account. High capital mobility alters the effectiveness of different monetary instruments in achieving the objectives of monetary policy. On the one hand, instruments that impose a high cost or administrative constraint on the banks—as is the case with credit or interest rate ceilings or high nonremunerated reserve requirements—may be circumvented more easily by disintermediation through the capital account, and therefore become less effective. On the other hand, with an open capital account, monetary instruments that operate on the overall cost of money or credit in financial markets may be transmitted more rapidly to credit and exchange markets and may allow the central bank to influence the decisions of financial institutions and markets that operate in its domestic currency, both locally and internationally. Indirect monetary instruments, such as open-market operations, therefore come to play a core role in steering interest rates, managing the liquidity situation in the market, and signaling the stance of monetary policy.

Fifth, as a practical matter, the distinction between capital controls and financial regulations may not be straightforward. Indeed, many controls on capital movements are often exercised through regulations on the underlying capital transactions rather than the associated payments and receipts. A number of capital controls are in the form of financial regulatory measures, including reserve requirements that discriminate between residents and nonresidents, or may be the consequence of the particular regulatory frameworks for financial markets and financial institutions. An analysis of the regulatory factors influencing capital movements therefore requires a more complete understanding of overall financial regulatory frameworks, and of the extent

[1]For a discussion of the sources of such market failures and the need for supporting reforms, see Johnston (1997).

to which limitations on capital movements are an incidental consequence of the need to protect investors and exercise prudential oversight over financial institutions or a deliberate attempt to influence the volume of capital movements for macroeconomic and balance of payments reasons.

Finally, the dynamics of reforms might also argue for synchronization of domestic financial sector reforms and the liberalization of capital movements. Financial sector reforms often involve a rapid monetization of the economy and a period during which the growth of credit exceeds that of money as agents adjust to the elimination of financial repression (see Chapter 3). Capital account liberalizations are often associated with initial surpluses in the capital account of the balance of payments—a factor reflecting the improved environment for investors and the return of flight capital (see Johnston and Ryan, 1994). If confronted separately, each of these factors can create problems for monetary and macroeconomic management. If confronted together, however, the adjustments in the monetary and external sectors can be offsetting to some extent (see Johnston, 1997). Thus, the more rapid growth of credit than money following domestic financial sector liberalization would, other things being equal, tend to place pressure on the balance of payments. This pressure may be offset through the return of flight capital that may accompany the liberalization of the capital account. Both adjustments of asset portfolios reflect the elimination of financial repression and are in this sense equilibrating, but circumstances could also arise where the capital inflows contribute to a more rapid expansion in bank credits. In such cases, simultaneous financial sector and capital account liberalization could compound the macroeconomic management difficulties. This is likely to be a particular concern when there is limited autonomy in monetary policy.

Capital Account Liberalization and Macroeconomic Policy Design

The second broad conclusion from the survey is that the pace of capital account liberalization needs to be adapted to macroeconomic policy. What is generally important for managing the volume of capital flows is the overall incentive structure that produces such flows. A number of items will tend to influence this incentive structure—including particular regulatory frameworks and the stage of development and soundness of the financial system. Another important consideration is the configuration of interest rates and exchange rates.

As a general proposition, stock-flow portfolio analysis can be applied to analyze the factors influencing capital movements, as well as to distinguish between the short- and longer-run effects of capital controls.[2] In the short run, the "grit-in-the-wheels" effect of capital controls might allow a country temporarily to reduce the rate of capital flows, but over time investors will adjust their portfolios to reflect portfolio balance considerations. The longer-run impact of controls on capital flows will thus depend on whether the regulations increase or reduce risk-adjusted rates of return. The observed capital flight in countries maintaining controls, and the observed net strengthening of the capital account when countries eliminate controls, suggests that capital controls are generally treated by investors as an additional risk factor. This leads to the seemingly perverse conclusion that a country restricting capital flows would have to maintain higher interest rates to compensate for the increased risks. Nevertheless, evidence from curb markets in countries with repressed financial systems would generally support this view. Thus, contrary to the usual assumption that capital controls can help reduce local interest rates and limit outflows, one of the major considerations in capital account liberalization is the management of the inflows that are likely to follow such liberalization in view of the decline in investor risk premiums. Similarly, the degree of protection that capital controls provide to individual markets and institutions will depend on the extent to which there would be second-round portfolio adjustments. For example, capital flows into security markets are likely to have an expansionary impact on the balance sheets of domestic banks as well, because of liquidity effects and portfolio adjustments that would follow changes in relative interest rates and asset prices, even if there are controls on inflows to commercial banks.

A portfolio-balance approach is complemented with the covered interest rate parity condition that is the consequence of arbitrage between short-term domestic and foreign interest rates, and the discount

[2]For an early discussion of stock-flow portfolio analysis as applied to international capital movements, see Mundell (1963). See also McKinnon and Oates (1966), and Branson (1974).

on the currency in the forward exchange market. The covered interest rate parity condition can be written as follows:

$$i_d = i_f + F_d ; \tag{1}$$

where $F_d = \frac{e^f - e^s}{e^s} \times 100$,

i_d is the domestic interest; i_f, the foreign interest rate of the same maturity, and F_d, the forward discount for that maturity; e^s is the rate of exchange (units of domestic currency in terms of a foreign currency) in the spot exchange market; and e^f, the forward exchange rate on the date of maturity of the interest rate contracts. Thus, where the foreign interest rate and forward exchange rate are predetermined, a country could determine the domestic interest rate or the spot exchange rate, but not both.

With greater freedom of capital movements, short-term interest rates will increasingly be determined by the covered interest rate parity condition. An attempt to set both interest rates and exchange rates, which are inconsistent with this condition, could give rise to incentives for significant short-term capital flows. The potential magnitude of such flows will, among other things, reflect the expectations for the currency and the particular exchange rate.

Thus, with increased capital mobility, the capacity to assign monetary and exchange policies to achieve different macroeconomic targets will be increasingly constrained. If monetary policy is targeted to constraining inflation, the exchange rate would not be free, for example, to be used as an expenditure switching instrument to achieve objectives for the current account. Fiscal policy could be used to influence the savings/investment balance to achieve such objectives but monetary and exchange rate policy could not. Conversely, if the exchange rate is targeted to achieve objectives for the current account, or if the exchange rate is fixed, monetary policy would be left with little autonomy to achieve domestic stabilization objectives.

Assigning monetary policy, and consequently exchange rate policy, the task of domestic stabilization may require that either exchange rates or domestic interest rates, or both, are allowed to become more flexible. Higher capital mobility may also result in greater volatility in interest rates or exchange rates in view of the sensitivity of capital flows to changes in market sentiment and the more rapid transmission of shocks and potential contagion affects. Greater flexibility of the exchange rate or interest rates may help discourage short-term speculative flows that exploit inconsistent interest rate and exchange rate alignments. Where capital is attracted by high domestic interest rates as part of a disinflationary program, temporary appreciation of the exchange rate may help to support the disinflationary strategy and allow for a more rapid lowering of domestic interest rates to international levels, while at the same time meeting the inflation target. Once inflation and interest rates have been brought down, the exchange rate should also adjust to a level consistent with a sustainable balance of payments. The costs would depend on whether export performance would be seriously affected by a temporary appreciation in the exchange rate, as well as whether markets exist to hedge the risks of greater volatility.

One of the risks of assigning exchange rate policy to current account objectives and relying on fiscal consolidation to achieve domestic stabilization with an open capital account is that the authorities' freedom to deal with speculative short-term flows is likely to be seriously constrained by the limited short-run flexibility of fiscal policy. Many countries have as a consequence resorted to capital controls in these circumstances. The extent to which capital controls can be used to manage the overall volume and structure of capital flows is questionable, however. Thus, the viability of such an assignment of instruments to targets also appears questionable with the increased volumes of capital flows.

Consequences of the Pace and Sequencing of Capital Account Liberalization

The above analysis argues for integrating capital account liberalization with the design of structural and macroeconomic policies. Maximizing the benefits from capital account liberalization while minimizing the risks requires a comprehensive approach to reforms.

A comprehensive approach will generally involve the coordination of the liberalizations of portfolio capital flows with domestic financial sector liberalization and reforms—that is, liberalization of interest rates, development of indirect monetary control procedures, and the strengthening of banks and capital markets through, among other measures, improved regulations. A lack of coordination between the domestic financial sector and capital account reforms can create distortions and regulatory incentives for capital movements that are unrelated to the underlying economic conditions, thus risking greater instability in capital movements. At the same time, there would be good reason to coordinate the liberalization of foreign direct investment with reforms aimed at strengthening the real sector and export potential of the economy, including reforms to the trade and investment regimes, exchange rate adjustments to improve competitiveness, and liberalization of exchange controls on current international transactions.

Where financial systems are weak, policymakers should address the institutional weaknesses in advance of, or concurrent with, the liberalization of the capital account. Countries that have not raised their institutional capacity to implement prudential regulations to the level of international best practice may also need to rely temporarily on selective capital controls as part of their financial regulatory frameworks. In view of the fungibility of capital, however, too much reliance cannot be placed on capital controls in protecting particular institutions and markets.[3] Consequently, it is important for countries to make rapid progress in strengthening financial markets and institutions generally.

A comprehensive approach would also require an appropriate and consistent mix of macroeconomic and exchange rate policies. This mix may well require a reorientation of monetary and exchange rate policy to provide appropriate autonomy of monetary policy in dealing with capital inflows.

Such a well-planned and sequenced program of reforms does not necessarily imply a gradualist approach. Rather, an effective program calls for coordinated and concurrent reforms irrespective of the pace of the reforms. In fact, in some cases liberalizing the capital account before implementing other parts of the economic and financial sector reform program may be desirable. More rapid capital account liberalization can provide momentum to the overall reform process by weakening entrenched vested interests and bureaucratic control of private sector activities. It can also help to develop markets by increasing competition and promoting a larger volume of capital flows. In such cases,

[3]For a discussion of the effectiveness of capital controls, see Johnston and Ryan (1994), Cardoso and Goldfajn (1997), and Dooley (1996).

faster liberalization of the capital account would require similarly rapid progress in the necessary concurrent reforms to domestic financial markets and institutions and in adapting the macroeconomic policy framework. Speeding up these reforms is desirable in any event in view of the limited extent to which countries can insulate themselves from the market.

Selected Country Experiences with Sequencing Capital Account Liberalization

This section discusses the experience of four countries with capital account liberalization from 1985 to 1996. For each country, a detailed country matrix describing the sequence of reforms to domestic and external transactions is provided in the Appendix with a summary of measures in the text. Domestic reforms have been grouped into reforms to the financial supervisory and regulatory framework; the development of money markets and instruments; and the development of capital markets. External reforms are grouped into reforms to the exchange market arrangement and system; direct investment; portfolio investment; the trade regime; and introduction of restrictions on capital flows. Where appropriate a distinction is made between capital inflows and outflows.[4] The Appendix tables also present selected macroeconomic and balance of payments indicators. For reference purposes, information on the stock position for the exchange and capital control regimes for the four countries can be found in the IMF's *Annual Report on Exchange Arrangements and Exchange Restrictions* (1997).

Chile

The sequencing of Chile's reforms of domestic and external transactions during the period 1985–96 is summarized in Table 6.1 and de-

[4]Whether a capital control measure would mainly affect capital inflows or capital outflows may not be evident. For example, a control on the liquidation and repatriation of foreign-held capital, while strictly a control of capital outflows, has often been maintained for the purpose of discouraging capital inflows. Moreover, there is overlap between certain measures classified as exchange system measures and measures classified as changes in the capital control regime.

Table 6.1. Chile: Sequencing of External and Domestic Financial Liberalization

(M represents major measures and m represents relatively minor measures)

	1985	1986	1987	1988	1989	1990	1991	1992	1993	1994	1995	1996
Monetary controls and financial system												
Capital market development	m					m	m	m	m	m	m	m
Money market and instruments	m		m				M	m	m		M	m
Financial supervisory and regulatory framework	M	M	m		M						m	
Exchange system, trade and capital flows												
Exchange regime	m[1]	m[2]		m[3]	m[4]		m[5]	M[6]		m[7]		M[8]
Exchange market arrangement and system	m	m		m		M[9]	m	m	m	m	M	m
Trade reforms	m		M	m		m	m	m	m			
Liberalization of portfolio investment												
Inflows	M	m	M			m	m	m	m		m	m
Outflows						m	M	m	M	M	M	M
Liberalization of direct investment												
Inflows	M				m				M			
Outflows									M			
Restrictions on capital flows												
Inflows						m	M	m		m	M	m
Outflows						m			m			

[1]The peso was devalued twice, the exchange rate band was widened from 0.5 percent to ±2 percent, and the peso was adjusted daily by 1.7 percent per month until August 1985. After August, the peso was adjusted daily based on the previous month's inflation less external inflation.

[2]The peso continued to be adjusted daily based on the previous month's inflation less external inflation leading to a 10.5 percent depreciation during the year.

[3]The exchange rate band was widened from ±2 percent to ±3 percent on each side of the center rate.

[4]The exchange rate policy to seek a real depreciation of the peso was abandoned and the exchange rate band was widened from ±3 percent to ±5 percent. In addition, the estimated rate of external inflation used in adjusting the exchange rate was lowered from 0.4 percent to 0.3 percent.

[5]The midpoint exchange rate was devalued three times during the year accumulating a total of 3.4 percent, and the reference rate of the peso was appreciated by 2 percent.

[6]The exchange rate arrangement of the peso changed from a peg to the U.S. dollar to a peg to a basket of currencies, the reference rate of the peso was revalued by 5 percent, and the exchange rate band was widened from ±5 percent to ±10 percent.

[7]The midpoint of the exchange rate band was revalued by 10 percent, and the weights of the reference currency basket were changed.

[8]The weights of the currency basket were changed, and the width of the exchange rate band was increased from ±10 percent to ±12 percent.

[9]The parallel foreign exchange market became an informal legal market in which the exchange rate was freely determined.

scribed in detail in Appendix Table 6.6; selected macroeconomic and balance of payment indicators are presented in Figure 6.1 and Appendix Table 6.7.

After an earlier experience with rapid liberalization and a banking crisis, Chile followed a gradualist approach to reforms. During the period covering 1985–89, the reforms focused on completing the restructuring of the banking system, establishing indirect methods of monetary control, carrying out trade reform, increasing the scope of transactions by banks, establishing the autonomy of the Central Bank of Chile, and selectively liberalizing direct and portfolio capital inflows. Later phases of reforms emphasized the development of financial markets, the adoption of more flexible interest rate and exchange rate policies, and selective relaxation of controls on capital inflows and outflows, accompanied by the introduction of controls on certain capital inflows mainly in 1991 and 1995.

Restoring the soundness of the banking system, which had been damaged in the earlier banking crisis, and reversing the earlier protectionist trade policies were given priority from 1985–87.[5] The earlier banking crisis and external shocks had led policymakers to reverse interest rate liberalization. Following the completion of the banking restructuring, the central bank eliminated the practice of announcing indicative interest rates in 1987, and influenced the level of domestic interest rates mainly through open-market operations in its indexed instruments. Capital market activity, which had been moderate, was promoted gradually—pension funds were allowed to invest part of their assets in selected domestic stocks beginning in 1985. In 1989, the law established the legal autonomy of the central bank.

Chile's liberalization of external transactions focused initially on trade liberalization—providing more liberal access to foreign exchange for current international transactions—exchange rate adjustment, and exchange market development. In 1985, previous tariff increases were rolled back in two steps, and, concurrently, the ex-

---

[5]For a discussion of the banking crisis and official responses, see Velasco (1991). In 1986, the General Banking Law and the Organic Law of Superintendency of Bank and Financial Institutions were substantially modified to give banks a broader scope of transactions in recognition of new types of financial services and to reduce the risks of another banking crisis. In October 1989, Congress enacted a constitutional law establishing legal autonomy for the central bank, which gave it the mandate to ensure the stability of the financial system.

Figure 6.1 Chile: Selected Macroeconomic Indicators

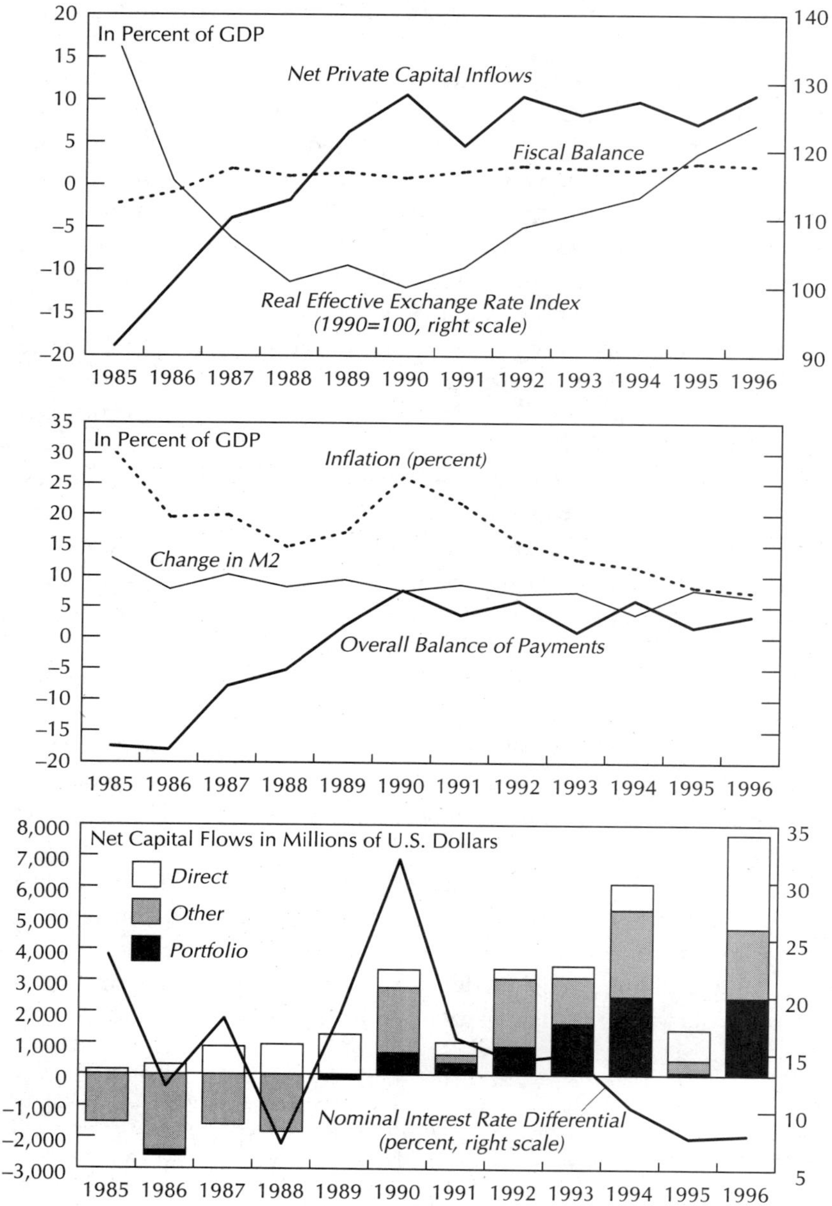

Sources: IMF, *International Financial Statistics, Direction of Trade Statistics*; and IMF staff estimates.

change rate was devalued to offset the impact of the lower tariffs and to bring the exchange rate to a more realistic level.[6] Limitations were eased on payments and transfers for current international transactions, and new instruments were introduced in the foreign exchange market.

Capital account measures were selective and focused initially on liberalizing capital inflows. In 1985, amendments to Chapter XIX of the central bank's foreign exchange regulations permitted foreign direct investment inflows through debt/equity swaps.[7] Capital from these investments, however, could not be repatriated for 10 years and profits for four years. Such swap operations were further promoted in 1987, with the authorization of External Investment Funds.[8] Also under an amendment to Chapter XVIII of the foreign exchange regulations, nonresidents were permitted to purchase selected debt instruments, but the source of foreign exchange and the conversions had to take place outside the official foreign exchange market. Allowable transactions were broadened in 1986, and again in 1987, when nonresidents were permitted to invest in publicly offered instruments with the repatriation of the original capital after five years and no limit on profit remittances. In 1989, the Additional Tax on the repatriation of profits by foreign investors under the Income Tax Law was reduced from 40 percent to 35 percent.

The capital account of the balance of payments showed a marked strengthening and recorded a surplus in 1989 reflecting much stronger foreign direct investment inflows (see Figure 6.1 and Appendix Table 6.7). In 1989, monetary policy was tightened to offset accelerating inflation, and portfolio capital inflows increased substantially, reflecting the large interest differentials. In this context, the authorities abandoned their previous policy of seeking a real depreciation of the ex-

---

[6]A 15 percent import surcharge was introduced on July 18, 1984, in addition to the existing 20 percent uniform import duty for products under 248 customs categories, partly replacing existing surcharges. The general tariff level was increased from 20 percent to 35 percent on September 22, 1984.

[7]The main legal framework for foreign investment in Chile was the Decree-Law No. 600, or Foreign Investment Statute, of 1974 as amended several times, and the Compendium of Foreign Exchange Regulations of the Central Bank of Chile, in particular Chapters XII, XIV, XVIII, XIX, XXVI, and XXVIII. For legal interpretations of the Regulations, see Mayorga and Montt (1995).

[8]Under the new mechanism, small external investors were able to participate in debt/equity conversions without having to go through the case-by-case conditions normally applied to such operations.

change rate, and widened the band for the fluctuations in the exchange rate.[9]

Beginning in 1990, the authorities emphasized the development of domestic financial markets and instruments. Several measures were implemented to broaden and enhance the efficiency and competitiveness of the stock exchange and local security markets: trading in futures contracts was introduced in 1990; pension funds were allowed to invest a greater percentage of their assets in equities; and electronic screen-based trading and settlement systems began functioning in 1993. The following year the stock market introduced trading in options, and during 1995–96, the investment activities of pension funds in the local securities markets were further liberalized. Concurrently, the money and foreign exchange markets were developed. The central bank enhanced its capacity to conduct monetary operations by widening the range of instruments and maturities used in open market operations (see Alexander, Baliño, and Enoch, 1995). Under new foreign exchange regulations, all foreign exchange transactions were permitted unless specifically prohibited by the central bank, and the parallel foreign exchange market became an informal legal market in which the exchange rate was freely determined.

In response to the large capital inflows recorded in 1990, the authorities began to liberalize capital outflows. In 1991, residents were allowed for the first time to use foreign exchange obtained in the unofficial market to invest abroad, and the period of investment after which capital could be repatriated by nonresidents was shortened to three years. In 1992, the pension funds were granted limited freedom to invest overseas, and remittances of profits and capital earned on foreign investments were allowed in advance of pre-existing schedules under certain conditions. Foreign inflows were also liberalized by allowing the issue of American Depository Receipts, and in 1991 the arrangements for trading shares sold through American Depository Receipts were expanded and taxes on dividends were reduced. At the same time, new restrictions were introduced on certain capital flows. In 1991, the central bank introduced a 20 percent reserve requirement on new foreign borrowing—except for trade credits—with the

[9]Under the crawling exchange rate parity, the peso was devalued daily on the basis of the difference between domestic inflation in the previous month and expected external inflation. The exchange rate had also been widened in 1985 and 1988; see Table 6.1.

objective of limiting short-term capital inflows. Subsequently, the reserve requirement was extended to most outstanding foreign borrowing and to foreign currency deposits, and increased to 30 percent. The stamp duties imposed on domestic loans were also extended to foreign loans.

Net capital inflows declined briefly in 1991 as interest rates were reduced, but recovered sharply in 1992. In response to continuing large capital inflows and upward pressure on the exchange rate, the reference rate of the peso was revalued, and modified from a peg to the U.S. dollar to a peg to a basket of currencies, and the fluctuation band for the exchange rate around the central rate of crawl was widened from ±5 percent to ±10 percent. Inflation was constrained through continued fiscal consolidation appreciation, in the real exchange rate, and sterilized foreign exchange intervention.[10] (See Figure 6.1 and Appendix Table 6.7.)

During the period 1993–96, the pace of capital account liberalization accelerated, with a greater emphasis placed on capital outflows. Certain restrictions on capital inflows were also intensified. In 1993, the minimum period for capital to remain in the country was reduced from three years to one, and the time limit for remittances of profits was eliminated. In 1994, foreign portfolio investment outflows were encouraged by allowing life insurance companies, pension funds, banks, and mutual funds to invest larger percentages of their portfolios abroad through the official market, allowing domestic banks to invest in financial institutions abroad, and granting individuals access to the formal exchange market for a limited set of capital transactions.[11] Capital outflows were liberalized further in 1995–96 by broadening the allowable assets and increasing the limits on foreign investments. Portfolio investment inflows were also encouraged by reducing the

[10]Sterilization policies were used throughout the entire period but more heavily during 1990–92 (see Lee, 1996). The main instrument used was that of open market operations in central bank paper (one-year promissory notes). Longer-term promissory notes (four- and six-year) were used in 1992. Also in 1992, the central bank raised the real annual interest rate posted by the central bank on auction of its 90-day indexed promissory notes, and in 1993 a more active use of repurchase agreements was introduced.

[11]Regulations on the surrender and repatriation of foreign exchange earnings were also relaxed, and authorized exchange houses were permitted to conduct forward and swap operations in the official exchange market.

minimum size of American Depository Receipts issues, lowering the rating requirement for corporations issuing bonds on the international market, and modifying the 30 percent reserve requirement on foreign borrowings. At the same time, due to circumvention of the existing restrictions, the authorities intensified restrictions on certain other inflows. In 1994, reserve requirements on foreign borrowing were required to be held solely in U.S. dollars, and in 1995 the ceiling on credit in Chilean pesos backed by deposits in U.S. dollars was reduced to avoid a circumvention of the reserve requirement on foreign borrowing. The reserve requirement on foreign liabilities was extended to secondary market transactions in American Depository Receipts, and to all investment inflows that did not constitute an increase in the capital stock of the bank.

Chile's overall capital account strengthened, and there were much larger gross capital movements (Figure 6.1 and Appendix Table 6.7). Direct investments abroad increased to $1.1 billion in 1996, while foreign direct investment inflows increased to $4.1 billion. The net capital account strengthened to $6.3 billion (9 percent of GDP) in 1996. The current account balance fluctuated and showed some tendency to widen on average. The government repaid foreign debt, reducing the surplus in the overall balance of payments, and continued to adapt the exchange rate arrangement by revising the weights of the currency basket and widening the exchange rate band. The real exchange rate continued to appreciate, and the inflation performance continued to improve (see Figure 6.1).

Chile's capital account liberalization appears to follow a distinct sequencing, with an initial focus on the completion of the restructuring of the banking system, trade reform, liberalization of the exchange system, and selective liberalization of capital inflows. Subsequently, the emphasis shifted to developing domestic money, bond, and equity markets. The capital account liberalization was also combined with the evolution of macroeconomic policies, strengthening of the instruments for indirect monetary control, and modification of the exchange arrangement to allow for greater flexibility of the rate within a crawling band exchange arrangement. Capital outflows were liberalized in response to a strengthening balance of payments. While liberalizing longer-term capital outflows and inflows, Chile introduced selective controls on capital inflows; however, such controls were circumvented and had to be broadened progressively.

Indonesia

The sequencing of Indonesia's reforms of domestic and external transactions during the period 1985–96 is summarized in Table 6.2 and described in Appendix Table 6.8; selected macroeconomic and balance of payments indicators are presented in Figure 6.2 and Appendix Table 6.9.

The economic reforms in Indonesia focused on reorienting the economy to reduce its dependence on the oil sector, expanding the role of the private sector, and encouraging the creation of a competitive non-oil, export-oriented industrial base that would absorb the rapidly growing labor force. The strategy entailed the pursuit of coordinated financial and exchange rate policies, aimed at providing a stable macroeconomic environment, accompanied by wide-ranging structural reforms to promote sustained growth and economic diversification. Key elements of reform during 1985–96 included the gradual liberalization of direct investment inflows to promote non-oil exports and economic diversification, maintenance of a competitive exchange rate, trade liberalization and tariff reform, and improvements in monetary management. Financial sector reform was also critical during the period and was carried out through the liberalization of external inflows, promotion of competition in the banking sector, strengthening of financial institutions, and encouragement of the growth of the capital market.

In 1985, Indonesia maintained a liberal regime for capital outflows by resident individuals and juridical entities, while prohibiting lending abroad by banks and financial institutions. Limitations on outflows through financial institutions remained in effect throughout the period (see the IMF's *Annual Report on Exchange Arrangements and Exchange Restrictions*, 1997). Selective controls applied to capital inflows; direct investment inflows were limited by domestic ownerships requirements; the purchase of equity by foreign investors in the local stock market was prohibited; and limits were imposed on foreign borrowings. Trade policy remained substantially protectionist.

Over much of the period, reforms focused on an opening of the real economy through a gradual promotion of direct investment inflows and liberalization of the tariff system as part of a restructuring of the real economy (see Appendix Table 6.8). Direct investment inflows were liberalized by expanding the fields where such investments were

Table 6.2. Indonesia: Sequencing of External and Domestic Financial Liberalization

(M represents major measures and m represents relatively minor measures)

	1985	1986	1987	1988	1989	1990	1991	1992	1993	1994	1995	1996
Monetary controls and financial system												
Capital market development			m				m	m			m	M
Money market and instruments	m		m	M	m	m						
Financial supervisory and regulatory framework				M	m	m	m	M		m	M	
Exchange system, trade and capital flows												
Exchange regime		M[1]	m							m[2]	m[3]	m[4]
Exchange market arrangement and system	m			M[5]	m		m					
Trade reforms	M	m	m	m	m	m	m		m	m	m	m
Liberalization of portfolio investment												
Inflows					M			m				m
Outflows												
Liberalization of direct investment												
Inflows	M	m	m	m	m		m	m	m	m		m
Outflows							m					
Restrictions on capital flows												
Inflows							m					
Outflows												

[1]The rupiah was devalued by 31 percent.

[2]Exchange rate movement allowed more flexibility. Bank Indonesia ceased to announce an indicative exchange rate in the morning and instead began announcing buying and selling rates at 3:00 p.m. computed on the basis of a basket of weighted currencies with a spread of ± Rp 15 (compared to ± Rp 10 previously).

[3]Exchange rate movement allowed more flexibility; the buying and selling rates computed on the basis of a basket of weighted currencies with a spread of ± Rp 22 (compared to ± Rp 15 previously).

[4]Exchange rate movement allowed more flexibility; in June the intervention band was widened to Rp 118 (5 percent) and in September widened to Rp 192 (8 percent).

[5]Indonesia accepted Article VIII of the IMF Articles of Agreement.

Figure 6.2 Indonesia: Selected Macroeconomic Indicators

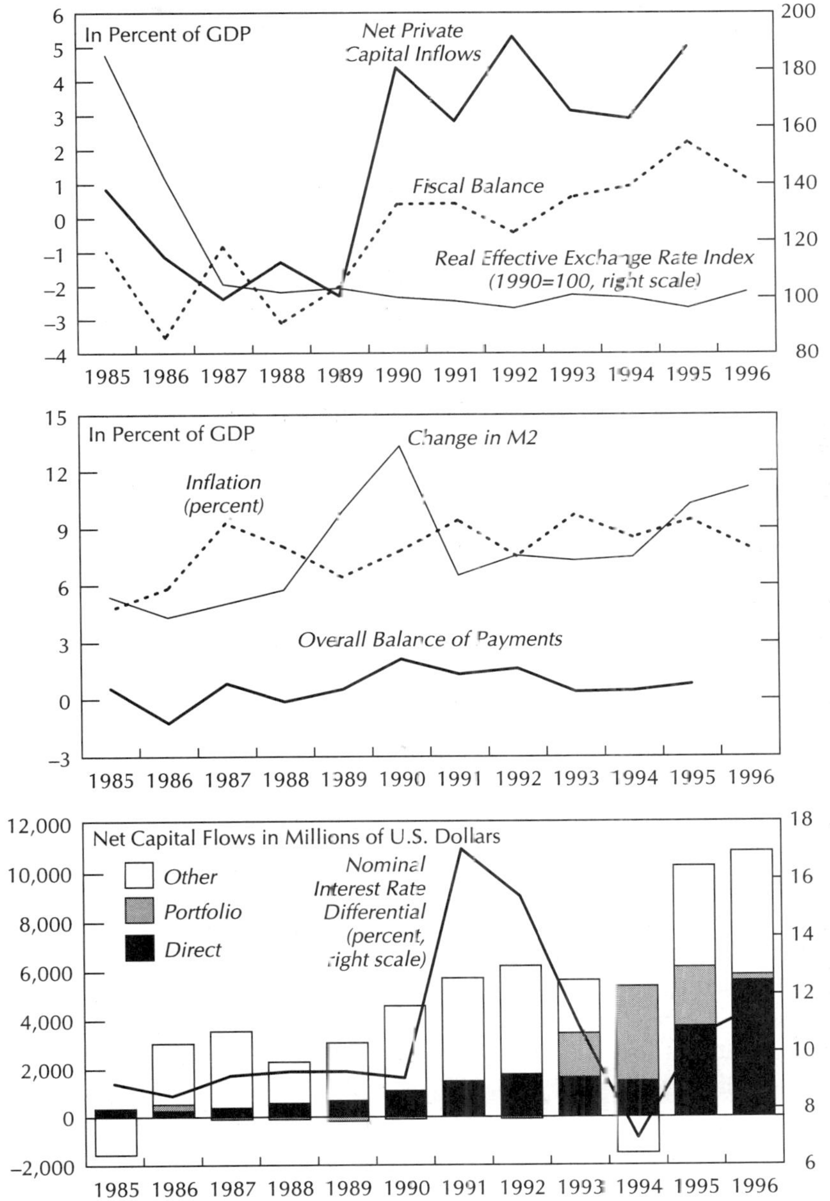

Sources: IMF, *International Financial Statistics, Direction of Trade Statistics*; and IMF staff estimates.

permitted. The expansion was accomplished by limiting the equity ownership rules to production of certain goods and investments in certain sectors, and by lengthening the period after which a company had to revert to domestic ownership.

The exchange rate was depreciated in 1983 and again in 1986 to bring it into line with market conditions as part of the economic restructuring package. Indonesia also liberalized payments and transfers for current international transactions and accepted the obligations of Article VIII of the IMF's Articles of Agreement in 1988. The foreign exchange market was developed and the selling of swaps in the foreign exchange market was liberalized. These reforms were associated with greater openness of the economy (as measured, for example, by the ratio of exports plus imports to GDP) and faster economic growth (see Appendix Table 6.9).

Reforms were undertaken concurrently in the financial and real sectors. These reforms focused initially on establishing the financial markets, institutions, and instruments for a more market-based system. Beginning in 1983, interest rates were liberalized and direct credit controls on the banking system were partially removed. Money market instruments were introduced in 1984. In 1987, institutional reforms were undertaken to strengthen the operations of the capital market, including reforms to the stock exchange and introduction of new capital market instruments. The authorities modified their monetary control framework by shifting toward targeting international reserves. They introduced daily auctions of money market instruments and allowed the market to play a bigger role in determining interest rates and the exchange rate.

The reforms in 1988 emphasized the functioning of the banking system, enhanced bank supervision, and development of the money market. Financial sector reform was promoted by permitting greater foreign participation in the financial sector through the licensing of new foreign banks and branches, creating a level playing field for foreign and domestic banks, and permitting foreign participation in other types of financial institutions and in the insurance business (see Appendix Table 6.8). Additionally, reforms were undertaken to improve the functioning of the capital market, including extending the role of the market in raising funds for investments, lengthening the maturity of money market instruments, and broadening the range of market makers.

Subsequently, in 1989, the authorities liberalized portfolio capital inflows by eliminating quantitative limits on bank borrowing from nonresidents. For the first time, foreigners were permitted to invest in the stock market, and to acquire up to 49 percent of the ownership of listed stocks. Restrictions on direct investment inflows were also relaxed further and foreign direct investors were allowed to sell foreign exchange directly to commercial banks instead of through the central bank.

In 1990–91, the Indonesian economy began to overheat, the current account deficit widened, inflation accelerated, and interest rates rose substantially. In the context of the maintenance of a stable real exchange rate, however, the increase in interest rates was accompanied by a substantial inflow of foreign capital, and total net private capital flows registered a surplus in 1990 for the first time since 1985 (see Figure 6.2).[12] The foreign capital inflow was mainly in the form of commercial bank borrowing, which was converted to domestic currency using the central bank's swap facility, thus contributing to an increase in the growth of money. Monetary restraint was supported by tightening fiscal policy to curtail domestic demand pressures; however, inflation continued on an upward trend (Figure 6.2).

Concerned that the inflows through the banking sector were excessive and were complicating macroeconomic management, the authorities reimposed in 1991 quantitative controls on offshore borrowing by banks and state enterprises. They also introduced stricter limits on the open foreign exchange positions of banks and reduced their foreign exchange swap positions as a percentage of their capital base. The limitations on public sector borrowing from abroad remained in place from 1992 to 1996. Nevertheless, the authorities continued to broaden the arrangements for foreign borrowing for trade finance by private entities. Sales of securities to nonresidents were permitted and foreign direct and portfolio investment through the stock markets was liberalized as part of the more general economic and financial sector development program. These measures were undertaken concurrently with other measures to strengthen the domestic capital markets and the

[12]The total net private capital account is defined as net direct portfolio and other investment minus net official capital plus net errors and omissions in the balance of payments plus an estimate of misinvoicing. For a discussion of this measure, see Johnston and Ryan (1994).

regulatory framework for banking operations.[13] In particular, in 1995–96, regulations were issued to strengthen financial institutions through the upgrading of accounting standards to ensure compliance with prudential guidelines and to safeguard against excessive risk taking through derivative tradings.

Large interest differential in the context of a stable exchange rate and very rapid growth in the domestic stock market continued to promote large net private capital inflows in 1992–96. These inflows took the form of both net direct and portfolio flows. The inflows were partly offset by a reduction in official capital inflows and by a widening in the current account deficit. Inflows were also sterilized through auctions of central bank paper and through swap operations in the foreign exchange market. Additionally, the authorities permitted somewhat greater exchange rate flexibility (1994–96).

In the first half of 1997, Indonesia continued to attract foreign investment flows. In response the central bank took measures to restrict the related credit growth, including partial sterilization from sales of central bank certificates, an increase in reserve requirements, and reduction in subsidized credit to public enterprises. Initially, Indonesia managed the regional currency crises that began in June 1997 better than its neighbors. This performance was attributed to stronger fundamentals, including a relatively smaller external current account deficit. Nevertheless, on July 11, 1997, to protect against speculation, Indonesia widened the trading band for the exchange rate against the U.S. dollar from 8 percent to 12 percent. Subsequently, concerns also emerged about the stability of the banking system, and the Indonesian rupiah came under speculative pressure and was allowed to float. The authorities also took administrative measures to counteract the pressure on the exchange rate. Nonresident transactions in the forward market were restricted to $5 million per customer, and each bank's net open position in the forward market was limited to $5 million. The authorities also lifted the 49 percent limit on foreign ownership on new initial public offerings in September.[14]

---

[13]For example, new banking law was issued in 1992 that provided guidelines consistent with accepted international banking.

[14]In July the central bank imposed limits on bank loans to real estate developers who wanted to purchase land, and restrictions were made on banks such that they were not permitted to buy commercial paper from developers raising finance to buy land.

Korea

The sequencing of Korea's reforms of the domestic and external transactions from 1985–96 is summarized in Table 6.3 and described in Appendix Table 6.10; selected macroeconomic and balance of payments indicators are presented in Figure 6.3 and Appendix Table 6.11.

Throughout the period, the Korean economy was characterized by significant government intervention and a financial sector that lagged behind the industrialization of the economy. The liberalization of the domestic financial system and the capital account was very gradual and selective, and a comprehensive plan was not adopted until June 1993. Monetary policy was conducted primarily through direct instruments, including ceilings on lending rates and guidance for lending to priority sectors. During the period, interest rate policy played little active role in external management. Developments in the balance of payments position, particularly in the current account, guided the government's interventions in the foreign exchange market and system and its policies with respect to transactions related to trade and the capital account.

Faced with a significant surplus in the current account balance of payments over the period 1986–89, the authorities progressively liberalized the import regime through a preannounced schedule of measures. Restrictions on payments for current international transactions were relaxed and Korea accepted the obligations of the IMF's Article VIII in 1988. Capital outflows were also promoted by liberalizing direct investment, purchases of real estate overseas, and certain portfolio investments outflows by institutional investors. At the same time, the central bank undertook various measures aimed at reducing net capital inflows, including encouraging the early repayment of external borrowing, tightening of the regulations on foreign commercial loans and foreign bank borrowing, and imposing restrictions on the volume of foreign exchange that could be brought in and sold to domestic banks (see Appendix Table 6.10). The fiscal position was consolidated to facilitate repayment of official foreign debt. In spite of the exchange measures, the overall balance of payments registered a widening surplus, as the current account surplus increased to reach 8 percent of GDP in 1988. The authorities used sterilization policies extensively—mainly through the issue of large quantities of liquidity control bonds and the reserve requirement on local currency deposits. The fiscal po-

Table 6.3. Korea: Sequencing of External and Domestic Financial Liberalization

(M represents major measures and m represents relatively minor measures)

	1985	1986	1987	1988	1989	1990	1991	1992	1993	1994	1995	1996
Monetary controls and financial system												
Capital market development		m	m	m	m	m	m		m		m	m
Money market and instruments	m	m	m	m	m	m	m	m	m	m	m	m
Financial supervisory and regulatory framework	m	m			m	m	M	m	m		m	m
Exchange system, trade and capital flows												
Exchange regime						M[1]		m[2]	m[3]	m[4]	m[5]	
Exchange market arrangement and system	m	m	m	M[6]	m	m	m	m	m	m	m	m
Trade reforms	m	m	m	m	m	m	m	m	m	m	m	m
Liberalization of portfolio investment												
Inflows	m				m		m	M	m	m	m	m
Outflows		m	m	m		m	m	m	m	m	m	m
Liberalization of direct investment												
Inflows	m		m	m	m	m	m			m	m	
Outflows	m	m	m	m	m			m	m	m	m	
Other investment												
Inflows							m	m				
Outflows				m			m	m				

[1]Adopted the "market average exchange rate" (MAR) system. The MAR for the Korean won-U.S. dollar would be based on the weighted average of the previous day's interbank rates for the Korean won-U.S. dollar spot transactions. During each business day, the Korean won-U.S. dollars exchange rate in the interbank market would be allowed to fluctuate within margins of ± 0.4 percent against the MAR.

[2]The margins within which the exchange rate for Korean won-U.S. dollars in the interbank market was allowed to fluctuate daily around the MAR were widened to ±0.8 percent.

[3]The margins mentioned in note number 2 were widened to ±1 percent.

[4]The margins mentioned in note number 2 were widened to ±1.5 percent.

[5]The margins mentioned in note number 2 were widened to ±2.25 percent.

[6]Accepted Article VIII of the Agreements.

Figure 6.3 Korea: Selected Macroeconomic Indicators

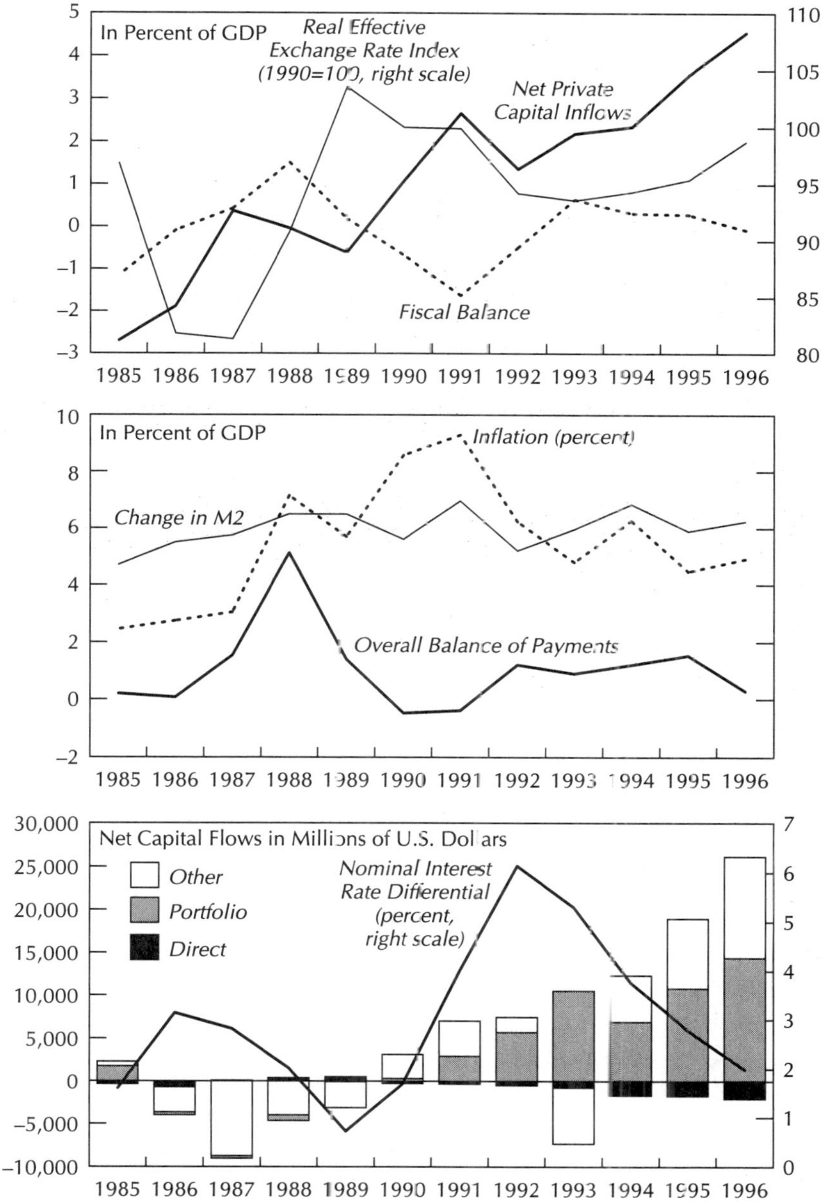

Sources: IMF, *International Financial Statistics, Direction of Trade Statistics*; and IMF staff estimates.

sition also improved and the nominal and real exchange rate appreciated (see Figure 6.3).

Beginning in 1989, the current account balance of payments began to weaken, reflecting the background of a weakening fiscal position (in an attempt to stimulate the economy), an appreciation in the real exchange rate, and rising inflation. The authorities responded by encouraging capital inflows. Some of the earlier measures aimed at limiting capital inflows were reversed—foreign exchange banks were allowed to raise funds offshore through certain instruments, and the limits on amounts of foreign exchange that could be imported and sold to local banks were raised. The authorities also accelerated the liberalization of direct investment inflows by lifting the ceilings on these inflows; replacing approvals with notifications; providing tax incentives; and expanding the sectors where foreign direct investment was permissible. However, with increasing labor costs at home, foreign direct investment registered a net outflow in 1990 as enterprises continued to locate manufacturing abroad. Nevertheless, the financial account registered a surplus, reflecting short-term inflows related to trade credits and borrowing for crude oil imports.

During the period 1988–96, Korea adopted a range of reforms aimed at the development of the domestic money, security, and foreign exchange markets. These measures paved the way for a broader opening of the capital account for portfolio capital flows in the 1990s. In 1988 the authorities allowed some initial interest rate liberalization. Two years later, they announced a four-stage plan for interest rate deregulation, and in 1993 the authorities liberalized a wide range of interest rates. Interest rates on deposits of one to two years were liberalized in 1994, followed by the liberalization of short-term deposits in two steps in 1995. The financial system was developed through a number of measures, including the strengthening of bank supervisory procedures, promotion of a bankers' acceptance and forward exchange markets, development of market makers, and the strengthening of regulations, trading procedures, and transparency of the local security markets. Operational improvements were introduced in the capital market, with the introduction of the "real-name" system for all financial transactions and the computerization of transactions in the stock market. In addition, various steps were taken to improve and strengthen the regulation and supervision of the financial sector, including a thorough revision of the General Banking Act and related prudential measures pertaining to accounting practices to promote transparency. Monetary stabilization bonds were auctioned, as opposed to being sold at administratively determined prices, and repurchase agreements using the liquidity control bonds became a major monetary instrument. Korea also moved from a multi-currency peg to the Market Average Exchange Rate system to allow market forces to play a greater role in exchange rate determination; the margins for the fluctuation of the exchange rate were also gradually widened.

Korea continued its policy of gradually promoting capital outflows by progressively liberalizing the limits on outward investments. The liberalization measures included extending the range of financial institutions eligible to invest abroad and raising the ceilings on their overseas investments; broadening the number of businesses eligible for overseas direct investment; liberalizing purchases of real estate; and allowing residents to retain larger foreign exchange balances abroad and to invest directly in foreign government bonds and equities up to a limit. For capital inflows, in 1992 nonresidents were permitted limited access to the stock market, and the types of securities that could be issued abroad by residents were expanded. The limits on foreign investments in Korea were gradually lifted, and sectors and markets gradually opened to foreign portfolio investment. For example, total foreign direct investment in domestic equities was increased from 10 percent in 1992 to 12 percent in 1994, to 15 percent in 1995, and to 20 percent in 1996. In 1996, nonresidents were permitted to invest in domestic bonds through Country Funds, and the Korean Bond Fund was listed on the London Stock Exchange.

The net private capital account strengthened sharply in 1991, reflecting an increase in foreign bond issues by Korean corporations, and in 1992 net portfolio inflows nearly doubled, reflecting the partial opening of the stock market to foreign investors. Net portfolio investment inflows continued to strengthen in subsequent years, with net private capital inflows reaching $16 billion in 1995. Korea continued to be a net exporter of direct investment, but increasingly became a major net recipient of portfolio investment inflows. These inflows were offset by a weakening in the current account balance of payments and an increasing surplus in the overall balance of payments. The exchange rate was permitted to adjust to some extent, but the degree of adjustment was limited. Nominal interest rates were also reduced, but, with inflation higher than elsewhere, the interest differentials with foreign rates remained positive.

Notwithstanding the significant steps taken during 1985–96 toward a deregulated financial sector, Korea's financial sector and capital account transactions continued to be subject to many regulations and government intervention. Moreover, the effectiveness of certain reforms—for example, interest rate deregulation—is unclear. Accordingly, further liberalization measures have been scheduled for the period 1997–2000, provided that stable macroeconomic conditions are maintained or the differential between Korean and international interest rates falls below 2 percent.[15]

Thailand

The sequencing of Thailand's reforms of domestic and external transactions from 1985 to mid-1997 is summarized in Table 6.4 and described in Appendix Table 6.12; selected macroeconomic and balance of payments indicators are presented in Figure 6.4 and Appendix Table 6.13.

Just before the start of the period under review, Thailand undertook a major adjustment effort: the baht was devalued by 14.8 percent in 1984, significant fiscal consolidation began, and a decisive change was made in the orientation of trade and industrial policies toward export-led growth. Thailand gave priority to promoting capital inflows through tax and institutional reforms while concurrently developing its financial markets. This policy, together with large positive interest differentials and a fixed exchange rate, promoted large net capital inflows. Such inflows contributed to strong economic performance and an increasing opening of the economy. Subsequent concerns about the sustainability of the exchange rate and the solvency of the financial system, however, resulted in a sharp reversal of capital inflows and a currency crisis.

---

[15]In the first half of 1997, several measures were taken to ease investment inflows. For example, a capital increase of about $200 million was authorized for the Korea Fund; the limit on foreign ownership of Korean equities was raised from 20 percent to 23 percent; foreign investors were allowed to purchase nonguaranteed bonds of small- and medium-sized companies with maturities of three years and above and up to 50 percent of the issue; and restrictions on the usage of long-term loans with maturities of over five years brought into the country by foreign manufacturers were abolished.

Table 6.4. Thailand: Sequencing of External and Domestic Financial Liberalization

(M represents major measures and m represents relatively minor measures)

	1985	1986	1987	1988	1989	1990	1991	1992	1993	1994	1995	1996	1997[1]
Monetary controls and financial system													
Capital market development		m	m	m	m	M	M	M	m		m	m	M
Money market and instruments	m	M	m	m	M	M	m	M	m	m	M		M
Financial supervisory and regulatory Framework	M			m				M	M	m	M	M	M
Exchange system, trade and capital flows													
Exchange regime													M[2]
Exchange market arrangement and system	m	m		m	M	M[3]	M	M	m	M	m		M
Trade reforms	M		m	m	m				m			m	
Liberalization of portfolio investment													
Inflows	m	M				m		m	m				
Outflows	m					m	M	m					
Liberalization of direct investment													
Inflows	m						M	M					M
Outflows							m			m			
Restrictions on capital flows													
Inflows											m	M	
Outflows											m		m

[1]Data are through August.

[2]The exchange rate arrangement of the Thai baht changed from being pegged to the U.S. dollar to a managed float.

[3]On May 4 the government accepted Article VIII obligations of the IMF Articles of Agreement.

Figure 6.4 Thailand: Selected Macroeconomic Indicators

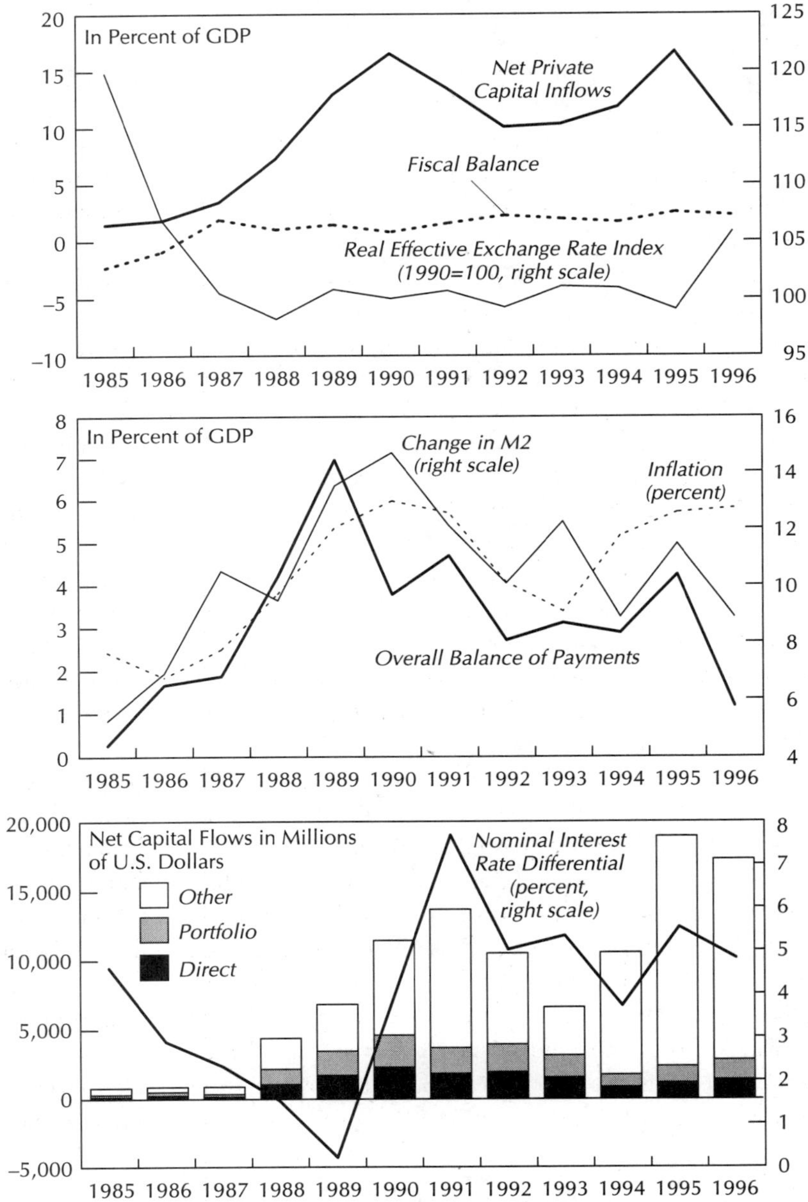

Sources: IMF, *International Financial Statistics, Direction of Trade Statistics*; and IMF staff estimates.

At the beginning of the period under review, Thailand maintained a relatively open capital account regarding capital inflows. The Alien Business Law of 1972 and the Investment Promotion Act of 1977 expanded the sectors open to foreign investment and liberalized the screening requirement for such investments. Portfolio investment inflows were treated liberally, although initially exchange controls applied to the repatriation of interest, dividends, and principal. Foreign borrowing could be conducted freely but had to be registered with the Bank of Thailand.

During the period, foreign inflows were promoted further through various measures, including eliminating restrictions on foreign investments and foreign ownership of export-orientated industries; granting tax incentives to encourage direct investments in special sectors; granting tax incentives to foreign mutual funds for investments in the stock market; creating new closed-end mutual funds; establishing rules for foreign debenture issues by Thai companies; reducing taxes on dividends remitted abroad; and allowing the free repatriation of investment funds, loan repayments, and interest payments by foreign investors.[16] In 1992, the authorities approved the establishment of the Bangkok International Banking Facility, which greatly eased access to foreign financing and expanded short-term inflows (see Figure 6.4); and in 1995 the Provincial International Banking Facility was established, which could extend credit in both baht and foreign currencies with funding from overseas.

Payments and transfers for current international transactions were also progressively liberalized, and in 1990 Thailand accepted the obligations of IMF Article VIII. Further liberalizations followed, with the removal of limits on the amount of foreign exchange that could be purchased, brought in, or taken out of the country; the relaxation of surrender requirements; and the broadening of the uses of nonresident baht accounts and resident foreign currency accounts.

In contrast to the promotion of capital inflows and the rapid liberalization of the exchange system, controls on capital outflows by residents were liberalized only gradually. In 1990, commercial banks were allowed to lend limited amounts to nonresidents in foreign currency

[16]Certain limitations on foreign ownership were retained on non-export orientated industries and on the maximum foreign ownership of companies listed on the stock exchange.

and to approve the repatriation of proceeds from sales of securities. The following year, Thai residents were permitted to invest abroad or to lend limited amounts to companies that had at least a 25 percent Thai equity participation. This ceiling was raised in 1994. Purchases abroad of capital and money market securities, foreign direct investments exceeding $10 million, and purchases of real estate remained subject to Bank of Thailand approval. Insurance companies were permitted to invest abroad under certain circumstances, but only up to 5 percent of their total portfolio. Locally issued mutual funds were restricted to investing their total portfolio in the domestic market.

Domestic financial market reforms focused initially on the development of the stock market. The Securities Exchange of Thailand was established in 1975, and the Securities Exchange Act was amended in 1984. Thailand adopted a number of subsequent reforms aimed at developing the stock exchange, including the establishment of the Securities and Exchange Commission in 1989; the creation of an automated trading system to replace manual transactions in 1991; and the passage of the Securities Exchange Act and the Public Company Act B.E. 2535 in 1992. The Acts, designed to support and promote the stock market, allowed public and private companies, listed and unlisted, to issue stocks and bonds. At the same time, the Thai Rating and Information Services was established as a credit rating agency to aid the development of corporate debt markets. Over the period, the number of companies listed on the exchange more than tripled, and the annual average growth in stock market capitalization was a remarkable 57 percent during 1987–94.

Following a crisis among the finance companies in the first half of the 1980s, measures to strengthen the banking system were introduced in 1985, including strengthened prudential standards and improved on- and off-site monitoring. Despite these improvements, the banking system continued to have an oligopolistic structure, which was reflected in large spreads between the deposit and lending rates (see Appendix Table 6.13). Moreover, the 1997 banking crisis indicated that there were a number of financial sector weaknesses that were not fully addressed following the earlier banking crisis.

Interest rates and credit controls were liberalized gradually, and in 1992 the ceilings on savings deposits and lending rates were removed. Nevertheless, indirect monetary instruments were not well developed, and the authorities relied to a considerable extent on foreign exchange swaps to manage the liquidity effects of capital inflows. In the context of the fixed exchange rate regime, such swaps generally involved the central bank setting a forward exchange rate that did not deviate significantly from the spot exchange rate.

Thailand's promotion of capital inflows, combined with a rapidly growing economy, contributed to substantial net capital inflows in the range of 9–13 percent of GDP between 1989 and 1995 (a much higher percentage than the other countries reviewed in this study). Net capital inflows were offset initially by repayments of official capital and subsequently by substantial deficits in the current account balance of payments, which reached 8 percent of GDP in 1995. Nevertheless the growth of broad money and inflation increased along with the surpluses in the overall balance of payments and in spite of fiscal consolidation (see Figure 6.4).

The composition of capital inflows evolved over the period and appeared responsive to the regulatory reforms and incentives for capital flows. Net direct investment inflows contributed to the initial strengthening of the capital account, but net portfolio inflows became more important with the subsequent reforms to promote investments in the Thai stock markets, the establishment of the Bangkok International Banking Facility, and the large positive interest differential. A growing proportion of the net inflows were short term in nature, reaching 60 percent of the total in 1995. Consequently in 1995, Thailand began to restrict short-term capital inflows by imposing 7 percent reserve requirement on banks' nonresident baht accounts. These restrictions were extended in 1996, among other reasons, to cover new foreign borrowing of less than one year.

In 1996 growth and investment levels deteriorated in the face of an appreciating real exchange rate and capital inflows and exports declined sharply. The large current account deficit, high interest rates, and increasing inflation left the country vulnerable to external shocks and a shift in market sentiment. Moreover, serious weaknesses appeared in the financial system due to exposures to the property sector and inadequate loan provisioning. High interest rates to counteract outflows aggravated the solvency and liquidity position of many banks and finance companies, and resulted in intervention by the authorities to support the financial system. In July 1997, faced with a banking crisis, a run on the currency, and large foreign exchange losses, the authorities floated the baht and adopted a managed floating exchange rate.

In response to the currency crisis, sales of foreign exchange were restricted for all foreign exchange transactions except those applied to exports and imports of goods and services, and direct and portfolio investment. Banks that had been free to lend to nonresidents subject to open position limits became subject to temporary restrictions on baht lending to nonresidents. Forward outright transactions in baht with nonresidents and the selling of baht against foreign currencies to nonresidents were temporarily restricted (see Appendix Table 6.12). However, such measures did not in general prevent the selling of the currency, which continued to depreciate.

Lessons from the Country Experiences

While the four country experiences reviewed here are diverse, the approach to and the consequences of the capital account liberalizations contain some lessons for managing such reforms.

Sequencing of Reforms

Liberalizations of direct investment inflows were generally undertaken as part of broader strategies aimed at restructuring the real sectors of economies. These strategies included eliminating barriers to trade, adjusting initial exchange rates, removing restrictions on current payments and transfers, and accepting the obligations of Article VIII of the IMF's Articles of Agreement, as well as liberalizing and promoting foreign direct investment inflows. Liberalizations of portfolio capital flows were generally coordinated with domestic financial sector reforms, especially the liberalization of domestic interest rates and movement toward indirect monetary instruments, strengthening of domestic security markets, and the reform of domestic banking systems and the foreign exchange market. In Chile and Korea, financial sector reforms tended to precede capital account liberalization, while in Indonesia opening the capital account helped to promote the restructuring and to improve the competitiveness of the domestic financial system. The currency crisis in Thailand illustrates the risks when liberalization does not cover all the necessary concurrent reforms. In that case, the strengthening of financial institutions and the development of indirect monetary instruments lagged the liberalization of the capital account.

The approach to the liberalizations of capital inflows and outflows varied depending on the particular priorities adopted by the country. In Korea, management of the current account balance of payments appeared initially to be the overriding consideration, and Korea sought to manage current account surpluses and deficits through regulatory and other changes that influenced capital inflows and outflows. Thailand actively promoted capital inflows while limiting outflows with the objective of supplementing domestic savings and promoting investment and rapid economic growth. Indonesia maintained a relatively liberal regime for capital outflows and gradually liberalized inflows with the aim of attracting foreign capital to assist the restructuring of its economy. Chile also liberalized capital inflows as part of its program of economic restructuring, and liberalized outflows in response to balance of payments considerations.

The pace of reforms varied. Chile and Korea followed a gradual approach to reforms. By contrast, Indonesia liberalized capital outflows early in the reform process; the liberalization of capital inflows occurred much later and more gradually. Thailand opened its economy to capital inflows, especially portfolio investment inflows, much more rapidly than the other countries surveyed but liberalized capital outflows only gradually.

Macroeconomic Management of the Liberalizations

Table 6.5 shows average comparative macroeconomic, financial sector, and balance of payments indicators for the four countries in the periods 1985–90 and 1991–96. In all cases, the capital accounts were more liberal in the second period than in the first. In all cases, net inflows of private capital accompanied the opening of the capital account, and all countries recorded surpluses in their overall balance of payments. In all cases, portfolio investment flows dominated direct investments. Indonesia's balance of payments was less affected than the other countries by the removal of capital account controls, perhaps because restrictions on capital outflows had been liberalized much earlier in Indonesia. In all countries but Korea, the surpluses were combined with fiscal consolidation.

The impact of the capital inflows on economic performance varied, however. Chile reduced its current account deficit as well as inflation, and also brought down the interest differential with foreign rates and

Table 6.5. Averages of Selected Economic Indicators

	Chile		Indonesia		Korea		Thailand	
	1985–90	1991–96	1985–90	1991–96	1985–90	1991–96	1985–90	1991–96
				(In percent)				
Selected economic indicators								
Real GDP growth	5.9	7.4	5.6	7.2	9.5	7.4	9.5	8.1
Inflation per year	21.3	12.8	7.0	8.8	5.0	6.0	3.6	5.0
M2 to GDP ratio	39.4	38.5	31.0	46.4	36.7	42.3	62.3	77.2
Currency to deposits ratio	10.9	8.9	19.1	10.6	12.0	10.6	11.4	9.2
Fiscal balance to GDP ratio	–0.1	2.0	–1.7	0.8	0.0	–0.1	–0.6	2.9
Private sector credit to GDP ratio	55.6	48.9	24.3	51.8	51.2	60.0	51.5	84.7
Exports plus imports of goods to GDP ratio	48.2	46.6	38.2	43.5	60.3	53.4	53.5	68.9
Current account to GDP ratio	–4.0	–1.8	–2.6	–2.5	3.4	–1.9	–3.1	–6.6
Financial account to GDP ratio	–2.3	5.8	3.6	4.1	–1.8	2.8	5.3	10.1
Of which: Direct investment	2.9	1.7	0.6	1.3	–0.1	–0.3	1.4	1.2
Portfolio & other investment[1]	–6.5	5.5	0.8	2.4	–0.5	2.6	4.2	8.9
Interest and exchange rates								
Nominal deposit rate (percent per year)	26.5	16.9	17.3	17.3	10.0	8.9	10.6	10.3
Real deposit rate (percent per year)	5.2	4.0	10.3	8.6	5.1	2.9	6.9	5.3
Interest rate differential[2]	18.5	11.9	9.0	12.0	2.3	4.0	1.7	5.3
Lending/deposit spread	7.8	5.3	3.6	3.7	0.2	0.3	5.7	5.4
Official exchange rate per U.S. dollar (end of period)	251.4	404.1	1,640.8	2,175.8	770.7	794.0	25.7	25.4
Real effective exchange rate index (1990=100)	110.6	92.2	122.9	98.8	92.4	96.0	104.4	101.1

(*In millions of U.S. dollars*)

Balance of payments								
Current account, n.i.e.	(803)	(1,014)	(2,238)	(3,792)	5,377	(7,730)	(2,182)	(9,428)
Financial account, n.i.e	(152)	3,103	3,178	6,337	(2,515)	11,454	3,668	14,216
Of which: Direct investment	692	988	551	2,030	(66)	(1,190)	953	1,474
Portfolio & other investment[1]	(1,017)	3,018	737	3,731	(373)	10,680	3,059	12,646
Net errors and omissions	(61)	(252)	(479)	(1,235)	(357)	(162)	618	(613)
Overall Balance[3]	(1,015)	1,837	462	1,310	2,555	3,613	2,104	4,175
Memorandum Item:								
Net private capital[4]	(235)	4,569	(1,928)	6,052	(460)	11,717	5,177	16,860

Sources: IMF, *International Financial Statistics*, *World Economic Outlook*, and *Direction of Trade Statistics*, various issues; and IMF staff estimates

Note: The averages cover the years where there is data available. Parentheses indicate a negative sign.

[1]Excluding official capital.

[2]Interest differential = deposit rate minus London interbank offer rate on three-month U.S. deposits.

[3]The overall balance includes: current account, financial account, capital account, and net errors and omissions. Capital account figures are not shown because they are zero throughout the period.

[4]Total capital – direct investment + portfolio investment + other investment minus official capital + net errors and omissions + misinvoicing.

the real deposit rate. The growth of broad money and domestic credit to the private sector was generally constrained in the context of a managed floating exchange rate. In contrast, Korea and Thailand experienced rapid growth of money and domestic credit in the context of stable exchange rates against the U.S. dollar, and in both cases, inflation accelerated and the current account balance of payments weakened. Thailand also faced a currency crisis. In Indonesia, broad money and private credit grew rapidly, inflation accelerated, the current account remained in deficit, and the rupiah came under speculative pressure.

How can the differences in performance be explained? One explanation begins with the observation that the ratios of broad money and private sector credit to GDP fell in Chile at the same time as private capital inflows increased as a percent of GDP, while in the other countries the ratios of broad money and private sector credit to GDP increased significantly (see Figure 6.5). Thus, for a time in Chile, net private capital inflows appear to have substituted for domestic intermediation, while in the other countries the inflows were associated with an increase in such intermediation, and with a rapid expansion in credit to the economy. In turn, this may explain the accelerating inflation and the weakening current account performances in the latter countries. Where the credit expansions were also associated with banking sector problems, this situation can create particular concerns about the efficiency of use of the capital inflows, and thus the sustainability of the balance of payments, and lead to a loss of confidence and capital outflows.

What may determine the different monetary and credit developments? Part of the explanation may reflect the fact that Chile implemented substantial financial sector reforms in the 1980s and adopted strengthened prudential standards earlier than in the other countries. The initial expansion in credit that often accompanies financial sector liberalization may therefore have occurred earlier in Chile than in the other countries surveyed, and the strengthened bank supervision may have led to a better pricing of risks and avoidance of banking problems.

Second, all of the countries sought to manage capital inflows through their regulatory regimes. In Thailand, the regulatory and institutional framework generally favored such inflows, while in other countries limits were applied to certain inflows or controls were liberalized gradually. As a consequence, net private capital inflows were larger as a percent of GDP in Thailand than in the other countries, and a large part of these inflows through the international banking fa-

Figure 6.5 Capital Flows, Private Sector Credit, and Current Account Deficit, 1985–96 *(In percent of GDP)*

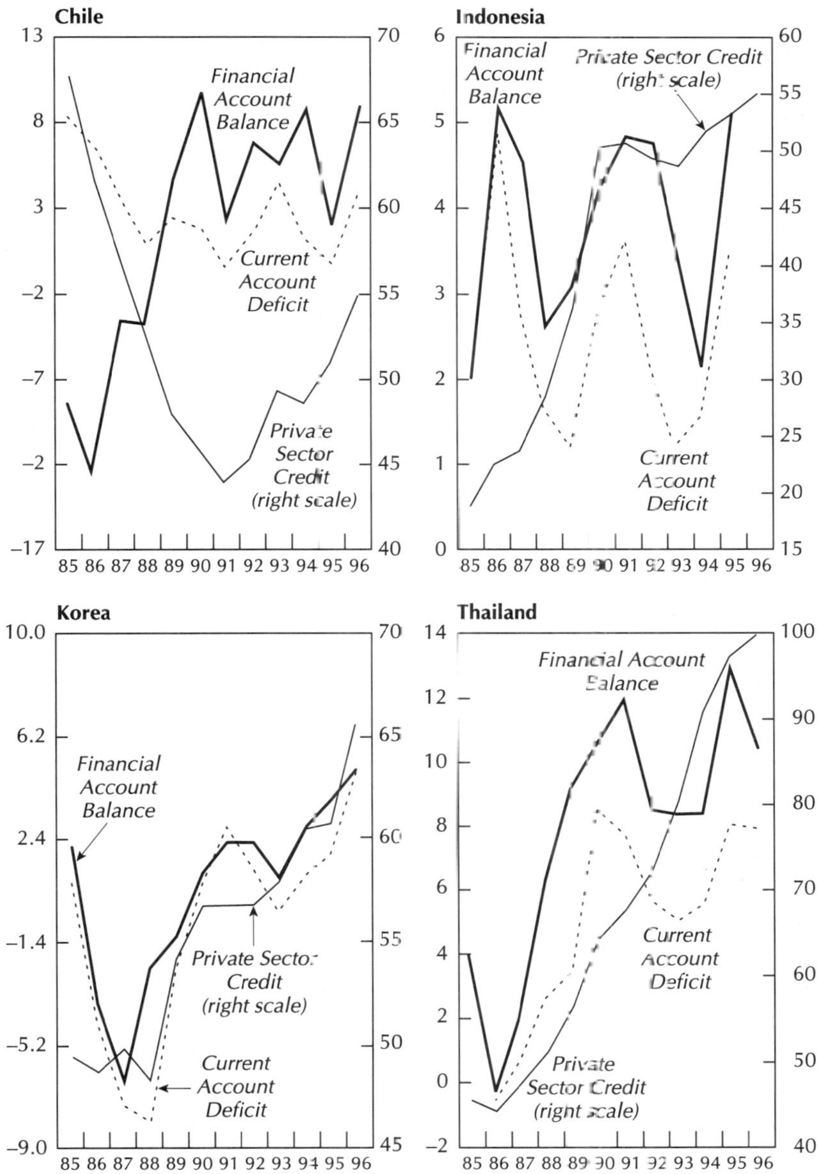

Sources: IMF, *International Financial Statistics*, and *World Economic Outlook*.

cility were short term in nature, which may have increased Thailand's vulnerability to a reversal of such flows.

There is no strong evidence that the reintroduction of controls was particularly effective in limiting overall capital inflows. The capital controls may have influenced the composition of such flows, and thus had some impact in determining whether the net inflows were directed to the domestic banking system. Chile actively sought to discourage capital inflows to the banking system. Indonesia and Thailand also became concerned by the volume of inflows to their banking systems, although in Thailand this concern came late in the reform process. The introduction in 1991 and subsequent intensification of controls in Chile did not appear to result in a marked growth of bank credit. In fact, private sector credit increased as a percent of GDP after 1991 (see Figure 6.5). Also, at a theoretical level it is not clear that a restriction on certain types of inflows would be particularly effective in limiting bank credit expansion in view of the potential fungibility of capital.

Finally, the countries had different exchange rate regimes. The countries that appeared to better manage the capital inflows followed more flexible exchange rate arrangements. Such flexibility generally created greater autonomy for monetary policy in managing the effects of capital inflows and may itself have helped to discourage short-term speculative capital flows. Part of Chile's successful management of capital account liberalization may be partly attributed to its more flexible management of the exchange rate within a preannounced crawling band. In contrast, Thailand's maintenance of a fixed exchange rate limited the flexibility of its monetary policy to constrain the growth of money and credit in the face of significant capital inflows. When combined with Thailand's policy of promoting capital inflows, the fixed exchange rate arrangement may have initially created unrealistic expectations about the rates of return. When market sentiment changed, the result was a sharp reversal of capital inflows.

Capital Account Liberalization and the Asian Currency Crisis

The currency crises in Asian countries were preceded by a sizable buildup of short-term foreign liabilities. This section investigates one aspect of the events leading up to the Asian crisis—namely, whether the nature of regulation of capital movements, and in particular, the sequencing of the liberalization of the capital account, contributed to the buildup of short-term debt in the three main Asian crisis countries—Indonesia, Korea, and Thailand.

Growth of Short-Term Liabilities

As the description of individual experiences indicate, Indonesia, Korea, and Thailand adopted markedly different approaches to the liberalization of their capital account regimes in the years leading up to the crisis. Generally, the capital account regulations were not directly biased toward short-term external borrowing:

- In Indonesia, there is no strong indication that regulations favored any particular maturity, especially shorter over longer maturities. In some instances (e.g., Presidential Decree No. 39 in 1991), ceilings were imposed on foreign commercial borrowing, except for purposes of financing long-term projects.
- Korea followed a very cautious approach to liberalization of capital inflows into its security markets (see Park, 1998). In 1992, nonresidents were permitted limited access to the stock market, and the types of securities that residents could issue abroad were expanded. Foreign exchange banks were authorized to borrow abroad, but direct foreign borrowing by corporations was controlled. Beginning in 1994, the ceiling on banks' foreign currency loans was lifted, but the Bank of Korea applied window guidance in the form of ceilings on banks' medium- and long-term borrowings from international financial markets.[17] The letter of the law, however, did not entail preferential treatment for short-term inflows, per se.[18] The Korean regulations did, however, favor for-

[17]One explanation that has been offered for the maintenance of controls on longer term external borrowing by banks is that the Ministry of Finance and Economy was seeking to prevent a loss of control over financial institutions through possible debt/equity swaps.

[18]Indeed, on joining the OECD in 1996, the authorities expressed their reluctance to ease capital controls further and explicitly stressed that they wished to maintain controls over short-term capital inflows that may "hamper macroeconomic and financial market stability." For this reason the authorities resisted the liberalization of access by nonresidents to domestic money market instruments during the accession to the OECD. Frequently the law established detailed quantitative limits on the amount of the transaction or on the size of the firms that were allowed to trade on international markets.

eign borrowing (and onlending) by banks, over direct access by corporations to international capital markets; and credits from nonresidents to nonbank residents—with the exception of trade credits—were subject to prior approval.

- In Thailand too, the general thrust of the regulatory framework did not differentiate between the maturity of the capital flows, per se, but it did tend to favor inflows directly intermediated by the domestic banking system. With the establishment of the Bangkok International Banking Facility in 1992, the government tried to improve the access of domestic entities to international capital markets through the banking system, and this helped to channel short-term inflows through the banking system. The authorities subsequently pursued a policy of promoting foreign investments into the country, and security markets were also liberalized. Nevertheless, the inflows of foreign capital through the capital and money markets, controlled by the Security and Exchange Commission, lagged behind those intermediated through the banking sector.

Thus, while there was no strong regulatory bias toward short-term flows except in one respect in Korea, the capital account regulations did bias flows toward the local banking system in Korea and Thailand in particular. This institutional bias seems to have *indirectly* favored short-term borrowing rather than longer-term flows, since banking institutions normally tend to rely on shorter-term finance. The heavy reliance on short-term flows also reflected inadequacies of risk assessment, management, and control.

The emphasis on bank-intermediated flows was, on the surface at least, consistent with the existing financial structure in these economies. Commercial banks dominated financial intermediation in all three countries, and the development of other financial markets was a more gradual process. For example, the bond market in Indonesia and Thailand barely reaches 10 percent of GDP, while in Korea it is currently equivalent to 50 percent of GDP, but with most corporate bonds guaranteed by financial institutions.[19] Moreover, foreign lenders may have generally preferred to channel their loans through the bank-

[19]By comparison, the bond market accounts for 110 percent of GDP in the United States, 90 percent in Germany, and 75 percent in Japan.

ing sector to the extent that they saw it as less risky, and in view of the difficulties in assessing individual corporations because of more limited information on their balance sheets and prospects. Perhaps even more important in this regard is the possibility that banks were seen to be not just supervised, but backed more directly by the authorities. As a number of economists have stressed there may well have been a strong element of implicit government guarantee associated with banks in these countries (see, among others, Dooley, 1997; and Krugman, 1998). To the extent such a perception was indeed held, both by the banks themselves and lenders to banks, this may have been an important factor in the lack of adequate currency and liquidity risk management in the banking sector. It is likely that the institutional biases in the capital account regulations interacted with these factors to exacerbate the buildup of inadequately-managed, short-term liabilities.

A second factor behind the buildup of short-term debt is that the underlying riskiness of the investments in these countries may have led to some preference by lenders for shorter maturities. The lack of well-developed bond markets, among other things, probably made pricing of longer-term debt more difficult. Residual uncertainty about the legal and financial infrastructure and relatively costly monitoring of local developments also tend to encourage external creditors to favor shorter-term investment over longer-term ones.[20] To some extent, this effect might have declined over time, as apparently robust macroeconomic trends continued to obscure underlying weaknesses. Nevertheless, as the outlook for either the specific borrowing institution or the country more generally became more uncertain, the tendency to prefer shorter-term exposure would have reasserted itself. In such a situation, the interest rates charged by lenders typically increase to reflect the higher risk or uncertainty premium, but the premium itself typically tends to rise more than proportionally with the maturity of the loan. This is particularly so when hedging instruments for foreign exchange risks are limited to very short-term maturities. In these

[20]The nature of the Basle capital adequacy requirements for OECD creditor banks might also have played some role here. While lending to other OECD banks is given a risk weight of 20 percent for capital adequacy purposes, irrespective of the term of the loan, lending to non-OECD banks carries this weight only for loans of less than one year, while loans longer than that carry the full 100 percent risk weight. Since all lending to corporations also carries the same 100 percent weight, there is also an incentive to favor (short-term) loans to banks, rather than nonbanks in non-OECD countries.

circumstances, the borrower would be squeezed into progressively shorter-term contracts, and could face difficulties in rolling over its obligations should conditions continue to deteriorate. Such a buildup of short-term liabilities can occur regardless of the regulatory environment, in view of the scope to effectively redenominate longer-term contracts into shorter-term ones, through derivative and other transactions.[21]

Developments in Indonesia seem to confirm a general market preference for shorter-term credit, except perhaps for the strongest and most sizable borrowers. Indonesia's capital account regulations contained neither an obvious direct bias toward shorter-term rather than longer-term flows, nor a bias toward bank-intermediated inflows (bank borrowing was more restricted than private corporate borrowing, in fact). Nevertheless, to the extent that larger private Indonesian corporations had close links of various sorts with the authorities, moral hazard issues (a perception of official support) may well have played a role in the excessive and inadequately managed external borrowing, similar to that in the buildup of bank debt in Korea and Thailand.

Beyond the underlying reasons for market preferences for shorter-term and/or bank-intermediated external borrowing, and beyond any additional biases that may have been created by capital account regulations, a third important factor in the buildup of shorter-term external debt in the Asian crisis countries has been the incentives created by the macroeconomic environment. The three countries considered here all quite actively pursued either nominal or real exchange rate targets (a de facto peg in Thailand's case), while orienting interest rates toward internal stability objectives. This resulted in significant periods of relatively high interest differentials, especially at the shorter end, and encouraged capital inflows that were substantially short term in nature, and in particular in the form of foreign currency borrowing. Such borrowing was largely unhedged because of expectations that relatively stable exchange rates would be maintained indefinitely.

[21]Though it is clear that relatively new and innovative instruments such as credit derivatives and options can be used to achieve this effect, it can also be done in much more basic ways. For example, a "synthetic sale" of direct investments can be created relatively quickly and cheaply by obtaining a bank loan in domestic currency.

Implications of the Crisis for Capital Account Liberalization

There are five main implications of the above analysis. First, the sustainability of inflows depends on the efficiency of the use of the funds, not least as regards the prudent management of the risks involved with external funding. Specifically, the channeling of funds through banking sectors where risk management was relatively weak and unsophisticated and where distorted incentive structures and moral hazard prevailed ultimately brought this efficiency into question. The rapid bank credit expansions strained credit assessment procedures and resulted in banks channeling newly borrowed funds into unprofitable or speculative activities, such as real estate lending, while the prudential supervision framework was not strong enough to curtail these trends effectively. The same issues arise where external borrowing by corporations is guaranteed by financial institutions, as in Korea. A major concern is, therefore, to ensure that commercial banks comply with appropriate prudential standards, including procedures for the management of asset and liability (liquidity) risks, and that banks face appropriate incentive structures (e.g., moral hazard is avoided as much as possible, and there are appropriate controls on lending to interrelated entities).[22]

Second, appropriate risk management incentives are also fundamental to avoiding excessive direct external borrowing by nonbank corporations. Prudential measures applied to financial institutions may have some indirect effect here (to the extent that corporations borrowing offshore also borrow from local banks). But more central is the need to avoid implicit government guarantees of corporations and associated moral hazard, as with the banks themselves. In addition, exchange rate regimes that avoid excessive rigidity tend to create a much greater awareness, both among banks and nonbanks, of the need to manage exchange rate risk.

Third, increasing recourse to shorter-term debt can be an indicator of growing uncertainty about economic prospects. The monitoring and disclosure of such debt is, therefore, important, both as a guide to domestic macroeconomic management, and as an input into

[22]Overall, currency mismatches (open foreign exchange positions) were not a very significant issue in Asian banks, but liquidity mismatches (arising from excessive maturity transformation) and inadequate credit assessment were.

better informed decision making by international financial markets. However, because of the scope to redenominate longer-term debt as short-term debt, statistical measures of short-term liabilities may not always be easy to interpret, particularly in the lead-up to a crisis when private lenders may seek to change quickly the composition of their assets.

Fourth, where restrictions remained on capital market issues abroad by resident corporations and on nonresident purchases of securities on the local market, it might well have been desirable to speed up the development of the longer-term security markets both through domestic capital market reforms (including greater disclosure of information by borrowers), and by removing the capital controls. With an appropriate public sector-private sector relationship that avoids moral hazard, allowing corporations access to the international bond markets could have an important market disciplining effect, since such access would require meeting higher financial disclosure standards. More broadly, policymakers need to be careful when liberalizing capital flows that they do not unduly favor some types of channels or instruments over others—a less than level playing field could skew the incentives for different groups in ways that are unhelpful for prudent competition and sound risk management.

Fifth, it is not clear that the reintroduction of controls helped much, either before the crisis, or especially once the crisis had begun. Thailand and Indonesia resorted to capital controls in an effort to reduce inflows before the crisis, and to restrict outflows during the crisis.[23] The more recent controls generally aimed to restrict forward or derivative transactions and their financing, but during the crisis they sent a negative signal to the market discouraging further capital inflows at a critical juncture. It is notable that most of the new controls introduced in Thailand were removed again in early 1998, while in Korea the emphasis was solely on liberalizing measures throughout the crisis. In Indonesia too, liberalization measures were taken in addition to the single restrictive measure.

---

[23]Outside the three main crisis countries, the Philippines took a number of successive measures to tighten certain capital controls from mid-1997, while Malaysia took one measure to tighten nonresident access to swap transactions.

Conclusion

Opening the capital account can have significant benefits for economic growth and welfare. Achieving the benefits of the liberalization, however, while minimizing the risks requires attention to the sequencing of the reforms and the pacing of capital account liberalization to macroeconomic and exchange rate policies. What is generally important for managing the volume of capital flows is the overall incentive structure that can give rise to such flows. This will be influenced by the regulatory regime for capital movements, the stage of development and soundness of financial systems, and the configuration of interest rates and exchange rates.

Therefore, countries should adopt a coordinated and comprehensive approach to reforms, of which capital account liberalization is an integral part. Such a public policy approach requires attention not only to the sequencing of the regulatory and institutional reforms that impact on capital movements, but also to the design of macroeconomic and exchange rate policies.

The experience of the Asian countries confirms that it is necessary to approach capital account liberalization as an integral part of a more comprehensive program of economic reform, coordinated with appropriate macroeconomic and exchange rate policies, and including policies to strengthen financial markets and institutions. The question concerns not so much speed, since some of the countries in Asia have followed a very gradualist approach. Rather, it concerns the appropriate sequencing of the reforms and, more specifically, what supporting measures need to be taken.

The liberalization of inflows through the banking system clearly needed to be more fully supported with reforms to encourage stronger management and supervision in that sector. There was also clearly a need to avoid moral hazard problems as much as possible for corporations as well as banks; and, in the more liberal market environment, to have adequate transparency and improved information flows so that there could be informed market decision making, which would in turn reduce the risks of sharps shifts in market sentiment in response to uncertainties. There was also a need to develop markets for hedging and managing risks, which are an essential part of efficient market-based financial systems and were notably lacking in many Asian economies.

Finally, policymakers need to recognize that with more open capital accounts a country's interest rate policy will be constrained by its choice of exchange arrangement and vice versa. Greater attention has to be given to an appropriate, internally consistent mix of macroeconomic policies to avoid creating incentives for excessive short-term capital inflows, and the risk of subsequent sharp reversals.

Appendix: Country Tables

This section contains tables that provide a detailed matrix of the sequence of reforms to domestic and external transactions in Chile, Indonesia, Korea, and Thailand. It also features tables containing selected economic indicators for the four countries.

Table 6.6. Chile: Sequencing of Reforms in the Domestic and Exchange Sectors

Monetary Controls and Financial System	Exchange System, Trade, and Capital Flows
1985	
Capital Markets Private pension funds were permitted to invest part of their assets in selected domestic stocks. *Financial Supervisory and Regulatory Framework* The process of recapitalization of the private financial system began in 1982 with the purchase of loan portfolios of banks up to an amount equivalent to 100% of the capital and reserves of each bank. This was followed in 1984 with the purchase of substandard loan portfolio of banks up to 150% of capital and reserves of each bank initially for cash, and up to an additional 100% of capital and reserves for non-negotiable, non-interest-bearing central bank notes. This scheme was extended to intervened banks in 1985. Legislation was enacted that allowed the government to recapitalize directly up to 49% of the capital of each bank. These banks were then sold to the private sector through the state development company, CORFO. A debt restructuring agreement was reached with foreign commercial banks, the third of a series of six agreements, beginning in 1983. *Money market and instruments* The CBC announced an indicative interest rate for 30-day deposits.	*Exchange Market Arrangement and System* In February the Central Bamk of Chile (CBC) announced that the exchange rate for the Chilean peso was devalued by 8.2% against the U.S. dollar. In June, the exchange rate of the peso was devalued again by 7.8%. At the same time, the CBC announced that the peso would be adjusted on a daily basis at a rate of 1.7% per month until August. After August, the rate would be adjusted daily on the basis of the previous month's inflation less an estimate of international inflation. The CBC also changed the width of the exchange rate band from 0.5% on either side of the daily rate to 2%. The limits on travel allowances were raised from $200 to $500 for travel to neighboring countries and from $800 to $1,500 for travel to other countries. Chapters XIX and XVIII of the *Compendium of Foreign Exchange Regulations of the Central Bank* were introduced in May. The amendments introduced two schemes for the purchase by foreign residents of specified Chilean foreign debt instruments in secondary markets abroad and their conversion into domestic peso obligations (see amendments below). *Direct Investment* Inflows: (Under *Chapter XIX*) Upon approval of the CBC, the foreign currency obligation can be exchanged into a domestic currency obligation, the proceeds of which must be used for direct investment purposes, with the intermediation of a financial institution. Special regulations apply to repatriation of such capital as well as to dividend payments, capital can be repatriated after 10 years and profits after four years. Profits of the first four years can be repatriated at 25% a year as of the fifth year.

Portfolio Investment

Inflows: (Under *Chapter XVIII)* Authorization was granted for residents and nonresidents to purchase selected debt instruments using foreign exchange not obtained in the official foreign exchange market for conversion into pesos without remittance rights. The peso assets could be used only to reduce domestic debt, third-party debt or to acquire specified assets or equity owned by domestic banks. Transactions under this chapter also need to be channeled through financial institutions, subject to an overall quota that would be assigned to the different institutions on the basis of an auction system.

Trade

The uniform tariff rate was reduced twice—from 35% to 30% and then to 20%.

A law was introduced giving exporters of specified export products an option of a subsidy equal to 10% of the net value of their sales not exceeding an overall value of $7.5 million, in lieu of benefits under the existing import duty drawback scheme.

1986

Financial Supervisory and Regulatory Framework

Two laws are substantially revised: the General Banking Law and the Organic Law of Superintendency of Banks and Financial Institutions.

The CBC restored five more banks that had been intervened in the private sector on a fully capitalized basis.

Exchange Market Arrangement and System

The official rate was adjusted daily during the year, representing a 10.5% depreciation.

A subsidy granted for debt service payments on foreign currency debt contracted before August 6, 1982 for debts greater than $50,000 through the preferential exchange rate arrangement was gradually phased out between July 1985 and December 1986.

The CBC allowed banks to conduct future foreign exchange operations for options with maturity between 15 to 180 days on a very restricted basis.

The limits on travel allowances were raised from $500 to $1,000 for travel to neighboring countries and from $1,500 to $3,000 for travel to other countries.

Portfolio Investment

Inflows: Restrictions on the use of peso assets (without remittance rights) by residents and nonresidents of debt purchased at a discount abroad with foreign exchange not obtained in the official market (under Chapter XVIII) were lifted.

Table 6.6 *(continued)*

Monetary Controls and Financial System	Exchange System, Trade, and Capital Flows
1987	
Financial Supervisory and Regulatory Framework The last two intervened banks were sold to private investors through stock auctions between 1986–87, marking the end of the privatization phase. One state-owned bank was not privatized or intervened during the banking crisis. *Money Market and Instruments* The CBC eliminated its practice of announcing indicative interest rates for 30-day bank deposits and began setting the rate on 90-day indexed promissory note (PRBC); short-term central bank paper sold through auctions on demand.	*Portfolio Investment* Inflows: Foreign Capital Investment Fund (FICE) Law was issued to attract foreign resources to be invested in publicly offered instruments. Original capital was allowed to be repatriated after five years, with no limit on profit remittances. All remittances not corresponding to the capital originally invested were subject to a 10% income tax. Inflows: External Investment Funds under Chapter XIX were authorized. This made it easier for small external investors to participate in debt equity conversions without having to go through the case-by-case conditions normally applied to such operations. Transactions under this chapter were progressively restricted. Chapter XVIII was modified to allow debt conversions by mortgage debtors, up to $6,000 without going through the auction system. *Trade* A fund to guarantee loans granted to nontraditional exporters for capital requirements was established. Regulations governing imports from Free Zones were modified. A preferential tariff treatment was suspended for those countries that had not adopted the new regional scheme of preferential tariffs. A system of deferred payment was introduced for custom duties on imports of capital goods. The list of goods eligible for export financing through rediscounts of the CBC was expanded. A subsidy of 5% was introduced for export values between a certain value and the indexation of these values, which are to be adjusted annually.

1988

Exchange Market Arrangement and System

The exchange rate band was widened from ±2% to ±3% on each side of the center rate.

Commercial banks were authorized to sell foreign exchange for payments of insurance premiums contracted in Chile up to $50,000; for larger amounts authorization was required from the CBC.

New minimum amounts for foreign exchange swap operations were set with the CBC.

The period for surrendering export earnings was lengthened to 90 days after repatriation, as long as the earnings were held as swaps or foreign currency deposits with Chilean resident banks.

Trade

Custom duties were lowered across the board from 20% to 15%.

The maximum surcharge was raised from 15% to 20%.

The drawback subsidy for small exporters was reduced from 10% to 8%.

The fiscal credit under the system of deferred import duty payments was lowered to 11% from 15%.

1989

Financial Supervisory and Regulatory Framework

Congress enacted a constitutional law establishing legal autonomy for the CBC of Chile (October).

Exchange Market Arrangement and System

In July the authorities announced that the policy adopted in late 1988 of seeking a small real appreciation of the peso had been reversed. The peso continued to be devalued daily on the basis of the difference between domestic inflation in the previous month and estimated external inflation. To reverse some of the real appreciation that had occurred since 1988, the band around the central rate was widened from ±3% to ±5% and the exchange rate moved to the top of the band.

In September the authorities reduced the estimated rate of external inflation used in adjusting the exchange rate from 0.4% per month to 0.3%.

Direct Investment

Inflows: The Additional Tax on the repatriation of profits by foreign investors under the Income Tax Law was lowered from 40% to 35%.

Table 6.6 *(continued)*

Monetary Controls and Financial System	Exchange System, Trade, and Capital Flows
1990	
Capital Markets The stock market introduced trading in futures contracts.	*Exchange Market Arrangement and System* The parallel foreign exchange market became an informal legal market in which the exchange rate was freely determined and access to the official market remained unchanged. Proceeds from exports of goods and services, payments for imports of goods and services, debt-service payments, remittances of dividends and profits, and authorized capital transactions, including loan receipts were to be transacted through the official exchange market. The repatriation period for export proceeds was extended to 120 days (up from 90 days). *Portfolio Investment* Outflows: Chapter XXVI was added to the rules on International Exchange. Under this chapter individuals and legal entities, domiciles and residents abroad, who met certain conditions, were permitted to remit abroad proceeds from the sale of stocks of registered corporations domiciled in Chile that were purchased with funds abroad through the official exchange market. The remittance of dividends and profits accruing from such stocks was also allowed through the official exchange market. Inflows: Under Chapter XXVI, American Depository Receipts (ADRs) were issued for the first time. *Trade* The minimum import financing requirement (120 days) was abolished. *Restrictions on Capital Flows* New regulations were introduced whereby all capital transactions had to be reported to the CBC and remained subject to approval.

1991

Capital Markets

Pension funds were permitted to invest a greater percentage of their assets in equities.

Money Market and Instruments

Credits granted by foreign commercial banks to Chilean commercial banks as part of restructuring packages were exempted from the 20% reserve requirement (see Introduction of Restrictions).

An alternative means of satisfying the 20% reserve requirement on new foreign borrowing in the form of a special repurchase agreement with the CBC was established.

Exchange Market Arrangement and System

In June the authorities announced that the reference exchange rate of the peso appreciated by 2%.

The midpoint exchange rate was devalued three times in 1991 for a cumulative amount of 3.4%.

The maximum amount of time allowed for exporters to make their returns was increased from 120 to 150 days.

The time allowed for exporters to liquidate advance payments received on their sale of their products was extended from 90 to 150 days.

Portfolio Investment

Inflows: Chapter XXVI was modified so that shares through ADRs could be traded and quoted, not only on official foreign stock markets but privately.

Outflows: Capital that entered through Chapter XIX could be repatriated after three years instead of 10 years. The minimum holding period for *other* investments remained at three years under both: the Decree Law No. 600; and Chapter XIV, which stipulates that capital brought into the country in the form of foreign borrowing must be sold through authorized banks when the investor has registered the transaction with the CBC.

Outflows: Under Chapter XIX foreign investors were allowed to sell their investments to domestic residents after paying a fee to the CBC.

Outflows: Chapter XII set out regulations and different channels for Chilean corporations to invest abroad. Chapter XII was revised to permit Chilean individuals and juridical entities to use foreign currency of their own or obtained from the informal exchange market to invest abroad. Prior approval from the CBC was no longer required but the CBC had to be notified within 30 days of the investment.

Inflows: Taxes on dividends on investments were lowered to 42% from 49.5%. The tax credit on repatriation of profits was increased from 10% to 15%.

Outflows: The CBC authorized banking companies to acquire low-risk financial assets abroad with a maximum value of up to 25% of the public's foreign currency term deposits.

Table 6.6 *(continued)*

Monetary Controls and Financial System	Exchange System, Trade and Capital Flows
1991 *(continued)*	*Trade* CBC allowed banks to assign 60% (up from 40%) of their dollar deposits to finance foreign trade. Banks were allowed to finance foreign trade transactions between third countries belonging to Latin American Integration Association (LAIA). The ad valorem import tariff was reduced to 11% from 15%. Stamp duties imposed on domestic loans were extended to foreign loans. *Restrictions on Capital Flows* Inflows: A reserve requirement of 20% was first imposed only on all new *foreign borrowings*, except for credits that are provided directly to Chilean exporters by foreign importers. The reserve requirement was to be held at the CBC for a time related to the maturity of the credit, with a minimum of 90 days and a maximum of one year. Inflows: The 20% reserve requirement was extended to all outstanding foreign borrowing, except for credits with maturity of less than six months, and the time period for which the CBC would hold a loan was increased to one year, irrespective of the maturity of the foreign loan. The requirement on existing credits maturing between July and December was phased out. Inflows: Stamp duties imposed on domestic loans were extended to foreign loans.
1992	
Capital Markets The Superintendent of Securities and Insurance announced the creation of a central securities depository to be implemented in stages beginning at the end of 1993. *Money Market and Instruments* Insurance companies were permitted to participate in the auctions of CBC promissory notes and treasury bills.	*Exchange Market Arrangement and System* The exchange system was changed from being pegged to the U.S. dollar to being pegged to a fixed basked of currencies consisting of the U.S. dollar, the deutsche mark, and the Japanese yen. The central exchange rate and the floating band are to be set daily according to the evolution of the value of the currency basket and the exchange rates of the currencies in the basket. The reference rate of the Chilean peso was revalued by 5% and the band was widened from 5% to 10% on each side of the midpoint rate.

The CBC modified the operating rules of auction system—declaring that transactions must be cleared at the cutting rate, and no auction could be declared void. The CBC introduced longer maturity (4-, 6-, 8-, and 10-year) promissory notes and increased size of auctions.	The CBC was authorized to intervene in the foreign exchange market and operate within the established 10% margin. Exchange arbitrage operations were undertaken abroad by banks were liberalized. Commercial banks were permitted to increase their foreign exchange exposure and deal in foreign exchange among banks, instead of only with the CBC. Foreign exchange could be bought for purposes of amortization of capital and payment of interest on debt duly registered at the CBC within 90 days after the due date. Export proceeds over $2,000 were permitted to be surrendered through commercial banks. Exporters were permitted to retain 10% (up from 5%) of the proceeds in special foreign currency accounts with a cumulative limit a year of $5 million from $500,000. Commercial banks were authorized to sell foreign exchange using their term deposits in foreign exchange. Limits on travel allowances were raised from $1,000 to $3,000 for neighboring countries and to $5,000 from $3,000 for travel to other countries. *Portfolio Investment* Inflows: Qualified residents were authorized to obtain foreign credits by issuing bonds abroad. Inflows: A-rated Chilean enterprises and banks were authorized to issue bonds in foreign markets. Outflows: Pension funds were permitted for the first time to invest abroad up to 1.5% of the total value of their assets. This percentage was increased again later in the year to 3%. Outflows: Chapter XIX was amended to allow applications for advance remittances of profits and capital earned on foreign investment under certain conditions. Inflows: In May the period of application of the reserve requirement on external credits entering under Chapter XIV was increased to one year from 90 days but the reserve requirement ratio for these inflows was left unchanged at 20% until August. *Other Investment* Inflows: In October, Chapters XIV and XXVI were amended such that external credit could be obtained through issuing of share-convertible bonds abroad.

Table 6.6 *(continued)*

Monetary Controls and Financial System	Exchange System, Trade, and Capital Flows
1992 *(continued)*	*Trade* The limit on import payments above which the prior approval of the CBC would be required was raised to $100,000. The limit on payments for invisibles was raised to $3,000 from $200. *Restrictions on Capital Flows* Inflows: In August the reserve requirement on external credits was first extended to foreign currency deposits and then subsequently increased to 30% from 20%.
1993	
Capital Markets An electronic screen began operating on the trading floor of the stock exchange, and the Centralized Financial Clearing and Settlement and Operations Settlement systems started functioning. *Money Market and Instruments* The CBC introduced auctions of 12-, 14-, and 20-year promissory notes.	*Exchange Market Arrangement and System* The maximum period to surrender foreign exchange proceeds of nonfinancial services exports (insurance payments, shipping fees and other commissions) was extended by 90 days to 150 days, in line with that in force for merchandise export proceeds. *Direct Investment* Outflows: Under an amendment of Decree Law No. 600 (DL 600), the main vehicle for foreign investment in Chile, the minimum period for the remittance of capital and earnings was allowed after one year instead of after three years for all investment flows under this law. Remittances of profits were not subject to any time restrictions. Inflows: The "guaranteed" corporate income tax (or "invariability rate") for foreign investors opting for a tax rate different from that used for domestic corporations (an option under DL 600 that is a rate guaranteed for the duration of the investment) is reduced to 42% from about 49.5%. Inflows: The tax on gross revenue for payments to nonresidents for the use of patents and trademarks was lowered from 40% to 35%. *Portfolio Investment* Outflows: The minimum period for the remittance of capital and earnings was allowed after one year instead of after three years for all investment flows also under Chapter XIX and Chapter XIV. Profit remittances from investments under Chapter XIX remained subject to certain restrictions until the full elimination of Chapter XIX in 1995.

Inflows: Corporations issuing bonds on the international capital market were required to obtain a credit rating from a foreign rating company that is equal to or better than the rating assigned to Chile.

Trade

Documents were required to provide information on imports that were previously issued only by the CBC were permitted to be issued by private agencies with respect to imports from Latin American Integration Association (LAIA) member countries.

Restrictions on Capital Flows

Outflows: Decree Law 600 was amended to clarify that access to the formal exchange market for the remittance of capital or profits abroad required the prior approval of the Foreign Investment Committee.

1994

Capital Markets

The stock market introduced trading in options.

Exchange Market Arrangement and System

The midpoint of the exchange rate band was revalued by 10% and the weights of the reference currency basket were changed.

The ceiling on foreign exchange positions held by commercial banks was eliminated in November.

The CBC authorized exchange houses operating in the formal exchange market to carry out forward and swap operations.

The proportion of export proceeds that exporters were allowed to retain was raised to 15%, then to 25%, and again to 50%. The limit on export proceeds in a 12-month period was raised to $10 million, then to $15 million, and again to $50 million a year.

The period to surrender foreign exchange from exports was extended from 150 to 180 days, then to 210 days and again to 270 days.

Table 6.6 *(continued)*

Monetary Controls and Financial System	Exchange System, Trade, and Capital Flows
1994 *(continued)*	*Portfolio Investment* Outflows: Life insurance companies that have a BBB+ risk rating were permitted to invest up to 10% of their resources in 32 selected countries. Outflows: General insurance companies with a BBB risk-rating were permitted to invest up to 15% of their resources in 34 selected countries. Outflows: Mutual funds were authorized to invest up to 30% of their resources, but did not have to meet any risk criteria. Nor were they limited to a specific number of countries. Inflows: It was made easier for nonfinancial enterprises to issue bonds in foreign markets or place ADRs abroad because their qualification rating was lowered to BBB+ from an A rating by the National Risk Classification Commission. In addition, the minimum amount of issue was halved to $25 million and authorization from the CBC was no longer required. Outflows: The maximum amount that pension funds, insurance companies, and mutual funds were allowed to invest abroad was raised to 4% from 3% of their portfolio. Outflows: The issuance of ADRs but not of bonds by banks was simplified: the minimum amount for each issue was lowered to $25 million from $50 million, and the requirement that the issuing bank be rated A by the National Risk Classification Commission was replaced by the requirement that it be rated BBB+ by two international rating agencies. Outflows: The CBC published new regulations with respect to investment abroad by pension funds. Pension funds were permitted to invest up to 6% of assets in international markets. Outflows: Chilean banks were permitted to invest in financial institutions abroad after obtaining authorization from the CBC and the Superintendency of Banks and Financial Institutions. The investment itself could not exceed 25% of the bank's capital plus reserves, and the banks risk-weighted assets could not exceed tenfold its effective patrimony. *Restrictions on Capital Flows* Inflows: All reserve requirements on foreign borrowing were required to be held solely in U.S. dollars.

1995

Capital Markets

The CBC allowed pension funds to invest up to 9% of their assets in risk-rating instruments.

The minimum risk rating requirement for instruments in which pension funds may invest was lowered from A– to BBB–.

The CBC raised the ceiling: (a) on pension funds' investment in domestic stock from 30% to 37% of their assets; and (b) on pension funds' investment in instruments issued by public finance institutions from 45% to 50% of their assets.

Financial Supervisory and Regulatory Framework

The CBC introduced regulations for exchange houses and brokerage companies through which pension funds can carry out domestic and foreign financial transactions.

Money Market and Instruments

Banks and financial institutions are allowed to open a "liquid deposit account" in the CBC.

The CBC limited the access of financial institutions to its liquidity credit lines to the following amounts, calculated as the average amount of credit outstanding during a given reserve period: starting September 9, 90% of the amount was assigned under the first tranche, and starting October 9, 60% of that amount.

The CBC announced that its 90-day indexed promissory notes (PRBC) would be sold through biweekly auctions; the auction of the 30-day promissory note (PDBC) would be limited only to banks and financial institutions that purchased PRBCs during the previous auction. These banks and financial institutions were allowed to purchase an amount equivalent to up to 10% of their PRBC purchases at a nominal interest.

Interest rates on daily indexed liquidity credit lines were

Exchange Market Arrangement and System

The CBC authorized exchange houses operating in the formal exchange market to purchase and sell foreign exchange in connection with ADR transactions (undertaken through Chapter XXVI).

Pension funds and insurance companies were granted access to the formal exchange market.

The CBC specified that mutual funds would not be granted access to the formal exchange market to carry out exchange operations related to their investments abroad.

The CBC authorized exchange houses operating in the formal exchange market to carry out exchange operations related to investment abroad by pension funds and insurance companies.

The CBC specified that the maximum amount of financial investment that banks and financial institutions can deduct from the foreign exchange position used to calculate their reserve requirement is equal to the maximum limit on such investments.

The CBC allowed exporters to no longer surrender export proceeds to the CBC, although they are still required to inform the CBC of these operations, until April 1996.

The obligation to surrender proceeds from foreign bond issues was eliminated.

Portfolio Investment

Outflows: Chapters XVIII and XIX were eliminated, thus lifting the restrictions on the purchases of selected Chilean foreign debt instruments.

Outflows: Restrictions on the remittance of profits abroad and the three-year holding period for capital repatriation for selected Chilean foreign debt instruments was lifted.

Inflows: The CBC lowered the minimum amount required to issue ADRs to $10 million from $25 million for companies that already had issued ADRs abroad.

Outflows: A minimum country risk rating of BBB– was established for investment in foreign stocks by insurance companies. (This rating refers to the risk in the ceiling in which the stock is trading.)

Outflows: The CBC raised the ceiling on investment abroad from 6% to 9% of total assets, with a subceiling of 4 ½% in stocks and stock-based instruments.

Table 6.6 *(continued)*

Monetary Controls and Financial System	Exchange System, Trade, and Capital Flows
1995 *Money Market and Instruments (continued)*	*Portfolio Investment (continued)*
lowered from 6.3% to 5.7% for the first credit tranche; from 6.55% to 6% for the second credit tranche, and from 7.05% to 6.5 % for the third credit tranche.	Outflows: The CBC lowered the minimum risk ratings of foreign investment by banks and financial institutions from A– to BB– for up to 30% of the total allowed (equivalent to 25% of the banks' capital and reserves) and to BBB– for the remaining 70%.
The CBC lowered the rate on daily deposits by commercial banks with the CBC from 5.22% to 5%.	Outflows: The CBC established the following ceilings on investments abroad by institutional investors: (a) for pension funds the ceiling was raised from 3% to 6% of their total assets; (b) for life insurance companies, 10% of their assets in foreign financial instruments, and up to 3% in urban nonresidential real estate; (c) for general insurance companies, 15% of their assets in foreign financial instruments, and up to 3% in urban nonresidential real estate; and (d) for mutual funds, 30% of their total assets, without reference to any minimum rating requirement or any specific number of countries.
The CBC raised the interest rate on its indexed liquidity credit lines from 5.7% to 6.7% for the first credit tranche, from 6% to 7% for the second credit tranche; and from 6.5% to 7.5% for the third credit tranche.	The Superintendency of Banks and Financial Institutions was authorized to determine the time period during which banks will be required to adjust the ratio between their foreign investment and their total assets to the ceiling established by the CBC (transitory provisions).
The CBC raised the rate on commercial bank liquidity deposit accounts with the CBC from 5% to 6%.	*Restrictions on Capital Flows*
The CBC moved from fixing the rate on its 90-day indexed paper to fixing the interest rate on its overnight operations with commercial banks.	Inflows: The ceiling on credit in Chilean pesos backed by deposits in U.S. dollars was reduced from 150% to 70%, to avoid a possible by-passing of the one-year 30% reserve requirement on foreign borrowing. The ceiling on credit in Chilean pesos backed by deposits in U.S. dollars was further reduced to 10%.
	Inflows: The 30% reserve requirement on foreign liabilities was extended to secondary transactions of ADRs.
	Inflows: The coverage of the existing 20% reserve requirement on foreign liabilities was broadened to include investment flows that do not constitute an increase in the capital stock but only a transaction of assets from residents to nonresidents.

1996

Capital Markets

The CBC announced that for the trading of securities by pension funds, it would consider two formal secondary markets: one domestic, and one external. The domestic formal secondary market would consist of stock exchanges, their brokers, and commercial banks with a risk rating of AAA– or higher on their long-term instruments and a rating of 1– or higher on their short-term instruments. The external formal secondary market would consist of stock and securities exchanges, further exchanges securities dealers and brokers authorized to trade in these exchanges as well as over the counter, open and closed end mutual funds, and banks authorized to receive deposits.

Money Market and Instruments

The CBC limited the access of financial institutions to its liquidity credit lines to 30% of the amount assigned under the first tranche.

Exchange Market Arrangement and System

The composition of the currency basket used to calculate the central reference exchange rate of the exchange rate band was adjusted by increasing the weight of the U.S. dollar from 45% to 80%, while reducing that of the deutsche mark and Japanese yen from 30% to 15% and from 15% to 5%, respectively.

The width of the exchange rate band was increased from ±10% to ±12.5%.

The CBC lowered the threshold over which banks are required to provide detailed information on sources and destination of foreign exchange transactions from $50,000 to $10,000 per transaction.

The CBC allowed foreign exchange houses to sell up to $15,000, or its equivalent in other foreign currencies, to any person for travel expenses, payments to international organizations, and payments for studies abroad.

The CBC required exporters to convert export advances into local currency through bank transfers on the formal exchange market, and banks to report such transactions to the CBC.

The CBC authorized debtors of external credits recorded under Chapter VI to settle amortization interest, commissions, and expenses corresponding to these operations directly abroad with export proceeds. It was required that the CBC be kept informed of these transactions.

Mutual funds were permitted to use the formal exchange market to make investments abroad.

Debtors of credits recorded under Chapter IV were allowed to access in advance the formal market to prepay the credits or maintain the resources in account abroad that could be given in guarantee to the creditor.

Table 6.6 ***(concluded)***

Monetary Controls and Financial System	Exchange System, Trade, and Capital Flows
1996 *(continued)*	*Portfolio Investment* Outflows: The CBC eliminated the restrictions on the share of mutual fund assets that can be invested abroad. Outflows: Several times in 1996 the authorities expanded the list of foreign investments in which domestic institutional investors are allowed to invest (including domestic pension and mutual funds). Outflows: The CBC granted individuals unrestricted access to the formal exchange market for transactions up to $15,000 a month. Inflows: External credits destined exclusively to prepay foreign credits that were previously authorized and recorded with the CBC were exempted from the 30% reserve requirement, provided the weighted average terms of each credit and residual of the original credit were similar. Outflows: The CBC granted individuals unrestricted access to the formal exchange market for transactions up to $15,000 a month (also applicable to Portfolio Investment). *Restrictions on Capital Flows* Inflows: The CBC limited the extension of outstanding foreign loans subscribed under Chapters VI and XIV to a maximum period of one year over their initial maturity. Receipts of foreign credits under Chapter XIV would not be obliged to repay these credits at their initial maturity since they still had access to the informal market. Fines of up to 4% of the value of the scheduled amortization were established to deal with late payments.

Sources: *Annual Report,* Central Bank of Chile (various issues); *International Tax Summaries: A Guide for Planning and Decisions,* Coopers and Lybrand (various issues); *Annual Report and Exchange Arrangements and Exchange Restrictions,* IMF (various issues); *Doing Business in Chile,* Price Waterhouse, 1995; *The Securities Market in Chile: 1980–1989,* Chile, Superintendencia de Valores y Seguros; and *Tax Laws of the World: Chile,* Foreign Tax Publishers, 1989.

Table 6.7. Chile: Selected Macroeconomic, Financial Sector, and Balance of Payments Indicators

	1985	1986	1987	1988	1989	1990	1991	1992	1993	1994	1995	1996
						(In percent)						
Selected economic indicators												
Real GDP growth	2.5	5.6	6.6	7.3	9.9	3.3	7.3	10.7	6.6	4.2	8.5	7.2
Inflation per year	30.7	19.5	19.9	14.7	17.0	26.0	21.8	15.4	12.7	11.4	8.2	7.4
M2 to GDP ratio	40.0	38.9	39.5	38.5	39.7	39.9	39.4	37.7	39.1	36.6	37.8	40.7
Currency to deposits ratio	11.4	12.2	10.8	11.0	10.0	10.1	9.2	9.5	9.2	9.4	8.5	7.7
Fiscal balance to GDP Ratio	–2.3	–0.9	0.4	–0.2	1.8	0.8	1.6	2.2	1.9	1.7	2.5	. . .
Private sector credit to GDP Ratio	68.1	61.7	57.0	52.7	48.1	45.9	44.0	45.4	49.3	48.5	51.1	55.0
Exports plus imports of goods to GDP ratio	41.7	43.0	46.5	51.1	54.0	52.8	49.5	47.1	44.5	44.9	47.6	46.1
Current account to GDP ratio	–8.6	–6.7	–3.6	–1.0	–2.5	–1.8	0.3	–1.6	–4.6	–1.2	0.2	–4.1
Financial account to GDP ratio	–8.5	–12.5	–3.6	–3.7	4.8	9.9	2.4	6.9	5.6	8.7	2.1	8.8
Interest and exchange rates												
Nominal deposit rate (percent per year)	32.0	19.0	25.2	15.1	27.7	40.3	22.3	18.3	18.2	15.1	13.7	13.5
Real deposit rate (percent per year)	1.3	–0.5	5.3	0.4	10.7	14.2	0.5	2.8	5.5	3.6	5.5	6.1
Interest rate differential[1]	23.6	12.1	18.0	7.1	18.4	32.0	16.3	14.4	15.0	10.3	7.7	8.0
Lending/deposit spread	8.8	7.3	7.6	6.1	8.2	8.6	6.2	5.7	6.1	5.2	4.4	3.9
Official exchange rate per U.S. dollar (end of period)	183.9	204.7	238.1	247.2	297.4	336.9	374.9	382.3	431.0	404.1	407.1	425.0
Real effective exchange rate index (1990 = 100)	136.6	115.6	107.1	100.8	103.2	100.0	96.4	93.2	95.7	94.6	86.4	86.8

Table 6.7 *(concluded)*

	1985	1986	1987	1988	1989	1990	1991	1992	1993	1994	1995	1996
						(In millions of U.S. dollars)						
Balance of Payments												
Current account, n.i.e.	–1,414	–1,192	–735	–231	–705	–540	113	–700	–2,072	–644	142	–2,921
Financial account, n.i.e	–1,395	–2,221	–742	–905	1,340	3,014	843	2,931	2,579	4,534	1,387	6,342
Direct investment abroad	–2	–3	–6	–16	–10	–8	–123	–378	–433	–926	–697	–1,080
Direct investment in reporting economy, n.i.e.	144	316	891	968	1,289	590	523	699	808	1,773	1,668	4,091
Net direct investment	142	313	885	952	1,279	582	400	321	375	847	971	3,011
Portfolio investment assets	. . .	. . .	. . .	. . .	. . .	. . .	. . .	. . .	–90	–351	–14	–137
Portfolio investment liabilities	. . .	–78	–8	–8	80	353	186	452	820	1,259	49	1,240
Net portfolio investment	. . .	–78	–8	–8	80	353	186	452	730	908	35	1,103
Other investment assets	434	576	257	370	297	553	1,298	–273	460	–163	–49	–141
Other investment liabilities	–1,971	–3,032	–1,876	–2,219	–316	1,526	–1,041	2,431	1,014	2,942	430	2,369
Net other investments	–1,537	–2,456	–1,619	–1,849	19	2,079	257	2,158	1,474	2,779	381	2,228
Of which, official capital	1,322	378	380	–104	–602	–335	–6	131	–895	–405	–2,151	–2,094
Net errors and omissions	–67	225	–144	–121	–119	–140	300	316	–80	–741	–391	–917
Overall balance[2]	–2,876	–3,188	–1,621	–1,257	516	2,334	1,256	2,547	427	3,149	1,138	2,504
Memorandum:												
Net private capital[3]	–3,115	–2,034	–814	–434	1,756	3,229	1,583	4,477	3,782	5,143	4,824	7,605

Sources: IMF, *International Financial Statistics, World Economic Outlook, and Direction of Trade Statistics,* various issues; and IMF staff estimates.

[1]Interest differential = Deposit rate minus London interbank offer rate on three-month U.S. deposits.

[2]The overall balance includes: current account, financial account, capital account, and net errors and omissions. Capital account figures are not shown because they are zero throughout the period.

[3]Total capital = direct investment + portfolio investment + other investment minus official capital + net errors and omissions + misinvoicing.

Table 6.8. Indonesia: Sequencing of Reforms in the Domestic and External Sectors

Monetary Controls and Financial System	Exchange System, Trade, and Capital Flows
1985	
Money Markets and Instruments	*Exchange Market Arrangement and System*
Interest rates are market-determined (liberalized in 1983) and money market instruments (SBIs) were introduced in 1984.	Government provided opportunity to foreign investors engaged in exports to obtain export credits at low interest rates through foreign exchange banks in Indonesia.
A standardized form of banker's acceptances (SBPUs) was introduced in February.	*Direct Investments*
	Inflows: Procedure simplified; beginning in April a proposal for a new project had to meet only 14 procedural requirements compared with 25 in the preceding year.
	Inflows: Certain fields closed to foreign direct investments might be opened if entire production exported.
	Trade
	Import tariff schedule revised; tariff ceiling was reduced substantially, with tariff rates ranging from 0% to 60% compared with 0% to 225%, previously; the number of tariff categories was also reduced from 25 to 12.
	A value added tax of 10%, which is applicable to the c.i.f. import price plus the tariff, was also introduced. Luxury goods and other specific goods were to incur higher import duties or specific taxes.
1986	*Exchange Market Arrangement and System*
	On September 12, the rupiah was devalued by 31% from Rp 1,134 per U.S. dollar to Rp 1,644 per U.S. dollar.
	Direct Investments
	Inflows: Government permitted foreign direct investment companies to extend their operations for 30 years after expansion approval (previously they were permitted to operate for 30 years from their actual establishment).
	Inflows: If foreign direct investment companies met certain criteria they were eligible for treatment equivalent to the domestic investment scheme. This allowed foreign direct investment companies to market their products locally, and to obtain working capital credit from commercial state banks and Indonesia's Development Bank.

Table 6.8 *(continued)*

Monetary Controls and Financial System	Exchange System, Trade, and Capital Flows
1986 (*continued*)	*Direct Investments* Inflows: Equity ownerships rules were relaxed for companies in several situations—those exporting all their products, businesses located in remote areas or facing high risk, or enterprises investing at least $10 million. Initially foreign ownership was allowed to as high as 95%, although after five years of operations it was to be reduced to at most 80%. Additionally, to encourage companies to reinvest their profits in Indonesia they were allowed to purchase shares of any existing enterprise and were not limited to those established with foreign participation, or under the domestic investment scheme. Inflows: Foreign investors who needed additional capital were permitted to invest in certain enterprises established under the domestic investment scheme. Inflows: To encourage exports, foreign investors were allowed to increase their share to 95% in an enterprise, although after five years the shares were to revert back to its original composition. *Direct Investment* Inflows: The investment priority list was revised and a wider sector was open to foreign direct investment. In addition, foreign investors were allowed to invest in sectors reserved for domestic investors as long as they were cooperative entities. *Trade* The government accepted GATT Code on subsidies and countervailing duties. Firms that export at least 85% of output were allowed to import input free of licensing restrictions and were exempt from import duties. Import licensing was liberalized on 321 CCCN items (mostly manufacturing), or 25% of restricted items. Changes in import duties became applicable to 333 products: Tariffs were reduced for imports not produced domestically and temporary surcharge imposed on 33 items.

1987

Capital Markets

Listing requirements on the Jakarta Stock Exchange (JSE) were simplified. Measures introduced to improve institutional framework and operation of capital market institutions (e.g., underwriters, guarantors, and stock traders).

Bearer securities were introduced.

Money Market and Instruments

Interest rates were allowed more flexibility.

Modifications were made to money market procedures to strengthen Bank Indonesia's ability to regulate liquidity. Bank Indonesia makes daily decisions to inject or withdraw liquidity through daily auctions in SBIs and SBPUs.

The government introduced the over-the-counter market.

SBPU discount ceilings were eliminated.

State-owned enterprises were forced to transfer part of their deposits to Bank Indonesia from state-owned banks.

Exchange Market Arrangement and System

Exchange rate was allowed more flexibility.

Direct Investments

Inflows: The transfer period of majority ownership from foreign to local was extended from 10 to 15 years with a possibility of further extension of five years.

Inflows: Companies exporting at least 65% (reduced from 85%) of their output were allowed to be established with a minimum of 5% local ownership, which had to be raised to 20% in 10 (previously five) years.

Inflows: Foreign companies in bonded zone and exporting 100% of output were allowed to be established with a national ownership of a minimum of 5% without the requirement to subsequently raise the local share of ownership.

Inflows: Government expanded the number of sectors open to foreign investment.

Inflows: Ownership rules were relaxed further to permit companies with foreign investment to be treated equally as those established under the domestic investment scheme—allowing them to sell output in the domestic market and to obtain working capital credit from state-owned commercial banks and the state development bank. To qualify, national ownership was required to be 51% (reduced from 75%) or 45% (reduced from 51%), provided at least 20% was sold through the stock market.

Inflows: The government abolished the license requirement for limited domestic purchases. This made it easier for foreign companies to purchase domestic products as inputs (previously two licenses were required now only one).

Inflows: Companies with presidential approval no longer had to obtain prior approval from the Capital Investment Coordinating Board to make imports. Only submission of a master list to authorized surveyors was required.

Inflows: To promote non-oil/gas exports, particularly manufacturing, companies established with foreign investments were allowed to export products manufactured by other companies and to establish joint-venture companies that would export manufactured goods.

Table 6.8 *(continued)*

Monetary Controls and Financial System	Exchange System, Trade, and Capital Flows
1987 *(continued)*	*Direct Investments*
	Inflows: Some enterprises under the domestic investment scheme or those established through foreign direct investment, whose outputs were mostly exported, were awarded permanent licenses. Some were exempt from licensing requirements if they were expanding or diversifying within the same industry.
	Inflows: Foreign direct investment companies exporting more than 65% of their output were allowed more freedom in hiring foreign experts.
	Portfolio Investments
	Inflows: Government announced plans to allow foreign investors to purchase securities on the stock market and on the over-the-counter stock exchange.
	Trade
	Import licensing was liberalized for 202 CCCN items (non-batik textiles), representing 89% of restricted non-batik imports (January).
	Import licensing was liberalized for 18 CCCN items (iron and steel sector), representing 13% of restricted iron and steel sector imports (January).
	Goods were freed from nontariff restrictions and were included in 111 tariff classifications (approximately 50% were steel and aluminum products; December).
	Due to removal of nontariff barriers, tariffs were increased on 91 CCCN items and tariffs were reduced on 65 items (December).
	Import duties were lowered on 65 CCCN items (December).
	Export licensing procedure was simplified (December).

1988

A financial policy package introduced on Oct. 27, 1988 included the following measures: an expectation to promote mobilization of funds, export of non-oil/gas commodities, efficiency in financial institution, and banks, and a more efficient monetary management, as well as a climate conducive to the development of the capital market.

A financial policy package introduced on December 20, 1988 was directed at further encouraging the development of the capital market and financing companies so as to mobilize more long-term funds to finance investment.

Financial Supervision and Regulatory Framework

To strengthen prudential bank supervision legal limits were established on financial institutions' exposure to individuals or groups of borrowers and supervisory responsibility for rural credit was transferred to Bank Indonesia from Agricultural Development Bank.

State banks, regional development banks, private national banks, and cooperative banks were permitted to open new branch offices throughout the country.

Nonbank financial institutions (NBFIs) and foreign banks were permitted to open one branch in each of seven cities, and joint-venture banks (with maximum foreign participation of 85%) could be established by foreign banks already represented in Indonesia.

New private banks were permitted to be established anywhere in Indonesia, while rural credit banks were allowed to be established outside main cities and municipalities. Two new private banks were licensed between October and December.

Requirements to become a foreign exchange bank were eased.

Exchange Market Arrangement and System

Article VIII was accepted on May 8.

The branch offices of foreign exchange banks, which were previously not allowed to manage foreign exchange, could do so now by simply informing Bank Indonesia.

Swap premium shifted to market-based determination and maximum maturity extended from six months to three years.

Direct Investments

Inflows: Foreign investors were allowed to establish joint ventures in the setting up of new financing institutions, such as factoring companies, venture capital, securities trading, and consumer financing, with a maximum share of 85% of the paid up capital.

Inflows: The government allowed joint ventures in the insurance industry but foreign partnership was limited to 80%. These companies were also allowed to offer life insurance policies either in rupiah or in foreign currency.

Inflows: Joint venture banks were also permitted with the foreign partner allowed at most a 85% share.

Trade

Nontariff barriers (NTBs) were replaced by tariffs on 300 products (including fertilizers, plastics, and most types of steel).

Tariff rates were reduced on 86 products and increased on 72 products. At least 22 products previously subject to specific duties, were made subject to ad valorem tariffs.

Table 6.8 *(continued)*

Monetary Controls and Financial System	Exchange System, Trade, and Capital Flows
1988 *(continued)* *Financial Supervision and Regulatory Framework*	
Foreign banks were allowed to establish sub-branch offices.	
Foreign banks were now allowed to introduce rupiah savings schemes, which were previously prohibited.	
Money Market and Instruments	
Reserve requirements were reduced from 15% to 2% on foreign currency deposits and on current liabilities. Time and saving deposits of all banks are now categorized as current liabilities.	
To increase competition, public enterprises were allowed to hold up to 50% of deposits at non-state financial institutions.	
New sub-branch offices of foreign banks were required to extend a major portion (at least 50%) of their credits to finance non-oil/gas exports.	
The share of export credits extended by the joint-venture bank were to be at least 50% of outstanding credits.	
Maximum maturity of money market securities was extended to six months.	
Weekly auctions of money market instruments introduced to supplement daily auctions.	
Several banks and NBFIs were authorized to act as market makers along with an investment company (FICORINVEST).	
NBFIs were authorized to issue rupiah CDs.	

1989

Money Market and Instruments

Previously, private national commercial banks were allowed to extend investment credit up to a maximum of 20% of their total lending and 10% of their equity for each borrower. For foreign banks, the maximum amount was 35% of their total lending. Under the new regulations the old limits had been removed, and all commercial banks including foreign banks were required to take into account the new regulation on legal lending limits.

Exchange Market Arrangement and System

Foreign direct investment companies were now permitted to sell their foreign exchange from their foreign exchange account directly to foreign exchange banks, thus eliminating the need to sell it to Bank Indonesia as was previously done.

Direct Investments

Inflows: To influence foreign direct investments the government replaced the priority list with a negative list.

Inflows: The minimum investment requirement was reduced to $250,000.

Inflows: Foreign investors were now permitted to own 100% of the shares if they were invested in the bonded zone of Batan Island and were exporting 100% of their output. Five years after commercial production, at least 5% of the shares had been sold to Indonesian partners.

Portfolio Investments

Inflows: The government regulated the purchase of stocks by foreign investors. Foreign investors were allowed to purchase up to 49% of stocks in the primary market or up to 49% of stocks listed on the stock exchange and OTC. However, foreigners were not allowed to purchase stocks issued by private banks.

Inflows: Since April, foreign exchange banks and NBFIs were no longer subject to ceilings on offshore borrowings. However, their net foreign exchange open position could not exceed 25% of their own equity.

Trade

The Harmonized System (HS) was adopted. Rates of tariffs and import surcharges on several products were modified.

State monopoly to import maize was revoked.

Table 6.8 *(continued)*

Monetary Controls and Financial System	Exchange System, Trade and Capital Flows
1990	
Capital Markets Steps were taken to further develop the capital market. Presidential Decree (Nov. 10) and Ministry of Finance Decree (Dec. 4) were issued to provide a new structure and policy framework (see below in 1991).	*Trade* Licensing requirements for 371 goods, including certain machinery steel products, electronic products, and pharmaceuticals were removed (restrictions on about 1,300 items still remain).
Financial Supervision and Regulatory Framework Joint-venture banks and foreign banks were permitted to open branch offices in Batan Island.	Tariffs on 2,363 products (out of 7,176 products) were reduced; tariffs above 40% were virtually eliminated (about 400 items remain). Split tariffs were eliminated; the surcharge on 53 products (out of 223) was removed.
Money Markets and Instruments Measures were introduced to reduce liquidity credits extended by Bank Indonesia. Liquidity credits would only be provided for activities that supported cooperatives, investment, and the achievement of self sufficiency in food.	Import tariff on 224 products was raised. In accordance with GATT, subsidized export credits were abolished.
1991	
Capital Markets Badan Pengawas Pasar Modal's (BAPEPAM) function was modified. It assumed responsibility for regulatory and supervisory aspects of the market and for protecting the investors' interests. Powers were increased to perform responsibilities.	*Exchange Market Arrangement and System* Bank Indonesia reduced the individual bank's swap limit from 25% to 20% of capital. In November 1991, Bank Indonesia started to provide two types of swaps—the liquidity type and the investment type (maturity of more than two years). Liquidity swaps were initiated by Bank Indonesia while the investment swap is initiated by the banks.
Based on principle of self-regulations, the operational role of BAPEPAM was transferred to private companies—PT Jakarta Stock Exchange (JSE) and PT Surabaya Stock Exchange (SSE).	*Direct Investment* Inflows: The government revised the direct investment negative list (items reduced to 60 from 70). Inflows: The government allowed foreign investors to own a maximum of 80% of the capital stock. Inflows: The government allowed venture capitalists to participate in the foreign direct investment scheme on a temporary basis not to exceed 10 years.

Financial Supervision and Regulatory Framework

Measures to strengthen regulatory framework of the banking system were to be implemented over a two-year period. These included stricter conditions for obtaining banking licenses and opening overseas branches; compliance with capital adequacy requirements; mandatory provisioning for doubtful or nonperforming assets; reduction in limits on banks' net open positions; and more detailed reporting by banks to Bank Indonesia.

Banks were required to keep the net open position in foreign currency including their off-balance sheet accounts at or below 20% of capital.

80% of all foreign exchange loans was to be allocated to businesses earning foreign exchange.

Inflows: The government broadened the scope of opportunities available to foreign direct investors. The minimum investment requirement of $1 million for setting up export-oriented enterprises was lowered to $250,000 if it involved the participation of cooperatives or small-scale economic groups. The share of the small scale participant was 5% at time of initial investment, but had to be raised to 20% in 10 years and to 51% in 15 years.

Inflows: Special concessions were granted to export-oriented foreign investment in eastern Indonesia to enable them to hire foreign workers

Outflows: Commercial banks (but not NBFIs) were allowed to open overseas branches or representative offices and undertake equity participation in banks and other financial institutions abroad. To be eligible the bank had to have the status of a foreign exchange bank for at least one year. Additionally, the bank's rating classification for overall performance and capital adequacy for the last 24 months could be at least sound for 20 months and fairly sound for the remaining months.

Restriction on Capital Flows

Inflows: A Foreign Commercial Borrowing Management Coordinating Team was established by Presidential Decree No. 39, in September. Ceilings on foreign commercial borrowings were introduced (on 10/12/91). This applied to Bank Indonesia, State Bank, commercial banks, private companies, and state-owned companies. Borrowings not subjected to ceilings or coordination included those required for regular trade, or in the context of money/capital market less than $20 million per creditor or depositor and not intended to finance new projects or expand projects related to public entities. Borrowings by private companies to finance private projects not related to public entities was also not subject to ceilings or coordination.

Inflows: Banks' short-term foreign exchange liabilities (up to two years, excluding trade related financing) were limited to 30% of capital.

Trade

Import restrictions replaced by tariffs on 322 items (in particular agricultural and vehicle assembly products), reducing proportion of imports subject to administrative restrictions to 12% from 15%.

The maximum tariff rate on finished goods was reduced to 30% from 40% and on intermediate goods to 15%. The number of items with tariffs higher than 35% was reduced. All these measures reduced total number of tariff items to 9,303 from 9,492 and the average (unweighted) tariff rate to 20% from 22%.

Surcharges on 137 products (out of 542) were removed.

Table 6.8 *(continued)*

Monetary Controls and Financial System	Exchange System, Trade, and Capital Flows
1992	
Capital Markets	*Direct Investment*
Commercial banks were allowed to issue securities through the stock exchange.	Inflows: Items on negative foreign direct investment list were reduced to 51 from 60.
Financial Supervision and Regulatory Framework	Inflows: 100% foreign ownership was permitted for (1) projects worth at least $50 million; (2) projects located in the 14 less developed provinces; and (3) projects situated in a bonded zone with 100% of output exported.
New banking laws were issued to replace laws issued in 1967.	
All specialized categories of financial institutions were eliminated.	Inflows: All new investments (except oil and gas, banks, and nonbank financial institutions) were required to have the prior approval of the Investment Coordinating Board (BKPM).
A phased reduction plan of banks' equity participation in nonfinancial institutions was initiated.	Inflows: Foreign banks were allowed to hold up to 85% of the equity of an NBFI. NBFIs were not permitted to compete with the commercial banks.
Permit bank ownership by foreigners (up to 49%) was allowed.	Inflows: Only Indonesian citizens were allowed to have the right to own land. However, foreign investors were allowed to acquire the right to build, right to use, and the right of exploitation.
State banks were converted to limited liability companies with up to 49% in private ownership.	*Portfolio Investment*
The supervisory authority of Bank Indonesia was strengthened.	Inflows: Foreign investors were allowed to purchase equity in commercial banks on the condition that they not hold the majority stock.
Stricter disclosure requirements were established.	*Trade*
Improved accounting standards were established.	Import licensing restrictions were reduced from 703 to 464—replaced with tariffs (mostly in manufacturing).
New insurance laws were issued on 2/11/92.	40% of existing import surcharges were removed.
	Krakatau Steel's monopoly import rights were eliminated.
	The ban on the export of unprocessed logs, raw skins and hides, and raw rattan was lifted, and export taxes on these items were introduced instead.

1993

Direct Investment

Inflows: The licensing procedure was simplified by requiring less paper work and some responsibilities were decentralized.

Inflows: 100% foreign ownership permitted for projects worth at least $2 million if inputs or components were produced for other industries.

Inflows: Divestment of 100% ownership was allowed to start in the eleventh year (instead of sixth). Divestment was to be carried out in 20 years, and could be transacted through capital market.

Inflows: For certain categories of investment, local ownership required to reach 20%–51% (previously 5%–20%) within 20 years, in particular, large investments (above $50 million). Government revised the negative list by reducing, restricting, or closing sectors from 51 to 33.

Inflows: Maximum length of land leases was increased to 30 years with easy renewal.

Trade

Items subject to restrictive import licensing requirements were reduced to 430 from 470.

Tariffs were lowered on 221 items (mostly machinery, equipment, paper, and paper products), generally by 5%.

NTBs were removed on 77 steel products. Imports surcharges removed on 58 steel products (accounting for 35% of steel imports).

Tariffs and surcharges were lowered on 72 glass products, 19 chemical products, 5 copper products, and certain machine tools.

Tariffs and surcharges were removed completely on inputs for electronic components industry.

Regulation was eased governing import of used machinery.

Restrictions on imports of pharmaceuticals were substantially relaxed.

Duty drawback system for exporters was simplified.

Table 6.8 *(continued)*

Monetary Controls and Financial System	Exchange System, Trade, and Capital Flows
1994	
Financial Supervision and Regulatory Framework	*Exchange Market Arrangement and System*
New regulation to strengthen prudential supervision by central bank was enacted so that bank examinations were to include examination of debtors and of bank subsidiaries operating in the financial sector.	Exchange rate movement was allowed more flexibility. Bank Indonesia ceased to announce an indicative exchange rate in the morning, and instead began announcing buying and selling rates at 3:00 p.m. The exchange rate was computed on the basis of a basket of weighted currencies with a spread of ± Rp 15 (compared to ± Rp 10 previously).
New regulation was established to provide the basis for operation of an independent rating agency that will provide more objective information to investors.	*Direct Investment*
Banks' net open position in foreign currency, including their off-balance sheet items, increased to 25% from 20% of bank capital and open position requirements no longer were applied to individual currencies.	Inflows: Foreign investors were allowed to retain a majority of the shares in the joint ventures indefinitely. Foreign ownership share could be as high as 95% with no further divestment required. There was no minimum capital investment requirement. Foreign ownership equivalent to 100% was permitted for certain categories of investment for an initial 15-year period. After that, some Indonesian ownership (greater than 0%) was required either through private placement or through capital market. Foreign investment was permitted in joint ventures in vital sectors (e.g., ports, power generation, and telecommunication). Foreign investors were allowed to locate operations anywhere in the country.
	Inflows: Foreign companies already operational were allowed to buy shares of other foreign companies or local companies.
	Inflows: Enterprises in bonded zones were permitted to subcontract locally outside zone.
	Trade
	Import facilities of up to two years were granted to enterprises that undertook capacity expansion of at least 30% or greater.
	NTBs were removed on 27 product lines and applied to five new alcohol-based products, resulting in 270 items remaining under restricted imports.
	Import surcharges were removed from 108 items and reduced for 13. The same surcharge continued to apply for the remaining 99 items.
	Import duties were raised on 38 tariff codes related to alcoholic products.
	Import duties were lowered on 739 items including manufactured and agricultural products.

1995

Capital Markets

Computerized trading was introduced on the Jakarta Stock Exchange.

Subrabaya Stock Exchange and the over-the-counter market merged to encourage participation by small investors.

Financial Supervision and Regulatory Framework

New regulations to promote better compliance with prudential principles and encourage self-regulation were issued, including: those on exchange of information between banks to facilitate banking operations and provide greater safeguards; credit policy guidelines to commercial banks to improve compliance with prudential lending principles; regulations pertaining to issuance and trading of commercial paper to lower risks borne by banks; guidelines on use of information technology to ensure secure transactions and backup systems to provide continuity of banking services; and those allowing the central bank to screen owners and managers of banks to preserve public confidence and integrity in the banking system.

A new regulation was issued to ensure public receives accurate and greater disclosure of financial conditions of banks and requires banks to standardize internal audit function. All banks with assets over Rp 10 billion were required to have their financial statements audited by public accountants approved by the central bank. Published annual financial statements must be based on audited financial statements.

New regulation was authorized to strengthen operations of pension schemes, including submission of financial reports audited by public accountants.

Exchange Market Arrangement and System

Exchange rate movement was allowed more flexibility. The buying and selling rates computed on the basis of a basket of weighted currencies with a spread of ± Rp 22 (compared to ± Rp 15 previously).

Bank Indonesia terminated the provision of investment swaps.

Trade

Tariffs lowered on 6,030 items of a total of 9,398 items.

Imports of 81 items previously restricted to selected importers could now be imported by general importers.

Table 6.8 *(continued)*

Monetary Controls and Financial System	Exchange System, Trade, and Capital Flows
1995 *(continued)* *Capital Markets (continued)*	
New regulation was passed to enhance supervision of finance companies covering borrowing, equity investment, and reporting.	
New regulations were issued on derivative transactions by banks to limit risks; banks were limited to dealing only in foreign exchange and interest rate derivatives; equity derivatives had to be approved by Bank Indonesia on a case-by-case basis; banks were required to give weekly report to Bank Indonesia on derivative transactions.	
1996	
Money Markets and Instruments	*Exchange Market Arrangement and System*
Bank Indonesia increased the reserve requirements to 3% from 2%, to be held at Bank Indonesia.	Exchange rate movement was allowed more flexibility. In June the intervention band was widened to Rp 118 (5%) and in September further broadened to Rp 192 (8%).
Bank Indonesia introduced various improvements in its clearing operations in Jakarta as a first step toward implementing an electronic clearing system in 1998.	*Direct Investment* Inflows: Foreign ownership of shares of securities companies was raised to 85% of paid-in capital.
Bank Indonesia introduced several improvements in its accounting system, including consolidating deposits held by commercial banks at Bank Indonesia into one account per bank, and internal accounting operations of Bank Indonesia and regional offices were brought on-line.	*Portfolio Investment* Inflows: Mutual fund companies were now permitted to be 100% foreign owned.
	Trade Tariff was reduced by 5% and 15% (mostly 5%) on 428 products, mainly capital goods; simplification of tariff code with removal of 1,100 items; reduction in import licensing, mostly steel; export taxes removed on processed animal leather, aluminum scrap alloy, and sandalwood; extension of duty drawback facility to goods supplied by existing exporters to firms in export processing zones.

Capital Markets

New capital market act was passed on Nov. 10, 1995 and enacted on Jan. 1, 1996. Supporting regulations and decrees were issued on Dec. 30, 1995. Under this Act, banks could act as custodians and trustees with the approval of supervisory agency BAPEPAM; mutual funds could now be allowed to be established; BAPEPAM was given powers to conduct criminal investigations and impose sanctions; simpler trading and book-entry settlement was guaranteed by clearing institution.

To stimulate bond market transactions, the rate of tax on interest income from bonds to be sold in the stock exchange, was set at 15%. Previously, interest income was subject to a progressive rate, which ranged between 10% and 30%.

The Indonesian Stock Deposit Clearing Corporation (DEI), which functioned as the clearing, guaranteeing, and settlement institution, was transformed into the settlement and custody institution. It also changed its name to Indonesian Stock Deposit Custodian Corporation.

The Indonesian Stock Clearing and Guarantee Corporation (KEPI) was established to function as the clearing and guaranteeing institution.

To boost trading on the SSE, the SSE implemented the Surabaya-Market Information and Automated Remote Trading (S-MART), which would enable members to conduct transactions from their offices. It also extended trading hours by one hour.

Tariff was increased by a 20% surcharge on propylene and ethylene imports.

Preferential duty arrangements established for approved national car manufacturers.

Import payments were allowed to be undertaken using letters of credit (LCs) opened in foreign exchange banks with payments due within 360 days.

The discount facility for export drafts was extended to suppliers of export-related products and the discount rate was reduced. Exporters (and export suppliers) were permitted to sell their export proceeds to Bank Indonesia, and to discount export drafts with a remaining maturity of between 30 and 720 days, with drafts being rediscounted in rupiah or dollars. Based on local LCs, suppliers of export-related goods could seek bank drafts and sell them to Bank Indonesia, provided their remaining maturity was between 30 and 90 days.

Fully owned foreign firms were allowed to export manufacturing, forestry, farm, fish, and mining goods; and foreign firms were allowed to import capital goods and raw materials for export from export processing zones.

General importers were permitted to import nine categories of goods previously restricted to producer importers.

The maximum limit for export of goods exempted from customs export declaration documentation was raised to Rp 100 million from Rp 10 million.

Pre-shipment inspection of exports by surveyors was discontinued; all inspection was undertaken within the framework of the customs act.

Requirements and procedures for certification of the origin on goods exported from Indonesia were simplified as follows: number of legal requirements was reduced to 4 from 31; number of supporting documents to be attached was reduced to 2 from 4; number of agencies permitted to issue certificates of origin was increased to 3 from 2; and number of officials vested with authority to issue certificates of origin was increased to 3 from 1.

Table 6.8 *(concluded)*

Monetary Controls and Financial System	Exchange System, Trade, and Capital Flows
1996 *(continued)*	
Financial Supervision and Regulatory Framework	
BAPEPAM introduced new regulation on financial reporting to improve transparency; guidelines were issued to cover the design, coverage, and requirements of financial statements to be submitted by issuers of stocks or public corporations to the public and BAPEPAM. These financial statements were required to conform to accounting standards and regulations in effect in the capital market.	
Government introduced regulations to promote mutual funds as a means of mobilizing investor funds, including issuing new income tax regulations for mutual funds and regulations concerning reporting of proper market value of mutual funds.	
The government introduced regulations concerning the procedure of revocation on operating licenses, dissolution, and liquidation of problem banks. This regulation described specific steps to be taken to try and save a problem bank. If no solution was found Bank Indonesia could propose to the Ministry of Finance to revoke the bank's operating license.	

Sources: *Report for the Financial Year,* Bank Indonesia, (various issues); *Annual Report on Exchange Arrangements and Exchange Restrictions,* IMF, (various issues); *Doing Business in Indonesia,* (various issues), Price Waterhouse; *International Tax Summaries: A Guide for Planning and Decisions,* Coopers and Lybrand International Tax Network, (various issues); and IMF staff esimates.

Table 6.9. Indonesia: Selected Macroeconomic, Financial Sector, and Balance of Payments Indicators

	1985	1986	1987	1988	1989	1990	1991	1992	1993	1994	1995	1996
						(In percent)						
Selected economic indicators												
Real GDP growth	2.5	5.9	4.9	5.8	7.5	7.2	7.0	6.5	6.5	7.4	8.5	7.2
Inflation per year	4.7	5.8	9.3	8.0	6.4	7.8	9.4	7.5	9.7	8.5	9.4	8.0
M2 to GDP ratio	23.9	26.9	27.2	29.6	35.0	43.3	43.7	45.8	43.4	44.9	48.3	52.5
Currency to deposits ratio	24.1	24.2	21.0	17.6	15.7	12.1	10.4	10.7	. . .	. . .	. . .	. . .
Fiscal balance to GDP ratio	–1.0	–3.5	–0.8	–3.1	–2.0	0.4	0.4	–0.4	0.6	0.9	2.3	1.2
Private sector credit to GDP ratio	14.1	16.4	18.7	22.3	23.8	50.6	50.7	49.5	48.9	51.9	53.7	55.8
ports plus imports of goods to GDP ratio	33.0	31.9	39.9	38.5	40.8	44.8	47.2	47.8	41.2	40.7	42.8	41.1
Current account to GDP ratio	–2.2	–4.9	–2.8	–1.7	–1.2	–2.8	–3.7	–2.2	–1.3	–1.6	–3.5	. . .
Financial account to GDP ratio	2.0	5.2	4.6	2.6	3.1	4.2	4.9	4.8	3.6	2.2	5.2	. . .
Interest and exchange rates												
Nominal deposit rate (percent per year)	18.0	15.4	16.8	17.7	18.6	17.3	23.3	19.6	14.6	12.5	16.7	17.3
Real deposit rate (percent per year)	13.3	9.6	7.5	9.7	12.2	9.7	13.9	12.1	4.9	4.0	7.3	9.3
Interest rate differential[1]	8.9	8.4	9.2	9.3	9.3	9.1	17.0	15.4	10.9	6.9	10.5	11.5
Lending/deposit spread	. . .	6.1	4.9	4.4	3.1	3.3	2.2	4.4	6.1	5.2	2.1	2.0
Official exchange rate per U.S. dollar (end of period)	1,125.0	1,641.0	1,650.0	1,731.0	1,797.0	1,901.0	1,992.0	2,062.0	2,110.0	2,200.0	2,308.0	2,383.0
Real effective exchange rate index (1990 = 100)	185.2	142.6	104.3	101.8	103.3	100.0	98.7	96.2	100.9	99.8	96.3	101.0

Table 6.9 *(concluded)*

	1985	1986	1987	1988	1989	1990	1991	1992	1993	1994	1995	1996
						(In millions of U.S. dollars)						
Balance of Payments												
Current account, n.i.e.	–1,923	–3,911	–2,098	–1,397	–1,108	–2,988	–4,260	–2,780	–2,106	–2,792	–7,023	. . .
Financial account, n.i.e	1,782	4,177	3,481	2,217	2,918	4,495	5,697	6,129	5,632	3,839	10,386	. . .
Direct investment abroad	. . .	. . .	. . .	. . .	. . .	. . .	. . .	. . .	–356	–609	–603	. . .
Direct investment in reporting economy, n.i.e.	310	258	385	576	682	1,093	1,482	1,777	2,004	2,109	4,348	. . .
Net direct investment	310	258	385	576	682	1,093	1,482	1,777	1,648	1,500	3,745	. . .
Portfolio investment assets	. . .	. . .	. . .	. . .	. . .	. . .	. . .	. . .	. . .	. . .	. . .	. . .
Portfolio investment liabilities	–35	268	–88	–98	–173	–93	–12	–88	1,805	3,877	4,100	. . .
Net portfolio investment	–35	268	–88	–98	–173	–93	–12	–88	1,805	3,877	4,100	. . .
Other investment assets	. . .	. . .	. . .	. . .	. . .	. . .	. . .	. . .	. . .	. . .	. . .	. . .
Other investment liabilities	1,507	3,651	3,184	1,739	2,409	3,495	4,227	4,440	2,179	–1,538	2,541	. . .
Net other investments	1,507	3,651	3,184	1,739	2,409	3,495	4,227	4,440	2,179	–1,538	2,541	. . .
Of which, official capital	1,345	2,886	2,537	1,756	2,604	218	1,287	770	552	137	131	. . .
Net errors and omissions	651	–1,269	–753	–933	–1,315	744	91	–1,279	–2,932	–263	–1,790	. . .
Overall balance[2]	510	–1,003	630	–113	495	2,251	1,528	2,070	594	784	1,573	. . .
Memorandum:												
Net private capital[3]	739	–901	–1,810	–12,090	–2,165	4,663	3,302	6,789	4,943	5,131	10,097	. . .

Sources: IMF, *International Financial Statistics, World Economic Outlook, and Direction of Trade Statistics,* various issues; and IMF staff estimates.

[1]Interest differential = Deposit rate minus London interbank offer rate on three-month U.S. deposits.

[2]The overall balance includes: current account, financial account, capital account, and net errors and omissions. Capital account figures are not shown because they are zero throughout the period.

[3]Total capital = direct investment + portfolio investment + other investment minus official capital + net errors and omissions + misinvoicing.

Table 6.10. Korea: Sequencing of Reforms in the Domestic and External Sectors

Monetary Controls and Financial System	Exchange System, Trade, and Capital Flows
1985	
Financial Supervision and Regulatory Framework Allowed 11 foreign bank branches to engage in trust business, which domestic banks already did. *Money Markets and Instruments* Interest rates on mortgages and convertible bonds were liberalized. The issuing rate of prime enterprises, commercial paper, was liberalized. Special trust accounts for households were introduced that earn dividends depending on fund performance (March). Two new deposit instruments were introduced—free savings account and household installment savings account (April). Certain share of lending was required to be allocated to small and medium-sized industries. Foreign banks were granted access to the discount window for export financing on the same terms as domestic banks. The reserve requirement on foreign currency deposits was raised from 1% to 10% on 7/23/85 effective from July and again to 20% on 8/1/85.	*Exchange Market Arrangement and System* Government reduced the limit of extra swap privilege of foreign banks' domestic branches. The guaranteed profit margin on swap transactions with foreign bank branches was also reduced from 1% to 0.75% per year. Residents were allowed to execute swap transactions with foreign financial institutions. Monthly travel allowance for studying abroad was reduced from $3,000 to $2,000 per person and from $2,000 to $1,000 per family. The central bank broadened the list of foreign currency loans that shipping firms were eligible for and lengthened their lending period for the purpose of repaying principal and interests of foreign loans. *Direct Investment* Inflows: Foreign investors were granted access to 102 of 339 restricted sectors, raising the liberalization ratio for capital to 76.3% from 66.1%. Total number of sectors open to foreign investors rose to 762 from 660. Outflows: Investments of over $1 million (previously $0.5 million) now had to be approved by the Overseas Investment Deliberation Committee. Outflows: Overseas investment regulations were streamlined so as to encourage domestic firm's investment in the exploitation of overseas natural resources and the development of high technology. *Portfolio Investments* Inflows: Korean companies were allowed to issue warrants and depository receipts in international capital markets under guidelines set by the government. The maximum issue was limited to 15% of the outstanding shares of the issuing company, and an individual foreign investor was limited to acquiring, at most 3% of any company's outstanding shares through the exercise of bond conversion or subscription rights. Inflows: Value limit on investment trusts was raised to $200 million.

Table 6.10 *(continued)*

Monetary Controls and Financial System	Exchange System, Trade, and Capital Flows
1985 *(continued)*	*Trade* Imports of 235 items were liberalized (ratio of liberalized to total imports rose to 87.7%). Number of automatically approved import items was raised from 6,712 to 6,945 from a total of 7,915 Customs Cooperation Council Nomenclature (CCCN) items.
1986	
Capital Markets Exchange Equalization Bonds were introduced. Six foreign banks were permitted to enter trust business. *Financial Supervision and Regulatory Framework* Two foreign firms were allowed to underwrite fire insurance, previously reserved for Korean firms. From August 21, the central bank prohibited foreign exchange banks from maintaining an oversold position of spot foreign exchange as an effort to restrain excessive growth of reserve money. *Money Market and Instruments* The issuing rates on negotiable CDs, secured corporate bonds, and bank debentures were liberalized. Guidelines on loans to small- and medium-sized firms were readjusted upwards for foreign banks. The obligatory lending ratio to small- and medium-sized firms was raised to 35%. That is, foreign banks were required to lend at least 35% of increased amount in loans to small- and medium-sized firms. Foreign banks were allowed access to the discount window for rediscounting of commercial bills and to issue CDs and CD loans.	*Exchange Market Arrangement and System* Bank of Korea reduced the yield on swaps from 0.75% to 0.5%. Limits on each bank's foreign currency swap were required to be reduced by amount of CDs sold. General swap limit extended to new foreign banks was reduced to $10 million from $15 million per branch. The general swap limit for new branches of foreign banks already established in Korea was removed. The central bank also got rid of the additional extra swap that had been allowed for increase of paid-in capital or retained profits. Authorization of expenses for emigration was delegated to heads of foreign exchange banks. Regulations were tightened on acquiring foreign currency loans through domestic banks and foreign bank branches. The supply of foreign currency loans for repayment of principal and interest on overseas borrowing, with a period over three years was restricted to small and medium enterprises that had weak fund raising capabilities. Foreign currency loan ceilings were introduced, which set an upper limit on the loanable amount for a bank's foreign currency loans outstanding at the level outstanding on August 20, 1986 or $500 million, whichever was greater. *Direct Investments* Outflows: Certain overseas investments not exceeding $200,000 were subject to automatic approval. *Portfolio Investments* Outflows: The government directed financial institutions to repay foreign short-term borrowings and bank loans that had unfavorable terms.[1]

Trade

Tariff rate on crude oil imports was raised from 1% to 15% in three steps.

302 items were removed from the restricted imports list and one item was added. The net effect raised the number of automatically approved items from 6,945 to 7,246 (or from 87.7% to 91.5%) of a total of 7,915 items.

1987

Capital Markets

The Securities and Exchange Law and the Law on Fostering the Capital Market were revised in order to protect firms that go public from takeovers by limiting individual holdings of each company's shares and to facilitate corporate expansions by permitting firms to issue new shares at market value instead of at par as was done previously (December).

Nine more foreign bank branches were permitted to handle trust business during the year, bringing the total to 19.

Money Market and Instruments

Minimum denomination of CDs was lowered.
An over-the-counter (OTC) market was established.

The reserve requirement on residents' foreign currency deposits was lowered from 20% to 4.5%, effective from February 20.

Exchange Market Arrangement and System

The monthly allowance for students abroad was raised to $1,500 from $1,000. In addition $500 and $300 was allowed for spouse and each child, respectively.

Foreigners employed in Korea were allowed to send their salary, except for basic living expenses, and retirement allowances to their home countries with approval from a foreign exchange bank rather than from Bank of Korea.

Korean residents could send up to $5,000 a year as living expenses to parents and children living abroad.

Korean residents could send up to $1,000 to relatives abroad for funerals or weddings, compared to $500 previously.

Koreans traveling abroad could carry $5,000 in cash for basic expenses regardless of purpose of travel. Additional $2,500 was permitted when traveling to countries whose currencies had appreciated significantly to the U.S. dollar. Credit card holders were allowed to charge all travel expenses without limit during business or official travel abroad.

The government abolished the restriction on the contract period for forward exchange transactions and permitted anyone holding a resident account to perform forward exchange transactions. In addition transactions using futures and options were allowed.

On November 1, the central bank reduced the fourth quarter swap ceiling that had been allocated to foreign bank branches by 10%. They also abolished the new swap facility of $10 million accorded to newly established foreign bank branches.

Inward remittances greater than $20,000 monitored to discourage speculation in stock market.

Table 6.10 *(continued)*

Monetary Controls and Financial System	Exchange System, Trade, and Capital Flows
1987 *(continued)*	*Direct Investment*
	Inflows: 26 manufacturing sectors were opened for foreign direct investment, leaving 13 of 522 manufacturing sectors still closed.
	Inflows: Certain tax privileges granted to attract foreign direct investment were reduced and after-investment controls relaxed to put foreign invested companies and local companies on an equal basis.
	Outflows: The limit over which overseas investment was subject to consideration by the Overseas Investment Deliberation Committee was raised from $1 million to $3 million in May and then to $5 million in December.
	Outflows: From December 28, overseas investment of $1 million was automatically approved.
	Outflows: Restrictions on the purchase of real estate abroad by Korean-owned companies were liberalized.
	Portfolio Investment
	Outflows: From April 15, overseas investment for the purpose of obtaining payment of dividends or interest income without participation in management was allowed, if undertaken to obtain advance technology or to overcome difficulties faced by export firms.
	Outflows: The government encouraged the early redemption of foreign borrowings on unfavorable terms by making foreign currency loans available for those companies wishing to redeem such foreign debt before its maturity.
	Outflows: On September 1, the government raised the maximum amount of investment profit that might be held overseas without approval by the central bank from $10,000 to $500,000.
	Outflows: The central bank made special foreign currency deposits with foreign exchange banks to encourage them to extend loans in foreign currency to companies importing machinery and equipment or redeeming foreign borrowings before maturity.

Trade

The government shortened the period to 120 days from 180 days during which advance receipt of export proceeds might be obtained. It also reduced the limit on such receipt by large companies from 3% to 1% of their export value over the previous calendar year.

Tariff rate on crude oil import was raised to 24.5%.

167 items were removed from the list of restricted imports, raising the number of automatically approved items to 7,408 of 7,911 items.

A new Foreign Trade Act came into effect on July 1, which included a revised system of import protection. The Korea Trade Commission was established under the Act.

From February 13, items eligible for import on a deferred payment basis were reduced to goods on which a tariff rate of less than 10% was applicable rather than the previous 20%. Imports for export use were also made subject to this restriction.

On April 1, the settlement period for import of crude oil on a deferred payment basis was shortened from 90 days to 60 days.

1988

Capital Markets

Effective March 1, the Korean Stock Exchange (KSE) was transformed into a nonprofit membership organization.

Money Market and Instruments

Interest rates on loans from banks and nonbank financial intermediaries, other than interest rates on loans subsidized by government funds, were fully liberalized.

Interest rates on time deposits with maturities of more than two years at banks, postal savings, and credit unions, and on time and savings deposits with maturities of over one year at mutual savings and finance companies, were liberalized.

Exchange Market Arrangement and System

An additional $5,000 was permitted to be purchased from banks for travel purposes.

The limit on remittances abroad for funerals and weddings was raised to $5,000.

Payments for sales promotion by businesses to foreign experts were liberalized.

Korean residents were permitted to retain up to $5,000 upon return from overseas travel.

Effective February 16, banking institutions were not permitted to exceed the foreign currency loan ceiling limit for lending to small- and medium-sized firms and export firms, as had been done in the past. However, loans for certain specific activities were excluded from this ceiling—loans for import funds for production facilities to diversify sources of imports and for early repayment of external debts.

Effective March 25, nonresidents were prohibited from exchanging into domestic currency amounts withdrawn from their nonresident foreign currency deposit accounts.

Table 6.10 ***(continued)***

Monetary Controls and Financial System	Exchange System, Trade, and Capital Flows
1988 *Money Market and Investment (continued)*	*Exchange Market Arrangement and System (continued)*
Yields on fund-type instruments, such as cash management accounts, bond management accounts, corporate money trusts, and pension trusts, were liberalized. Interest rates on repurchase agreements, commercial paper (with a face value greater than 30 million won and maturity more than 91 days), financial debentures, and corporate bonds were fully deregulated. "New" commercial paper and conventional commercial paper were merged into one.	Effective March 25, the maximum amount of foreign exchange allowed to be brought in without the obligations of registering and reporting to tax authorities, by residents and nonresidents, was *reduced* from $30,000 to $5,000; this was further *reduced* to $3,000 on September 1. Effective May 9, the central bank reduced the swap ceilings of foreign bank branches. It also reduced the guaranteed profit from 0.5% a year to 0.3% a year. Sales of foreign currency by nonresidents to domestic foreign exchange banks was limited to a maximum of $20,000; *reduced* to $10,000 on September 1. Effective September 15, overseas investments in the form of provision of technology or services were no longer classified as capital transactions but as invisibles and hence free from any post-check by regulations concerning overseas investment. Accepted Article VIII (November). *Direct Investment* Inflows: Advertising and motion picture distribution sectors were opened to foreign investment. Inflows: Restrictions on foreign investment in the insurance industry were liberalized (joint ventures with the 15 largest domestic companies were still restricted). Inflows: Foreign subsidiaries and joint ventures were authorized to import and distribute all products except for 12 restricted items. Outflows: Effective March 25, any noncorporate private business was permitted to make investments, regardless of business type, of up to $1 million. Also, overseas investors were allowed to retain all investment profits in their host countries without prior approval from the central bank—the previous limit on such retention was $500,000.

Outflows: Effective November 1, the central bank raised the limit on automatic approval of overseas investments from $1 million to $2 million.

Portfolio Investment

Outflows: The government permitted some domestic institutional investors to invest in foreign stock markets for their own account: up to $30 million by securities companies and $10 million by insurance and investment trust companies.

Outflows: Effective July 1, the government allowed investment in foreign securities, previously restricted to securities companies, by investment trust companies and insurance companies up to a maximum of $10 million. It also raised the maximum amount of investment permitted by securities companies from $10 million to $30 million.

Other

Outflows: Foreign exchange allowance for emigrants was raised to $200,000 a household for current expenses and to $300,000 for investment purposes.

Trade

Tariff rates on a large number of products were reduced during the year.

Restrictions on imports by manufacturing firms partly or wholly owned by foreign investors were liberalized.

275 items were removed from the list of restricted imports during the year, raising the number of automatically approved imports to 7,680 of 7,911 items.

Import of beef was subject to a quota.

The Bank of Korea reduced the loanable ratio (i.e., the amount of funds that could be borrowed) for selected imports of machinery and equipment and for repayment of prior external or foreign currency loans.

Table 6.10 ***(continued)***

Monetary Controls and Financial System	Exchange System, Trade, and Capital Flows
1989	
Capital Markets More *foreign banks* were allowed to engage in individual trust business. Effective December 30, in line with the 1988 plan for internationalization of the capital market, *foreign investors* were permitted to engage in direct transactions among themselves of Korean stock held in Korea that had been acquired through stock-related bonds (conversion of CBs issued abroad or excising the warrants of bonds with warrants (BWs) issued abroad). *Money Market and Instruments* The minimum maturity of CDs issued by banks to other banks, including development institutions, was reduced from 91 to 30 days. A bankers' acceptance market for trade bills was established. Legal barriers for the integration of the two call markets (the interbank market and the OTC market for nonbank financial institutions) were removed. Three new commercial banks were established. The Korean Exchange Bank was granted permission to change its status from a specialized to a nationwide commercial bank.	*Exchange Market Arrangement and System* Effective June 2, the central bank set a ceiling of $200 million on special foreign currency loans that could be given to one firm during a year. Effective December 1, the government introduced a professional brokerage system in the foreign currency call money market in an effort to speed up development of the foreign exchange market. Effective December 1, the central bank unified ordinary and additional swap ceilings. It also reduced the swap ceiling allocated to foreign bank branches at the end of the third quarter by 10%. Effective December 1, the maximum amount of foreign exchange that might be brought into the country with no registration and subsequent reporting to the tax authorities by residents and nonresidents was *raised* to $5,000 from $3,000. A U.S. dollar call market was opened. Maximum amount of foreign currency that nonresidents were allowed to exchange into won at domestic foreign banks was *raised* to $50,000 from $10,000. *Direct Investment* Inflows: Restrictions on foreign direct investment in six manufacturing sectors were removed. Inflows: Amount of foreign investment permitted without deliberation of the capital review committee was raised to $5 million from $3 million. Outflows: Effective February 13, the procedures and approval conditions for overseas investment were simplified. Balance sheets and three other documents for would-be investors were no longer required. In case the funds are loaned, repayment should be guaranteed by an international bank or an equivalent institution, and in the case of acquisition of securities, a would-be investor should hold at least 20% of the equity or send a full-time executive to the overseas company.

Financial Supervision and Regulatory Framework

Effective September 20, the ceiling on overbought positions of foreign exchange banks was raised to 200% of the average value of bills purchased and held in the previous month for all foreign exchange banks. Previously, the above percentage could vary from 20% to 150% depending upon the type of foreign exchange bank. In addition, the government required all foreign exchange banks to maintain overbought spot-exchange positions equivalent to at least 1% of the average value of bills purchased and held in the previous month (to be changed to 2% from January 1, 1990).

Outflows: Effective June 2, overseas investments other than those in overseas real estate or personal investment could now qualify for foreign currency loans. The maximum term of such loans was set at 10 years and the ceiling on them was fixed at 60% of the required funds for large firms and 80% for small- and medium-sized firms.

Outflows: Effective August 10, business firms were allowed to invest in foreign real estates for business purposes. The expanded scope of possible purchases included parking lots for commercial purposes, hotels, sporting facilities, laundries, gas stations, research institutes, job training facilities, and welfare facilities for employees. Previously, business had been limited to purchases of office buildings, factories, warehouses, exhibitions, employee residences and parking lots associated with offices.

Portfolio Investments

Inflows: Effective December 1, foreign exchange banks were allowed to raise off-shore funds by issuing foreign currency denominated bonds or borrowing from the off-shore accounts of other domestic foreign exchange banks. The banks were authorized to underwrite foreign-currency denominated bonds issued by nonresidents and to purchase and sell them, or to lend or deposit them with the offshore accounts of other domestic foreign exchange banks.

Inflows: The limit on equity investment by foreign securities firms was increased to 40%.

Trade

The import surveillance list, which required approval of the Korean Traders' Association before an import license could be awarded, was abolished. The system of emergency tariffs was abolished. Under the first phase of the second Five-Year Tariff Reduction Program, the average tariff was reduced to 12.7% from 18.1%.

The Bank of Korea lowered and then raised to its original level the loanable ratios for special foreign currency loans for import funds for production facilities to diversify their sources of imports.

Effective November 17, the central bank removed the overall ceiling for the year of $5 billion on special foreign currency loans for import funds for production facilities to diversify import sources. For countries with a bilateral trade surplus the overall ceiling on special foreign currency loans for imports was retained at $300 million for large firms while for small- and medium-sized firms it was raised from $500 million to $800 million.

Table 6.10 *(continued)*

Monetary Controls and Financial System	Exchange System, Trade, and Capital Flows
1990	
Capital Markets Coupon rates of new corporate bond issues with a maturity of over three years were deregulated. Banks were allowed to underwrite privately placed corporate bonds. Effective June 11, the government allowed each of the three domestic investment trust companies to establish a matching fund in line with the "Mid-Term (1988–92) Plan for Internationalization of the Securities Market." Capitalization of each fund was set at $100 million. Of this amount, $60 million was to be raised in international markets and the remaining $40 million domestically, with 70% of the funds being invested in Korean securities and the balance in foreign securities. *Financial Supervision and Regulatory Framework* Law was promulgatedto convert investment and finance companies into: (1) banks; (2) securities companies; or (3) money market broker. *Money Market and Instruments* Ceiling on CD issues was increased from 120% to 150% of net worth for specialized banks and for *foreign banks* to 150% of net worth or W 10 billion, whichever is greater. The Bank of Korea introduced direct sales of MSBs to retail investors and changed the minimum trading unit of MSBs from W 10 million to W 1 million. The maturity period of MSBs was extended to two years.	*Exchange Market Arrangement and System* The "market average exchange rate" (MAR) system was adopted. The MAR for the won-U.S. dollar was established using the weighted average of the previous day's interbank rates for the won-U.S. dollar spot transactions. During each business day, the won-U.S. dollar exchange rate in the interbank market would be allowed to fluctuate within margins of ±0.4% around the MAR. Restrictions on invisibles: Effective May 1, the right to purchase up to $5,000 in foreign currency was *withdrawn*. Foreign exchange banks were again required to enter the amount of foreign currency purchased by overseas travelers in their passports. Effective September 24, the upper limit on basic expenses for teenage overseas travelers was *reduced* from $5,000 to $2,000. No additional allowances were permitted for any overseas traveler whose stay abroad was less than 30 days. *Direct Investment* Inflows: Effective January 1, the maximum amount of foreign direct investment in manufacturing that could be automatically approved was raised from $3 million to $100 million. Inflows: Up to 99% foreign equity ownership in advertising firms was permitted. Inflows: Wholesale business of toiletries and cosmetics was opened to foreign investors. *Portfolio Investment* Outflows: Effective March 2, securities companies, which had an international securities business license, were authorized to invest up to $50 million, up from the previous $30 million. For investment trust companies issuing international beneficiary certificates and insurance companies having total assets in excess of W 5 trillion, the ceiling on portfolio investment abroad was raised from $10 million to $30 million. Outflows: Effective December 20, the central bank abolished foreign currency loans for the early redemption of foreign loans, in view of the current account deficit.

Effective March 8, reserve requirements on foreign currency deposits held in resident accounts were raised from 4.5% to 11.5%.

Trade

Under the second phase of the 1989–93 Five-Year Tariff Reduction Program, tariff rates on a large number of products were lowered, reducing the average unweighted tariff rate on total imports to 11.4% from 12.7%.

Effective September 1, the overall ceiling on special foreign currency loans for import funds for production facilities and for overseas investment funds was abolished. However, the overall ceiling on special foreign currency loans for imports from those countries running a bilateral trade surplus with Korea was raised from $0.4 billion to $0.8 billion for large firms and from $0.6 billion to $1.2 billion for small- and medium-sized firms.

Effective December 20, the central bank abolished foreign currency loans for import of production facilities for the import diversification scheme, in view of the current account deficit.

Effective December 20, the central bank revised the loanable ratios so that manufacturing and small and medium-sized firms receive preferential treatment in importing facilities and equipment. The foreign currency loan system was reclassified such that firms were categorized as Manufacturing or Others instead of General and Special.

1991

Capital Markets

Effective September 16, nonresidents who had exchanged convertible bonds into stocks were permitted to sell them and to purchase stocks listed on the Korean Stock Exchange.

Foreign bank branches' entry into the trust business was eased.

Financial Supervision and Regulatory Framework

The General Banking Act was revised and became effective December 31.

The Industrial Bank of Korea Act was revised and became effective December 31.

Exchange Market Arrangement and System

Documentation requirements for foreign currency deposits were liberalized. Firms whose annual external transactions exceeded $10 million were exempted from documentation requirements for foreign currency deposits up to 10% of their amount of annual foreign currency transactions (up to a limit of $100 million).

On May 6, won-dollar *forward contracts*, previously limited to overnight transactions, were diversified to give 13 maturities ranging from one day to a year.

Documentation requirements for foreign exchange transactions up to $1 million between banks and nonbanks were eased.

The prohibition of sales of foreign currencies from foreign currency accounts for purposes of making domestic payments was abolished.

Table 6.10 *(continued)*

Monetary Controls and Financial System	Exchange System, Trade, and Capital Flows
1991 *Financial Supervisory and Regulatory Framework* The Long Term Credit Bank Act was revised and became effective December 27. The Act concerning the Merger and Conversion of Financial Institutions became effective March 8. Effective July 1, foreign exchange banks' compulsory overbought position in spot transactions was lowered from the previous 2% to 1% of the average outstanding of bills bought in the preceding month. This ceiling was abolished on January 3, 1992. *Money Market and Instruments* A four-stage plan for *interest deregulation* was announced in August. The first phase was launched on November 21. The following lending rates were liberalized: bank overdrafts, discounts of commercial paper (CP) and trade bills. The following deposit rates were liberalized: CDs of banks and nonbank financial institutions. and issue rate of corporate bonds with over two-year maturity. Effective July 1, the ceiling limits on CDs set in June 1990 for *foreign exchange banks* were raised from 10 billion won or 150% of the sum of the paid-in capital and reserves, whichever is greater to W 12.5 billion or 175% of the sum of the paid-in capital, whichever is greater. Effective October 5, the limits were raised to W 15 billion or 200% of the sum of the paid-in capital, whichever is greater.	*Direct Investment* Inflows: Investments with a foreign participation of less than 50% in manufacturing projects were made subject to notification rather than approval. Decision whether or not to accept the investment is made within 30 days, in principle. Thereafter, two years are allowed for completion of the payment of the subject matter of investment. From January 3, 1992, this notification system was to be introduced in some service industries. Inflows: The tax system was amended such that foreign-invested enterprises became wholly exempt from corporate income tax and their expatriate employees from income tax, for only three years following commencement of business operations. In the subsequent two years a 50% reduction on both these taxes was granted. Foreign investment was permitted in ventures involving importation of alcoholic beverages at the wholesale level. Inflows: Restrictions on the scope of foreign investment in the retail sector were eased with the number of retail shops per investment increasing from 1 to 10 and the maximum permissible floor space per shop to 1,000 square meters from 700 square meters. Outflows: Maximum amount of foreign currency loans for overseas investments was decreased from 60% to 40% for large firms and from 80% to 60% for small and medium firms. *Portfolio Investment* Inflows: Effective March 2, nonresident Koreans were allowed to sell foreign currencies exceeding $50,000 to entrust their proceeds to development trusts with a maturity of two years or more. Effective July 15 the limit was raised to $100,000 and would be abolished from January 3, 1992. Inflows: Effective March 8, the government permitted the issuance of foreign currency denominated securities to finance the import of production facilities and equipment for which no domestic substitute is available. Outflows: Domestic institutional investors were permitted to invest in securities issued by foreign governments and public organizations with a high credit rating.

Restrictions on activities of *foreign banks* were eased significantly. They could now set up multiple branches under the same standards and procedures as those applied to domestic banks. An increase was made in the ceiling on foreign banks' paid-in capital, as was an increase in local currency funding opportunities for foreign banks.

Electronic information service was introduced in the OTC market.

Other

Inflows/Outflows: Restrictions on financing options for overseas offices were eased. Firms were permitted to raise funds abroad regardless of the amount, subject only to the approval of a class A foreign exchange bank. The limitations on the use of these funds were eased so as to include purchase of production facilities, equipment for overseas branches and subsidiaries, the purchase (or construction) of office buildings using mortgage finance, and the refinancing of existing debt on more favorable terms.

Trade

Imports of 93 items, mostly agricultural products, were liberalized in accordance with the 1989–91 import liberalization program.

The maximum amount of foreign currency loans was revised downwards for the following categories, effective September 6. For manufacturing firms the loanable ratio was reduced from 80% to 60% for large firms and from 100% to 90% for medium and small firms. Similarly for other firms they were reduced from 60% to 40% and 80% to 60%, respectively. For the purposes of redemption of principal of foreign currency borrowings the loanable ratio was reduced from 100% to 80%. For import of machinery for use in shipbuilding, it was lowered from 80% to 60% and co-financing from export-import bank from 100% to 80%.

1992

Financial Supervision and Regulatory Framework

Measures were introduced to increase transparency of regulations and procedures on bank supervision.

Investments in stocks by resident foreign financial institutions were subject to the same limits as those by institutions owned by nationals. Resident foreign financial firms were allowed to undertake over-the-counter transactions in listed bonds.

Foreign banks became free to become full members of the Korea Federation of Banks and the Korea Financial Telecommunications and Clearing Institute, the latter providing access to the nationwide electronic banking network (July).

Exchange Market Arrangement and System

Effective July 1, the margin within which the exchange rate of the won against the U.S. dollar is permitted to fluctuate was widened to ±0.8% around the MAR.

Effective January 3, 1992, residents' external remittances above $10,000 would have to be reported to the Office of National Tax Administration instead of the previous $15,000 and above.

Effective September 1, the range of *forward exchange contracts* that foreign exchange banks were permitted to enter into was extended. In the case of contracts with residents, forward transactions were also allowed for funds for overseas direct investment, operating funds for overseas branches of domestic financial institutions, funds for portfolio investment by institutional investors, and operating funds for domestic branches of foreign financial institutions. For contracts with nonresidents, funds for

Table 6.10 *(continued)*

Monetary Controls and Financial System	Exchange System, Trade, and Capital Flows
1992 *Financial Supervision and Framework (continued)*	*Exchange Market Arrangement and System (continued)*
Effective September 1, the oversold position ceiling of foreign exchange banks was raised from $5 million to the greater of $10 million, or 20% of the average outstanding of bills bought in the previous month. In addition, these banks were permitted to take oversold positions in spot transactions, which had previously been barred. The ceiling limit on such positions was set at the greater of $5 million or 5% of the average outstanding of bills bought in the previous month. Foreign exchange used to hedge exchange rate risk on capital transactions was exempted from the limit on the overall overbought position.	inward direct investment and stock investment were added to the list of eligible transactions. The objective of the extension of eligibility was to enable residents who conduct business overseas or foreigners who invest in Korea to manage exchange risk more efficiently.
	Effective September 1, the ceiling on foreign currency deposits maintained by resident firms (which is based on the amount of external transactions) was increased to 10%. Companies with records of external transactions were exempted from documentation requirements irrespective of the amount of annual transactions (previously exemptions were granted only to companies with transactions of less than $10 million).
Money Market and Instruments	In accordance with the revised Foreign Exchange Management Act of December 27, 1991, the relevant enforcement decree and the associated foreign exchange management regulations were revised and brought into force on September 1.
Effective May 1, the ceiling limit on CDs on *foreign bank branches,* which had been set at the greater of W 15 billion or 200% of the sum of in-country capital and reserves, was raised to the greater of W 17.5 billion or 225%, respectively. Effective December 19, the maximum maturity of CDs was extended from 180 days to 270 days.	Restrictions on capital account transactions were also eased. Capital account transactions were reclassified into three groups: transactions requiring permission, transactions that need prior notification, and transactions not requiring approval or notification. Additionally, underlying documentary requirements for capital transactions were greatly simplified and made more transparent.
The maximum maturity of call loans was extended to one month from 15 days.	Effective September 1, remittances for emigration of up to $100,000 were allowed for a householder and up to $50,000 for each other member of the household.
Over-the-counter interest rate and currency option transactions were expanded (in September 1992, banks were permitted to deal in interest rate and currency option trading on the over-the-counter market, though local firms were limited to call options only and options prices had to be "reasonable").	For emigration under a business investment scheme, remittance of the excess amount was allowed where the minimum investment required by the country of immigration was higher than the combined sum remittable as emigration settlement expenses and business investment fund.

Direct Investment

Outflows: Effective September 1, the government raised the ceiling from $2 million to $5 million on overseas direct investment subject to notification rather than permission. Also, direct investments in those countries with which Korea does not maintain diplomatic relations, until now requiring approval in all cases, were subject only to notification where the amount involved was less than $5 million.

Outflows: The range of overseas direct investment to be examined by the Overseas Investment Deliberation Committee was reduced. Now only investments above $10 million or on the restricted list were reviewed by them.

Outflows: Maximum amount of foreign currency loans for overseas investments was increased from 40% to 60% for large firms and from 60% to 70% for small and medium-sized firms.

Portfolio Investment

Inflows: Effective January 3, the domestic stock market was opened to foreign investors, subject to certain limitations. Nonresidents were allowed to invest in any domestic stocks, unless specified in some particular act. A 3% limit on investment by an individual foreigner and a 10% limit on total foreign investment was imposed. In the case of public utilities companies and those companies in infant industry, however, the total foreign investment limit was set at 8%.

Inflows: Previously, types of securities that could be issued abroad by Korean residents were restricted to ordinary bonds, convertible bonds, bonds with warrants, and stock depository receipts. Effective September 1, the list was expanded to include negotiable certificates of deposit and commercial paper.

In addition, the three-stage procedure for the authorization of the issue of these securities was reduced to a two-stage process—issuance approval and ex-post facto report (whereas previously approval for issuance negotiation, issuance notification, and ex-post facto report). Moreover, funds raised from issuance of these securities were permitted to be deposited either in a resident account established with the designated foreign exchange account or in an account with an overseas branch of a domestic exchange bank.

Table 6.10 *(continued)*

Monetary Controls and Financial System	Exchange System, Trade, and Capital Flows
1992 *(continued)*	*Portfolio Investment (continued)* Outflows: Effective September 1, the government raised limits on portfolio investments abroad by domestic securities companies, investment and trust companies, and insurance companies. Securities companies and investment and trust companies could invest up to $50 million, and those dealing with international businesses up to $100 million. Insurance companies could invest up to $50 million, and those with assets in excess of W 5 trillion up to $100 million. *Other* Inflows/Outflows: Restrictions on financing options for overseas offices were eased. The previous limit of raising overseas funds by Korean subsidiaries of $5 million was completely liberalized. Overseas financing was previously limited to 11 items. Effective September 1, project eligibility was expanded to include the raising of funds for mergers and acquisitions involving foreign enterprises and funds for the purchase of commodities. In addition, the limit on overseas financing by a local subsidiary was raised to an amount equivalent to 50% of the actual currency earnings of the relevant year. *Trade* Imports of 43 products were liberalized. Import liberalization ratio for manufactured products had risen to 99.9% and that for agricultural products to 87.1%. First the maximum amount of foreign currency loans was revised down to improve the balance of payments position and later adjusted upwards to influence equipment investment.

1993

Capital Markets

In February, a computerized on-line system of securities transactions was introduced in the stock market.

Financial Supervision and Regulatory Framework

Effective August 12, a real-name system in all financial transactions was introduced; i.e., transactions including deposits, installment savings, checks, CDs, stocks and bonds must be made only in real names.

Increasing transparency of regulations governing mandatory lending to small- and medium-sized enterprises occurs.

Effective July 1, the ceiling on overall oversold position of foreign exchange banks was raised from the greater of $10 million, or 20% of the average balance of foreign exchange bought in the preceding month, to the greater of $20 million, or 30% of the average balance of foreign exchange bought in the preceding month.

Effective October 1, for purposes of monitoring their overbought oversold position, banks were given the option of applying a 10% ratio to their capital base, instead of the

Changes in loanable ratios of foreign currency loans (in %)

	Previous	1/17	8/21	10/16
Import of equipment				
Manufacturing				
Large firms	60	50	60	80
High-tech industries	—	—	80	90
Small and medium firms	90	70	80	90
Research institutions	80	70	80	90
Import of machinery and materials for use in planned shipbuilding	60	50	50	80
Co-financing with the EXIM Bank of Korea	80	70	70	80

Exchange Market Arrangement and System

Effective October 1, the margin within which the exchange rate of the won against the U.S. dollar is permitted to fluctuate was widened to ±1% around the MAR.

Effective January 1, the Bank of Korea abolished the temporary annual ceiling limits on loans handled by individual foreign exchange banks that were imposed to curb foreign currency loans when the balance of payments had deteriorated.

Regulations regarding forward transactions were further liberalized.

Effective April 1, residents were allowed to hold up to $10,000 in foreign exchange free of concentration requirements and to sell, deposit, or hold foreign exchange freely within that limit (previous limit was $5,000).

Effective July 1, the government raised the ceiling on individual domestic enterprises' foreign currency deposit holdings from 20% to 30% of external transactions recorded in the previous year. Effective October 1, these limits were abolished.

Effective October 1, the regulations on foreign exchange transactions including forward transactions were liberalized as follows: (1) the ceiling on foreign exchange deposits payable in domestic currency, which was exempted from the documentation requirement, was abolished; and (2) forward transactions involving foreign or domestic currencies in amounts not exceeding $3 million were exempted from documentation requirements, provided that they are declared and conform to the "real demand" principle.

Table 6.10 *(continued)*

Monetary Controls and Financial System	Exchange System, Trade, and Capital Flows
1993 *Fianancial Supervision and Regulatory Framework (continued)*	*Exchange Market Arrangement and System (continued)*
existing ratio that is based on the volume of foreign exchange transactions. The differentiation between nationwide commercial banks and regional banks for purposes of monitoring foreign exchange exposure limits was abolished.	Effective October 1, it was possible to pay the overseas travel expenses of business travelers from deposits held in resident accounts under the company's name, whereas previously payment had only been possible from resident accounts held under the traveler's own name.
	Nonresidents were allowed to hold free won accounts.
Money Market and Instruments	Effective October 16, the central bank raised the amount of foreign exchange reserves earmarked for supporting foreign exchange bank foreign currency loans from $1 billion to $4 billion.
Effective June 1, the ceiling on CDs for *foreign bank branches* was raised to greater of W 20 billion or 250% of net worth.	*Direct Investment*
Interest rates were liberalized on all loans (except policy loans), as were time deposits with maturities of two years or more, corporate and financial bonds with less than two years' maturity, and MSBs, treasury and public bonds.	Outflows: Effective April 1, small-scale overseas investments of not more than $1 million no longer were investigated regarding their reasonableness of fund supply and the profitability of the investment project. The validity of projects involving more than $10 million in which successive investments are made for a period of more than three years was lengthened from one year to three years.
An auction system was introduced to place MSBs.	
Simplification of credit control criteria and procedures for large corporations were enacted.	Outflows: Effective December 7, 13 businesses were removed from the list of those in which overseas investment is restricted. Types of real estates where purchase was newly permitted comprised those held by insurance companies in connection with the management of their portfolios and residential housing for individual ownership by the staff of overseas offices. In addition, the government appointed the Korea Development Bank and the Industrial Bank of Korea as overseas investment authorization institutions.
	Outflows: Effective April 1, the government abolished the approval renewal system under which approval had to be obtained for an overseas branch office from a designated Class A foreign exchange bank every three years after its establishment. At the same time the remittance ceiling on the payment of operating funds was raised from $1 million to $2 million per year (this included funds for establishment expenses, maintenance and operating expenses, working capital for business activities, and funds sources through overseas borrowing).

Portfolio Investments

Outflows: Effective April 1, the government added investment and finance companies, pension funds, and companies with a record of performance of external transactions in excess of $100 million to the category of institutional investors eligible to make outward portfolio investment.

Outflows: Effective April 1, the government permitted enterprises with a record of performance of external transactions in excess of $100 million to hold foreign currency overseas, and it raised the limit on the foreign currency that may be held in foreign countries from $10 million to 10% of the value of external transactions (maximum $100 million). Previously, only general trading companies were permitted to hold foreign currency overseas. Also, the form of foreign exchange holdings overseas that had been restricted to bank deposits was allowed to diversify although real estate holdings are still barred.

Outflows: Effective October 1, the government revised the investment limits upwards.

	Ceilings on portfolio investment abroad (*$ millions*)	
	Previous	10/1
Securities companies	50	100
dealing with international business	100	200
Investment trust companies	50	100
dealing with international business	100	200
Insurance companies	50	100
with more than W 5 trillion in assets	100	200
Eligible companies (external transactions in excess of $100 mil.)	10	10% of external transactions within past 12 months (max $100 mil.)
Pension funds and Investment and Finance companies	0	50
Individual investors aggregate portfolio investment through investment trust companies	0	50

Table 6.10 *(continued)*

Monetary Controls and Financial System	Exchange System, Trade, and Capital Flows
1993 *(continued)*	*Portfolio Investments (continued)*
	Inflows: Effective April 1, instead of obtaining permission before issuing foreign currency denominated securities, now it only needed to be reported. The range of eligible funding objects financed through these issues was expanded to include early repayment of external debt and funds for inducement of technology. Eligible issuers were widened as they included those that had recorded a net profit on a cumulative basis over the preceding three years where as previously it was required that they record a net profit in each of the previous three years.
	Inflows: Overseas branches of domestic banks were in principle prohibited from supplying loans to residents of Korea. Effective February 1, the government permitted them to extend loans to residents of Korea engaged in the trading of commodities futures or financial futures.
	Trade
	Effective January 1, manufacturing industries were eligible for foreign currency loans for all imports of production facilities and equipment.
	Effective January 8, the central bank began supplying foreign exchange reserves to support foreign exchange banks' foreign currency loans for the import of production facilities, such as those for the high-tech industry.
	Effective June 11, the central bank expanded eligibility to include imports of all kinds of manufacturing production facilities and of production facilities for research.
	Effective October 1, settlements of exports and imports (including reinsurance) in won were permitted for transactions up to the equivalent of $100,000.
1994	
Money Market and Instruments	*Exchange Market Arrangement and System*
Interest rates on time deposits with maturities of one to two years and on installment savings deposits with maturities of over two years were liberalized.	The fluctuation limit of the won against the U.S. dollar was widened from ±1% to ±1.5% around the MAR.
Bank of Korea Financial Wire Network was introduced.	Residents were permitted to hold foreign exchange freely without limit (once converted into won, foreign exchange can only be converted back to foreign currencies within the limits determined by foreign exchange sales of the past three months).

Residents were allowed to retain foreign exchange proceeds from exports without surrendering them to a foreign exchange bank or depositing them in foreign currency accounts in banks.

Direct Investment

Inflows: Foreign firms were allowed to engage in business operations within three hours after submitting notification (previously this time requirement was 20–30 days).

Inflows: Rules governing land acquisition were liberalized.

Outflows: The number of businesses restricted from overseas direct investment was reduced to 14 from 17.

Outflows: The limit on the amount banks were allowed to approve for direct investment overseas was raised to $300,000.

Portfolio Investment

Inflows: The ceiling on portfolio investment in stocks of Korean firms by nonresidents was raised to 12% from 10% of a firm's equity.

Inflows: The ceilings on the amounts that resident corporations and their branches operating abroad may borrow from nonresident financial institutions located abroad were abolished.

Inflows: The overseas borrowing limit for high-technology foreign-financed manufacturing companies was raised from 50% to 75% and then to 100% of the foreign-invested capital. General manufacturing industries were included in the types of foreign-financed companies that are eligible for short-term overseas borrowing.

Outflows: Overseas stock investments of institutional investors were liberalized (these include securities companies, investment trusts, and insurance companies).

Outflows: Direct overseas stock investments by residents up to a limit of W 100 million (W 300 million for general juridical persons) were allowed, as were foreign direct investments in equity-linked bonds, including nonguaranteed convertible bonds issued by listed small and medium-size enterprises, up to an aggregate of 30% and individual bonds up to 5% of the amount of money listed (per company). Also, the purchase of government and public bonds, with interest rates comparable to international interest rates, was allowed in the primary market.

Table 6.10 *(continued)*

Monetary Controls and Financial System	Exchange System, Trade, and Capital Flows
1994 *(continued)*	*Portfolio Investment (continued)* Outflows: The limit on the amount of foreign exchange resident business firms may retain abroad was increased to the equivalent of 30% of their total import and export values, with the maximum increased to $300 million from $100 million. Outflows: The limit on the amount of investments foreign exchange banks were authorized to approve was raised to $300,000. Outflows: Companies whose total export and import value exceeded $10 million were given institutional investor status (investment limit was raised to $300 million, or 30% of the total export and import value, whichever is greater). *Trade* The deferred payment period for imports of consumer goods was extended to 90 days from 60 days and for imports of raw materials for exports to 150 days from 120 days; the upper limit on import and export transactions that can be settled in won was raised to $300,000 from $100,000.
1995 *Money Market and Instruments* The following interest rates were liberalized (July and November): Deposit rates offered by banks, mutual credits, credit unions, community credit cooperatives, mutual savings, and finance companies on: time deposits (maturity less than 6 months); installment savings (maturity less than 1 year); mutual savings (maturity less than 1 year); and preferential savings deposits and company savings deposits maintained three months or more. All lending rates were liberalized.	*Exchange Market Arrangement and System* The fluctuation limit of the won against the U.S. dollar was widened from ±1.5% to ±2.25% around the MAR. Individuals were not required to register foreign currency holdings of $50,000 and above with foreign exchange banks. Firms involved in foreign trade with no record of foreign earnings were allowed to establish overseas offices after one year of having registered, whereas previously this was permitted only to firms earning foreign currency of more than $300,000. Settlement period on trade-related transactions was lengthened.

A more flexible operation of the aggregate credit ceiling system was developed; lending was promoted to small- and medium-sized enterprises; the eligible enterprise system was abolished, as were restrictions on real estate as collateral in connection with loans to small- and medium-sized enterprises; the rule was revised to limit bank credit risk arising from the extension of large credits to single parties; and the limits on large credits were lowered.

The maturity of CDs, repurchase agreements (Rps), and CP was lowered to 30 days from 60 days. Minimum denominations were also lowered.

Competitive bidding system was initiated for banks purchasing MSBs.

Issuance of CDs by nationwide commercial and local banks was raised from 100% to 150% of net worth and from 300% to 400% for specialized banks.

Issuance of CDs by foreign banks was raised to greater of W 35 billion or 100% of net worth.

Banks could offer time and installed savings deposits of maturities of up to five years. The minimum maturity of installment deposits was shortened to six months.

Interbank financial network was extended to include post office and agriculture, fisheries, and livestock cooperatives.

Loans to foreign exchange banks that had been allocated by the Foreign Exchange Equalization Fund were now based on competitive interest rate bidding.

Capital Markets

Financial Institutions could place orders through Bank of Korea-Wire system for purchase or sales of government or public bonds as well as the existing paper-based system.

Individual residents were permitted to purchase up to $10,000 or equivalent per year without restrictions. Current account payment of less than $5,000 could be made without supporting evidence of underlying real demand. For those staying overseas for over 60 days an additional $10,000 per month was allowed compared to $3,000 before. Resettlement allowances for those staying abroad over a year was raised from $20,000 to $50,000 including the travel allowance of $10,000. Donations to international institutions were now freely permitted up to $50,000, compared to $10,000 earlier which had required endorsement from relevant ministry. Limits on use of domestic credit card for purchases abroad were raised from $3,000 per month to $5,000 per month for individuals and from $30,000 per quarter to $100,000 per quarter for firms.

The limit on the amount of domestic banknotes permitted to be imported/exported was raised to W 3 million.

Direct Investment

Inflows: Investments in 53 sectors were either newly permitted or the extent of access was greatly increased with effect from January 1. On November 15, 48 sectors concentrated in services and manufacturing out of 105, which had been barred or only partially opened to foreign direct investment, were either fully opened or extent of participation was widened.

Outflows: Number of sectors in which outward direct investment had been restricted, was reduced to 3 from 17. Projects under $50 million were required of only notification, compared to $30 million previously. Projects of $50 million required approval from Bank of Korea subsequent to favorable review by the Overseas Investment Deliberation Committee.

Portfolio Investment

Inflows: Total foreign investment by nonresidents in a listed company's outstanding stocks was raised from 12% to 15% and for public corporations from 8% to 10%. Investments in bonds through securities investment trust companies' beneficiary certificates was permitted up to $300 million.

Inflows: Overseas issuance of exchangeable bonds permitted, limited to 15% of total associated stocks.

Table 6.10 *(continued)*

Monetary Controls and Financial System	Exchange System, Trade and Capital Flows
1995 *(continued)*	*Portfolio Investment (continued)*
Financial Supervision and Regulatory Framework Bank supervision guidelines were strengthened to include specific information on derivatives trading and banks were instructed to follow new accounting standards to reflect derivatives trading.	Inflows: Limits lowered for small- and medium-sized firms on issuance of securities abroad. Inflows: Eight leasing companies were permitted to undertake medium- and long-term borrowing overseas without intermediation from foreign exchange banks.
Securities companies were allowed to engage in foreign exchange transactions related to domestic stock investments by nonresidents.	Inflows: Direct foreign borrowings by firms were permitted for purposes of redeeming debts or for imports if firms were engaged in social overhead capital projects or foreign invested high-tech firms; small- and medium-sized firms or public corporations were permitted to borrow 100% directly and up to 90% was permitted for large firms.
	Outflows: Limits on outward portfolio investments abolished for Investment and Finance Companies and Pension Funds. Limits were raised for corporations from W 300 million to W 1 billion and for individuals from W 100 million to W 500 million. Institutional investors were permitted to invest in foreign unlisted stocks up to 10% of their total investment holdings and 10% of total outstanding of any one issue.
	Outflows: Institutional investors and other corporations were allowed to entrust up to $10 million and $300,000, respectively, to overseas nonresidents for asset management.
	Outflows: Restrictions on resident holdings of overseas deposits were eased; institutional investors were allowed up to $100 million; other corporations $1 million; and individuals up to $30,000.
	Outflows: Enterprises with external transactions in excess of $5 million (lowered from $10 million) were permitted to hold foreign currency overseas. Limits on overseas holdings on overseas construction companies were raised from 10% to 20% of outstanding business contracts.
	Outflows: Resettlement allowance for emigration was raised from $250,000 to $500,000 and from $300,000 to $500,000 to satisfy any related investment conditions.
	Outflows: Domestic issuance of won-denominated securities by international financial institutions was allowed.

Trade

Ratio of foreign currency loans for import of production facilities to large firms was reduced from 90% to 70% and from 70% to 80% for commercial imports of used ships and aircraft. To encourage development of engineering techniques, eligibility for foreign currency loans was widened to include import of production facilities and equipment in engineering business.

Ratio of foreign currency loans available for import of machinery and equipment was lowered to 70% from 90% of total cost in the case of manufacturing firms and to 70% from 80% in the case of non-manufacturing firms.

The deferred import payments period was extended as follows. For large enterprises, and re-exports to the general area to 180 days from 150 days; re-exports to the regional area to 90 days from 60 days; and for domestic consumption purposes to 90 days from 60 days for imports from the general area and to 60 days from 30 days for imports from the regional area. For small- and medium-sized enterprises, and for re-exports to the regional area to 120 days from 90 days; for domestic consumption purposes to 120 days from 90 days for imports from the general area; and to 90 days from 60 days for imports from the regional area.

1996

Money Market and Instruments

The Bank of Korea lowered reserve requirement ratio in two steps, for demand deposits and time and savings deposits with a maturity of less than two years to 7% from 11.5%; for time and savings deposits with a maturity of two years or more to 4% from 8%; and on resident's deposits in foreign currency to 7% from 11.5%.

The reserve requirement ratio for certain long-term savings products was lowered to 2% from 3%.

Exchange Market Arrangement and System

The government changed the procedure required in making overseas payments for current account transactions from a system of validation by foreign exchange banks to a notification system, and abolished the need for service transactions to receive authorization.

Remaining underlying documentation requirement was abolished for forward exchange and financial futures transactions. However, transactions were still based on real demand.

Ceiling on the swap facilities provided to foreign bank branches was lowered by 10%.

Procedures for remittance of funds for operation of overseas branches of domestic firms were liberalized.

Table 6.10 *(continued)*

Monetary Controls and Financial System	Exchange System, Trade, and Capital Flows
1996 *Money Market and Instruments* (*continued*)	*Exchange Market Arrangement and System (continued)*
The Bank of Korea removed the restriction on the size of the premium a bank could charge over its prime lending rate.	Ceiling of $300,000 on the amount allowed to be deposited and withdrawn from the free won account for the purpose of current transactions was abolished.
The Bank of Korea enhanced the efficiency of open market operations by increasing the use of a competitive bidding system for Rps and sale of MSBs to 99% (from 76%) and 89% (from 33%), respectively.	Deposits overseas in won were allowed below the ceiling on the amount of won that could be carried out when traveling abroad. Also, residents were allowed to purchase and sell won below the ceiling on the amount of won permitted to be carried out when traveling abroad at both the domestic foreign exchange banks overseas and at branches and subsidiaries of foreign banks.
The central bank introduced MSBs with a maturity of two years.	The limit on won permitted to be taken out when traveling abroad was raised to W 8 million from W 3 million.
Korea Money Brokerage Corporation (KMBC) was established as a specialist brokerage house that would not only broker call loans and money-at-call but also short-term money market instruments like CDs, Rps, and other bills.	Individual remittances overseas of sums exceeding $10,000 per year had to be declared to the Bank of Korea. The annual receipt of over $20,000 or the annual remittances of at least $10,000 for more than three years by an individual had to be notified to the national tax administration.
The Bank of Korea abolished guideline ratio for commercial bank credit to the manufacturing sector. Regulations governing credit to select businesses—for example, hotels and restaurants—were eased.	The Bank of Korea introduced a foreign currency swap system for foreign portfolio investment by securities companies, insurance companies, and investment trust companies. The swapped funds could be invested only in those instruments open to institutional investors.
The Bank of Korea revised its rules for credit control on conglomerates. It also exempted the conglomerates ranking between 11th and 30th largest from the rules for credit control.	The Bank of Korea started to conduct spot transactions according to international practice. Won-Japanese yen spot and forward markets were established.
To encourage credit to small- and medium-sized enterprises, the Bank of Korea introduced new credit evaluation standards.	*Direct Investment* Outflows: Restrictions on overseas investment in three real estate-related sectors were eased.
Minimum maturity of trust account products was lengthened to 18 months from 12 months.	*Portfolio Investment* Nonresidents were permitted derivative transactions between foreign and domestic currencies based on their real demand.

Capital Markets

Stock index futures started trading on the stock exchange.

Securities companies and general investors were permitted to buy and sell in the domestic OTC market any securities in which overseas investment could be made.

Financial Supervision and Regulatory Framework

In line with the opening and globalization of financial markets, the General Banking Act was revised to strengthen accountability of bank management and to increase bank soundness.

To promote the restructuring of the financial industry, the Act Concerning the Merger and Conversion of Financial Institutions was extensively revised and retitled "Financial Industry Restructuring Act." This act empowered the regulatory authority to take corrective measures in the event of a financial institution failing and also simplified the merger process.

Regulations governing the foreign exchange positions of banks were modified, whereby the basis of the calculation was related to the volume of transactions or capital, whichever is greater. The ratios with respect to capital were set as follows: overall overbought position, 15% of capital; overall oversold position, 10% of capital; and spot oversold position, 3% of capital or $5 million.

Entry barriers to foreign exchange business were lowered, including simplification of the licensing process.

The government revised the Foreign Capital Inducement Law and renamed it the "Foreign Investment and Foreign Capital Inducement Law," which became effective February 1997. Revisions were designed to induce larger inflows and bring the system into line with international standards. For example, the system of approval of foreign direct investment projects was converted to a system of notification.

Inflows: Nonresidents were permitted to open free-won accounts in overseas branches/subsidiaries of a foreign exchange bank. Won currency funds deposited in a free-won account were allowed to be withdrawn to invest in domestic stocks.

Inflows: The aggregate ceiling on investments in the stock market by nonresidents was raised to 20% from 15% and to 15% from 10%, on purchases of stocks of a listed firm and those issued by a public corporation, respectively. The ceiling on holdings by an individual was raised to 5% from 3%.

Inflows: Indirect investment in domestic bonds was allowed by means of a country fund.

Inflows: Access of nonresidents to the stock index of the futures market was allowed, but limited to 15%; limit was raised to 30% in November.

Inflows: Nonresidents were allowed to purchase and trade bonds with warrants.

Inflows: The Korea Bond Fund, capitalized at $100 million, was listed on the London stock exchange.

Inflows: For small- and medium-sized non-manufacturing firms in certain sectors, restrictions on direct foreign borrowings were dismantled.

Inflows: Opening of branches by foreign companies involved in securities-related business no longer required the approval of the Ministry of Finance; procedure replaced by acceptance through examination.

Outflows: Limits on overseas deposits for asset diversification purposes raised incrementally to $3 million and $50,000 a year for juridical persons and individuals, respectively.

Outflows: Limits on investments in foreign securities by individuals and general corporations were abolished. List of eligible investments was widened to include unlisted foreign stocks traded in authorized OTC markets, CP issued by foreign enterprises, and CDs sold by foreign financial institutions.

Outflows: The extension of foreign currency credits abroad by resident institutional investors was liberalized.

Outflows: Limit on amount of foreign currency permitted to be held abroad by construction companies was raised to 30% of the balance of construction contract or $3 million, whichever is greater, from 20% of contract or $2 million, whichever is greater.

Table 6.10 *(concluded)*

Monetary Controls and Financial System	Exchange System, Trade, and Capital Flows
1996 *(continued)*	*Portfolio Investment (continued)*
	Outflows: The limit on the amount of foreign currency that could be held abroad by general trading companies was raised to 50% with the maximum of $500 million of the trading value from 30% with the maximum of $300 million.
	Outflows: Ceiling of $10 million on loans that an institutional investor could extend to nonresidents was abolished; limits were set at $10 million and $300,000 for general trading firms and other firms, respectively.
	Outflows: Head of emigrating family was allowed to transfer up to $400,000 (previously $200,000); and other family members were allowed to transfer up to $200,000 (previously $100,000).
	Outflows: Resident foreign exchange banks and institutional investors were allowed to extend loans denominated in domestic currency to nonresidents up to W 100 million per borrower.
	Domestic issue of won denominated securities was expanded to include governments, local governments, public institutions, financial institutions, and enterprises of foreign countries; 50% of the total issue was allowed to be sold overseas.
	Trade
	Export credits in the form of deferred receipts were liberalized.
	The ceiling on export advances for large enterprises was raised in two steps to 20% from 10% of the export value of the previous year.

Sources: *Annual Report*, Bank of Korea (various issues); *Annual Report on Exchange Arrangements and Exchange Restrictions*, IMF, (various issues); *Doing Business in Korea*, (various issues), Price Waterhouse; *International Tax Summaries: A Guide for Planning and Decisions*, Coopers and Lybrand International Tax Network, (various issues); and *Securities Market in Korea*, 1992, Korea Securities Dealers Association; and IMF staff estimates.

[1]As a result, over the year, the refinancing outstanding of the financial institutions decreased by $1.8 billion and bank loans totaling $1 billion were repaid before maturity (*Annual Report*, Bank of Korea, 1986, p. 28).

Table 6.11. Korea: Selected Macroeconomic, Financial Sector, and Balance of Payments Indicators

	1985	1986	1987	1988	1989	1990	1991	1992	1993	1994	1995	1996
						(In percent)						
Selected economic indicators												
Real GDP growth	6.9	11.6	11.5	11.3	6.4	9.5	9.1	5.1	5.8	8.6	8.9	7.1
Inflation per year	2.5	2.7	3.0	7.1	5.7	8.9	9.3	6.2	4.8	6.3	4.5	5.0
M2 to GDP ratio	34.8	35.3	35.9	36.8	39.3	38.3	38.8	40.0	42.0	43.5	43.8	45.7
Currency to deposits ratio	13.0	12.2	12.3	11.7	11.6	11.3	10.4	9.8	12.1	10.9	10.9	9.5
Fiscal balance to GDP ratio	–1.1	–0.1	0.4	1.5	0.2	–0.7	–1.6	–0.5	0.6	0.3	0.3	0.1
Private sector credit to GDP ratio	49.4	48.7	49.9	48.3	54.2	56.8	56.8	56.8	58.3	60.8	61.2	66.0
Exports plus imports of goods to GDP ratio	65.1	61.0	64.8	61.8	55.8	53.2	52.1	51.4	49.9	52.1	57.1	57.8
Current account to GDP ratio	–0.8	4.4	7.4	8.0	2.4	–0.7	–2.8	–1.3	0.3	–1.0	–1.8	–4.8
Financial account to GDP ratio	2.1	–3.7	–6.6	–2.4	–1.2	1.1	2.3	2.3	1.0	2.8	3.8	5.0
Interest and exchange rates												
Nominal deposit rate (percent per year)	10.0	10.0	10.0	10.0	10.0	10.0	10.0	10.0	8.6	8.5	8.8	7.5
Real deposit rate (percent per year)	7.5	7.3	7.0	2.9	4.3	1.4	0.7	3.8	3.8	2.2	4.4	2.5
Interest rate differential[1]	1.6	3.1	2.8	2.0	2.7	1.7	4.0	6.0	5.3	3.8	2.8	2.0
Lending/deposit spread	0.0	0.0	0.0	0.1	1.3	0.0	0.0	0.0	0.0	0.0	0.2	1.3
Official exchange rate per U.S. dollar (end of period)	890.2	861.4	792.3	684.1	679.6	716.4	760.8	788.4	808.1	788.7	774.0	844.0
Real effective exchange rate index (1990 = 100)	96.8	81.8	81.3	90.8	103.5	100.0	99.9	94.2	93.6	94.3	95.4	98.8

Table 6.11 (*concluded*)

	1985	1986	1987	1988	1989	1990	1991	1992	1993	1994	1995	1996
						(In millions of U.S. dollars)						
Balance of Payments												
Current account, n.i.e.	–758	4,747	10,092	14,538	5,387	–1,745	–8,291	–3,939	1,016	–3,855	–8,251	–23,061
Financial account, n.i.e	1,935	–4,010	–8,963	–4,279	–2,640	2,866	6,714	6,969	3,188	10,610	17,221	24,025
Direct investment abroad	–587	–1,185	–540	–643	–613	–1,056	–1,500	–1,208	–1,361	–2,524	–3,529	–4,424
Direct investmnet in reporting economy, n.i.e.	234	460	616	1,014	1,118	788	1,180	727	588	809	1,776	2,325
Net direct investment	–353	–725	76	371	505	–268	–320	–481	–773	–1,715	–1,753	–2,099
Portfolio investment assets	. . .	. . .	. . .	–37	–66	240	492	845	232	–230	–311	–2,414
Portfolio investment liabilities	1,738	–332	–296	–606	–2	82	2,442	4,857	10,298	7,097	11,136	16,787
Net portfolio investment	1,738	–332	–296	–643	–68	322	2,934	5,702	10,530	6,867	10,825	14,373
Other investment assets	–1,136	–738	–113	–1,958	–1,382	–2,330	–6,378	–2,515	–4,224	–7,627	–13,084	–11,822
Other investment liabilities	1,686	–2,215	–8,630	–2,049	–1,695	5,142	10,478	4,263	–2,345	13,085	21,233	23,573
Net other investments	550	–2,953	–8,743	–4,007	–3,077	2,812	4,100	1,748	–6,569	5,458	8,149	11,751
Of which, official capital	1,989	–862	–7,092	–3,787	–2,098	–610	818	1,806	249	2,450	2,544	3,920
Net errors and omissions	–882	–546	1,185	–590	691	–1,998	757	1,101	–720	–1,704	–1,444	1,040
Capital account balance	–103	–114	–210	–353	–318	–331	–328	–407	–475	–437	–487	–598
Overall balance[2]	345	241	2,364	9,719	3,488	–827	–770	4,181	3,534	5,101	7,576	2,054
Memorandum:												
Net private capital[3]	–2,547	–2,047	507	–74	–1,345	2,745	7,806	5,295	9,960	8,948	16,225	22,067

Sources: IMF, *International Financial Statistics, World Economic Outlook,* and *Direction of Trade Statistics,* various issues; and IMF staff estimates.

[1]Interest differential = deposit – Londoninterbank offer rate on one-year U.S. deposits.

[2]The overall balance includes: current account, financial account, capital account, and net errors and omissions.

[3]Total capital = direct investment + portfolio investment + other investment – official capital + net errors and omissions + misinvoicing.

Table 6.12. Thailand: Sequencing of Reforms in the Domestic and External Sectors

Monetary Controls and Financial System	Exchange System, Trade, and Capital Flows
1985	
Monetary Policy: The government pursued a less restrictive monetary policy than in 1984 aimed at giving greater stability and flexibility to the financial system, as well as to promote priority economic sectors. This policy emphasized a change in loan policies of financial institutions and adapting the interest rate structure to economic circumstances. *Financial Supervisory and Regulatory Framework* Regulations concerning rediscounting of finance company promissory notes were liberalized. Regulations governing commercial bank sales of government bonds, held as required by branching regulations in the repurchase market, were liberalized. Regulations concerning the rediscounting of promissory notes arising from exports, small industrial undertakings, and animal husbandry were liberalized (method of computing interest on promissory notes is changed). Bank of Thailand exempted interbank loans of up to 6-month maturity from a classification as a risk asset. The Act on the Undertaking of Finance Businesses BE 2522 (1979) was amended by the Second Emergency Decree BE 2528 (1985) by providing a better legal framework for finance, and securities companies and credit fonciers. To broaden participation in interbank markets and increase the volume of transactions, commercial banks created the Bangkok Interbank Offer Rate (BIBOR), which operates along with the interbank market.	*Exchange Market Arrangement and System* Outflows: Regulations continued to exist on the repatriation of interest payments abroad. Prior approval from the Bank of Thailand was required. *Direct and Portfolio Investment* Inflows: Bank of Thailand required every individual borrowing from abroad to register with the Bank within seven days of making the loan agreement. *Portfolio Investment* Outflows: Limits continued to be imposed on commercial bank lending to nonresidents in foreign currency. *Trade* Regulations regarding rediscounts of export bills were liberalized. Credit ceiling was increased from 50% to 60% of warehouse receipt value. The Bank of Thailand temporarily extended the rebate period for penalty fees levied against rice and tapioca exporters, from 60 to 150 days. A surcharge of 10% of the c.i.f. value was imposed on imports of goods and services under customs tariff heading No. 95.08. Regulations on the opening of letters of credit for imports were relaxed. The Bank of Thailand provided special assistance to exporters affected by the baht exchange rate adjustment by giving an exemption from paying penalty fees when unable to export goods within the specified time in the promissory notes. Manufacturers of goods exported by international trading companies were allowed to rediscount directly at the Bank of Thailand their own promissory notes issued against domestic letters of credit, sales contracts, or purchase orders received from promoted international trading companies (as an alternative to these international companies rediscounting their own promissory notes at the Bank of Thailand and then giving the proceeds to the manufacturers within 60 days).

Table 6.12 *(continued)*

Monetary Controls and Financial System	Exchange System, Trade, and Capital Flows
1985 *(continued)*	
Money Market and Instruments Commercial banks were asked to cooperate and offer concessionary interest rates or discounts to priority sectors (including the allocation of more credit to these sectors). The minimum maturity of promissory notes held by credit fonciers as collateral was increased. Bank of Thailand established a line-of-credit on overdrafts at commercial banks (to help commercial banks avoid excess liquidity). Bank of Thailand required commercial banks to cease paying interest monthly on time deposits.	
1986	
Monetary Policy: The Bank of Thailand continued with less restrictive policies with the aim at boosting the economy and investment, including official financial assistance to priority economic sectors. At the same time, the Bank of Thailand helped improve the stability and financial position of financial institutions. *Capital Markets* For interest paid on debentures Stock Exchange of Thailand (SET), the income tax (deducted at source) was set at 15% tax, lower than the personal income rate and excludable from personal assessable income.	*Exchange Market Arrangement and System* The Bank of Thailand increased the amount of foreign exchange a person going overseas can purchase to a more appropriate level, and increased the amount of foreign currency an authorized foreign exchange dealer can sell to such a person. *Portfolio Investment* Inflows: The tax on income earned from mutual funds was lowered for nonresidents and juristic persons, if they used foreign funds transferred to Thailand to purchase them. Inflows: For dividends and other forms of compensation earned from mutual funds, the government gives: (1) groups of persons not resident in Thailand a reduction in the income tax (deducted at source) from over 10% to no more than 10%; such earnings are also excludable from assessable personal income; and (2) juristic persons or partnerships established according to foreign law and without business in Thailand a reduction in income tax (deducted at source) from 20% to 10%.

Money Market and Instruments The Bank of Thailand consolidated its two-tier rate into a single rate, maintaining the ceiling credit line at 1% of total commercial bank deposits. Bank of Thailand used the 1985 base of deposit levels rather than the 1979 level. The Bank of Thailand added two more maturities for bond repurchases—90-day and 180-day to the existing four—1-, 3-, 30-, and 60-day. The CB reduced the refinancing rate of promissory notes arising from exports from 7% to 5% per annum, and those arising from exports of new products with no traditional markets and those issued by small exporters and small-scale industries, from 5% to 4% per annum. The financing rates were correspondingly reduced to 7% for all exports. The regulation on refinancing of promissory notes arising from exports was amended. The maximum value for refinancing export bills issued against receipts was increased from 50% to 60% of the value assessed by commercial banks. The penalty rate was reduced from 11% to 8%, bringing it in line with the rate in the money market. The decrease of the penalty rate was also accompanied by a relaxation of penalty collection methods.	Inflows: For capital gains earned from selling shares in mutual funds listed on the SET, an investor received a reduction in the income tax (deducted at source) from 25% to 12.5%. To qualify an investor must use foreign funds transferred into Thailand to purchase the mutual fund shares. Inflows: The Bank of Thailand introduced a regulation requiring the registration of all private foreign borrowing at the Bank of Thailand within seven days of the signature date, and not after the loan funds were imported and sold to authorized banks.
1987	
Monetary Policy: The Bank of Thailand carried out policies to expand credit, to promote production and investment, especially of small-scale industries in rural areas, and to solve the problem of excess liquidity in the banking system. The Bank of Thailand continued to promote stability of financial institutions and to encourage them to respond more flexibly to changing economic conditions.	*Trade* In order to promote border trade, the license fee was reduced from B 20,000 to B 2,000 per license for those exporters residing in border provinces and exporting an amount not exceeding B 20,000 per day. The maximum amount of each export and import transaction that is allowed without approval from the Bank of Thailand was increased to B 50,000 for all kinds of merchandise goods in order to facilitate border trade.

Table 6.12 *(continued)*

Monetary Controls and Financial System	Exchange System, Trade, and Capital Flows
1987 *(continued)*	
The *Sixth National Economic and Social Development Plan* was introduced (1987–91). The main objectives are increasing efficiency of development, production, and marketing and promoting equitable distribution of income.	
Capital Markets	
The minimum margin loan ratio at 35% was set by the SET. Subsequently it was changed three times to 50%, 70%, and back to 50%.	
Bonds issued by the Bank of Thailand were exempted from business tax and stamp duty.	
Maximum withholding tax on dividends and distributed profits from companies registered in the SET, mutual funds, and financial institutions that were set up under specific Thai law to provide credit were lowered from 30% to a rate not exceeding 15% of income.	
Capital gains arising from transfers of debentures issued by non-government agencies in the SET became subject to a 15% withholding tax at source on the excess of the return over the invested amount.	
Money Market and Instruments	
The Bank of Thailand revised the regulations concerning the amount of cash or promissory notes to be placed by clients as collateral against margin loans extended by finance companies. Instead of prescribing a fixed minimum rate of 25% of total borrowing, the requirement was changed to either 25% of borrowing or the ratio prescribed by the SET, whichever is higher.	

The Bank of Thailand revised the regulations on the financial facility extended to exporters by allowing the participation of commercial banks in joint credit extension, so as to help them adjust their liquidity positions. In this regard, the interest rate that the Bank of Thailand charges commercial banks varies in accordance with their shares in total credits extended to exporters—for example, 4%, 3%, 2%, and 1% a year for shares of 20%, 40%, or 80% respectively. However, the rate charged to customers by commercial banks remained unchanged at 7% a year.

1988

Monetary Policy: The Bank of Thailand implemented stricter monetary policy and at the same time emphasized the promotion of rural development by encouraging the diversification of credit extensions.

Capital Markets

Dividends and distributed profits from companies or partnerships not registered with the SET were allowed to be excluded from other taxable income for the year-end assessment if tax payers consented to a 15% withholding tax at source (such income otherwise is subject to withholding at the personal income tax rate).

The business tax exemption period for sales of securities in the SET was extended for two years until the end of 1990.

Financial Supervisory and Regulatory Framework

The Bank of Thailand revised regulations covering financial institutions in order to facilitate their operations and raise their efficiency.

Exchange Market Arrangement and System

Commercial banks were authorized to open foreign exchange accounts and to accept deposits in foreign currencies at an amount not exceeding $5,000 from foreigners who were in transit or resided temporarily in Thailand within 15 days after their arrival.

The regulation governing the use abroad of credit cards and the collection of money therefrom, including withdrawal of funds through ATMs, was modified. The change involved an increase in the ceiling for the use of credit cards in foreign countries to $2,000 in addition to the expenses that can be approved by authorized representatives on behalf of the Exchange Control Officer.

Trade

Credit card holders in Thailand were permitted to use credit cards abroad for import payments by submitting an application prior to their departure.

Table 6.12 *(continued)*

Monetary Controls and Financial System	Exchange System, Trade, and Capital Flows
1988 *Financial Supervisory and Regulatory Framework* (*continued*) To allow small entrepreneurs access to working capital and to maintain stability of crop prices, the Bank of Thailand modified regulations governing financial assistance to entrepreneurs in priority economic sectors and introduced new categories of credit extension. *Money Market and Instruments* The Bank of Thailand's total financial assistance line was raised from B 38.5 billion to B 40 billion, of which B 2 billion was allocated to small industries to invest in agricultural and industrial activities in rural areas.	
1989	
Monetary Policy: Monetary measures were focused on economic growth, income distribution, exports, and investment promotion as well as internal and external funds mobilization. *The Sixth Plan* was revised because all its goals were attained sooner than planned. The revision was aimed at sustaining high growth with stability to tackle major problems such as the trade and current account deficits, the widening of savings investment gap, and concentration of investment around Bangkok. *Capital Markets* Income tax exemption amendments were made on interest from government bonds and on income from the transfer of government bonds inside and outside the SET.	*Exchange Market Arrangement and System* The first round of relaxation of foreign exchange regulations is introduced. The maximum amount of: (1) Thai baht that an individual could bring into or take out of the country was increased to B 10,000; (2) Thai baht that could be sent through the money order service was increased to B 2,500 at a time; (3) foreign currency allowed to be bought from and sold to an individual customer by commercial banks without prior submission of the Exchange Control form was increased to B 1,000 and B 500, respectively; and (4) foreign currencies that commercial banks were allowed to sell to expatriate families as well as Thai nationals were raised to $5,000 per annum. Commercial banks were given authorization to sell foreign exchange and transfer Thai baht into transferable nonresident baht accounts of foreign investors or borrowers of foreign loans who had registered the funds with the Bank of Thailand. The transferred funds required (1) proceeds from sales of shares in the SET financed with foreign capital, or (2) dividends transferred by registered or authorized companies on behalf of an investor.

Money Market and Instruments

Interest rate ceiling on time deposits with maturity over one year was removed, while the interest rate ceilings on savings accounts and time deposits with one-year maturity or less and on lending rate were maintained.

Repayments of principals, interest, other expenses related to foreign loans, dividends, and transfer of relevant certificates of share ownership were allowed without the Bank of Thailand's approval. Sale of foreign exchange for bona fide transactions was limited to $500 or its equivalent without the submission of supporting documents. Sale of foreign exchange was permitted for remittances of family expenses and savings up to a limit of $5,000.

Commercial banks were allowed to approve foreign currency purchases for various purposes, including the exchange of foreign currency held by foreign travelers into another currency up to $3,000 or its equivalent at market rates.

Trade

Payments in domestic currency for imports and trade-related services, such as freight charges and insurance premiums, into nonresident transferable baht account could be approved by authorized banks on behalf of the competent officer.

Authorized banks were allowed to approve exchange control forms in connection with payments for imported materials for the manufacture of export products and with deferred import payments. They were also authorized to approve an exchange control form for exports under certain circumstances.

The limit on the value of imports and exports that do not require the filing of an exchange control form was increased to B 100,000 from B 50,000.

1990

Monetary Policy: Measures were aimed at improving the financial structure and international payment system with a view to enhancing competition in the financial sector, reducing inflation, and inducing more flexibility in the asset-liability management of domestic financial institutions. Policies were also implemented to assist the development of financial instruments and investment in the capital market.

Capital Markets

Bank of Thailand revised a regulation to allow finance companies to invest a greater amount of their funds in registered or listed securities (from 60% to 100% of their capital funds).

Exchange Market Arrangement and System

On May 4, the Government announced the acceptance of *Article VIII obligations of the IMF Articles of Agreement.*

A *second round, partial relaxation of foreign exchange regulations* was introduced. (1) commercial banks were allowed to grant permission to all applications of foreign exchange transactions relating to international trade; (2) the maximum limits entrusted to commercial banks on foreign exchange applications relating to service accounts were raised; the maximum limit on traveling allowances was increased to $20,000 per trip, and the limits on family allowances and educational expenses were also increased to $50,000 per year; (3) commercial banks were authorized to approve remittances of funds to families and relatives living abroad within the maximum limit of $100,000 per

Table 6.12 *(continued)*

Monetary Controls and Financial System	Exchange System, Trade, and Capital Flows
1990 *(continued)*	*Exchange Market Arrangement and System (continued)*
Bank of Thailand introduced new regulations for the setting up of security trading offices in the provincial areas. Eligible companies were required to have licenses to perform security brokerage service and be members of the SET.	person per year, and the limits of remittances of funds by emigrants were raised to $1 million per person per year (4) commercial banks were allowed to approve the repatriation of interest payments (net of taxes), payments for the repayment of foreign loans, and transfers of baht into and from nonresident baht accounts and into "transferrable" and "blocked" accounts for the purchase of foreign currency (up to $500,000 per transaction).
Money Market	Commercial banks was allowed to lend to nonresidents in foreign currency not exceeding $5 million or its equivalent.
The Bank of Thailand removed the requirement on the minimum denomination of promissory notes that finance companies can issue (from B 5,000 to B 10,000 to zero).	The maximum amount allowed to be transferred to each nonresident Baht account was increased to B 5 million a day.
The Bank of Thailand lifted the official ceiling on interest rates charged to nonbanks on promissory notes (rate that was charged used to be 1% higher than that offered at bank accounts in commercial banks).	*Portfolio Investment*
	Inflows: Three new closed-end mutual funds were approved to mobilize foreign capital: Thai Capital Fund, Thai Equity Growth Fund, and Thai Emerging Fund, all with maturity of 25 years.
	Outflows: Commercial banks are allowed to approve the repatriation of proceeds from sales of securities.
1991	
Monetary Policy: The Bank of Thailand continued to implement cautious monetary policy to achieve a balanced growth of money supply and credit, and to keep the expansion in domestic expenditure in line with growth in production capacity. Measures to promote a more efficient financial system were also undertaken in step with the changing economic structure, both at home and abroad, as well as to prepare domestic financial institutions for competition with foreign counterparts.	*Exchange Market Arrangement and System* The *third round of the relaxation of foreign exchange regulations* was undertaken following the acceptance of Article VIII: (1) residents were permitted to purchase an unlimited amount of foreign exchange currency from authorized banks (with some exceptions); (2) the period for surrender of foreign currency receipts was extended from 7 to 15 days, or the amount could be deposited in foreign currency accounts with authorized commercial banks in Thailand (upon checking that currencies originated abroad); and (3) the limit on foreign currencies brought into the country or taken out of the country was removed. Limits on the amount of Thai baht allowed to be taken out of the country were raised.

Capital Markets

The Securities and Exchange Bills were drafted.

The Thai Credit Rating Agency (CRA) to be established to support the issuance of financial instruments.

Computerized trading system was introduced in the SET.

Money Market and Instruments

Policies were further pursued to allow interest rates to adjust in accordance with market mechanism. Preparations were made for the eventual removal of the ceiling on savings deposit and lending rates (see 1992).

Lending rates of banks and finance companies became subject to ceilings of 19% and 21%, respectively.

Foreign exchange earners were allowed to open foreign exchange accounts with commercial banks up to $500,000 for individuals and $2 million for corporations.

Direct Investment

Inflows: The Investment Promotion Act was amended to induce more foreign investment.

Outflows: Thai investors were permitted to transfer freely up to a certain amount in U.S. dollars abroad for direct investment.

Inflows: Government allowed 100% foreign ownership of firms that export all of their output.

Portfolio Investment

Outflows: The maximum amount Thai residents could invest abroad or lend to companies abroad, which had at least 25% Thai equity participation, was set at $5 million per year, without the authorization of the Bank of Thailand.

Outflows: The repatriation of investment funds, loan repayments, and interest payments by foreign investors could be made without any restrictions.

Outflows: The tax on dividends remitted abroad was reduced from 20% to 15%. The tax on payments to nonresidents on income from royalties was lowered from 20% to 15%.

Restrictions on Capital Flows

Inflows: Joint ventures and foreign ownership were restricted to a maximum of 49% in certain investment projects.

1992

Monetary Policy: Major monetary policies were aimed at facilitating continued economic growth and development of the financial system and of Thailand into a regional financial center.

The *Seventh National Economic and Social Development Plan* was introduced (1992–96). Its main objectives were to sustain economic expansion with stability, to distribute income to regions, and to develop human resources.

Exchange Market Arrangement and System

The *fourth round of changes in exchange regulations* occurred. Changes included: (1) exporters were allowed to receive payments in baht from nonresident baht accounts in addition to those in foreign currencies, and could use such foreign currency receipts to pay for imports or debit foreign liabilities to nonresidents; (2) exporters were permitted to use the proceeds to service external obligations and pay for imports without depositing the proceeds in domestic banking accounts (previously proceeds were required to be deposited within 15 days of receipt); (3) residents could withdraw from their foreign currency accounts to repay debt on behalf of their subsidiaries, or transfer to creditors' foreign currency accounts at commercial banks in Thailand; and (4) expatriates temporarily working in Thailand were allowed to purchase foreign currencies to deposit in their foreign currency accounts at commercial banks

Table 6.12 *(continued)*

Monetary Controls and Financial System	Exchange System, Trade, and Capital Flows
1992 *(continued)* *Capital Markets* The Securities and Exchange Act came into force in May 1992. All activities relating to the securities business, including securities companies that were formerly under the Bank of Thailand's supervision, now came under the supervision of the SET. Afternoon trading was introduced on the stock exchange (July). Unlisted companies were permitted to issue corporate bonds and debentures. *Financial Supervisory and Regulatory Framework* Policies were focused on the development of the financial system. Authorities deregulated financial institutions' operations and expanded their scope of operation. New financial acts were promulgated and existing ones amended, and a subsequent phase of exchange control deregulation was undertaken. The government approved the establishment of the *Bangkok International Banking Facility (BIBF)*. Commercial banks that were registered to conduct international banking facilities were allowed to accept deposits or borrow in foreign currencies from abroad and from foreign banks or nonresidents; accept deposits or borrow in foreign currencies from abroad from foreign persons who lent foreign currencies in Thailand (limited to $500,000); conduct cross-currency transactions with overseas customers; give acceptance or guarantee debts in foreign currencies; deal in	*Exchange Market Arrangement and System (continued)* The daily ceiling on foreign notes and coins, which was allowed to be deposited in a foreign currency account, was removed. Government agencies, state organizations, or enterprises, or juristic persons established under specific laws were allowed to conduct any transactions through their foreign currency accounts. *Direct Investment* Inflows: Under the Seventh Plan, foreign ownership requests were to be decided by the individual ministries on a case-by-case basis. Inflows: Under the Seventh Plan, the criteria for granting tax incentives was designed to promote investment in special sectors. Exceptions were made for enterprises exporting at least 80% of their output. Inflows: Commercial banks, which were allowed to carry operations under the BIBF, were given a tax break: the corporate income tax was lowered from 30% to 10%; exempted from the withholding tax on interest paid to a foreign depositor or lender on the deposit or loan used for offshore lending; exempted from specific business tax and municipal tax (the typical 3.3% tax on gross income); and exempted from stamp duty (typically 0.5%) not exceeding B 10,000. An NIBF licensed bank remained subject to a 10% remittance tax on net profits sent out of Thailand. *Portfolio Investment* Inflows: In an effort to induce foreign investment in the Thai stock market, several taxes were reduced: dividend taxes, tax on interest payments from debentures to foreign juristic persons, and tax on capital gains from the sale of securities by juristic persons. Outflows: Tax on dividends remitted abroad was lowered from 15% to 10%

letters of credit when both buyer and seller resides abroad and import and export of goods do not enter or leave Thailand; and managing loan procurement of foreign currency loans from foreign sources.

The Financial Institutions' Lending Rate Act and the Commercial Banking Act were amended. Amendments were made to the second and third amendments of the Acts on the Undertakings of Finance Business, Securities Business, and Credit Foncier Business.

Financial institutions were allowed to jointly establish mutual funds management companies, and jointly apply for such licenses.

The Public Company Act came into effect in June 1992. Regional offices of transnational corporations within Thailand were allowed to be formed.

Money Market Instruments

The interest rate ceiling on savings deposits at commercial banks was abolished (January).

The interest rate ceilings on finance companies' and credit foncier companies' borrowing, deposits, and lending together with the ceiling on commercial banks' lending were lifted (June).

The interest rate ceiling on mortgage lending to low-income individuals was maintained for all loan contracts that were made before June 1992. For commercial banks, the ceiling for such a loan was fixed at the minimum lending rate, and for finance companies and credit foncier companies, it was fixed at the maximum lending rate less 1.5%.

Commercial banks and finance companies were permitted to issue certificates of deposits.

Table 6.12 *(continued)*

Monetary Controls and Financial System	Exchange System, Trade, and Capital Flows
1993	
Monetary Policy: Monetary measures were implemented cautiously within the framework of a more liberalized financial market. The policy stance was somehow restrictive; the measures aimed at increasing the efficiency of the domestic financial markets and at facilitating growth. Measures aimed at ensuring that the adjustment in interest rates were consistent with monetary conditions; there were further measures on financial deregulation and liberalization of foreign exchange controls. *Capital Markets* Financial institutions were allowed to seek permission to undertake securities businesses limited to trading or placing debt instruments. The SET introduced measures to improve the efficiency of its operations. Rules and procedures on the management of new types of mutual funds were established. *Financial Supervisory and Regulatory Framework* Thailand's offshore banking facility, the *Bangkok International Banking Facility (BIBF),* commenced operations. The Bank of Thailand relaxed some of the regulations governing the BIBF. This relaxation was extended especially to foreign commercial bank branches pertaining to required maintenance of assets in the country, capital maintenance, ratio of commitments to capital, and liquidity reserve requirement.	*Exchange Market Arrangement and System* Authorities increased the limit on baht that can be carried to bordering countries and Vietnam, to not more than B 250,000. *Portfolio Investment* Inflows: Rules governing the issuance of debentures in foreign countries, as well as subordinate debentures, were specified in order to increase alternatives for the private businesses in mobilizing funds. Issuers of such funds must obtain permission from the SET. *Trade* The Export-Import Bank of Thailand was established with the purpose of strengthening the financial standing of Thai export-oriented business.

Money Market and Instruments

The Bank of Thailand reduced the bank rate and the refinancing rate on finance companies' promissory notes.

The Bank of Thailand gave a directive to commercial banks to announce the Minimum Loan Rate and Minimum Retail Rate.

The Bank of Thailand provided financial assistance to the new investment projects, each with capital not exceeding B 200 million, that had been granted investment promotional benefits by refinancing, through commercial banks and the Industrial Finance Corporation of Thailand.

1994

Monetary Policy: Policy was aimed at supporting the stable economic expansion and development of the financial system.

Financial Supervisory and Regulatory Framework

Regulations on, and requirements for, the expansion of financial institutions were introduced.

Permission was granted to open the Provincial International Banking Facility. Requirements for the issuance of the various types of securities, conditions, and procedures related to mutual funds, guidelines for reports in information disclosure, requirements for the establishment of securities brokerage offices and branches of securities companies, revisions of regulations and procedures regarding the registration of securities and security holders, measures to maintain capital market stability, and revisions of other SET regulations were introduced.

Exchange Market Arrangement and System

The ceiling on the amount authorized banks are permitted to lend to nonresidents in foreign currency was eliminated.

Residents were permitted to use foreign exchange that originated abroad for servicing external obligations without having to surrender it or deposit it in a domestic bank account.

Foreign currency borrowed by residents from the BIBF, or borrowed by nonresidents from authorized banks or from withdrawal from nonresident baht accounts, could all be freely deposited in foreign currency accounts.

Limits on amount of foreign exchange that could be taken out for traveling expenses was eliminated.

Foreign exchange controls on the outward transfers of funds and lending in foreign currency were relaxed.

Authorities increased the limit on baht that could be carried to bordering countries and Vietnam, to not more than B 500,000.

Table 6.12 *(continued)*

Monetary Controls and Financial System	Exchange System, Trade, and Capital Flows
1994 *(continued)*	
Money Market and Instruments The Bank of Thailand raised the base interest rate and the discount rate (refinancing rate) for promissory notes of finance companies and finance and securities companies arising from agricultural, industrial, and commercial activities. The Bank of Thailand required commercial banks to inform their customers in writing about the benchmark rate (Minimum Loan Rate or Minimum Retail Rate) and the margin added on to such rate, as well as to clearly post the deposit interest rate and the benchmark rates for credit.	*Direct Investment* Outflows: The maximum amount permitted for direct investment abroad by Thai residents or lending to companies abroad that have at least 25% Thai equity participation was increased to upwards of $10 million.
1995	
Monetary Policy: Authorities tightened money policy to strengthen economic stability, at the same time financial reform measures were undertaken. *Capital Markets* The authorities introduced Bank of Thailand Bonds, which are auctioned every week according to a preannounced schedule. *Financial Supervisory and Regulatory Framework* The Provincial International Banking Facility (PIBF) was established. PIBF's funding must be from overseas like that of the BIBF, but PIBF can extend credit in both baht and foreign currencies.	*Exchange Market Arrangement and System* The authorities imposed constraints on bank lending including restrictions on non-priority lending in foreign exchange. *Restrictions on Capital Flows* Inflows/Outflows: The authorities imposed a 7% reserve requirement on nonresident baht accounts and on finance companies' short-term promissory notes. The previous regulation required 2% minimum deposits with the Bank of Thailand, and the remaining 5% in the form of vault cash and eligible securities.

Commercial banks with BIBF licenses were required to set up provisions for doubtful debts of 75% of the doubtful debt as of June 1994, and 100% as of the end of 1995.

Banks were not allowed to count loans in foreign currencies to purchase unused land or for personal reasons, as foreign assets; and only 50% of certain other loans could be counted as foreign assets, unless the borrower fully covered his exchange risk by buying the exchange forward at the same bank that extended the loan.

The Bank of Thailand required banks to submit detailed information on risk control measures on trading in foreign exchange and derivatives.

The Bank of Thailand adopted a new method of calculating nontrade net open foreign exchange positions (on which there are limits set as a percent of capital) for foreign and locally incorporated banks.

Finance and securities companies' daily long and short foreign exchange positions were restricted to a maximum of 25% and 20%, respectively, of first-tier capital funds.

The maximum for commercial banks' average weekly net long and short foreign exchange position was reduced to 20% and 15%, respectively, of first-tier capital funds, or $5 million, whichever is larger.

Money Market and Instruments

The central bank rate was increased by 1 percentage point to 10½%. The interest rate charged to finance companies on borrowing from the Bank of Thailand under the securities repurchase agreement was also raised to the same level as the central bank rate.

Authorities extended the coverage of the credit plan to include finance companies and banks in the BIBF.

Table 6.12 *(continued)*

Monetary Controls and Financial System	Exchange System, Trade, and Capital Flows
1995 *Money Market and Instruments* (*continued*)	
The Bank of Thailand improved the trading mechanism in the repurchase market whereby the prevailing best bid and best offer prices are matched continuously throughout the trading session.	
The Bank of Thailand permitted finance companies to issue bills of exchange or certificates of deposit denominated in foreign currencies with maturity of over one year to investors overseas or commercial banks authorized to undertake foreign exchange transactions.	
1996	
Capital Markets	*Restrictions on Capital Flows*
The authorities introduced three rescue funds during 1995–96 to slow the stock market's decline.	Inflows: A reserve requirement of 7% on banks' nonresident baht accounts with maturity of less than one year was imposed.
Authorities allowed securities companies to apply for licenses to undertake comprehensive securities businesses under the rules of the SE Act B.E.2535.	Inflows: A similar 7% reserve requirement was imposed on nonresident baht borrowing, with maturity of less than one year, by finance companies.
The SEC increased the "initial margin" from 30% to 40%.	Inflows: A 7% reserve requirement was imposed on new foreign borrowing with maturity of less than one year, by commercial banks and BIBF banks. This reserve requirement applies also to nonresident deposits. The following types of borrowing were exempted from this reserve requirement: international trade financing, overdrafts and liabilities arising from currency trading and derivatives transactions, and nonresident deposits at the BIBFs.
Financial Supervisory and Regulatory Framework	*Trade*
The Bank of Thailand revised the method for the calculation of finance companies' foreign exchange position in regard to lending whereby borrowers bear the foreign exchange risk.	The three-year tariff reduction program, covering about 4,000 product items, was designed to reduce the average tariff rate from about 30% to 17%, and ended in January 1, 1997.
The minimum capital adequacy requirement for commercial banks was increased.	

The Bank of Thailand tightened further the limits on banks' net foreign exchange positions by excluding loans in foreign currency to certain high-risk sectors from the banks' assets.

The preferential tax rate on BIBF profits was reduced.

The Bank of Thailand allowed financial institutions to choose custodians who have strong financial positions and a network of services in important financial centers and are given a credit rating from Standard and Poor's of not less than AA⁻.

The Bank of Thailand requested commercial banks to report monthly figures on credit card services every three months instead of six months.

The Bank of Thailand demanded that finance companies and finance and securities companies maintain liquid assets as deposits at the Bank of Thailand.

The Bank of Thailand required domestically incorporated commercial banks wishing to issue financial instruments to be counted as second-tier capital fund to seek permission from the Bank of Thailand not less than one month before offering securities for subscription.

The Royal Decree Regulating Affairs of the Bank of Thailand (No.8) B.E.2539 was enacted. Under the new decree, finance companies, authorized to undertake foreign exchange business upon obtaining a license, were allowed to purchase and sell foreign exchange with the Bank of Thailand like that of commercial banks.

The Bank of Thailand required foreign bank branches licensed to undertake businesses of commercial banking to maintain funds at not less than 7.5% of assets and contingent liabilities.

Table 6.12 ***(continued)***

Monetary Controls and Financial System	Exchange System, Trade, and Capital Flows
1996 *Financial Supervisory and Regulatory Framework (continued)*	
The Bank of Thailand required domestic commercial banks to maintain capital funds at not less than 8.5% of assets and contingent liabilities and the first-tier capital funds shall not be less than 6% of risk assets.	
Finance companies, finance and securities companies, and credit foncier companies were required to maintain reserves at no less than 100% of doubtful assets within the accounting period ending in June 1996.	
The Bank of Thailand permitted BIBF to sign contracts against risks for the amount maintained as liquid assets such as buying forward or option against the baht.	
The Bank of Thailand allowed foreign bank branches to include deposits maintained as liquid assets of BIBF in the calculation of foreign assets. The middle exchange rate announced by the Exchange Equalization Funds must be used in converting baht into U.S. dollars.	
The Bank of Thailand allowed foreign bank branches to maintain assets required under the Commercial Banking Act 2522 in foreign currency except for deposits at the Bank of Thailand, which have to be in baht.	
The Bank of Thailand prescribed that the amount of money with which a commercial bank engages in any or several types of the following transactions, namely credit granting, investment, and formation of contingent liabilities for any person, must not exceed 25% of its first-tier capital fund at the end of any day.	

The Ministry of Finance issued a notification stipulating regulations governing the permission for finance companies to manage private funds.

The Bank of Thailand issued a notification on financial assistance to six business undertakings.

The Bank of Thailand set a standard for the calculation of risk-weighted assets.

1997–Aug.

Financial Supervisory and Regulatory Framework

The Bank of Thailand required all financial institutions to submit daily reports of foreign exchange transactions with nonresidents, including all spot, forward, and swap transactions, as well as purchases of debt instruments from nonresidents.

Sixteen of the ninty-one finance companies were suspended in June and forced to merge with new domestic or foreign partners, absorbed by five "core" finance companies, or liquidated after the due diligence process had been completed.

Twenty-two finance companies were asked to raise new capital while two companies underwent negotiations with foreign investors.

A further 35 finance companies were suspended in August and were subject to similar procedures as those outlined in the June order.

Support to financial institutions was given through the Financial Institutions Development Fund (FIDF), except for those suspended in June and August.

A compulsory contribution to the FIDF on all protected liabilities of financial institutions was introduced.

Exchange Market Arrangement and System

On July 2, the exchange rate system was changed to managed floating, whereby the baht would be managed within an unpublished band

All affected financial institutions were required to submit daily reports of foreign exchange transactions with nonresidents, including all spot, forward, and swap transactions, as well as purchase of debt instruments from nonresidents to the Bank of Thailand.

In June, the baht proceeds from sales of stocks by nonresidents were required to be converted into foreign currency at the onshore exchange rate. The authorities introduced a two-tier currency market that creates separate exchange rates for investors who buy baht in domestic markets and those who bring it overseas. Effective September 8, 1997, the Thai authorities modified the exchange control regulation as follows: (i) foreign exchange earners were allowed to deposit their foreign exchange received in their foreign currency deposit account only if they had obligations to pay out such amounts to nonresidents abroad within three months from the deposit date; and (ii) exporters receiving packing credit from the Bank of Thailand through the Export-Import Bank of Thailand were required to sign a forward contract to sell their foreign exchange with a commercial bank selling promissory notes to the Export-Import Bank. The forward contracts must specify the amount of foreign currencies in terms of baht, which cannot be less than 50% of the face value of the promissory note.

Table 6.12 *(concluded)*

Monetary Controls and Financial System	Exchange System, Trade, and Capital Flows
1997–Aug. *Financial Supervisory and Regulatory Framework (continued)*	*Direct Investment*
The government announced it will not make available public funds to aid corporate and household borrowers, domestic or external.	Inflows: The restriction on foreign ownership of office buildings and condominiums was lifted in end-April 1997 in an effort to shrink the country's oversupply of real estate. Inflows: In April, foreigners investing more than B 25 million in the country were permitted to buy land.
Banks were required to make loan loss provisions on the basis of more stringent asset classification rules, and were allowed full tax deductibility for specific provisions required by the Bank of Thailand (as part of the structural performance criterium set by the IMF).	Inflows: In April, the foreign ownership limit of 25% for financial institutions was lifted on a case-by-case basis. *Restrictions on Capital Flows* Outflows: The Bank of Thailand temporarily limited baht lending to nonresidents through foreign exchange swap transactions, and all other transactions that could facilitate the buildup of baht position in the offshore market. These include direct loans, overdraft, currency swaps, interest rate swaps, forward rate agreements, currency options, and interest rate options.
Commercial banks and remaining finance companies were required to raise their capital in anticipation of possible further deterioration of their asset quality (as part of the structural performance criterium set by the IMF).	Outflows: The Bank of Thailand temporarily limited forward outright transactions in baht with nonresidents.
A 0.5% fee was introduced on the protected liabilities of financial institutions (as part of the performance criterium set by the IMF). After the banking crisis is normalized, institutions will be allowed to make public their exit from the current protection scheme.	Outflows: The Bank of Thailand temporarily limited selling baht against foreign currencies to nonresidents. Outflows: Any purchases of foreign exchange from nonresidents before maturity of certain securities must use the exchange rate prevailing in the domestic market on the purchase date. These securities included baht-denominated bills of exchange, promissory notes, certificates of deposit, and other debt instruments such as debentures and bonds.
Capital Markets In March, the SEC ordered a halting of trade in financial sector stocks.	Outflows: The Bank of Thailand tightened a remittance ban in response to stock sales by foreign investment funds that were trying to acquire Thai currency for short-covering purposes.
In May, Thai commercial banks offered to pool up to 50 billion baht to shore up the stock market.	The measures above were introduced in June and were not applied to foreign exchange transactions related to export and import of goods and services, and direct and portfolio investment, and were aimed mainly at short-term speculative activity.

Money Market and Instruments

In March the Bank of Thailand announced measures to issue zero coupon bonds to raise B 100 billion to buy substandard assets from property developers and the Thai cabinet set up an agency to manage a 100 billion baht rescue fund for property companies.

In April, the Bank of Thailand cut lending rates to finance companies by 50–100 basis points aimed at helping any financial institution that had liquidity problems.

In May, the Bank of Thailand floated another 20 billion baht of seven-year, zero-coupon bonds through weekly auctions. The government set aside another B 10 billion for confessional mortgage loans to first-time buyers.

In July, the FIDF lending rates were kept at above the highest deposit rate in the system and all liquidity support became subject to conditionality.

In August, the bank rate was increased from 10.5% to 12.5%.

In August, deposit rates in the financial system were capped at 1 percentage point above the average deposit rate of the five largest commercial banks.

Sources: Bank of Thailand, *Annual Report*, various issues, IMF, *Annual Report on Exchange Arrangements and Exchange Restrictions*, various issues; IMF, *Quarterly Report on Exchange Rate Arrangements*, various issues; *Doing Business in Thailand*, Price Waterhouse, 1992; *The Thai Stock Market: Leading in Sustained Growth*, Association of Members of the Stock Exchange, 1991; *Finance Industry in Thailand*, Association of Finance Companies, 1991; *Foreign Direct Investment in Asia*, by E.K.Y. Chin - Asian Productivity Organization, 1990; *Tax Laws of the World: Thailand*, Foreign Tax Publishers, 1989; *Guide to the Investment Regimes on the Fifteen APEC Member Countries*, 1993; Thailand's Laws and Policies on Foreign Investments, S. Sathirathai, and Y. Sudharma in *Current Developments in International Investment Law* ed. by Ho Peng Lee, 1992; *Asian Stockmarket Factbook*, SWIFT, 1994/95; and *The Emerging Asian Bond Market: Thailand*, World Bank, 1995.

Table 6.13. Thailand: Selected Macroeconomic, Financial Sector, and Balance of Payments Indicators

	1985	1986	1987	1988	1989	1990	1991	1992	1993	1994	1995	1996
						(In percent)						
Selected economic indicators												
Real GDP growth	6.9	11.6	11.5	11.3	6.4	9.5	9.1	5.1	5.8	8.6	8.9	7.1
Real GDP growth	4.6	5.5	9.5	13.3	12.2	11.6	8.1	8.2	8.5	8.9	8.7	6.4
Inflation per year	2.4	1.8	2.5	3.9	5.4	5.9	5.7	4.1	3.4	5.2	5.7	5.8
M2 to GDP ratio	56.2	59.3	62.2	61.3	65.0	69.8	73.1	74.7	78.9	77.8	78.9	79.5
Currency to deposits ratio	12.1	11.9	12.0	11.6	11.0	9.9	8.9	9.3	9.1	9.4	9.4	8.9
Fiscal balance to GDP ratio	–5.2	–4.2	–2.2	0.7	2.9	4.5	4.7	2.8	2.1	1.9	2.9	. . .
Private sector credit to GDP ratio	45.6	44.3	47.4	51.1	56.3	64.3	67.7	72.1	79.8	90.9	97.5	100.1
Exports plus imports of goods to GDP ratio	42.1	41.9	48.9	58.8	63.5	65.5	67.0	65.5	66.1	69.0	77.0	69.0
Current account to GDP ratio	–4.0	0.6	–0.7	–2.7	–3.5	–8.5	–7.7	–5.5	–5.1	–5.6	–8.1	–7.9
Financial account to GDP ratio	4.0	–0.3	2.1	6.2	9.1	10.6	12.0	8.5	8.4	8.4	13.0	10.5
Interest and exchange rates												
Nominal deposit rate (percent per year)	13.0	9.8	9.5	9.5	9.5	12.2	13.7	8.9	8.6	8.5	11.6	10.3
Real deposit rate (percent per year)	10.6	7.9	7.0	5.7	4.1	6.3	8.0	4.8	5.3	3.3	5.9	4.5
Interest rate differential[1]	5.2	1.3	–1.2	0.8	0.6	3.9	7.7	5.0	5.3	3.7	5.5	4.8
Lending/deposit spread	6.0	7.3	5.5	5.5	5.5	4.3	5.3	8.7	7.0	5.9	. . .	. . .
Official exchange rate per U.S. dollar (end of period)	26.6	26.1	25.1	25.2	25.7	25.3	25.3	25.5	25.5	25.1	25.2	25.6
Real effective exchange rate index (1990=100)	119.9	106.9	100.5	98.2	100.8	100.0	100.7	99.2	101.0	100.9	99.0	105.8

(*In millions of U.S. dollars*)

Balance of payments												
Current account, n.i.e.	–1,537	247	–366	–1,654	–2,498	–7,281	–7,571	–6,303	–6,364	–8,085	–13,554	–14,692
Financial account, n.i.e	1,538	–131	1,062	3,840	6,599	9,098	11,759	9,475	10,500	12,167	21,909	19,486
Direct investment abroad	–1	–1	–170	–24	–50	–140	–167	–147	–233	–493	–886	–931
Direct investment in reporting economy, n.i.e.	163	263	352	1,105	1,775	2,444	2,014	2,113	1,804	1,366	2,068	2,336
Net direct investment	162	261	182	1,081	1,726	2,303	1,847	1,966	1,571	873	1,182	1,405
Portfolio investment assets	. . .	. . .	. . .	. . .	. . .	. . .	. . .	. . .	0	–5	–2	–41
Portfolio investment liabilities	895	–29	346	530	1,486	–38	–81	924	5,455	2,486	4,083	3,585
Net portfolio investment	895	–29	346	530	1,486	–38	–81	924	5,455	2,482	4,081	3,544
Other investment assets	–242	–150	141	269	313	164	352	104	–3,265	–1,027	–2,738	2,661
Other investment liabilities	722	–213	393	1,960	3,700	6,996	9,642	6,479	6,739	9,839	19,383	11,876
Net other investments	481	–363	534	2,228	3,387	6,833	9,993	6,584	3,474	8,812	16,645	14,537
Of which, official capital	807	419	196	121	–834	–1,938	255	–313	–165	–34	292	542
Net errors and omissions	103	598	248	411	928	1,419	431	–142	–230	87	–1,196	–2,627
Overall balance[2]	104	713	943	2,596	5,030	3,236	4,618	3,029	3,907	4,169	7,159	2,167
Memorandum:												
Net private capital[3]	568	783	1,737	4,476	9,338	14,162	13,243	11,209	12,924	17,061	28,098	18,625

Sources: IMF, *International Financial Statistics, World Economic Outlook,* and *Direction of Trade Statistics,* various issues; and IMF staff estimates.

[1]Interest differential = deposit rate – London interbank offer rate on three-Month U.S. deposits.

[2]The overall balance includes: current account, financial account, capital account, and net errors and omissions. Capital account figures are not shown because they are zero throughout the period.

[3]Total capital = direct investment + portfolio investment + other investment + official capital + net errors and omissions + misinvoicing.

Bibliography

Agarwala, R.K., 1983, "Price Distortions and Growth in Developing Countries," World Bank Working Paper No. 575 (Washington: World Bank).

Alexander, William, Tomás J.T. Baliño, and Charles Enoch, 1995, *The Adoption of Indirect Instruments of Monetary Policy*, IMF Occasional Paper No. 126 (Washington: International Monetary Fund).

"All Countries Share in Effects of Globalization," 1996, *IMF Survey*, July 15, pp. 235–37.

Anderson, D., 1987, *Economic Growth and the Returns to Investment*, World Bank Discussion Paper No. 12 (Washington: World Bank).

Arellano, José P., 1983, "De La Liberalización a la Intervención: El Mercado de Capitales en Chile, 1974–1983," Colección Estudios CIEPLAN No. 14, (Santiago, Chile: Corporacion de Investigaciones Economicas Para Latinoamerica).

Baliño, Tomás J.T., 1987, "The Argentine Banking Crisis of 1980," IMF Working Paper No. 87/77 (Washington: International Monetary Fund).

_____, Omotunde E.G. Johnson, and V. Sundararajan, 1996, "Payment System Reforms and Monetary Policy," *Finance and Development*, Vol. 33 (March), pp. 2–5.

Bank Indonesia, *Report for the Financial Year*, (Jakarta: Bank Indonesia) various issues.

_____, *National Financial Statistics* (Jakarta, Indonesia).

Bank for International Settlements, 1989, "Changes in Central Bank Money Market Operating Procedures in the 1980's," BIS Economic Papers No 23 (Basle, Bank for International Settlements, January).

Bank of Korea, *Annual Report* (Seoul, Korea), various issues.

_____, *Financial System in Korea* (Seoul, Korea), various issues.

_____, *Monthly Statistical Bulletin* (Seoul, Korea), various issues.

Bank Negara Malaysia, 1984, *Money and Banking in Malaysia* (Kuala Lumpur).

Bank of Thailand, *Annual Report* (Bangkok), various issues.

Barro, R., 1991, "Economic Growth in a Cross Section of Countries," *Quarterly Journal of Economics*, Vol. 104, pp. 407–33.

Barth, Richard, Alan R. Roe, and Chorng-Huey Wong, eds, 1994, "Coordinating Stabilization and Structural Reform," IMF Institute (Washington: International Monetary Fund).

Basle Committee on Banking Supervision, 1996, *Amendment to the Capital Accord to Incorporate Market Risks* (Basle: Bank for International Settlements, January).

Beattie, V., P. Casson, R. Dale, G. McKenzie, C. Sutcliffe, and M. Turner, 1995, *Banks and Bad Debts* (New York: John Wiley and Sons).

Bencivenga, V., and B. Smith, 1991, "Financial Intermediation and Endogenous Growth," *The Review of Economic Studies*, Vol. 58, No. 2, pp. 195–209.

"Benefits of Capital Flows Tied to Strong Risk Management," 1995, *IMF Survey*, June 19, pp. 185–88.

Berggren, Arne, 1996, "Asset Valuation and the Appropriate Structure of Support—An Illustrative Example," paper prepared for workshop on systemic restructuring (unpublished; Washington: International Monetary Fund, Monetary and Exchange Affairs Department).

Bernanke, Ben S., 1983, "Non-Monetary Effects of the Financial Crisis in the Propagation of the Great Depression," NBER Working Paper No. 1054 (Cambridge, Massachusetts: National Bureau of Economic Research).

_____, and Mark Gertler, 1987, "Banking and Macroeconomic Equilibrium," in *New Approaches to Monetary Economics*, ed. by William A. Barnett and Kenneth J. Singleton (Cambridge: Cambridge University Press), pp. 89–111.

Bernanke, Ben S., and Alan S. Blinder, 1988, "Credit, Money, and Aggregate Demand," *American Economic Review*, Papers and Proceedings Vol. 78, No. 2, pp. 435–45.

Blejer, Mario, 1982, "Interest Rate Differentials and Exchange Risk: Recent Argentine Experience," *Staff Papers*, International Monetary Fund, Vol. 29 (June), pp. 270–79.

Borio, Claudio E.V., 1990, "Leverage and Financing of Non-Financial Companies: An International Perspective," BIS Economic Papers No. 27 (Basle: Bank for International Settlements, May).

_____, 1995, "The Structure of Credit to the Non-Government Sector and the Transmission Mechanism of Monetary Policy: A Cross-Country Comparison," BIS Working Paper No. 24 (Basle: Bank for International Settlements, April).

Borish, Michael S., Millard F. Long, and Michel Noël, 1995, *Restructuring Banks and Enterprises, Recent Lessons from Transition Countries*, World Bank Discussion Paper No. 279 (Washington: World Bank).

Brainard, Larry, 1990, "Reform in Eastern Europe: Creating a Capital Market," *The AMEXBANK Review*, Vol. 17, No. 9 (November), pp. 2–3.

Branson, William H., 1974, "Stocks and Flows in International Monetary Analysis," in *International Aspects of Stabilization Policies*, ed. by Albert Ando, Richard Herring, and Richard C. Marston, (Boston: Federal Reserve Bank of Boston).

Calvo, Guillermo A., 1983, "Trying to Stabilize: Some Theoretical Reflections Based on the Case of Argentina" in *Financial Policies and the World Capital Market: The Problem of Latin American Countries*, ed. by P. Aspe-Aramella, R. Dornbush, and M. Obsfeld (Chicago: University of Chicago Press).

———, 1988, "Servicing the Public Dept: The Role of Expectations," *American Economic Review*, Vol. 78, pp. 647–61.

Calvo, Guillermo, and Pablo E, Guidotti, 1991, "Speculative Attacks," IMF Working Paper 91/10 (Washington: International Monetary Fund).

Calvo G., L. Leiderman, and C. Reinhart, 1993, "The Capital Inflows Problem: Concepts and Issues," IMF Paper on Policy Analysis and Assessment 93/10 (Washington: International Monetary Fund, July).

Cameron, R., 1967, *Banking in the Early Stages of Industrialization* (New York: Oxford University Press).

Cardoso, Eliana, and Ilan Goldfajn, 1997, "Capital Flows to Brazil: The Endogeneity of Capital Controls," IMF Working Paper 97/115 (Washington: International Monetary Fund).

Cardoso, J., and B. Laurens, forthcoming, *The Effectiveness of Capital Controls on Inflows: The Case of Chile*, IMF Working Paper (Washington: International Monetary Fund).

Central Bank of Argentina, *Memoria Anual* (Buenos Aires: Central Bank of Argentina), several issues.

Central Bank of Chile, *Annual Report* (Santiago: Chile), various issues.

Central Bank of the Philippines, *Annual Report* (Manila, Philippines), various issues.

Cheng, Hang-Sheng, ed., 1986, *Financial Policy and Reform in Pacific Basin Countries*, (Lexington, Mass.: Lexington Books).

Chile, Superintendencia de Valores y Seguros, *Revista de Valores* (Santiago, Chile), various issues.

———, *The Securities Market in Chile: 1980–1989* (Santiago, Chile).

Cho, Yoon Je, 1986, "Inefficiencies from Financial Liberalization in the Absence of a Well Developed Equity Market," *Journal of Money, Credit, and Banking*, Vol. 18 (May), pp. 191–99.

_____, and David Cole, 1986, "The Role of the Financial Sector in Korea's Structural Adjustment," Harvard Institute for International Development Studies, Discussion Paper No. 230 (Cambridge, Mass. May).

Choi, Chang-Nak, 1984, "Putting the Nation's Finances in Order," *Business Korea* (Seoul, Korea, September), pp. 28–29.

Cole, David, and Betty Slade, 1996, *Building a Modern Financial System: The Indonesian Experience*, Trade and Development series (New York: Cambridge University Press).

Connolly, Michael, and Claudio Gonzalez-Vega, eds., 1987, *Economic Reform and Stabilization in Latin America* (New York: Praeger).

Coopers and Lybrand, *International Tax Summaries: A Guide for Planning and Decisions*, various issues.

Corbo, Vittorio, 1985, "Reforms and Macroeconomic Adjustments in Chile During 1974–84," *World Development*, Vol. 1 (August), pp. 893–916.

_____, and Jamie De Melo, 1985, "Overview and Summary," *World Development*, Vol. 13 (August), pp. 863–66.

_____, and James Tybout, 1986, "What Went Wrong with the Recent Reforms in the Southern Cone," *Economic Development and Cultural Change*, Vol. 34 (April), pp. 607–40.

De Gregorio, J., and P. Guidotti, 1992, "Financial Development and Economic Growth," IMF Working Paper 92/101 (Washington: International Monetary Fund).

de Juan, Aristóbulo, 1995, "Building Sound Banking in Transition Economies" paper presented at the seminar held during Annual Meetings of the European Bank for Reconstruction and Development (London).

Demirgüç-Kunt, Asli, and Ross Levine, 1994, "The Financial System and Public Enterprise Reform—Concept and Cases," Policy Research Working Paper No. 1319, Policy and Research Department (Washington World Bank, July).

Diaz-Alejandro, Carlos, 1985, "Good-Bye Financial Repression, Hello Financial Crash," *Journal of Development Economics*, Vol. 19 (September–October), pp. 1–24.

Dittus, Peter, 1994, "Corporate Governance in Central Europe: The Role of Banks," BIS Economic Papers No. 42 (Basle: Bank for International Settlements, August).

Diwatripont, Mathias, and Jean Tirole, 1994, "The Prudential Regulation of Banks," *The Walras-Pareto Lectures* (Cambridge, Mass.: MIT Press).

Dooley, Michael, 1996, "A Survey of Academic Literature on Controls over International Capital Transactions," *Staff Papers*, International Monetary Fund, Vol. 43, No. 4 (December), pp. 639–87.

_____, 1997, "A Model of Crises in Emerging Markets," NBER Working Paper No. 6300 (Cambridge: National Bureau of Economic Research, December).

_____, Jeffrey Frankel, and Donald J. Mathieson, 1987, "International Capital Mobility: What Do Savings-Investment Correlations Tell Us?" *Staff Papers*, International Monetary Fund, Vol. 34 (September).

Drees, B., and C. Pazarbaşıoğlu, 1995, "The Nordic Banking Crises: Pitfalls in Financial Liberalization?," IMF Working Paper 95/61 (Washington: International Monetary Fund, July).

Dziobek, Claudia, Olivier Frécaut, and Maria Nieto, 1995, "Non–G-10 Countries and the Basle Capital Rules: How Tough a Challenge is it to Join the Basle Club?" IMF Paper on Policy Analysis and Assessment 95/5 (Washington: International Monetary Fund, March).

Ealdama, E., Jr., 1986, "The Auction Market for Treasury Bills," *Philippine Central Bank Review*, Vol. 38 (December), pp. 15–38.

Edwards, Sebastian, 1984, "The Order of Liberalization of the External Sector in Developing Countries," *Essays in International Finance*, No. 156 (Princeton, New Jersey: Princeton University, December), pp. 59–68.

Eichengreen, B., James Tobin, and Charles Wyplosz, 1995, "Two Cases for Sand in the Wheels of International Finance," *The Economic Journal*, Vol. 105, No. 428, pp. 162–72.

European Central Bank, 1998, "The Single Monetary Policy in Stage Three," General Documentation on ESCB Monetary Policy Instruments and Procedures (September).

Feldstein, M., and C. Horioka, 1980, "Domestic Saving and International Capital Flows," *Economic Journal*, Vol. 90, No. 357 (June).

Fernández, Roque, 1985, "The Expectations Management Approach to Stabilization in Argentina During 1976–82," *World Development*, Vol. 13, No. 8 (August), pp. 871–92.

Foreign Tax Publishers, 1989, *Tax Laws of the World* (Ormond Beach, Florida).

Frenkel, Jacob, 1982, "The Order of Economic Liberalization: A Comment," in *Economic Policy in a World of Change*, ed. by K. Brunner and A. Meltzer (Amsterdam: North-Holland).

Friedman, B., 1975, "Targets, Instruments and Indicators of Monetary Policy," *Journal of Monetary Economics*, Vol. 1, No. 4, pp. 443–73.

Fry, Maxwell, 1988, *Money, Interest, and Banking in Economic Development* (Baltimore: The Johns Hopkins University Press).

Galbis, V., 1994, "Sequencing of Financial Sector Reforms: A Review," IMF Working Paper 94/101 (Washington: International Monetary Fund, September).

Gallagher, M., 1991, *Rent-Seeking and Economic Growth in Africa* (Boulder, Colorado: Westview Press).

Garber, P., 1996, "Managing Risks to Financial Markets from Volatile Capital Flows: The Role of Prudential Regulations," *International Journal of Finance and Economics*, Vol. 1 (July), pp. 183–95.

Garcia, Gillian, 1995, "Comparing and Confronting Recent Banking Problems in Foreign Countries: Applying a Framework for Analysis," paper presented at the Annual Conference of the Western Economic Association at the Sheraton Harbor Island, San Diego, July 5–9.

Gelb, Alan H., 1989, *Financial Policies, Growth, and Efficiency* (Washington: World Bank, June).

Gertler, Mark, 1988, "Financial Structure and Aggregate Economic Activity: An Overview," *Journal of Money, Credit, and Banking*, Vol. 20 (August), pp. 559–88.

_____, and A. Rose, 1991, "Finance, Growth and Public Policy," World Bank Working Paper Series No. 814 (Washington: World Bank, December).

Goldsmith, R., 1969, *Financial Structure and Development* (New Haven: Yale University Press).

Gray, Cheryl W., and Arnold Holle, 1996, "Bank-Led Restructuring in Poland—An Empirical Look at the Bank Conciliation Process," World Bank Policy Research Working Paper No. 1680, Policy Research Department (Washington: World Bank, September).

Greenwood, J., and B. Jovanovic, 1989, "Financial Development, Growth, and the Distribution of Income," *Journal of Political Economy*, Vol. 98, No. 4, pp. 1076–107.

Grilli, Vittorio, and Gian Maria Milesi-Ferretti, 1995, "Economic Effects and Structural Determinants of Capital Controls," *Staff Papers*, International Monetary Fund, Vol. 42, No. 3 (September), pp. 517–51.

Guitián, Manuel, 1998, "The Challenge of Managing Global Capital Flows," *Finance and Development*, Vol. 35, No. 2 (June), pp. 14–17.

Gulde, Anne Marie, and Lorena Zamalloa, 1997, "Liquid Asset Ratios and Financial Sector Reforms," IMF Working Paper 97/144 (Washington: International Monetary Fund).

Gurley, John G., and Edward S. Shaw, 1960, *Money in a Theory of Finance* (Washington: Brookings Institution).

Hanson, James, 1992, "Opening the Capital Account: A Survey of Issues and Results," World Bank Staff Working Paper No. 901 (Washington: World Bank, May).

_____, 1994, "An Open Capital Account: A Brief Survey of the Issues and the Results" in *Financial Reform: Theory and Experience*, ed. by G. Caprio, Jr., I. Atiyas, and J. Hanson (Cambridge: Cambridge University Press).

Hsiao, C., 1986, *Analysis of Panel Data*," (Cambridge; New York: Cambridge University Press).

International Finance Corporation, 1989, *Emerging Stock Markets Factbook* (Washington: International Finance Corporation, April).

International Monetary Fund, 1983, *Interest Rate Policies in Developing Countries*, IMF Occasional Paper No. 27 (Washington: International Monetary Fund, October).

_____, 1991, "*Determinants and Systemic Consequences of International Capital Flows*," IMF Occasional Paper No. 77 (Washington: International Monetary Fund, March).

_____, *Annual Report of Exchange Arrangements and Exchange Restrictions*, various editions.

_____, *Directions of Trade Statistics*, various issues.

_____, *International Financial Statistics* (Washington: International Monetary Fund), various issues.

_____, *World Economic Outlook*, various issues.

_____, and the World Bank, 1980, *The Philippines: Aspects of the Financial Sector* (Washington: IMF/IBRD).

Jao, Y.C., 1976, "Financial Deepening and Economic Growth: A Cross-Section Analysis," *Malayan Economic Review*, Vol. 21, No. 1 (April), pp. 47–58.

Jappelli, T., and M. Pagano, 1992, "Saving, Growth and Liquidity Constraints," CEPR Discussion Paper No. 662 (London: Centre for Economic Policy Research, May).

Johnston, R. Barry, 1983, *The Economies of the Euromarket* (London: MacMillan).

_____, 1991a, "Sequencing Financial Reform," in *The Evolving Role of Central Banks*, ed. by Patrick Downes and Reza Vaez-Zadeh (Washington: International Monetary Fund).

_____, 1991b, "Distressed Financial Institutions in Thailand: Structural Weaknesses, Support Operations, and Economic Consequences," in

Banking Crisis: Cases and Issues, ed. by V. Sundararajan and T. Baliño (Washington: International Monetary Fund).

_____, 1993, "Aspects of the Design of Financial Programs with the Adoption of Indirect Monetary Controls," IMF Paper on Policy Analysis and Assessment 93/16 (Washington: International Monetary Fund, October).

_____, 1997, "The Speed of Financial Sector Reform: Risks and Strategies," in *Sequencing? Financial Strategies for Developing Countries*, ed. by A. Harwood and B.L.R. Smith (Washington: Brookings Institution Press).

_____, 1998, "Sequencing Capital Account Liberalization and Financial Sector Reform," IMF Paper on Policy Analysis and Assessment 98/8 (Washington: International Monetary Fund).

_____, and C. Ryan, 1994, "The Impact of Controls on Capital Movements on the Private Capital Accounts of Countries' Balance of Payments: Empirical Estimates and Policy Implications," IMF Working Paper 94/78 (Washington: International Monetary Fund, July).

Kane, Edward, 1987, "No Room for Weak Links in the Chain of Deposit Insurance Reform," *Journal of Financial Services Research*, Vol. 1, No. 1, pp. 77–111.

_____, 1992, "How Incentive-Incompatible Deposit Insurance Funds Fail" in *Research in Financial Services: Private and Public Policy* (Greenwich, Conn.: JAI Press), Vol. 4, pp. 51–91.

_____, 1995, "Difficulties of Transferring Risk-Based Capital Requirements to Developing Countries," *Pacific Basin Finance Journal*, Vol. 3, pp. 193–216.

Kashyap, Anil K., and Jeremy C. Stein, 1994, "Monetary Policy and Bank Lending," in *Monetary Policy*, ed. by Gregory N. Mankiw (Chicago: University of Chicago Press), pp. 221–62.

Khatekhate, D.R., 1988, "Assessing the Impact of Interest Rates in Less Developed Countries," *World Development*, Vol. 16, No. 5, pp. 577–88.

King, R.G., and R. Levine, 1992, "Financial Indicators and Growth in a Cross Section of Countries," World Bank Working Paper No. 819 (Washington: World Bank, January).

_____, 1993a, "Finance and Growth: Schumpeter Might be Right," *Quarterly Journal of Economics*, Vol. 108, pp. 717–37.

_____, 1993b, "Finance, Entrepreneurship, and Growth: Theory and Evidence," *Journal of Monetary Economics*, Vol. 32, pp. 513–42.

Kneeshaw, J.T., 1995, "A Survey of Nonfinancial Sector Balance Sheets in Industrialized Countries: Implications for the Monetary Policy Transmission Mechanism," Working Paper No. 25 (Basle: Bank for International Settlements, April).

Korea Securities Dealers Association, 1992, *Securities Market in Korea* (Seoul).

Krueger, Anne, 1984, "Problems of Liberalization" in *World Economic Growth*, ed. by A. Harberger (San Francisco: ICS Press).

Krugman, Paul, 1998, "What Happened in Asia?" Available via the Internet at http://web.mit.edu/krugman/www/disinter.html.

Kwack, S.Y., and U.C. Chung, 1986, "The Role of Financial Policies in Korea's Economic Development Process" in *Financial Policy and Reform in Pacific Basin Countries*, ed. by Hang–Sheng Cheng (Lexington, Mass.: Lexington Books).

Lee, C.K., 1986, "Financial Reform Experiences in Korea," in *Financial Policy and Reform in Pacific Basin Countries*, ed. By Hang-Sheng Cheng (Lexington, Mass.: Lexington Books).

Lee, Jan-Yung, 1996, "Implications of a Surge in Capital Inflows: Available Tools and Consequences for the Conduct of Monetary Policy," IMF Working Paper No. 53 (Washington: International Monetary Fund).

Leite, S.P., 1985, "Notes on Open Market Operations in Mexico," (unpublished; Washington: International Monetary Fund, July).

_____, and V. Sundararajan, 1988, "Issues in Interest Rate Management and Liberalization" (unpublished; Washington: International Monetary Fund, April).

_____, 1990, "Issues in Interest Rate Management and Liberalization," *Staff Papers*, International Monetary Fund, Vol. 37 (December), pp. 735–52.

Levine, R., 1992, "Financial Structure and Economic Development," World Bank Working Paper No. 849 (Washington: World Bank, February).

_____, and D. Renelt, 1992, "A Sensitivity Analysis of Cross-Country Growth Regression," *American Economic Review*, Vol. 84, pp. 942–63.

Lindgren, Carl, Gillian Garcia, and Matthew Saal, 1996, *Bank Soundness and Macroeconomic Policy* (Washington: International Monetary Fund).

Little, Ian, Tibor Scitovsky, and Maurice Scott, 1970, *Industry and Trade in Some Developing Countries: A Comparative Study* (London: Oxford University Press).

Long, Millard, and Izabela Rutkowska, 1995, "The Role of Commercial Banks in Enterprise Restructuring in Central and Eastern Europe," Policy Research Working Paper No. 1423 (Washington: World Bank, February).

Markelew, Victoria, 1995, *Cash, Crisis, and Corporate Governance—The Role of National Financial Systems in Industrial Restructuring* (Ann Arbor: The University of Michigan Press).

Mathieson, D.J., and Richard Haas, 1994, "Establishing Monetary Control in Financial Systems with Insolvent Institutions," IMF Paper on Policy

Analysis and Assessment 94/10 (Washington: International Monetary Fund, June).

Mayorga, Roberto, and Luis Montt, 1995, *Foreign Investment in Chile* (Boston: M. Nijhoff).

McKinnon, Ronald, 1973, *Money and Capital in Economic Development* (Washington: Brookings Institution).

_____, 1982, "The Order of Economic Liberalization: Lessons from Chile and Argentina," *Carnegie-Rochester Conference Series on Public Policy*, Vol. 17 (Autumn), pp. 159–86.

_____, 1989, "Financial Liberalization and Economic Development: A Reassessment of Interest Rate Policies in Asia and Latin America," *Oxford Review of Economic Policy*, Vol. 5, No. 4, pp. 29–54.

_____, 1991, *The Order of Economic Liberalization: Financial Control in the Transition to a Market Economy* (Baltimore: The Johns Hopkins University Press.).

_____, and Wallace E. Oates, 1966, *The Implications of International Economic Integration for Monetary, Fiscal, and Exchange-Rate Policy*, Princeton Studies in International Finance No. 16, (Princeton, N.J.: International Finance Section, Department of Economics, Princeton University).

Michaely, Michael, 1986, "The Timing and Sequence of a Trade Liberalization Policy" in *Economic Liberalization in Developing Countries*, ed. by A. Choksi and D. Papageorgiou (London: Basil Blackwell).

Mishkin, Frederic, 1978, "The Household Balance Sheet and the Great Depression," *Journal of Economic History*, Vol. 38 (December), pp. 45–88.

Moody's Investors Service, 1998, "Indonesia—Recapitalization Required," *Banking System Outlook* (June).

Mundell, Robert A., 1963, "Capital Mobility and Stabilization Policy Under Fixed and Flexible Exchange Rates," *Canadian Journal of Economics and Political Science*, Vol. 29.

Nascimento, Jean-Claude, 1990, "The Crisis in the Financial Sector and the Authorities' Reaction: The Case of the Philippines," IMF Working Paper 90/26 (Washington: International Monetary Fund).

Odedokun, M., 1992, "Multi-Country Evidence on the Effects of Macroeconomic, Financial and Trade Policies on Efficiency of Resource Utilization in the Developing Countries," IMF Working Paper 92/53 (Washington: International Monetary Fund, July).

Pagano, Marco, 1993, "Financial Markets and Growth: An Overview," *European Economic Review*, Vol. 37 (April), pp. 613–22 .

Park, Daekeun, 1994, "Foreign Exchange Liberalization and the Viability of a Fixed Exchange Regime," *Journal of International Economics*, Vol. 36.

Park, Yung Chul, 1998, "Gradual Approach to Capital Account Liberalization: the Korean Experience," a paper prepared for IMF Seminar on Capital Account Liberalization (unpublished; Washington: International Monetary Fund, March).

Patrick, H.T., 1966, "Financial Development and Economic Growth in Under-developed Countries," *Economic Development and Cultural Change*, Vol. 14, pp. 174–89.

Price Waterhouse, 1995, *Doing Business in Chile* (New York).

_____, 1992, *Doing Business in Thailand* (New York).

_____, *Doing Business in Indonesia* (New York), various issues.

_____, *Doing Business in Korea*, (New York), various issues.

Persson, Torsten, and Guido Enrico, 1990, "Macroeconomic Policy, Credibility, and Politics," *in Fundamentals of Pure and Applied Economics* (New York: Harwood Academic Publishers).

Petrie, A. Humberto, and James R. Tybout, 1985, "Microeconomic Adjustments in Argentina During 1976–81: The Importance of Changing Levels of Financial Subsidies," *World Development*, Vol. 13 (August), pp. 949–67.

Quintyn, Mark, 1994, "Government Securities Versus Central Bank Securities in Developing Open Market Operations—Evaluation and Need for Coordinating Arrangements," IMF Working Paper 94/62 (Washington: International Monetary Fund).

Roubini, N., and X. Sala-i-Martin, 1992, "Financial Repression and Economic Growth," *Journal of Development Economics*, Vol. 39, pp. 5–30.

Saal, Matthew I., and Lorena M. Zamalloa, 1994, "Use of Central Bank Credit Auctions in Economies in Transition," IMF Paper on Policy Analysis and Assessment 94/11 (Washington: International Monetary Fund, June).

Schadler, S., M. Carkovic, A. Bennett, and R. Khan, 1993, *Recent Experiences with Surges in Capital Inflows*, IMF Occasional Paper No. 108 (Washington: International Monetary Fund, December).

Shaw, E., 1973, *Financial Deepening in Economic Development* (New York: Oxford University Press).

Sheng, Andrew, 1991, "The Art of Bank Restructuring: Issues and Techniques," (unpublished; Washington: Economic Development Institute of the World Bank, June).

Soto, Claudio G. 1997, "Control of Capital Flows: An Empirical Assessment of the Case of Chile," Central Bank of Chile (October).

Sprenkle, C.M., and M.H. Miller, 1980, "The Precautionary Demand for Narrow and Broad Money." *Economica*, Vol. 47, (November).

Sundararajan, V., 1985, "Debt-Equity Ratios of Firms and Interest Rate Policy: Macroeconomic Effects of High Leverage in Developing Countries," *Staff Papers*, International Monetary Fund, Vol. 32 (September), pp. 533–44.

_____, 1987, "The Debt-Equity Ratios of Firms and the Effectiveness of Interest Rate Policy: Analysis with a Dynamic Model of Savings, Investment, and Growth in Korea," *Staff Papers*, International Monetary Fund, Vol. 34 (June), pp. 260–310.

_____, 1991, "Financial Sector Reform and Central Banking in Centrally Planned Economies," in *The Evolving Role of Central Banks*, ed. by Downes and Vaez-Zadeh (Washington: International Monetary Fund).

_____, 1992, "Financial Sector Reforms and Their Appropriate Sequencing," in the 19th Southeast Asia, New Zealand, and Australia Central Banking Course (unpublished; Tokyo: Bank of Japan, October–November), pp. 177–203.

_____, 1994, "Interaction Between Monetary Control and Financial Sector Reform," in *Coordinating Stabilization and Structural Reform*, ed. by Richard Barth, Alan R. Roe, and Chorng-Huey Wong. (Washington: International Monetary Fund).

_____, and Tomás J.T. Baliño, 1990, "Issues in Recent Banking Crises," IMF Working Paper 90/19 (Washington: International Monetary Fund).

_____, eds., 1991, *Banking Crises: Cases and Issues* (Washington: International Monetary Fund).

Sundararajan, V., Peter Dattels, and Hans J. Blommestein, eds., 1997, *Coordinating Public Debt and Monetary Management* (Washington: International Monetary Fund).

Tobin, James, 1965, "The Theory of Portfolio Selection" in *The Theory of Interest Rates*, ed. by F. Hahn and F. P. R. Brechling (London: MacMillan).

Velasco, Andrés, 1991, "Liberalization, Crisis, Intervention: The Chilean Financial System, 1975–1985," in *Banking Crises: Cases and Issues*, ed. by V. Sundararajan and T. Baliño (Washington: International Monetary Fund), pp. 113–74.

Villanueva, Delano, and Abbas Mirakhor, 1990, "Strategies for Financial Reform: Interest Rate Policies, Stabilization, and Bank Supervision in Developing Countries," *Staff Papers*, International Monetary Fund, Vol. 37 (September), pp. 509–36.

World Bank, 1984, *Economic Memorandum on Argentina* (Washington: World Bank).

_____, 1986, *Philippines, Financial Sector Study* (Washington: World Bank).

_____, 1988, *Philippines: Financial Sector Study*, The World Bank Report No. 177–PH (Washington: World Bank, August).

_____, 1989, *Financial Systems and Development*, World Development Report 1989 (New York: Oxford University Press), pp. 70–83.